# Reviews from *Sacred Places North America*

"An interesting book for both the armchair and the adventurous traveler, this (book) is recommended." —*Library Journal*

"The book is filled with fascinating archeological, geological, and historical material. These 108 sacred places in the United States, Canada, and Hawaii offer ample opportunity for questing by spiritual seekers." —*Spirituality & Health*

"A revealing, useful, and enthusiastically recommended guide for the vacationer seeking to fulfill their spiritual as well as their recreational yearnings." —*Midwest Book Review*

"World traveler Brad Olsen has compiled a book that documents 108 destination spots for 'feeling the energy' of our spiritual historical roots. Pilgrimage is one way we can find ourselves and this book will provide a guide." —*Twin Cities Wellness*

"The book's chapters correspond to ten regional sections of the U.S. and Canada, which are further subdivided into specific U.S. States and Canadian provinces. No less than 38 of the 50 United States are revealed to contain sacred sites — some of which are very public and easy to access, such as the House of David in Michigan, and some of which are more obscure, like Shiprock, 'the stand-alone neck of an ancient volcano core' in New Mexico. But never fear: Olsen provides lucid and detailed directions, as well as tantalizing and historically well-informed essay-portraits, for each destination. The book is also peppered with excellent maps, illustrations, and photos." —*Fearless Books*

"For travelers who prefer destinations with spirit ... juxtaposing local folklore and Native American legend with scientific theories to provide context." —*Orlando Sentinel*

"It's an odd lot, the places that have a way of touching your heart: mountains and homesteads, caves and monasteries, lakes and pathways. Author Brad Olsen has recognized that variety in this bringing together of 108 places that stir the soul. Many of the destinations mentioned come as no surprise in a collection of the hallowed: Ohio's Serpent Mound, Wyoming's Yellowstone, Colorado's Mesa Verde, for instance. But other entries serve as a delightful reminder that there is room in our hearts to expand the definition of sacred: Massachusetts' Walden Pond, Michigan's House of David, and Tennessee's (and Elvis') Graceland, for instance." —*Chicago Tribune*

"Olsen maps out obscure destinations brir̶ history, places where you will not have to ists. You'll find lots of maps, drawings and for the individualist." —*Ashley Tribune*

# Reviews from *Sacred Places Around the World*

"... the ruins, mountains, sanctuaries, lost cities, and pilgrimage routes held sacred around the world." —*Book Passage*

"For each site, Brad Olsen provides historical background, a description of the site and its special features, and directions for getting there." —*Theology Digest*

"(Readers) will thrill to the wonderful history and the vibrations of the world's sacred healing places." —*East & West*

"Sites that emanate the energy of sacred spots."
—*The Sunday Times*

"Sacred sites (to) the ruins, sanctuaries, mountains, lost cities, temples, and pilgrimage routes of ancient civilizations."
—*San Francisco Chronicle*

"Many sacred places are now bustling tourist and pilgrimage desti-nations. But no crowd or souvenir shop can stand in the way of a traveler with great intentions and zero expectations."
—*Spirituality & Health*

"Unleash your imagination by going on a mystical journey. Brad Olsen gives his take on some of the most amazing and unexplained spots on the globe—including the underwater ruins of Bimini, which seems to point the way to the Lost City of Atlantis. You can choose to take an armchair pilgrimage (the book is a fascinating read) or follow his tips on how to travel to these powerful sites yourself."
—*Mode*

"Should you be inspired to make a pilgrimage of your own, you might want to pick up a copy of Brad Olsen's guide to the world's sacred places. Olsen's marvelous drawings and mysterious maps enhance a package that is as bizarre as it is wonderfully acces-sible. The historical data and metaphysical ruminations make it an intriguing read. So pick a mystical corner of the world, be it Mount Shasta, Delphi or Borobudur, and plan out a pilgrimage real or imag-ined among the Tungus shamans of Siberian Russia, the ghosts of Mohenjo-daro, the Muslim faithful at the Grand Mosque in Mecca, and more." —*San Francisco Examiner*

# SACRED PLACES

# NORTH AMERICA

**Second Edition**

## 108 DESTINATIONS

Written, photographed, and illustrated by

**BRAD OLSEN**

**CONSORTIUM OF COLLECTIVE CONSCIOUSNESS**

www.cccpublishing.com    www.bradolsen.com    www.stompers.com

# Sacred Places North America:
## 108 Destinations

second edition

Copyright © 2008 by Brad Olsen

Published by the Consortium of Collective Consciousness ™

All rights reserved.

Reproduction or translation of any part of this work beyond that permitted by section 107 or 108 of the 1976 United States Copyright Act without the permission of the copyright owner is unlawful. Requests for permission or further information should be addressed to CCC Publishing, 530 8th Avenue #6, San Francisco, CA 94118 USA. FAX (415) 933-8132.

As is common in a historic and reference book such as this, much of the information included on these pages has been collected from diverse sources. When possible, the information has been checked and double-checked. Even with special effort to be accurate and thorough, the author and publisher cannot vouch for each and every reference. Because this is a book about traveling, many specifics can change overnight and without prior warning. The reader will find ample information collected from experienced adventurers, writers, and travel industry experts. The author and publisher assume no responsibility or liability for any outcome, loss, arrest, or injury that occurs as a result of information or advice contained in this book. As with the purchase of goods or services, *caveat emptor* is the prevailing responsibility of the purchaser, and the same is true for the traveler.

Library of Congress Cataloging-in-Publication Data:

Olsen, Bradford C.

  Sacred Places North America: 108 Destinations / Brad Olsen

   p. cm.

  Includes index

  ISBN 10: 1-888729-13-9 (Pbk.)

  ISBN 13: 978-1-888729-13-9

  1. Spirituality — Guidebooks. 2. Travel — Guidebooks. I. Title

  Library of Congress Catalog Card Number: 2005904373

Printed in the United States of America.

10 9 8 7 6 5 4 3 2

**Front Cover Photos:** © 2008, Brad Olsen: Waubansee Stone, IL; Old Oraibi, AZ; Aztalan, WI. National Park Service: Devils Tower, WY.

# ALSO BY BRAD OLSEN

*Sacred Places Europe: 108 Destinations*
2007

*Sacred Places Around the World: 108 Destinations*
2004

*World Stompers: A Global Travel Manifesto*
2001

*In Search of Adventure: A Wild Travel Anthology*
1999

*Extreme Adventures Northern California*
1997

*Extreme Adventures Hawaii*
1997

The Dating System used in this text is based upon the modern method of using Before Current Era (BCE) instead of Before Christ (B.C.), and Current Era (CE) rather than "in the year of the Lord" *anno Domini* (A.D.). Those unfamiliar with this dating system should take note that 1 B.C. is the same as 1 BCE and everything then counts backward just the same. Similarly, 1 A.D. is 1 CE with all the years counting forward to the present, or Current Era. To assist in universal understanding, all measurements of length, distance, area, weight, and volume are listed both in the old British standard and the metric system.

# 108 SACRED PLACES in NORTH AMERICA

## THE SOUTHWEST

## WEST COAST STATES

## ALASKA AND HAWAII

## WESTERN CANADA

## ROCKY MOUNTAINS

# AUTHOR'S KARMA STATEMENT

*"Society today has corrupted humans. All seem to be caught up in the search for money, fame and power. But a smaller few of us have kept the values of the old world and try to live this way. We come to the mountains and commune with nature. We visit the relics of humankind's glorious past to remember our own. We have not lost sight of God and moral reasoning. Therefore, with our quests, I can safely say we are bettering societal values; we are helping future generations."*

**-Anonymous journal entry, Mount Shasta Base Camp**

It has been over a decade since I climbed Mount Shasta and copied this quote. That climbing trip in 1997, much like my full moon ascent of Egypt's Great Pyramid in 1994, inexorably changed my life by overwhelming me with the power of sacred places. It occurred to me then, and I still believe it today, that the best aspect of a civilization is almost always expressed in the holy locations that were honored. No matter who the people were or where they lived, some kind of priority was given to divine interpretation. They are the settings where the population worshipped, performed ceremonies, and erected buildings to define their collective vision of the divine. They remain an interpretation to eternal questions. Others traveled long distances, sometimes under adverse conditions, to worship at a holy place. From the most primitive of shrines to the tallest cathedral, from legendary mountains to prehistoric medicine wheels, the discovery of sacred places takes on many forms. Therefore, we must be helping society and

▲ Author's self-portrait atop Dreamer's Rock in Canada.

ourselves with our journeys to visit the relics of humankind's glorious past. There is a collective wisdom that resides at these worldwide locations, something that resonates with those reverent few who decide to pay a visit. This book is, after all, a travel guide.

My readers routinely tell me of their own profound experiences regarding trips they've taken to a sacred place. There are people who experience past life recalls, others a deeper understanding of the folklore or history of a location. Some have reported being witness to supernatural phenomena during their visit, such as a UFO flyby or a ghost sighting. Others report a feeling of deep serenity. Some

10

come away with great vacation memories and photographs to share. There is no invalid experience. Developing a personal relationship with a sacred place is akin to our own fingerprints—that which is entirely unique to each person. In a similar way this is how I view all religions. Each contains wisdom and beauty, but the true meaning lies within the believer, the one who has a personal revelation.

Every so often I hear from readers how they would love to undertake a trip, but life's obligations keep them occupied in their hometown. What is special about this book is that most of us live within one day driving distance to a dozen of these sites. I highly recommend roadtrips! Besides driving to the locations near their homes, I tell these people to locate their own private sacred place. A personal location for reflection in a beautiful natural setting always works best. Unusual rock formations attracted the Native Americans, as they can for you! I have several of my own in San Francisco, California. One is social and full of people (similar to many of the locations in this book), and the other is remote where I rarely see another person.

I am delighted to revise and update *Sacred Places North America* into a second edition. When I embarked on several cross country trips from 2001 until 2003 researching the first edition, I was amazed at the diversity and mystery embedded into the fabric of North American history. Habitation of this continent is much older, and encompasses more diverse cultures, than was previously understood. The idea that pre-Columbian visitors from far away lands came to the New World is known as "cultural diffusion theory." It is recognized by diffusion historians that North American prehistory features a variety of people arriving, settling, trading and exploring in anomalous locations. Evidence in the last few decades has confirmed the Scandinavian Norse as the first recorded discoverers of North America, predating Christopher Columbus by nearly 500 years. What about before the Vikings? Tantalizing clues suggest that other visitors arrived much earlier, sometimes by at least a thousand years. It would therefore be reasonable to assume that each group would have brought with them unusual cultural traits that influenced, and eventually assimilated, with the numerically dominant Native American populations. The newcomers would have built shrines in North America devoted to their imported religions. The evidence pointing to multiple "diffusions" is overwhelming, but opposition to the idea remains strong within academic circles.

To compile a transcendental book such as this I found myself seeking guidance from many

▲ My now deceased car at Mount Saviour Monastery, New York, in 2002.

varied sources. I sought out experts on the subject of sacred sites, whether they were fellow world travelers, Native Americans, park rangers, tour guides, travel writers, or anyone else with an intuitive sense into the power of a place. In writing this volume, it was necessary for me to engage in some supposition unconfirmed by conventional archaeology. If I have surpassed the usages academic historians consider acceptable, I have done so in an effort not to mislead anyone. It is my belief that archaeological evidence should speak for itself; no matter how much it changes the historical status quo. Just as American academics stubbornly held onto the unique discovery of North America by Columbus viewpoint for centuries, so are the anomalous findings of other people who arrived centuries before Columbus being routinely dismissed to this day. Sometimes radical revision is a hard pill to swallow. A footnote from Edward Gibbon's *History of the Decline and Fall of the Roman Empire* explains how the master historian grappled with the revisionist dilemma. Gibbon writes: "I owe it to myself and to historic truth to declare that some circumstances in (what follows) are founded only on conjecture and analogy." The perspective of cultural diffusion is new and open to different interpretations. Mine is the voice of a lifelong world traveler with an insatiable curiosity for uncovering the truth.

–Brad Olsen
CCC Publishing
San Francisco, CA
Spring Equinox, 2008

"The fundamental purpose of all leaders, messiahs or visionaries is to find some means by which the two sides of the earth can live together in peace and harmony. Time is very short–it is necessary to achieve this harmony as soon as possible to avoid complete disaster. Philosophies, religions and other such movements have all failed to accomplish this aim, and the only possible way to accomplish it is through the individual development of humans. As an individual develops their own, unknown potentialities, they will become strong and will, in turn, influence many more people. If enough individuals can develop themselves–even partially–into genuine, natural human beings, able to use the real potentialities that are proper to humankind, each such individual will then be able to convince and win over as many as a hundred other people, who will, each in their turn, upon achieving development, be able to influence another hundred, and so on. ... The separate, distinct growth of each individual in the world is the only possible solution."
–George Gurdjieff

# FOREWORD

## by David Hatcher Childress

I first met Brad when he contacted me about doing a story for his co-written book *In Search of Adventure*. Of course, I was happy to do a story for his anthology and was flattered that I would be included. Brad's next book, *Sacred Places Around the World* reminded me of my own *Lost Cities* series of books, and I was amused by his maps and drawings that accompanied the text.

The world is a fascinating place with many wonderful sites and "sacred places." I began traveling the world back in 1976 when I was 19 years old. As I journeyed across Asia, the Middle East, Africa, Europe, South America and Pacific islands, I became extremely interested in the many pyramids, megalithic walls, earthen mounds, and unusual rock formations that literally cover the globe. These sacred places were oftentimes said to be linked together in some way. Some were said to be connected by invisible energy lines that went from one sacred site to another. In Britain, these ancient energy paths were called "Ley Lines" and usually named after their "discoverer." The Chinese had a name for energy lines that connected certain spots with others; they called them Dragon Lines. The native aboriginals of Australia have a similar tradition of energy lines called "Song Lines" or sometimes referred to as "Dreaming Tracks." This concept of an interconnectedness between these ancient sites is often called the World Grid concept. That many ancient sites—including the Great Pyramid of Giza, Stonehenge, Mont St. Michel, Mount Olympus, Mount Shasta and even the vortices of Sedona—are connected by energy lines and become "power points" where certain of these energy lines cross. Hence, a world grid of power places and energy lines seems to unfold across the globe, reaching even remote islands. Did ancient man discern these energy lines and their crossing paths and then turn many of them into sacred sites? Was there a mathematical formula or map of these power points that could be plotted on a piece of parchment or in book of collected pages? Many have attempted to do this difficult task to varying success.

*Sacred Places North America* is a valiant attempt to take on such a task for North America. Brad has literally criss-crossed the continent many times in search of little-known, as well as well-known, sites that dot the land from sea to shining sea. One point to be made with the notion of sacred sites is that they were not only connected to each other, but that ancient humans apparently sought these sites out and used them for sacred ceremonies or pilgrimages. While most history and archaeology professors are teaching the theory of isolationism—that ancient cultures were essentially isolated from each other—the connection between sacred sites is more in line with the theory of diffusionism. The theory of cultural diffusion is a theory that gains more and more academic ground every year as archaeologists gather increasing evidence that ancient man loved to travel and explore.

Diffusionism says that oceans, lakes and rivers are not barriers but highways. There is ample evidence that ancient traders not only followed ancient Roman roads to Scotland and the Silk Road to China and India, but also by boat across the Atlantic, Indian and Pacific Oceans. As they reached various trading cities located at river deltas or mountain valleys, they would be told of other cities and sacred sites that might be visited. To travel and know the world, and visit these sacred sites is to gain knowledge and wisdom. Often it was the journey itself that really mattered; the destination was but a point of reference; a place to be obtained before setting off to another point. These sacred journeys to sacred sites form a larger part of our life than we even know. While many persons specifically set out on a specific pilgrimage to a specific site—whether it be the trip to a religious shrine or the family of four on the way to the Grand Canyon—our lives in general take us from one sacred site to another on a never ending pilgrimage. Everyone's life is a journey from one sacred site to another—and these sacred sites are all around us. There is an infinite amount of them, as many as we care to perceive. This pilgrimage is on such a grand scale that we can hardly perceive it.

What is a sacred site then? It can be the pyramid-shaped mound that one sees from a distance, or the sanctuary of the grandparent's back country farm. Sacred sites are everywhere for us to find, but we must open our eyes to see them. *Sacred Places North America* takes us to 108 of these sites with some friendly commentary and advice. From here the reader can move forward and find some sacred sites of his own, perhaps just out their backdoor! Whether it is the wandering Zen monk or someone on a vision quest, the journey from sacred site to sacred site begins with one step ...

–David Hatcher Childress

author of *Lost Cities of North & Central America, The Anti-Gravity Handbook, Technology of the Gods*, and 19 other books.

▲ David Hatcher Childress (middle, left), Brad Olsen (right) and friends visit Ground Zero in New York City a few months after 9/11.

# INTRODUCTION TO NORTH AMERICAN SACRED PLACES

*Every continent has its own spirit of place. Every people is
polarized in some particular locality, which is home, the homeland.
Different places on the face of the earth have different vital
effluence, different vibration, different chemical exhalations,
different polarity with different stars: call it what you like, but
the spirit of place is a great reality.*
-D.H. Lawrence

In the depths of the human spirit resides an inclination to trace the paths long venerated by our ancestors. Such journeys are food for the soul. These travels on ancestral trails touch upon that which is vital to our humanity. They open our minds to the world around us, to our collective history and to the cosmos above. When we arrive at a physical destination, we can find ourselves in a spiritual one as well—closer to our own individual reality, and the larger universe. But the other reality is that this education into ourselves comes almost by definition with a crush of other people. To see beyond the souvenir stands we need to know what we are looking for. Sacred places represent the essential spirit of humankind.

Seeking out a sacred place is no new concept. Since the beginning of time, humans have doubtless journeyed to distant locations to discover a spiritual relationship with themselves, our planet and the cosmos. Pilgrims pursue a prophesized destination; shamans prepare for vision quest; priests lead their flock; visionaries dream of a temple where there once was none; and modern travelers load up their packs and set forth.

Some discernible qualities exist at every sacred place. Perhaps it's the design, the physical proximity of the site, the building materials used, the story left behind, the shape of the monument, or how the sacred site inspired, or continues to inspire, religious movements. The most important quality of a sacred site is the feelings these places evoke in us. People venture to sacred sites, consciously or unconsciously, to satisfy the human spirit's desire for communion with themselves, our collective humanity, and the cosmos above.

## Visiting Natural and Human Wonders

In most world religions, specific areas hold great spiritual significance. The grand monuments of antiquity retain their age-old mysterious wisdom in this accelerated modern age. While most sacred places are bustling tourist and pilgrimage destinations, one can still find quiet moments at off-hours. The location, orientation, structure, and function of a sacred site are usually based on universal principles of balance and harmony, which no tourist group can obstruct.

It is important to note that anyone visiting a sacred place should go with sincere intentions and no expectations. Having expectations usually sets the traveler up for disappointment. You can view a sacred site as an interesting pile of rocks or a place long venerated by our ancestors. You can see these locations as tourist traps or places where others may commune with a higher force—no matter how many tourists are wandering around. Go to them! Go with respect, reverence and a clear conscience. Some are very difficult to locate, some very easy. Some will inspire, others may disappoint. But without a doubt, no matter where you go, you will return a much more understanding and perhaps enlightened person. A simple travel mantra: "Open your mind; enrich the soul. Make time to travel your ultimate goal." Indeed, "seek and ye shall find!"

In the last few hundred years, the indigenous people of North America have gone through tremendous change. Before modern European contact, the Native American population lived off the plentiful abundance of the land, and communed peacefully with the Great Spirit. It is estimated that at least 57.3 million people lived in the Americas prior to 1492 when Columbus first dropped anchor in the Caribbean. Within the first month of contact the native population began to decrease due to genocide, disease and forced enslavement. In North America, the open territory of the Indians gave way to European colonists who settled on the land and created productive agricultural communities. In turn, agriculture gave way to the Industrial Revolution as the growth measure of America. Today, almost all indigenous people in North America continue to reside on reservations. Some of the sacred sites listed in this book are situated on their reservations or had once been located on their traditional homelands. If venturing to a Native American site, or any sacred place listed in this book, please go there with respect for the location.

## The Earliest Sacred Sites: Caves and Mountains

Before early humans started building freestanding structures, they resided in caves. In the dark caverns of Europe and Asia, the first signs of religion began to take form. Similarly, caves in North America provided shelter from the elements and wild animals. Survival of the clan depended on hunting and fertility, and most prehistory artifacts represented this concern. Later, as religion evolved, certain caves and grottoes took on spiritual connotations when they were adorned with religious icons or acted as safe houses for sacred texts.

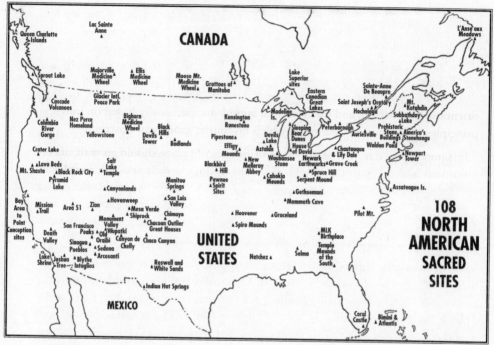

"From time immemorial the mountains have been the dwelling place of the great sages: Wise men and sages have all made the mountains their own chambers, their own body and mind." So spoke Dogen, a 13th century founder of the Soto Zen tradition, which is famous for its tenant of communing with nature. Pilgrimages to sacred mountains have been made for thousands of years. Hundreds of mountain ranges cover the planet, but spiritual seekers revere only a few. These pristine peaks are the ones worshipped through indigenous folklore and ancient religious texts; many have long been considered the home to immortal gods. The Hopi regard the San Francisco Peaks as the legendary residence of the kachinas. The kachinas are Hopi gods who are said to live underground in the mountains, much like the Lemurians inside Mount Shasta. Several other sacred mountains are the keystone to indigenous religions, including Pilot Mountain in North Carolina, Devils Tower in Wyoming, and the many impressive peaks in the Cascade Range and the Rocky Mountains.

## Temples, Shrines, and Churches

Back in the time when North America was free of human influence, there were obvious places that people perceived as special. Here, the first shrines were built. Then large settlements rose, and in the hallowed parts of early cities enormous temple mounds and platforms were erected. Oftentimes the original temple would denote the origin of the principality. These sacred precincts were home to the priestly caste and the molders of civilization. In almost every case, the original

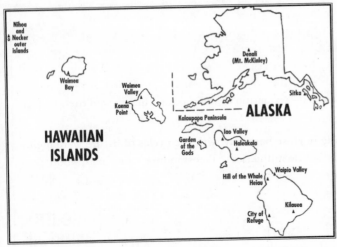

center of an ancient city contained a temple or shrine devoted to a pantheon of pagan gods. Sometimes the temples of antiquity would also be a location of sacrifice. This could be strictly devotional, but oftentimes it adopted the more grizzly practice of animal or human sacrifice.

Modern temples, shrines and churches all share one common feature: They were built to help people come closer to God. These structures are sources of spiritual power that help seekers recover some peace of mind in a seemingly crazy world. They bring people together in acts of faith and love. The temples, shrines and churches of the world are devotional sanctuaries for those seeking divine inspiration, regardless of religion, denomination, or sect.

## Pyramid Mounds and Astronomical Arrangements

Among the most intellectually advanced civilizations of early history—the Egyptian, Sumerian, Chinese, Mexican and Tibetan—all were pyramid builders. When humans began to construct artificial structures they used numbers and measurements derived from the natural world. The idea was to reflect the order of heaven on earth. Particularly in the context of a flat plain, pyramids represented an effort to measure an elevated aspiration uniting humans with the cosmos. Aesthetic awareness in relation to universal principles could alter states of consciousness, and enhance psychological and spiritual development. As a towering geometrical shape, the many types of pyramids functioned as astronomy platforms, ritual centers and sometimes deep within, as tombs. In eastern North America, the lost Mississippian Culture erected enormous earthen pyramids fronting central plazas, similar in design to their Mayan and Aztec neighbors in Central America.

Most of North America's prehistoric earthen pyramids feature alignments or were situated near wooden circular henges that served as astronomical calendars. Archaeoastronomy became a part of North American archaeology following Warren Wittry's 1964 discovery of a series of woodhenges at Cahokia Mounds in Illinois. Wittry demonstrated that these wooden features were solar observatories. Sadly, most of the earthen pyramids and geometric earthworks that once dotted the eastern landscape are now lost. Sometimes new investigations can only be conducted by the reports of earlier researchers. Many archaeologists consider the 19th century work of E. G. Squier and E. H. Davis to be the first archaeological investigation in the United States. Although Squier and Davis did not record alignments in the mound sites they charted, their maps are invaluable in aiding archaeoastronomers in their re-evaluation of the mound builders and their incredible architecture.

Prehistoric people living in close harmony with the cycles of nature were highly sensitive to the planet's subtle influences. Freestanding stone and wood post arrangements represent a profound understanding of the cosmos, especially the earth's relationship with the sun and moon. Stone, wood, and earthen circles were used as calendars to predict seasons, as planetariums to study the movement of stars, and as meeting places where native people could gather and exchange information. Although many have been lost, thousands of alignments remain on the continent—with the most famous being the medicine wheels on the western plains of Canada and certain megalithic arrangements in New England.

## New World Colonization Revisionist Theories

The most widely-accepted theory concerning the peopling of the New World is that the first human inhabitants were the Clovis people, who are thought to have arrived approximately 13,000 years ago. This is the Bering Straits migration theory proposed in the 1930s, which still remains a popular belief today. After all, artifacts of the Clovis culture are found throughout most of the United States and as far south as Panama. This standard theory

## MAP ICON LEGEND

### PREHISTORIC NATIVE AMERICAN

| | | | |
|---|---|---|---|
| Pictographs = | 🔥 | Unusual Human Remains = | 💀 |
| Medicine Wheel = | ⊕ | Geoglyphs = | 🏃 |
| Early Artifact Site = | 🔥 | Effigy Mounds = | 🐻 |
| Petroglyphs = | 🕺 | Temple Mounds = | ▱ |
| Cliff Dwellings = | 🏚 | Burial Mounds = | ▴▴▴ |

### PRE-COLUMBUS EUROPEAN

| | | | |
|---|---|---|---|
| Dolmens = | 🗿 | Celtic Artifacts = | † |
| Chambers = | ▦ | Norse Artifacts = | ⚔ |
| Standing Stones = | ⋯ | Phoenician Artifacts = | 👁 |
| Script or Carving = | ✳ | Norse Longhouses = | 🏠 |

### MODERN NATIVE AMERICAN

| | | | |
|---|---|---|---|
| Reservation = | 𝕏 | Sacred Hill or Mound = | ⛰ |
| Totem Poles = | 🗿 | Early Footpaths+Routes = | ∼∼∼∙∙ |
| Sacred Peak = | ⛩ | Haunted Site = | 👻 |
| Pueblo = | 🏘 | Hawaiian Heiau = | ▦ |

### GENERAL SYMBOLS

| | | | |
|---|---|---|---|
| County Road = | ⬛ | Mountain Range = | ⛰ |
| State Highway = | (105) | Woodlands = | 🌲 |
| Interstate = | (H20) | Grassland = | 𝔀𝔀 |
| Mesa or Butte = | ⬛ | Swampland = | 𝔀 |
| Volcano = | 🌋 | Dominant Mt. Peak = | ⛰ |
| Waterfall = | 🏞 | Pagoda or Eastern Garden = | 🎋 |
| Lava Tube = | 🌊 | Sunken Ruins = | ⚓ |
| Vortex = | ◆✦ | Christian Site = | † |
| Hot Spring = | ♨ | Mission = | ⛪ |
| Geyser = | 🌿 | Church or Cathedral = | ⛪⛪ |
| Fossils = | 🦴 | Capital City = | ⊕ |
| Cave = | 🦇 | UFO Sightings = | 🛸 |

### Sacred Places North America

has been challenged in recent decades by a growing number of archaeologists, with newly identified Preclovis sites including Cactus Hill, Virginia and Monte Verde, Chile. Other experts claim no conclusive evidence of Preclovis inhabitation has yet been definitely established. The Topper site in South Carolina may change everything we think about the peopling of North America. Radiocarbon tests of carbonized plant remains from the Pleistocene era were found with stone artifacts dated to be at least 50,000 years old, below the level where Clovis and Preclovis tools were found. This 2004 finding along the Savannah River in Allendale County by University of South Carolina archaeologist Dr. Albert Goodyear indicates that humans inhabited North America long before the last Ice Age, more than 20,000 years ago. Until the recent challenges to the Clovis theory, it was unusual for archaeologists to dig any deeper than the sediment layers of the Clovis culture, based on the belief that no human artifacts would be found older than Clovis.

The new findings in South Carolina are potentially explosive revelations in archaeology. Not only does this disclosure cause North American archaeology to question its own basic premises, but the whole conception of human migrations around the world is now in question. We are told the dawn of modern *Homo sapiens* occurred in Africa between 60,000 and 80,000 years ago. Evidence of modern human's migration out of the African continent has been documented in Australia and Central Asia at 50,000 years, and roaming into Europe around 40,000 years ago. The fact that humans could have been in North America at or near the same time has sparked many debates among archaeologists worldwide, raising new questions on the origin and migration of the human species. "Topper is the oldest radiocarbon dated site in North America," says Dr. Goodyear. "However, other early sites in Brazil and Chile, as well as a site in Oklahoma also suggest that humans were in the Western Hemisphere as early as 30,000 years ago, to perhaps 60,000." One possible solution to this riddle, but routinely ignored by archaeologists, is that an earlier Atlantis civilization existed in this distant timeframe and may have been partially responsible for the peopling of the Americas.

## New Evidence of Very Early Arrivals

Unlike Asia, Europe and Africa, the New World of the Americas contains not a single human fossil deposit other than *Homo sapiens*. This fact implies that humans arrived independently in North America via the "land bridge" known as Beringia, or ocean bound from the east and west by boat. The Mongolian stock of Indians were known to have traveled across the Bering Strait land bridge and down an ice-free corridor east of the Rockies as the last glaciers began to melt about 13,000 years ago. An ongoing genetic investigation suggests wider cultural diffusion, building support for the theory that ancient Asian seafarers began populating western North America thousands of years before the migration of big-game hunters from Siberia. Attracted by the food-rich kelp beds ringing the Pacific coasts of present-day Russia, Alaska and British Columbia, the earlier maritime migrants are believed to have plied the coastal waters in sealskin boats, moving in small groups over many generations from their traditional homelands in the Japanese islands or elsewhere along Asia's eastern seaboard. Other genetic matches of

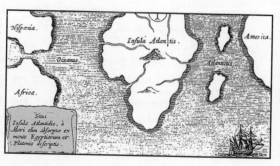

▲ Athanasius Kircher's map of Atlantis, here depicted to be in the center of the North Atlantic Ocean.

ancient North Americans are linked to Pacific Islanders and Japan's indigenous Ainu people. Interest in the theory has been stoked by recent DNA studies showing characteristic links between a 10,000-year-old skeleton found in an Alaskan cave and genetic traits also identified in modern Japanese and Tibetan populations. These Asian groupings are also linked to aboriginal populations along the west coasts of North and South America. The rise of the "coastal migration" theory has been advanced by a sprinkling of other ancient archeological finds throughout the Americas—several of them being too old to fit the traditional theory of an exclusive overland migration. Proponents of coastal migration argue that Ice Age migrants in boats might have island-hopped southward along North America's west coast as early as 16,000 years ago, or traveled in oceangoing vessels across the South Pacific even earlier. The travelers would have taken advantage of tropical islands or small refuges of land that had escaped envelopment by glaciers. The difficulty proving this theory is that nearly all of the land that might contain traces of human settlement or activity is now under water. The mounting evidence to support this contentious new theory about the peopling of the Americas is gradually gaining support in scholarly circles.

On the Atlantic side of the continent, diffusionist historians maintain that earlier European seafarers arrived long before Christopher Columbus' Caribbean visit in the late 13th century. Evidence is now being established that Egyptian and Phoenician traders from the Mediterranean, Celtic sailors of Spain, Basque explorers, Irish monks and the Scandinavia Norse were also North American colonizers, primarily in the regions of eastern Canada and New England. A much older migration may have occurred when survivors from the legendary continent of Atlantis arrived about 50,000 years ago. All of these early arrivals would have blended genetically with the indigenous people over time. When modern European explorers reached the North American continent in the early 14th century, the Historic or Modern Period in the Americas began. In Hawaii the first contact with Europeans came in the late 16th century. The new European explorers, who later became permanent settlers, brought with them new technology, diseases, and political, social, and religious systems completely foreign to the native inhabitants. The introduction of guns, germs and steel were utterly new concepts to the native populations, and the changes brought to their age-old lifestyles were profound and, almost without exception, disastrous.

The highly controversial theory that Caucasians traveled to America before, after, or contemporaneously with the Bering Straits migration is not without detractors. For one, it would diminish the special position held by the aboriginal people of North America that they are the only true "Native Americans." For reasons of political correctness, and the racial implications that would result, the facts surrounding this theory have been suppressed. The persistent view of most "old school" historians that North America was not contacted anytime before Columbus, fails to take into account even the most basic evidence. Beyond the hard proof, there have been many justifications to keep these theories underreported and out of the history books. The first was a dilemma for biblical scholars who literally interpreted the Scriptures of the Old Testament, which describes the settlement of only three continents after Noah's flood. Either the Scriptures were wrong, or the aboriginal people of North America did not exist. Another justification was legal ownership. Certainly the Native Americans were here first, but by regarding them as "uncivilized savages," the new settlers were able to feel warranted in taking over the land they occupied. But what if there were prior European settlements in North America before the pilgrims of the Mayflower? This presents a much greater dilemma. If historians acknowledged such a presence, European powers from Scandinavia to Ireland to Spain could all have claimed legal ownership of the New World that was actively being established in North America by the British and French. Not only that, but earlier conquests would belittle the feats of modern explorers, especially the "discoverers" of North America who loaned their name to the many places of their conquest and influence. Such motivations would have been ample reason for 19th and 20th century historians, as well as modern Native American special interest groups, to suppress and deny any evidence of previous European settlements or exploratory incursions into the continent.

## What Happened to the First Caucasians in North America?

New evidence indicates that the first Caucasians in North America were either killed in open warfare with the Indians, or more likely were absorbed into what became the numerically dominant Native American groupings. The discovery of the Kennewick Man and Spirit Cave Man and their related gene string supports the genetic tracking between non-Mongoloid body traits of ancient skeletal remains in North America and recent genetic studies with ancient Caucasian peoples (see: Columbia River Gorge; Lake Lahontan sites). The successive waves of Caucasians in America therefore disappeared, presumably with their culture, through a long process of racial integration and warfare, leaving behind only tantalizing clues such as skeletons, tools, weapons, petroglyphs, earthworks, language fragments, stone structures, runic writings, and genealogical anomalies as evidence of their existence. The sacred places they utilized must be fully explained and integrated into this survey.

As would happen with anyone who endeavors to present an all-inclusive survey of prehistoric (as well as historic and modern) sacred sites in North America, these anomalies can sometimes be central to establishing a location long out of use. Sometimes the "spirit of the place" lingers on and deserves mention, no matter how inconvenient it may be to others. I have endeavored to do so with a straightforward approach by presenting each leading theory objectively. I fully expect those who conduct surveys similar to mine to be objective as well. If this is done, useful insights will be gained, which might be applied to the betterment of all.

## Why the Number 108?

Numbers, it can be argued, carry as much significance as letters. Numbers convey a different method of communication altogether, forming the basis for commerce and all the sciences. Numbers are deeply rooted in many cultural traditions, oftentimes contemporary with a civilization's original literary works. Such is the case with the number 108 in most East Asian religious cultures. 108 is the number of beads on sacred mala necklaces worn by millions of reverent Buddhists and Hindus. To them, the number 108 is associated with the precessionary cycles of Earth and

the cosmos above. If a Buddhist or Hindu pilgrim can endure a trip to the most sacred mountain in Asia, the inhospitable Mount Kailash on the Tibetan Plateau, that seeker is on a true path to nirvana. If that same pilgrim can manage 108 circuits around the base of Kailash in a single lifetime, their entry into heaven is assured.

▲ Signs of 108 span the continent.

## Mapping the Sacred

The artistic technique of illustrating maps or charts is called cartography. The information contained on maps was a highly protected secret in ancient times. Not until the 19th century did the physical properties of the planet at last become common knowledge. In antiquity the best cartographers were usually travelers themselves, studying shorelines, weather patterns and mountain ranges; trying to accurately convey their knowledge in maps for other explorers and sea captains by way of contrast. Amerigo Vespucci, the man who loaned his first name to identifying the continents of the New World, was an "Age of Discovery" cartographer who put his prominent signature over the landmass of North America.

Following the age-old tradition of cartography being passed on from mapmaker to mapmaker, my maps are hand drawn based on other source maps. I could have completely created the maps digitally, but I feel the hand drawn look better enhances my text and adds a personal touch. I designed them to look like they are out of a field notebook, and in some cases they were! Usually I worked on the text, maps, and illustrations simultaneously during production, going from one to the other when new information was collected. I included many additional minor sacred sites that I was not able to include with the 108 described sites in the text. I eliminated some modern cities and highways unless they were necessary to add for point of reference. I desire to include an eclectic assemblage of maps reflecting the long heritage of diverse cultures in North America.

## DISCLAIMER

In assembling the contents of this book, and all the books I write for that matter, my sole objective is to present every viewpoint with equal balance and respect. Some of the theories I present may be offensive to some groups, or may be ridiculed as outrageous nonsense. Atlantis survivors or ancient Mediterranean seafarers coming to North America thousands of years before Columbus may seem farfetched, but there is evidence suggesting that these early migrants may be a part of North American prehistory. When paranormal experiences such as ghosts, UFOs and Bigfoot sightings are associated with a sacred place, they too are mentioned. Lest we forget it is the message that is important, not the messenger. I see myself as that messenger; the scribe who collects a wide range of relevant data and distills it into a comprehensive volume. I realize there are vested interests in keeping some of the information presented out of a book like this, but like a defendant who is presumed innocent before being proven guilty, new theories also need their day in court. I respectfully ask the reader to be the judge and jury in this case by carefully considering all sides to the various theories presented in this volume, and to formulate his or her own conclusions.

# THE SOUTHWEST

*There are some secrets which do not permit themselves to be told.* -**Edgar Allan Poe,** *The Man of the Crowd*

T HE AMERICAN SOUTHWEST IS A LAND OF DRY and sometimes very hot desert conditions, separated by treacherous mountain ranges and intermittent streams cut by long empty canyons. The rugged terrain is ideal for small land reptiles, clumps of cactus, and dry scrub forests of juniper and piñon trees. Much of the region is semi-arid and seemingly devoid of life, but this makes it a land of stark contrasts and impressive scenery. Bisecting the entire region, the flowing waters of the Colorado River carved the Grand Canyon more than a mile (1.7 km) deep in some locations on its long journey to the Gulf of California. Like a long series of cascading steps from north to south, starting at an elevation over 5,000 feet (1,600 m), expansive flat-topped tablelands break off into steep edges known as mesas and feature the spectacular stand-alone rock formations called buttes that can resemble the shape of a cathedral or ghost ship. This fantastical landscape was carved by the elements of wind, rain, volcanic activity and flowing water erosion over many millennia. The climate occasionally changed during the long march of time, with some periods being wetter and allowing a wider proliferation of life.

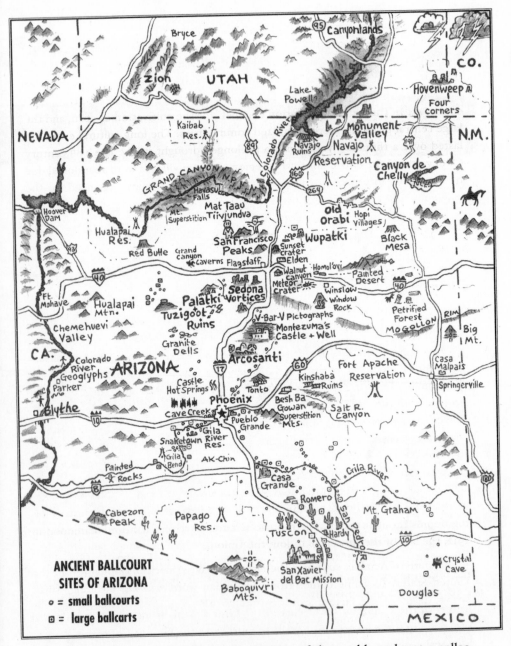

No area of North America and few countries of the world can boast a collection of archaeological ruins equal to that of the American Southwest, a cultural region that extends from the Great Basin of what is today Nevada and Utah, the Colorado Plateau, and the whole of Arizona and New Mexico. Only from the point of view of *norteamericanos,* the Spanish word for people north of Mexico, is the southwestern region of the United States known as the "Southwest." To the ancestral Pueblo Indians and Spanish *conquistadors,* the land of the Southwest was

26

the *Gran Chichimeca*, meaning the "Great Land of Nomads." These prehistoric wanderers for a time became the settled Hohokam, Fremont, Anasazi, Mogollon and Sinagua cultures, but were considered barbarians from the viewpoint of the more refined Valley of Mexico inhabitants. Prehistoric Mexican influence can be found in the architectural style of Southwestern cliff dwellings, pottery, ball-courts, *kivas*, trade items, irrigation channels for the cultivation of corn, and the large central plazas in more urbanized communities. The long cultural evolution lasted over a thousand years until a prolonged drought in the late 13th century CE devastated the entire Southwest region. Anasazi villages were abandoned due to starvation, internecine strife, and migrations. Life abruptly changed for the survivors, who centuries later became the ancestral Puebloan people. Today, surviving indigenous Southwest communities have retained their cultural heritage perhaps better than any other North American Indian segment. At a time when many ancient rituals have been forgotten elsewhere, the native people of the Southwest proudly display their age-old traditions on the largest reservations in North America.

# ARIZONA

Spanish conquistadors first entered what is today Arizona in 1540 on an unsuccessful expedition to locate the legendary Seven Cities of Gold. Instead they found a land of ghost cities left by the Hohokam, Arizona's earliest known people, and the cliff-dwelling ancestral Puebloans, also called the Anasazi. Franciscan priests started building a network of missions in their effort to save souls. Thwarted in 1680 by the Pueblo Revolt, the Spanish returned in the 1700s to crush Indian resistance. Over 300 years of Spanish domination ended with the 1848 treaty ending the Mexican War, but much of Arizona territory reverted to the victorious United States government. Apache and other Native American resistance continued until the end of the 19th century, even as railroads and mining booms brought thousands into the territory. Arizona achieved statehood in 1912, the last of the Lower 48 to join the Union.

The state of Arizona supports the largest Native American population in the United States. Its name comes from the Indian word *arizonac,* meaning "small spring." One of the fastest growing states in the country, Arizona is home to such famous natural wonders as the Painted Desert, the Petrified Forest, Meteor Crater and the Grand Canyon. The Navajo and Hopi reservations corner the northeastern part of the state in a vast land marked by towering red rock formations, spectacular canyons and green, forested mountains. Navajo territory, the larger of the two, completely surrounds the Hopi land, and overlaps into western New Mexico and southern Utah. In this part of Arizona primitive Navajo *hogans,* Hopi mesa adobe homes, traditional attire and lively ceremonies color the atmosphere. The Navajo and Hopi reservations are a place of limitless horizons, stark mesas, and reflective inspiration.

# Arcosanti

In the high desert of central Arizona is a prototype city called Arcosanti, built as an example on how urban congestion and social isolation can be eliminated. The city is designed according to the concept of "arcology"—the blending of architecture and ecology as one integral process—to address the wastefulness of modern urban sprawl. Arcology advocates a new city design, one that maximizes the interface of urban inhabitants, and to minimize the use of energy, pollution, raw materials and land, all the while allowing human interaction with the surrounding natural environment. "In a successful arcology arrangement," says Italian-born architect and philosopher Paolo Soleri, "the built and the living interact as organs would in a highly evolved being." Thus, Soleri specifically designed Arcosanti to be "the City in the Image of Man." As such, many systems at Arcosanti work together with efficient circulation of people and resources, multi-use buildings, and a proficient application of solar orientation for lighting, heating and cooling. In this complex, creative environment all aspects of the city are accessible, while personal privacy in a resourceful use of space is paramount to the overall design. As such, Solari proclaims, "A central tenet of arcology is that the city is the necessary instrument for the evolution of humankind."

Arcosanti is a three-dimensional, pedestrian-only urban environment developed entirely by Paolo Soleri, who studied under the eminent architect Frank Lloyd Wright. Under construction since 1970, Arcosanti is only about 10% completed and already houses nearly a hundred construction and artesian workers. When completed, Arcosanti will house 7,000 people, demonstrating ways to improve urban conditions and lessen our destructive impact on the earth. Its large yet compact structures and solar greenhouses will occupy only 25 acres (10 ha) of a 4,060-acre (1,624-ha) land preserve, keeping the natural countryside in close proximity to urban dwellers. Visitors report a "surge of inspiration" from being immersed in the advanced esthetic of geometric forms and utopian concepts applied at Arcosanti.

> The urban experiment called Arcosanti is
> located near an old Indian village. Both
> Arcosanti and the prehistoric pueblo are
> built under the concept of arcology, that is,
> architecture coherent with ecology.

Arcosanti is constructed on the top of a low mesa. On a cliff wall behind Arcosanti are two prehistoric petroglyphs of a human and mountain goat depicted in harmony with their natural environment. The petroglyphs are located near the entrance to a large cave. Native Americans presumably occupied the cave, and sustained a living in the fertile valley. Not far from the cave, atop the next mesa to the north of Arcosanti, is an unexcavated Indian settlement. The ruins incorporate the walled remains of several pit houses joined next to

▲ The City of Arcosanti was only one tenth completed in 2008.

each other in a townhouse fashion, built into the natural contours of the mesa. It may be a coincidence that an Indian pueblo community, so similar in concept to an arcology city, exists within a stone's throw from Arcosanti. Or maybe Paolo Soleri planned it that way.

### Getting to Arcosanti

Arcosanti is conveniently located just off Interstate 17, only 70 miles (113 km) north of metropolitan Phoenix. The exit for Arcosanti is at Cordes Junction, where signs lead motorists a few miles to the Visitor's Center. 50,000 tourists drop in every year for a free tour of the city. For those wishing to actively participate, there is a five-week workshop program at Arcosanti to teach Soleri's building techniques and arcological philosophy, while working to continue the city's construction. The current city was built almost entirely by the more than 4,000 past workshop participants.

## Canyon de Chelly

Within the four sacred mountains are a series of deep red-rock canyons intrinsic to the identity of the Navajo Nation. The sheer sandstone canyons and rock formations collectively known as Canyon de Chelly feature hundreds of Indian sites, including prehistoric pueblo dwellings and rock art murals spanning several thousand years. The two primary canyons, Canyon del Muerto and Canyon de Chelly, shelter an almost tropical oasis of trees and flowers through the high desert terrain. The two gorges and multiple tributaries create one of the Southwest's most impressive landscapes. The Navajo traditionally called the canyon *tsegi*, meaning variously "in the rock" or "canyon." The Spanish spelled it *chegui*, a Hispanicized version of the Navajo word. As they often did, American settlers later anglicized the name to "de Chelly," pronounced de shaye. Although the canyons are spiritually significant to the Navajo, the Navajo were not the first to settle in the canyon. The Navajo arrived in the late 1600s following three centuries of an intermittent Hopi presence, preceded by much older inhabitations.

Canyon de Chelly is home to several periods of prehistoric Indian civilizations dating from 2500 BCE until the Great Drought in 1300 CE. The earliest arrivals, a vague cultural classification called the Archaic, were a people who built

▲ The White House ruins in Canyon de Chelly.
Lithograph circa 1890.

no permanent homes but left images on the canyon walls to tell their stories. Next on the scene were the pithouse-dwelling Basketmaker people, who were attracted to the canyon by the presence of water to irrigate their primitive farms. They remained for several hundred years before the Anasazi moved into the canyon and built upon the older Basketmaker home sites. Between 1050 and 1300 CE, human habitation reached a peak in the canyon with the building of dramatic cliff dwellings, including the White House, Antelope House, Sliding Rock, and the Mummy Cave settlement. Eventually the Anasazi would vacate the canyon as mysteriously as the Basketmakers did, leaving behind abandoned pueblos, rock art murals and assorted artifacts. To the Hopi people, whose modern reservation is only 50 miles (80 km) away, some sites in the canyon are considered highly sacred, like the *kachina* paintings in a cave near Antelope House. The Hopi farmed in Canyon de Chelly during the summer months and erected only temporary housing. Although most of the pictographs and petroglyphs in Canyon de Chelly were created by the Anasazi, some examples can be traced to the Archaic people, the Basketmakers, the Hopi as well as modern Navajos. Each culture brought with them their own colorful and distinct style of rock art.

> The Navajo people retain a mystical bond to Canyon de Chelly, considering it the physical, historical, and spiritual center of their nation.

For many years the canyon served as a refuge and fortress to the Navajo people. The Athapaskan speaking Navajos, originally a branch of the Apaches and still recognizably Apachean, moved into the Southwest from the Great Plains in the 15th and 16th centuries. The mysterious serpentine ravines allowed protection from their enemies, as well as fertile farming and grazing lands. So important was the canyon to the Navajo that it was specifically outlined in the original 1868 treaty with the United States: "(the reservation boundary) embraces the outlet of the Canon-de-Chilly (sic), which canyon is to be all included in this reservation, shall be, and the same is hereby, set apart for the use and occupation of the Navajo tribe of Indians, and for such other friendly tribes or individual Indians." When the first boundary lines for the Navajo Reservation were drawn, Canyon de Chelly was intentionally placed dead center. Navajo tribal members remain in the canyon leading a simple lifestyle herding sheep and growing crops. Many Navajos living outside the canyon and other Colorado Plateau tribes return to Canyon de Chelly on pilgrimage to make prayer offerings or perform age-old rituals as their ancestors have done for many generations.

### Getting to Canyon de Chelly National Monument

Canyon de Chelly National Monument is located 3 miles (4.8 km) from Route 191 near the town Chinle in northeastern Arizona. The 26-mile (42-km) canyon's sheer cliffs range from 30 to more than 1,000 feet (9 to 300 m) in height, providing a spectacular backdrop for hundreds of prehistoric ruins, as well as modern Navajo farms and houses. The Visitor's Center offers exhibits and cultural displays. A drive around the canyon offers excellent rim viewpoints. A Navajo guide is required for all canyon access, except for the 2.5-mile (4-km) round trip White House Trail.

## The Navajos

In the 15th century, the *Díne* (the original Navajo name meaning "The People") migrated south from the far northern tundra regions of North America into the Central Plains. A hundred years later part of the tribe migrated once again, this time to what is today northeastern Arizona and northwestern New Mexico. Here they encountered the Pueblo Indians already established on the land for many centuries. Similar to the Romans adapting to the traditions of older Greek mythology, the Navajo emulated the legends of their older Hopi counterparts. Navajo legend describes the Díne as having to pass through three different worlds before arriving on this earthly plane, called the fourth world, or the Glittering World. On this plane the Díne believe there are two classes of beings: the Earth People, and the Holy People. The Earth People are the Navajo themselves, while the Holy People are the equivalent of Navajo gods. The Holy People are said to have the power to aid or harm Earth People, and centuries ago the Holy People taught the Díne how to live correctly in their everyday life. They were taught how to harmoniously exist with Mother Earth, Father Sky, animals, plants, and insects. The Holy People assisted the First Man and the First Woman out of the third world into the Glittering World, where the first man and woman found

▲ A mural in the Navajo Nation inspires pride in their traditional ways.

pueblos already existing. The Holy People put four sacred mountains in four different directions: Mount Blanca near Alamosa, Colorado to the east; Mount Taylor near Grants, New Mexico to the south; the San Francisco Peaks near Flagstaff, Arizona to the west; and Mount Hesperus near Durango, Colorado to the north. Collectively these mountains established the ancestral Navajoland of the fourth world. The Díne (named the "Navajo" by Spanish explorers in 1540) mark their emergence into the fourth world from a hole in the La Plata Mountains of southwestern Colorado. The story of Díne creation is recounted in the tribe's most important ceremony, called the Blessing Way Rite. This ritual had been given to the tribe shortly after the emergence of the Holy People who created the natural world and humans. Navajo religious doctrine holds that the first Blessing Way ceremony was performed during the emergence of First Man and First Woman. The Navajo people and the Blessing Way came into being simultaneously and symbiotically, thus establishing the ceremony's importance for all time. The two-day ceremony begins by recounting in song First Man's creation of humankind. The next day more songs are sung about other stages of the world's creation, and a bathing ritual in yucca (cactus) suds is performed to symbolize renewal. Crushed flower blossoms, corn meal, and pollen are sprinkled upon the ground to bless and bring good fortune to the Navajo people. The ceremony concludes with a 12-stanza song designed to satisfy the Holy People and reinforce the Navajo ideal of harmony between humans and nature. Blessing Way is performed at least once every six months for each Navajo family, in addition to special occasions such as weddings, impending births and the consecration of a new home. The Navajo regard this ceremony as fundamentally life-giving because the Díne founders bestowed it, defining the tribe and its world purpose. Indeed, the Navajo believe that when the Blessing Way ceremony ceases to be performed, the world will come to an end.

# Monument Valley

In a high desert climate where fresh water and wild game are scarce, the pre-historic Anasazi Indians thrived in the area for over 700 years. The Anasazi first came to Monument Valley at least 1,500 years ago, constructing cliff dwellings and carving mysterious petroglyphs before suddenly disappearing. Some Navajos claim there are a few Anasazi ruins in Monument Valley that no white man has ever seen. The Athapaskan speaking Navajo arrived hundreds of years after the Anasazi disappeared, adapting well to the arid environment. In Monument Valley, where the past seems eternal and history is all around, the Navajo have maintained harmony with "Mother Earth and Father Sky," blending what is modern with what is traditional in this fourth, or Glittering World. The valley features spires, buttes, and mesas towering over the mile-high terrain by a thousand feet (300+ m) or more. The landscape speaks eloquently of nature's own creation technique by using wind, erosion, rain and time.

Much of Navajo culture remains unchanged and preserved in Monument Valley. Their art has been passed down from generation to generation and many artistic techniques continue as they have since ancient times. Potters still use the coil method, adding liquid colored clay to create exquisite designs. Hand woven carpets and other textiles continue to be dyed and spun at Monument Valley. Traditional homes called *hogans* dot the landscape. The domed, hexagon-shaped hogan is regarded as a sanctuary to the families who take up permanent residence. Native Americans usually assigned religious significance to their dwellings, which would oftentimes double as ceremonial centers. For example, the hogan entrance always faces east toward the rising sun. Some of the 300 Navajos still living in Monument Valley reside in the traditional earthen homes, although most now include modern stoves for heat and cooking.

> Monument Valley is among the most photo-graphed landscape in the world. The Navajo Nation considers it a healing place with deep spiritual meaning.

Several important Navajo ceremonies started within Monument Valley, including the origination of the Squaw Dance and the Yei Bi Chei Dance. Both dances were first held in Monument Valley and continue to be performed at different locations on the reservation where needed. Yei Bi Chei was a holy figure to the Navajo. Distinguished Navajo men dress as the Yei Bi Chei and dance for healing purposes in a very sacred nine-day ritual called the Night Way Ceremony. A prominent rock formation in Monument Valley resembles a line formation of several different Yei dancers. The Squaw Dance involves winter stories about animals when they are hibernating. In addition to group ceremonies, individual Navajo families have their own favored "prayer places" in different locations around Monument Valley.

▲ The bizarre, eroded landscape of Monument Valley. Each of the mesa formations has a Navajo legend associated with its unique shape.

Modern visitors are equally inspired when traveling among the mammoth monoliths and immense rock spires stretching skyward from the desert floor. Transpersonal healing experiences are often reported. Monument Valley is especially enchanting at sunrise and sunset when the sandstone rock formations transform into various hues between orange to crimson red as the light changes. Monument Valley is an ever-changing landscape holding many secrets. The Navajo name of the valley is *Tsé Bii Ndzisgaii* meaning "white streaks inside rock." Many mineral and silver deposits are known in the valley, but mining is strictly prohibited. The Navajo killed two soldiers serving under Kit Carson after they attempted to mine silver in the sacred valley. The Mitchell Butte and Merrick Butte were named after the slain silver poachers. The Navajo retain many creation tales and stories about everyday life in association with the various buttes and mesas.

## Getting to Monument Valley

The vast landscape of Monument Valley is completely enclosed on the Navajo Reservation, located on the border of northern Arizona and southern Utah. Monument Valley Navajo Tribal Park is located 4 miles (6.5 km) east of U.S. 163 on the Arizona side. The nearest town is Kayenta, Arizona at the intersection of U.S. 160 and U.S. 163. An unpaved scenic drive winds among red sandstone buttes and spires rising above the desert floor. The Navajo Reservation is the largest reservation in the United States, encompassing 25,000 square miles (65,000 sq km) across northwestern Arizona, southern Utah and northeastern New Mexico. Climbing any of the buttes or mesas in Monument Valley is prohibited without a Navajo guide.

## The Mysterious Anasazi

There is no accurate account of what these people called themselves; the term *Anasazi* is a Navajo word meaning variously the "Ancient Ones," or "Ancient Enemies." These early pueblo dwellers are known to Arizona's Hopi people as *Hisatsinom*, meaning the "People of Long Ago." For the Zuni, these people were the *Ashiwi*. Modern Puebloan people (Hopi, Zuni, Tiwa, Acoma and others) do not advocate the cultural division and scientific names often applied to their ancient ancestors, such as the anglicized "Anasazi" and "Sinagua." Ironically, even "Pueblo" is a Spanish term for clustered homes in a village, given by the conquistador Coronado during an expedition to the Southwest. Yet for purposes of greater clarity and understanding, the term "Anasazi" and other common usage names will be featured throughout this book.

The early Anasazi (100 BCE) were nomadic hunter-gatherers ranging over great expanses of territory throughout much of the Southwest. By 700 CE they had begun to live in settled communities of which New Mexico's Chaco Canyon was the largest and best-preserved pueblo village. The extensive ruins are the greatest architectural achievement of prehistoric Native Americans. Intensive construction occurred throughout Chaco Canyon between 900 to 1120 CE, resulting in the development of several sophisticated dwelling complexes. The Chaco Canyon complex was the main social and ceremonial center of the Anasazi culture.

The Anasazi people had no written language, yet were bound by a complex religion based on weather patterns. Since rain was vital to their very existence, the coming of storms, especially thunder and lightning, must have evoked a supernatural feeling for the pueblo's inhabitants. A wide variety of items have been excavated and determined to be ceremonial offerings. These offerings include traditional tools, beads, and pots, but also include sacrificed animals such as black bear, dog and puma.

Just as the Anasazi religion is a mystery, so is their demise. Sometime after the 12th century CE the population of Chaco and its outlier Great Houses went into steep decline, until most of the communities were completely abandoned. An invading tribal force is unlikely because the pueblos were well-fortified and do not show signs of being attacked. A more likely reason is overused land, lack of trees, lack of water and failing crops. All this suggests a tragic

▲ Navajo hogans may have been based on earlier Anasazi homes.

human drama of famine, death and cultural decline. It is likely that the remaining Anasazi assimilated with other tribes, migrated south to establish new communities or became the Hopi nation. Still today the Hopi regard the Hisatsinom as their forefathers.

## Old Oraibi

High atop the Third Mesa with sweeping views of the San Francisco Mountains, live the fourth world descendents of the Hopi Nation. The rich Hopi tradition, adopted by the Navajo, teaches that three worlds existed prior to the one in which we now live. Legend says that a very long time ago, in the first world, their ancestors witnessed destruction of civilization with fire. The second world was destroyed by ice, and the third inundated by water. Sometime in the early 12$^{th}$ century of the fourth world, the Hopi left their traditional homeland and arrived on the Three Mesas in northeastern Arizona. Their first settlement, known today as Old Oraibi, has the longest unbroken cultural roots on the continent by a single people. A series of severe droughts in the late 13$^{th}$ century forced the Hopi to abandon several smaller villages in the region and consolidate within Oraibi and a few other settlements. Once the most populous and influential Hopi pueblo community, Old Oraibi fell into decline in 1907 when economic disturbances and internal dissension split the village. Many residents went to live in other pueblos or form new communities, such as Hotevilla and Bakavi, but the heart and soul of pueblo living remained at Oraibi. And while never completely abandoned, Old Oraibi today looks like a living archaeological site with original adobe walls still intact and scattered potsherds littering the ground. Many of the last inhabited Hopi pueblo homes at Old Oraibi date back hundreds of years.

> Old Oraibi, established around 1100 CE, is the longest continuously inhabited settlement in North America.

The Hopi Nation is made up of 34 clans, each with its own distinct role. The people of the Badger Clan, for instance, are the keepers of healing plants. Those of the Eagle Clan are the spiritual leaders. Other clans are the Bear, Butterfly, Cloud, Corn, Crow, Snake and dozens more. Each clan has its own history that is passed down through its members. Each clan is responsible for certain ceremonies and for honoring certain sacred objects. Clan membership determines which ceremonial offices a person may hold. With such a division of knowledge, it is said that no single Hopi person could know absolutely everything about the Hopi Nation. Hopi society is matrilineal, meaning the clan of the mother determines the clan membership of the children. Property is passed on from mother to daughter. Parents have the role of only showing love to their children, while

36

the families' uncle has the role of disciplining the children if necessary. In times of death, clan members are usually buried near other clan members. The clan members of Old Oraibi are still buried in the traditional manner of bundling the body with yucca ropes and placed into hidden caves in the western cliff walls of the Third Mesa near Oraibi.

Hopi spirituality is intertwined with everyday life. Most Hopi still pray to the *kachina* supernatural beings as their outward expression of spirituality. The roots of the Hopi people can be traced back 100 generations or more. Today approximately 40% of Hopi are Christian, while the rest adhere to the indigenous religion of their ancestors. When the Hopi pray, they pray first for family, then for clan and then for the rest of the world. To stay close to the land, each clan and each person has a personal plot for growing food or sacrament items. The three mesas making up the Hopi homeland are considered the "Center of the Universe." Old Oraibi is on the outer tip of the Third Mesa, with abundant petroglyphs of kachinas featured on the eastern and southern bluff walls. Each of the three contiguous mesas features three distinct dialects of the Hopi language. The kachina gods are different on each mesa too, unique to each pueblo community in appearance and meaning.

In the pueblos of the various cliff-dwelling tribes are semi-subterranean ceremonial rooms, referred to as *kivas*, where the traditional entrance is through the roof using a ladder. Here appointed priests set out sacred objects in preparation for multi-day ceremonies, the most complex of which centers around the kachina

▲ A Spanish church in ruins on the Third Mesa of the Hopi Reservation.

▲ House of Chief Talti, Old Oraibi.
Lithograph circa 1875.

cult. On a specific date, usually twice per month in the season they are performed, masked and plumed members dance through the pueblo to bestow happiness onto the tribe and reaffirm the promise of ample, life-giving rain. In Old Oraibi there are three kivas left out of an original 23, and the settlement has been hosting kachina dances for many centuries. Only on the Third Mesa are held the dances open to the public. The First and Second Mesas hold kachina dances, but they are closed to non-indigenous people due to fear of exploitation. When Old Oraibi lost most of its population in 1907, it also lost its position as the center of Hopi spirituality and culture. Although the 1939 Hopi tribal constitution provides each village with a seat on the tribal council, Oraibi has declined to elect a representative and maintains relative independence from the tribal council. Old Oraibi has since retained a more traditional way of life and has resisted the adoption of modern culture that is visible in other Hopi villages.

### *Getting to Old Oraibi*

Old Orabi is located on Hopi land in northeastern Arizona, surrounded completely by the Navajo Nation. Arizona Route 264 crosses east-west directly through the Hopi Indian Reservation and accesses all communities on the three mesas. Old Oraibi is on the Third Mesa, just east of the village Hotevilla. No photographs are allowed in Old Oraibi, unless permission is granted from a Hopi member in the community. Kachina dances are held on weekends, usually twice per month, starting on winter solstice, and finishing on summer solstice. Admission is free, but photography or the drawing of dancers is strictly prohibited. Many other villages sit atop the Hopi Nation's three mesas: Walpi, Shungopavi, Polacca, Sipaulovi, Bakavi, and Kykotsmovi, sometimes called New Oraibi and the seat of the Hopi tribal government. Most of the Hopi elders and mystics live in the town Hotevilla. Old Oraibi is listed on the National Register of Historic Places and was declared a National Historic Landmark in 1964.

# San Francisco Peaks

Northern Arizona's San Francisco lava field is an area of young volcanoes sprinkled along the southern margin of the Colorado Plateau. The vast volcanic field spreads over 1,935 square miles (3,100 sq km) and includes more than 600 vents and cinder cones. Most of the vents are erupted basalt lava flows, interspersed with scattered scoria cones. The individual peaks and vents are the eroded remnants of a larger compound stratovolcano, which is a moderately steep volcano formed by multiple eruptions. The stratovolcano features lava domes, characterized by bulbous masses built by internal inflation. San Francisco Mountain is the only stratovolcano in the San Francisco volcanic field and was built by several eruptions occurring between about 1 and 0.4 million years ago. Since then, much of the mountain has been displaced to create the "Inner Basin." The missing material may have been removed quickly and explosively by an eruption similar to the 1980 eruption of Mount Saint Helens in Washington, or it may have been removed slowly and incrementally by a combination of water erosion, glacial scouring, internal cone collapses or large landslides. Although inactive for a thousand years, the San Francisco volcanic field is believed to be situated on top of a geothermal "hot spot," so another eruption in the future is very likely.

> Most of the Southwestern tribes believe the
> San Francisco Peaks are the sacred abode of
> spiritual beings named kachinas by the Hopi.

A kachina is considered an ancestral spirit to the Hopi and several surrounding Puebloan people including the Zuni and Acoma. Kachinas are not gods. They are spiritual helpers who have been with the Hopi since their emergence from the base of the mountain. The kachinas live atop the San Francisco Peaks within sight of the Hopi and Navajo reservations. Every winter the kachinas come down from the mountains and visit the Hopi and other Native Americans who request their help. In Hopi life there are three versions of kachinas. First, there are the mystical deities themselves who reside high atop the San Francisco Peaks and govern elements like rain and wind. Second, there are masked dancers and impersonators who are actually men of the tribe portraying their favorite gods in Hopi ceremonies. The third version is kachina dolls or carvings. The age-old Hopi tradition of carving various kachina figurines from cottonwood roots carries on to this day. The dolls were first created as a remembrance and teaching aid to be handed over to children during a ceremony by a kachina dancer. Now the carvings are popular tourist gifts and collector items.

The Hopi recognize over 300 different kachina deities, varying from desert animals to vegetables, each one playing an integral role in their living mythology. Each deity has a job to do or a lesson to teach. The kachinas arrive at the Hopi mesas in the winter disguised as Hopi men dressed in traditional attire to represent the various gods. The Hopi believe that when an impersonator wears

▲ The San Francisco Peaks soar above ancient ruins.
(Photo courtesy U.S. Geological Survey)

a kachina mask, he becomes empowered with the characteristics of the spirit being represented and should therefore be regarded as sacred. Each kachina has an important role in the daily lives of the Hopi people. Ogres teach discipline, chief kachinas teach wisdom and have powers comparable to that of a religious elder. The cricket, with his wheat-shock antennae, is a symbol of fertility. There are also female kachinas who, with the exception of only one kachina called *Pachavuin Mana*, are portrayed strictly by the men of the villages. The "women" instruct on the importance of values, such as a mother would teach their children. There are cloud spirits called *shalakos* who bring rain. There are also light-hearted clown kachinas, such as the formidable mudheads, whose primary function is one of amusement during pauses in kachina dancing, or to dampen the seriousness of a major ceremony. "Borrowed" kachinas are deities that have traveled from one pueblo to another at an earlier date and have since been "adopted" by that pueblo. A relatively new Third Mesa kachina is called the Priest-Killer, seen touting a bloody knife and a spindly cross, who harkens back to the Pueblo Revolt against the Spanish clergy. In 1680, many pueblo tribes, including the Hopi, rose up and killed the Spanish priests who had often cruelly forced their ways onto the native people.

Some of the most elaborate kachina rituals are devoted to rain-god worship. Similar to other southwestern Native American rituals, the rain deities are associated with ancestral spirits who return each year in the form of rain clouds from their western homelands. The winter rains of the American Southwest typically come from the west. According to Hopi mythology the kachinas inhabit the San

Francisco Peaks for only part of each year, until the rain comes and then they fly as clouds to provide precious rain to the mesa country. They stay until midsummer when they return to the coolness of high elevation forests. Hopi spirits also carry the prayers of their people. The arrival of the kachinas in December for the *Powamu,* or the Bean Dance, starts the cycle of kachina appearances. They appear regularly until just before harvest time around the summer solstice, ending with the *Niman* Dance, or the Home Dance, at which time all kachinas return to the underworld through the *sipapu* in the San Francisco Peaks, the entrance where the first humans emerged. The area directly surrounding the towering San Francisco Peaks is protected as the Kachina Peaks Wilderness, so named because of its spiritual significance to the Hopi people.

### Climbing the San Francisco Peaks

San Francisco Mountain, Arizona's tallest peak at 12,633 feet (3,790 m), serves as a scenic backdrop to Flagstaff and much of the northwestern part of the state. The greater San Francisco region offers the hiker plenty of solitude and high altitude exploration possibilities. A good selection of trails abound, including the Sunset Trail, the Kachina Trail, and the Inner Basin Trail offering access to the various peaks and features many spectacular views that reward the sometimes strenuous hiking effort. The arduous "Humphreys Trail" is 4.5 miles (7.3 km) to the top of San Francisco Mountain. This is the only trail that leads to the highest point in Arizona. The trail ascends through alpine scenery of huge rockslides, avalanche chutes and a bristlecone forest as it climbs from 9,300 to 12,633 feet (1,890-3,790 m). The last part of the summit trail is rocky, steep and unshielded from the elements. The view from the top is a full 360-degree panorama of the Grand Canyon, the three mesas of the Hopi, the Painted Desert, and Oak Creek Canyon. From Flagstaff, drive 7 miles (11.3 km) on Highway 180 to the northbound Snowbowl Road (Forest Road 516). The trailhead begins at the north end in the first parking lot of the Snowbowl Ski area. Note that off-trail hiking and camping are prohibited above the treeline.

## Sedona Vortices

The Sedona landscape is commonly described as magical, with its impressive red rock canyon walls towering majestically against the clear, blue sky of central Arizona. The mesas in the region are stark and tall, and dominate the panorama. Sedona is a popular New Age center, attracting millions of tourists from around the world every year. Nearby, the canyon opens up into a gorgeous, rock-rimmed amphitheater, and south of Sedona stands the famous Chapel of the Holy Cross. Yet most people come to Sedona to experience the unique earth energies residing just outside of town, called the vortices. A recent study by Northern Arizona University concluded that two thirds of the near four million annual visitors to Sedona came seeking some sort of spiritual experience.

▲ On the trail to the Boynton Canyon Vortex.

The surrounding red rock country of Sedona is believed by many to be a vortex meditation site. Vortices are defined as specific global power spots that enhance prayer, contemplation, and reflection for people of all faiths. A vortex is a potent energy pattern emitting from the earth where the planet is at its healthiest and most alive. Vortices appear when there is a combination of rock cracks, fissures, fault lines, ley lines, underground rivers, high amounts of magnesium or iron in the soil content, and a negative ion count. Of course, Sedona is not the only vortex site—there are dozens or perhaps hundreds worldwide and they are usually associated with a known sacred place. The energy of a vortex acts as an amplifier, working to enhance or magnify any physical, mental, emotional, or spiritual levels of the visitor. This amplifier effect of the vortices supposedly helps augment thoughts and intuitions, heighten emotions, or may allow unexpected insights at an interpersonal or spiritual level. The terms "electric" or "magnetic" does not apply to the kind of energy found at a vortex, but to its effect. One scientific explanation of vortices has suggested that the mineral composition found within the Sedona red rocks creates a magnetism that may have a discernible effect on people. As a result of their popularity, vortex sites are among the most visited and impacted locations within the Coconino National Forest.

Sedona, Arizona has been termed the New Age capital of the United States, mainly because of at least four major energy vortices detected near the town. The Sedona Vortices are supposedly the strongest and most readily apparent in the world.

Most of the natural features in the Sedona area were held sacred by prehistoric people who recognized the potent energies of the land. Native Americans speak of the universal Grandmother Spirit who still resides in Sedona, continuously welcoming her spiritual family home. Several medicine wheels of stacked rocks have been constructed in the area, both by Native Americans and by New Age visitors. The reverence of

▲ The strangely eroded red rock formation called Bell Rock is said to contain powerful vortex energy.

Sedona as a sacred place by people of more than one cultural tradition is readily apparent. Nearly all Christian denominations have a church around town. Several Hollywood celebrities own property in Sedona. Native American legends color virtually every aspect of the region. Ever since Sedona became a New Age mecca it has attracted artists, writers, musicians and spiritual seekers from all walks of life. The strong natural energy vibrations seem to be quite conducive in magnetizing others of a like mind.

## Getting to the Sedona Vortices

There are four frequently visited energy vortices in the Sedona area. **Boynton Canyon Vortex** is located 3.2 miles (5.2 km) west of Sedona on Highway 89A past the Highway 179 junction. Follow the signs for Boynton Canyon. From the parking area, visitors follow the well-marked trails to a 30-foot (10-m) rock knoll where the energy is strongest, a place called "Kachina Woman." The **Bell Rock Vortex** emanates near the base of an almost perfectly symmetrical butte. Bell Rock has a distinctive shape, and is easy to spot just north of the village Oak Creek on Highway 179. **Airport Vortex** is the closest vortex to the town Sedona itself. Going 1.1 miles (1.8 km) west on 89A, turn south on Airport Road and park a half-mile up at the distinct curve before the road continues to the top of the mesa. The vortex is a small hill with twisted junipers and a clear view of Sedona on both sides. Finally, there is the **Cathedral Rock Vortex.** This vortex is located 4.3 miles (7 km) west on 89A past the junction of 89A and Highway 179. Turn west on Back O' Beyond Road to the car turnoff and the trailhead to Cathedral Rock. It is now required for all motorists to obtain a "Red Rock Pass" before parking at any of the vortex turn-off areas. The cost is based on a daily or per week basis, and is available in numerous park service offices and the Chamber of Commerce in downtown Sedona.

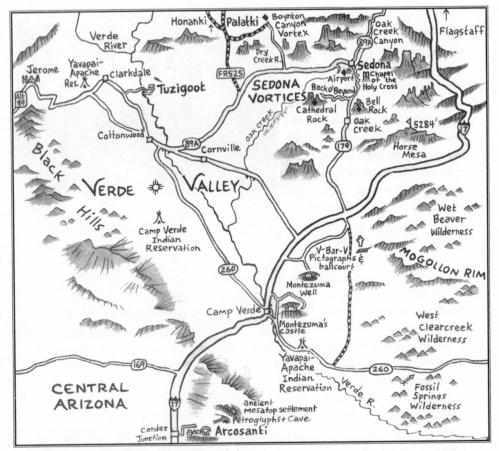

## Southern Sinagua Pueblos

Water is the desert's most elusive natural resource and has always been the key to survival for humans, plants and animals alike. Prehistoric inhabitants enjoyed either a high standard of living when water was in abundance, or suffered and disappeared without it. The Spanish word for "without water" is *sinagua,* a name the Spaniards bestowed on the long-lost people who abandoned their pueblos in the Verde Valley, presumably because of a lack of water. Despite their given name, the Sinagua people did have water. Early in their development they discovered an unusual and effective method of farming based on water conservation. Later, they adopted the art of irrigation farming.

In and around the Verde Valley region of Sedona are several advanced prehistoric settlements of the Southern Sinagua people, whose culture is often referred to as the "People in Between." The Sinagua were strongly influenced from all directions by their surrounding Anasazi, Mogollon, and Hohokam neighbors. They eagerly adopted Hohokam buff colored pottery, Anasazi above-ground pueblo building techniques, as well as Mogollon-style ball courts and canal irrigation systems. The Southern Sinagua became a unique synergistic culture among several already clearly defined. Similar to their Northern Sinagua kinfolk at Wupatki, the Verde Valley became a human melting pot of successive cultural influences coming together in cooperation and peace. About 1150 CE, the Southern Sinagua began building their large pueblo communities, the three most notable in the Verde Valley are the neighboring Tuzigoot, Palatki and Montezuma's Castle settlements. These cliff-dwellings came to prominence in the 1300s during the drought years, and were occupied for another century. Yet sometime in the early 1400s, the Sinagua abandoned the entire valley. No one knows why, but suggestions include continuing drought conditions, too much

▲ Montezuma's Castle occupies a cave in a nearly sheer cliff face.

pressure on the land, or conflicts with the encroaching Yavapai tribe who were living in the Verde Valley when the Spanish arrived in 1583. Whatever the reasons for leaving, the survivors were absorbed into northern pueblo communities and are generally regarded as the ancestors of the modern Hopi people. A Hopi legend tells of a southern people merging with them around this time because they did not have priests or ceremonies of their own, and were thus spiritually deficient.

> The Verde Valley around Sedona supported a rich cultural melting pot of prehistoric people, the most prolific being the Southern Sinagua. Their culture is best defined by the large pueblo hill town called Tuzigoot, and the Palatki Ruins located alongside the highest concentration of pictographs in the region.

Tuzigoot (Apache for "crooked water") is the remains of a Sinaguan pueblo community built between 1125 and 1400 CE. The ruins crown the summit of a 120-foot (36-m) limestone ridge overlooking the meandering Verde River. The original pueblo was two stories high in places and consisted of 77 ground-floor rooms. Like most pueblo dwellings, there were few exterior doors, because entry

Roof top view from Tuzigoot looking down on the hillside settlement.

by way of ladders through an opening in the roof was the preferred way to access the rooms. The Sinagua were prolific traders, and Tuzigoot appears to be a primary outpost for foreign trade. Found on site were Anasazi black-on-white pottery shards, parrot feathers from Mexico (likely used for ceremonial purposes), fine jewelry featuring turquoise, and seashells from the Gulf of California. In exchange, the Sinagua traded salt from nearby lake deposits, a soft ornamental stone called argillite, and copper ore extracted from the Jerome area. Along with physical items for trade, news of neighboring tribes followed along with the goods, as well as adaptations in customs and ideas. Religious practices from Mexico, such as stargazing from the rooftop of the highest pueblo, also likely influenced the people of Tuzigoot. A main feature of Tuzigoot is the central plaza that was a community-gathering place. Here residents displayed their wares for barter, gossiped about the latest news, and gathered for religious dance ceremonies or games of skill with neighboring villages.

About eight miles (14 km) away as a bird flies from Tuzigoot is another prominent Sinagua pueblo site called Palatki, a Hopi name meaning "Red House." Palatki consists of two large dwellings built at the base of a sheer cliff in a box canyon. Like Montezuma's Castle, the pueblo ruins are interesting and fairly well-preserved. But what makes Palatki more impressive is the adjoining rock art area called Red Cliffs. Several different native cultures contributed their own pictographs and petroglyphs to the various rock art panels suggesting this was an area of special spiritual importance. The definition of a pictograph is an illustration painted or applied to a surface, while a petroglyph is one scratched or scraped onto a surface. Collectively, the four Palatki Red Cliff alcoves represent the finest example of rock art and the largest single panel in the Verde Valley. The first alcove is called the Grotto Site where a concentration of pictographs, mostly snakes and water figures, surround a pool of water that has always been present. To many Indians, snakes are associated with water, lightning, and the underworld. Just around the corner, the Bear Alcove is named after a grouping of bears found near the top of the roof. Large mammals such as deer, mountain sheep, and antelope are also depicted. This may have been an area where hunting rituals were performed to improve a hunters' chance of killing one of these animals. The third alcove depicts the faint remnants of two sun or shield-like designs of the Sinagua, thought to be clan symbols of the former residents. These shields were traced over

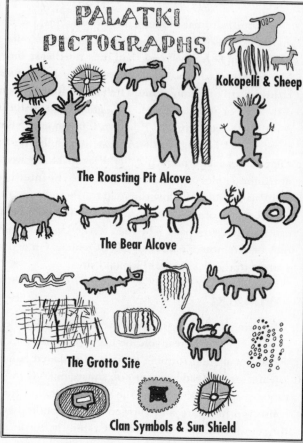

PALATKI PICTOGRAPHS

Kokopelli & Sheep

The Roasting Pit Alcove

The Bear Alcove

The Grotto Site

Clan Symbols & Sun Shield

with charcoal by the Yavapai or the Apache, likely as an attempt to rejuvenate the supernatural powers of the prehistoric pictograph, obtain it for themselves, or negate the power. The fourth alcove is called the Roasting Pit where the agave plant was roasted and the red rock ceiling is charred black from countless fires. Archaic, Sinagua, Yavapai, Apache, and Hopi people have drawn on the walls of this shelter, suggesting it was an important ceremonial center to all these people for thousands of years. A great variety of designs can be found at Palatki, including large sun shields, rattlesnakes, and mysterious ghost-like figures in several places. Perhaps the most identifiable pictograph at the Roasting Pit is the Hopi image of Kokopelli, the hump-backed flute player, jokester, womanizer, and fertility figure often associated with water. He is also a sort of Pied Piper who can attract game animals by playing his flute. Below Kokopelli are mountain sheep and raindrops, testifying to his magical powers. A pictograph depicting two spiraling "caduceus," resembling a pair of DNA strands, are a favorite mystery to New Age visitors. They call it the "Blue Door" because of a slit between the rocks, allegedly a supernatural entranceway to the Pleiades star system.

### Getting to the Southern Sinagua Pueblos

Tuzigoot National Monument is located just off Route 279, the road connecting the towns of Cottonwood and Clarkdale. Route 279 connects at both ends to Highway 89A, the road that runs northeast into Sedona. The well-marked Montezuma Castle National Monument is located a few miles east of Interstate 17, just north of Camp Verde. The Palatki Red Cliffs Heritage Site is a 30-minute drive west of Sedona, located on a grated dirt road called FR 795. One way to go is on Dry Creek Road to Boynton Canyon and follow the signs to Palatki, the other is to take Highway 89A west for 7 miles (12 km) and turn north on Red Canyon Road, alternatively called FR 525. This grated dirt road will continue due north for 6 miles (9 km) until it comes to the intersection for the Honanki Ruins and Palatki Ruins. Follow the road to the right for 2 miles (3.5 km) further north on FR 795. Normal cars can make the trip to Palatki, but should proceed at a cautious and slow pace. The road to the Honanki ruins is very rutted and should only be attempted in a sturdy 4WD vehicle. Guided jeep tours from Sedona take visitors to the Palatki and Honanki sites.

## Wupatki

Tree-ring data analysis in northern Arizona has determined that in the winter of 1064-1065 CE a great volcano exploded and set in motion a two centuries-long volcanic tantrum, forming what is now called Sunset Crater. Volcanic cinders, ash and sand spread out over 800 square miles (1,280 sq km) surrounding the volcano. Instead of devastating the land, the cinders formed a kind of mulch, which conserved moisture and allowed better conditions for growing crops. During the sustained eruption of Sunset Crater, the fertile soil in a dry area encouraged prehistoric farmers to move into the area. The region around the volcano became a melting pot of different Southwest cultures, including the Anasazi from the east and north, the Hohokam from the south, and the Mogollon from the southeast. All of these groups and more set up farming communities next to the less-sophisticated Northern Sinagua people, who had been living near Sunset Crater before the eruption. These very different prehistoric cultures, collectively called the Hisatsinom by their Hopi descendents, lived together and learned from each other for about 150 years. Perhaps by then the land was exhausted. For whatever reason, the last inhabitants left about 1225 CE, shortly before Sunset Crater emitted its last burst

▲ Sunset Crater is a near perfect cone.
(Photo courtesy U.S.G.S.)

48

of activity in 1250 and became an extinct volcano. The Hopi and other local tribes consider the region as a highly energized "spot of power," one of several particularly sacred places on the planet. According to Hopi traditions, Sunset Crater in northern Arizona is a sacred mountain where angry gods once threatened to destroy evil people with its volcanic fire.

> **The people who constructed the Wupatki pueblos were a collection of several different prehistoric cultures. The result is an amalgamation of people interacting peacefully with each other in a harsh environment.**

The name *Wupatki* derives from a Hopi word meaning "tall house," referring to the multistory dwellings, which during the 1100s, contained more than 100 rooms and housed perhaps 150 people. Although there are about 800 ruins in the Wupatki National Monument, the Wupatki Pueblo near the Visitor Center was the most developed of the four primary settlements in the vicinity of Sunset Crater. Other accessible pueblos include Wukoki, Nalakihu, the Citadel, Lomaki, and the Box Canyon Dwellings. In one area there are nearly 100 individual ruins scattered within a single square mile. Wupatki was by far the largest pueblo and likely served as the administrative and cultural center to the other farming settlements in the outlying areas. Wupatki has been partially excavated and includes two pueblo complexes, an old spring, a large circular community "amphitheater," a ballcourt, and a blowhole, which may offer a clue as to why the Sinagua decided on this location. The blowhole, or "breathing cave," sends negative ionized air rushing through it and was held extremely sacred by prehistoric Indians. The blowholes are openings in the earth where water-cooled air rushes out when the air pressure below ground is greater than that above. Several other breathing caves in the Four Corners region can be heard for miles around when the conditions are just right, and some have be measured to emit air at 30 M.P.H. (50 km P.H.) under certain circumstances. The fact that one of

▲ The ballcourt at Wupatki.

these curious geological anomalies is located at the Wupatki Pueblo further attests to its importance as a spiritual site. Hopi Indians refer to the blowhole as the breath of *Yaapontsa,* the wind spirit.

Another significant feature of Wupatki is an ancient ballcourt, one of only several discovered in northern Arizona. The Wupatki ballcourt measures 78 feet (23.4 m) wide, 102 feet (30.6 m) long, with a 6-foot (1.8-m) high wall. While ballcourts are far more common in southern Arizona—over 200 have been uncovered throughout the state—it is commonly believed the Hohokam people built them all between the years 750-1200 CE. The game balls, also found at Arizona archaeological sites, were made of carefully shaped rocks and covered in pine pitch or other materials. Similar to ancient Mesoamerican ball games, the objective seems to have been to move the ball toward a goal by using a curved stick or kicking it with feet and legs only. This game was introduced to the Hohokam from Mexico where, in the 16th century, Spanish observers indicated that it was strenuous and had a religious or ritualistic overtone. Its significance and method of playing in Southwestern culture, however, are not clearly known. With such a profound similarity to Mesoamerican cultures, the Hohokam are sometimes referred to as the Northern Toltecs by researchers. A common feature of Arizona ballcourts is that they are located along major natural drainages and known travel routes. As such, ballcourts may have provided social exchanges between villages because most were clustered within a one-day walk of other neighboring villages. The Wupatki ballcourt is the only one in the Sunset Crater region and was likely an important feature to their way of life. It is one of the last to be constructed and the only known masonry-built court in the Southwest.

### Getting to Wupatki National Monument

From Flagstaff, drive 32 miles (52 km) north on U.S. 89 to the second Wupatki-Sunset Crater Loop Road entrance, then continue 14 miles (23 km) east to the Visitor Center. Before reaching the Wupatki Pueblo Visitor Center, the Nalakihu and Citadel Ruins are located on the Loop Road, while the Lomaki and Box Canyon Dwellings are down a short side road. The Wukoki Pueblo is located on another side road just past the Visitor Center. 18 miles (29 km) from the Visitor Center, by the 36-mile (58-km) loop road, is Sunset Crater National Monument. The tossed particles of iron and oxidized sulphur on the rim of the volcano gave Sunset Crater its red-orange color and name. The dead mouth of the volcano is visible within the crater, the same one that spewed out prodigious amounts of cinders that covered the surrounding area. Climbing Sunset Crater is prohibited, but there is the scenic Lava Flow Trail at the volcano's base. A single entrance fee covers both parks.

# NEVADA

During the last Ice Age much of northwestern Nevada was a vast inland sea called Lake Lahontan. The same planetary warming period that gradually melted the Sierra glaciers also dried up Lake Lahontan, but many shallow lakes and marshes remained until historic times. Lake Lahontan was intact during the arrival of early man in Nevada. At 9,500 years ago the lake was still high, and it is known that humans lived in the Truckee Basin 11,000 years ago and probably earlier. Nevada was a much different place back then, a lush lake district with plenty of animals, including huge ground sloths, mastodons, and rhinos. Today Nevada is a land of desert extremes, noted for its range of high and low annual temperatures. Precipitation averages about nine inches (23 cm) per year across the entire state.

Nevada was likely visited by Spanish explorers in 1776, but half a century passed before the arrival of new foreigners. Eminent explorer John C. Fremont conducted the first systematic survey of Nevada in 1844, the same year when he chanced upon Pyramid Lake. His mapping helped guide the gold-crazed hordes heading for the California foothills after 1848, the same year when the United States won the region from Mexico. The first permanent town named Genoa was founded by Mormons. It was from here Snowshoe Thompson set off for Sacramento carrying the mail, first passing by Lake Tahoe and then across the Sierras. The famous Pony Express would follow the same route. The call of "Eureka!" was heard all across Nevada in 1859 when prospectors discovered gold and one of the biggest silver deposits in U.S. history—the Comstock Lode of Virginia City. Nevada quickly grew fabulously wealthy allowing its entry into statehood by 1864, but after the boom went bust in the 1880s, the state's fortunes and population soon dwindled. A new kind of boom came to Nevada in the mid-20th century with the advent of legalized gambling.

## Area 51

In one of the most rural parts of the continental United States is a top-secret military installment called Area 51 that officially does not exist. Its 200-plus buildings are undisclosed, what goes on there remains classified, and anybody who gets too close to the facility is promptly arrested. Signs posted outside the

▲ Nevada State Highway 375 runs adjacent to Area 51.

base ominously warn, "Use of deadly force authorized." Although downplayed by military brass, clandestine photographs of Area 51 have been taken and widely distributed showing an extensive base clustered next to the world's longest runway. The Air Force and Department of Defense facility in southern Nevada at Groom Lake has become the best-kept secret everybody knows about. Popularized by the 1996 movie *Independence Day*, featuring fictionalized scenes of Area 51, the base has entered the mind of our collective psyche. Yet admission of any covert operations or testing of secret aircraft at Area 51 is resolutely denied by Air Force officials. Furthermore, the base does not appear on any public U.S. government maps. According to Federal Aviation Administration pilots' charts and U. S. Geological Survey topographic maps, this air base simply does not exist.

The first wave of Area 51 notoriety came in 1989 when a man named Bob Lazar appeared in a broadcast on Las Vegas television station KLAS, claiming to be a physicist working on backward-engineered propulsion systems of various saucer shaped aircraft, supposedly based on recovered alien technology. The craft he reportedly worked on were kept in a secret complex called S-4 at Papoose Lake, a dry lakebed only a few miles south of Groom Lake. Subsequent interviews with Lazar on KLAS transformed Area 51 into a top destination for UFO watchers. The second wave of notoriety came when two mountain peaks, Freedom Ridge and White Sides Mountain, located less than 13 miles (21 km) away from Area 51, became prime viewing platforms for nighttime aerial activity. The nearby mountains became so popular that the Air Force acquired the land from the federal Bureau of Land Management (BLM) and closed access in April, 1995 "for the public's safety." More Area 51 infamy involved the known testing of the Star Wars Defense Program, the Stealth Cruise Missile, hypersonic spy airplanes that can reach speeds up to Mach 7, and the training of top-secret pilots from around the world. Finally, eyewitness reports of disc-shaped craft hovering over nearby mountains, rumors of at least 15 underground levels, and the remains of alien bodies and extraterrestrial aircraft only enhance the urban legend of Area 51. Such notoriety draws dozens, sometimes hundreds, of tourists to this remote region every day.

> Area 51 is a mecca for UFO enthusiasts, paranormal researchers, and the just plain curious. Thousands of annual visitors make the journey to Nevada Highway 375, alternatively named the "Extraterrestrial Highway," to get a peak of this ultra top-secret Air Force base.

Area 51 is as much of an enigma today as it ever was. The military still keeps the area cloaked in tight secrecy, and seeks to acquire more BLM land to keep the curious "watchers" even farther away. Although Area 51 is in Nellis Air Space, the base itself is controlled by Edwards Air Force Base in California. The

Nellis Bombing and Gunnery Range is the largest restricted airspace in the world and the largest restricted ground area in the United States. The entire base is 4,687 square miles (7,546 sq km), approximately the same size as the state of Connecticut. Although enormous in size, the Nellis Air Space is the greater whole surrounding Area 51. Even the name Area 51, a title given by the Atomic Energy Commission, remains ambiguous. The designation "Area 51" can be found on old government maps, but the base has other nicknames too. Pioneers named the dry lakebed "Groom Lake" and blazed the first roads into the region long before the land was acquired by the Air Force. Another popular nickname is "Dreamland," referring to the name of the restricted airspace over Area 51. Military contractors call Area 51 "The Ranch," or "Paradise Ranch." The CIA Director of 1955 was from Watertown, New York, and CIA staffers reportedly refer to Area 51 as the "Watertown Strip."

▲ Archive satellite image of Area 51.

Other nicknames include the "Pig Farm," and "The Box." Rumors continue to circulate as to whether the Air Force has moved its most sensitive operations out of Area 51, or if the top-secret testing continues to this day.

## Getting to Area 51

Area 51 is strictly off-limits to civilians. Along the unmarked perimeter of Area 51, including the now closed Freedom Ridge and White Sides Mountain, are inconspicuous trespasser detection devices. There are trip sensors, buried motion sensors, geo-phones to pick up vibrations, ammonia sensors to pick up human scents, radar stations, car sensors and hundreds of video cameras. Just stepping past the warning signs is enough reason for military police subcontractors to come out and detain any trespassers. Suspects will be held at gunpoint until a Lincoln County Sheriff's Deputy arrives to impound any vehicles and make an arrest for "Government Trespassing on the Nellis Bombing and Gunnery Range." Suspects can expect a night in jail, a $600 fine, and all associated vehicle towing fees. The only legal way to view Area 51 is to stop at the famous "Black Mailbox," (now painted white) just off Nevada State Route 375 (the Extraterrestrial Highway). The mailbox is located exactly halfway between mile marker 29 and mile marker 30, and is by far the most popular viewing location. Another legal option for viewing Area 51 is to climb Tikaboo Peak, located on BLM land approximately 30 miles (48 km) away from the base. Visitors may access Tikaboo Peak via Highway 93, just south of Pregnant Valley Lakes and the town of Alamo. A 4WD vehicle is necessary for the rutted dirt road, and sturdy climbing shoes are recommended to climb the summit. Tour guides to Tikaboo Peak can be arranged in the tiny town of Rachel at the Area 51 Research Center, or maps can be obtained at the Little A'Le'Inn Bar and Restaurant, also in Rachel. Since Rachel is the nearest settlement to the base, it enjoys minor celebrity status as being "the official home of Area 51." Located three hours north of Las Vegas by car, Rachel receives a modest number of visitors all year round, and several small businesses offer food and lodging, as well as aerospace and "alien-themed" merchandising.

## Black Rock City

Like a mirage in the desert, the Burning Man Arts Festival appears and disappears in less than a fortnight. Every late summer during the final week of August leading into the Labor Day weekend thousands of digerati geeks, pyrotechnic enthusiasts, aging hippies and too-hip yuppies descend on a prehistoric dry lakebed in the Nevada desert known to insiders as Black Rock City. It's not perhaps the ideal place to go camping or consume a heady cocktail of drugs and alcohol—temperatures can exceed 100 degrees Fahrenheit (24° C) by day. The area is also prone to white-out storms fueled by fierce dust winds. It is an environment that is either very harsh or very gentle. Over exposure to the harsh elements can be life threatening. But the 50,000-odd anarchists, experimental scientists and bizarre performance artists who make a pilgrimage here from all over the world try their best to prove this wrong every year. Burning Man is a solemn gathering too—it is the largest display of mythological ritual in modern America—one that is not dogmatic.

Burning Man chronicles its birth to 1986, the year when a San Francisco artist named Larry Harvey inadvertently lit the first match in what would become a legacy. He torched a life-sized wooden stick figure in memory of an ex-girlfriend amidst the ceremonial cheers of a handful of friends. For the next four years, on the summer solstice, he continued with this ritual at Baker Beach in San Francisco until the police interceded. Harvey and about one hundred friends then started to transport the now 40-foot (12-m) "Man" across state lines to Nevada's Black Rock Desert. At 3,910 feet (1,173 m) above sea level and 120 miles (192 km) northeast of Reno, just beyond the tiny town of Gerlach, it was about as far away from the rules and regulations of the city as one could get. In the early years, as the event began attracting more and more outsiders, the new motto of playa Burners became "No Spectators." The event morphed into a totally different way of gathering, one based on sacred geometry and the principles of community building. Today's Black Rock City is a utopian art community that allows optimum interconnectivity with all participants. According to founder Larry Harvey, "Burning Man as an event acts like a sacred place, because the design is based on a Stone Age model. The central location of the Man conditions perceptions, lending all the classic qualities of a sacred place."

> Burning Man founder Larry Harvey describes Black Rock City as "Noeticsphere," a location best comprehended by the intellect and creativity of its citizen population.

The wide 400-square-mile (640-sq-km) spread is an alkaline salt stretch called the playa, supposedly so expansive that the curvature of the earth is visible. The barren, cracked-mud landscape is the perfect surreal tableau to the even more surreal adult bacchanal that is Burning Man. A population size rivaling the largest cities in Nevada arrives each year to inhabit the cozy five-square-mile (8-sq-km) encampment. The whole thing culminates with the Man being torched to the ground on the second-to-last night of the festival—an event that can be anticlimactic after the laser-filled skies, electroluminescent wired bodysuits, fire-breathing mechanical dragons, oversized, fuel-oozing metal faces and techno tribal dance parties that illuminate each and every evening. But the event is much more than the burning of an effigy constructed from wood and neon and stuffed with fireworks. Basically, Black Rock City is the most artistic,

▲ The shape of Black Rock City, as viewed from the air at left, is remarkably similar to the ancient city discovered at Poverty Point, Louisiana, at right.

survivalist, futuristic and utterly surreal spectacle on earth. Despite its whimsical, anything-goes appearance, Burning Man is extremely well-organized. Not only is there plenty of breathing space for everyone, but there is also relative assurance that participants will be safe, have a decent place to pee, and good vibes will abound.

Art and interactivity are at the very core of the Burning Man ethos. The largest work of art on the playa might be the city itself. Theme camp groups must be entirely self-reliant, provide their own power source, and be able to protect its mechanisms and props against the elements, while ensuring safety. Villages and theme camps are located along the innermost streets of Black Rock City, and they usually provide entertainment or a service to the temporary residents. Theme camps are usually a collective of people representing themselves under a single identity. Villages encompass an assembly of smaller theme camps. The city grid is laid out in a large semicircle "horseshoe" with the Man in the middle. The center of the circle is empty and nearly a mile wide. Art installations are allowed in this space but people are not permitted to camp outside the residential rings. The streets are arranged in a radial design according to the hours on a clock face, ranging from 2:00 to 10:00. Center Camp is always at 6:00. The concentric streets are bisected by streets with names inspired by the annual theme. The inside of the horseshoe is where much of the action takes place, such as art installations, temporary performance stages, motorized wet bar parties, or the somber atmosphere surrounding the temple. In addition to the burning of the Man, the burning of a temple has become an anticipated final-night activity. Black Rock City attracts a consistently intelligent, accomplished and eclectic group of people. Larry Harvey's social experiment in radical self-reliance requires participants to bring in all food, shelter, water, and be prepared for volatile and spontaneous desert elements—high winds, rain, dust storms, scorching sun and cold nights are all apt to make an appearance. The advance planning required for attending Burning Man, and the potential for extreme weather conditions, automatically weeds out the weaklings from the diehards.

▲ Black Rock City is host to dozens of weddings per year. Most take place at the "Temple" or at other art installations on the playa. The ceremony itself usually becomes a performance for the enjoyment of other "Burners."

### Getting to Black Rock City

Motorists coming from all directions need to navigate towards the small town of Gerlach, 12 miles (19 km) south of Black Rock City. From Gerlach, go northwest on Highway 447 for a mile. At the fork go right on Highway 34—from here the Burning Man entrance will soon come into view. More detailed directions starting from further away can be obtained from the Burning Man official website: www.burningman.com. The official site has ticket info, directions, great photos and a helpful "First-Timers' Guide." Bring all necessary gear and food or stop at one of the many shopping plazas near Reno. The grocery store in the town of Empire, 3 miles (5 km) from Gerlach, is the last supply outlet before Burning Man. Once inside, bicycles are the festival vehicle of choice, since driving is prohibited on the playa, except for specially approved art cars. Black Rock City also has a FAA-approved airport for private airplanes to land and park.

## Lake Lahontan sites

Ancient Lake Lahontan was a large inland sea that existed during the last Ice Age, expanding over much of northwestern Nevada, with fingers extending into northeastern California and southern Oregon. Lake Lahontan was at its highest-level 14,000 to 12,600 years ago, corresponding with the final retreat of the glaciers in the Sierra Nevada mountain range. At its highest level the lake had a surface area of 8,665 square miles (13,950 sq km), with its widest section centered at the current location called the Carson Sink. The depth of the lake was approximately 900 feet (290 m) at present day Pyramid Lake, and 500 feet (150 m) at the Black Rock Desert. During the Ice Age, Lake Lahontan would have been one of the largest lakes in North America. Climate change around the end of the Pleistocene epoch led to a gradual evaporation of ancient Lake Lahontan as the planet became increasingly warmer. The lake had largely disappeared in its extended form by approximately 9,000 years ago. As the surface elevation dropped, the lake broke up into a series of smaller lakes, most of which rapidly drained, leaving only a dry alkaline playa. These playas include the Black Rock Desert, the Carson Sink and the Humboldt Sink. The only modern day remnants existing as true lakes are Pyramid and Walker Lakes. The surface area of Pyramid Lake today is 828 square miles (1,333 sq km), a mere fraction in size to the original Lake Lahontan. Winnemucca Lake has been dry since the 1930s, and Honey Lake in California periodically desiccates. The ancient Lahontan shoreline is evidenced by tufa formations throughout the area.

The existence of ancient Lake Lahontan coincided roughly with the first appearance of humans in the Great Basin. Abundant and unusual archaeological evidence of early human habitation has been uncovered around the prehistoric lakeshore. In 1911, two workmen started removing bat guano for commercial use from a cave near Lovelock, Nevada. Debris and guano had piled up to a few feet in depth to almost 15 feet (4.5 m) thick in some places. After removing several

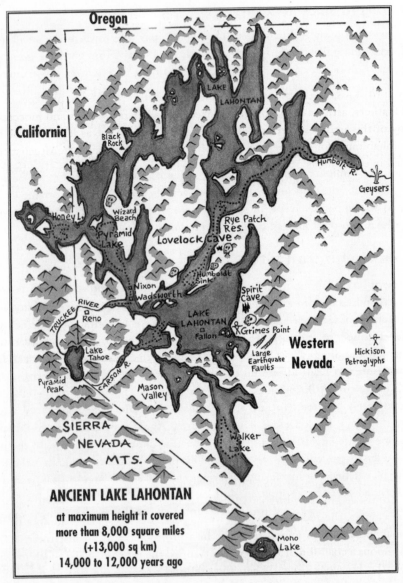

Oregon

California

Black Rock

LAKE LAHONTAN

Humbolt R.

Geysers

Honey L.

Wizard Beach

Pyramid Lake

Rye Patch Res.

Lovelock Cave

Nixon

Humboldt Sink

Wadsworth

Spirit Cave

RIVER

TRUCKEE

Reno

LAKE LAHONTAN

Grimes Point

Fallon

Western Nevada

Hickison Petroglyphs

Lake Tahoe

CARSON R.

Large Earthquake Faults

Pyramid Peak

Mason Valley

SIERRA NEVADA MTS.

Walker Lake

**ANCIENT LAKE LAHONTAN**
at maximum height it covered
more than 8,000 square miles
(+13,000 sq km)
14,000 to 12,000 years ago

Mono Lake

cartloads of guano from the small cave, the men uncovered human remains, animal bones, and a wide variety of artifacts. Acknowledging the find, the two prospectors notified authorities and the next year an archaeologist from the University of California was called to the scene. Professor Llewellyn Loud began collecting thousands of specimens, and what he found buried under the multiple layers of bat excrement astonished everyone. The artifacts themselves were much different than what the Paiute Indians had used in pre-contact times, and the curious human remains belonged to a very tall race of people with reddish hair. In all, 60 bodies were recovered and many of them showed signs of being mummified. Over 4,500 artifacts were uncovered in Lovelock Cave, including a large assortment of objects considered among the oldest discovered in the New World. Some of the artifacts include rock, bone and wood sculptures of animals, realistic duck decoys, exquisite coiled basketry, many varieties of woven textiles, and a "keep" for husbanding fire. Also found were a large assortment of bone, stone, horn and leather objects that had various uses. There were fishhooks, fishnets, bird skins, feathers bundled together, stuffed birds' heads, blankets of fur and feathers, articles of clothing, and exceptionally large sandals and moccasins. Many of the artifacts were found in storage pits or caches, as if left by the former inhabitants for safekeeping. Groupings of the tall bodies were ritualistically buried in select areas of the cave. Some of the bodies were represented by fragments of bones, some by complete skeletons, and others by remarkably preserved mummies. Grouped together, the artifacts and skeletons are so very unique in the Great Basin that they have been classified as belonging to the distinct Lovelock Culture. The stone, bone and wood sculptures make the Lovelock artists unsurpassed in their field with a high degree of realism not found in subsequent cultures. The artwork reflects the individual interacting in a social setting, and their role in a hunting, gathering and foraging society, based on the resources available. Descendents of the Lovelock Culture harvested wild grass seeds for winter storage, crafted a wide variety of projectile points for hunting, and carved an extensive assortment of animal figurines for religious purposes. The animal carvings probably functioned in native shamanistic rituals concerned with healing, curing, propagation, fertility and death.

For many centuries, red-haired enemies with boats featured prominently in local Indian legends, or what were thought to be legends until the discovery of the Lovelock mummies. According to these legends, the red-haired people were a tall band of troublemakers whom the Paiutes called the "Si-Te-Cah." Significantly, the name Si-Te-Cah means "tule eaters,"—tule being the fibrous reed which is the base material of the mats found in Lovelock Cave. Tule no longer grows in the region and was probably imported along with the people who used it. According to the Paiutes, the red-haired giants were hostile enemies, and a number of the regional Indian tribes joined together in a protracted war against them. After many moons a coalition of Indian tribes trapped the remaining Si-Te-Cah in what is now the Lovelock Cave. When they refused to come out, the Indians piled brush before the cave mouth and set it aflame. The remaining Si-Te-Cah were completely exterminated. The strange legends of red-haired giants in ancient Lake Lahontan were recounted by Sarah Winnemucca Hopkins, daughter of Paiute Chief Winnemucca. In the first ever book written by a Native American woman called *Life Among the Paiutes* she relates many stories about the Si-Te-Cah, including this account on page 75: "My people say that the tribe we exterminated had reddish hair. I have some of their hair, which has been handed down from father to son. I have a dress which has been in our family a great many years, trimmed with the reddish hair. I am going to wear it some time when I lecture. It is called a mourning dress, and no one has such a dress but my family."

Astonishingly, this book was published in 1882, a full 30 years before the discovery of the red-haired mummies at Lovelock Cave.

Such findings of tall, Caucasian mummies in Nevada did not bode well with mainstream archaeologists or Paiute historians. After the fanfare surrounding the Lovelock Cave discoveries simmered down, much of the skeletal remains were stolen, destroyed or lost. And since the remains did not fit the local Indian profile with regard to stature and hair color, most modern Native American historians hoped those red-haired giants would just go away. Yet discoveries of extremely tall Caucasian skeletons kept popping up all around the ancient Lake Lahontan region. In 1931, further skeletons were discovered in the Humboldt Lake bed region. Eight years later, a mystery skeleton was unearthed on a nearby ranch. Collaborating the Si-Te-Cah theory was the 1940 discovery of Spirit Cave Man found 13 miles (20 km) east of Fallon, Nevada. Spirit Cave Man was buried on tule mats and preserved in the same manner as the Lovelock mummies. Local Paiutes continue to object to the scientific investigation of the Spirit Cave Man, even after it was radiocarbon dated at 9,400 years old, making it the oldest known human mummy in North America. In each case, the skeletons were exceptionally tall, dwarfing in size any of the surrounding Native American peoples. Skeletal remains of a tall male termed the "Wizards Beach Man" were recently uncovered near Pyramid Lake. This skeleton has been radiocarbon dated at 9,225 years old. The skull shape is distinctly "long" and remarkably Caucasian. The skull bears little resemblance to the Mongoloid shape of earlier Native American races. The Wizards Beach Man's non-Indian features, similar to the mummified remains found at Lovelock and Spirit Cave, continue to puzzle archaeologists. The archaeological and anthropological findings around ancient Lake Lahontan establish a very strong case for cultural diffusion over many thousands of years. Some of the bones, including a giant skull and some femurs, can be seen at the museums in Lovelock and Winnemucca, Nevada.

> Pyramid Lake is the largest remnant of ancient Lake Lahontan. It is a "sacred healing lake" to the Northern Paiute tribe who still possess a reservation encompassing the entire lake and all surrounding mountains.

For over 10,000 years, various Native American groups maintained a near changeless existence along the shores of Pyramid Lake. Nomadic peoples hunted and gathered in the surrounding area, but primarily lived in a culture based on fishing. The latter migrating Northern Paiute Indians came to the lake over a thousand years ago and settled where the Truckee River drains into Pyramid Lake. At 27 miles (43.5 km) long and 8 miles (13 km) wide, the lake level today is much lower than in the time when the first Paiutes arrived. They called themselves "Kuyuidokado," meaning Pyramid Lake Paiutes and eaters of cui-ui fish. The native cui-ui is a rare, sucker-type fish found only in Pyramid Lake. Suddenly everything changed for the Northern Paiutes in 1844 when the American explorer John C. Fremont arrived. It must have seemed incredible to stumble upon this desert lake out in the middle of nowhere. Fremont and other settlers set in motion water diversions for

▲ The entrance to Lovelock Cave.

farming along the Truckee, and encouraged the Paiutes to move from a fishing based culture to an agriculture based society. The cui-ui and Lahontan cutthroat trout are two endangered fish that can no longer spawn all the way up the Truckee River due to major water diversions. A millennium old lifestyle suddenly came to an abrupt halt.

The Northern Paiutes used the physical landmarks around Pyramid Lake to interpret their existence. The lake provided their food supply and also the basis for a rich mythology. Along the lakeshore are many geological curiosities, including hot springs, strange rock formations and the Needle Rock towers. Bizarre tufa outcroppings, similar to Mono Lake in California, appear like above-water coral reef formations. The most impressive setting on the lake is the Fremont Pyramid named after the pyramid-shaped tufa island located on the eastern shore. Accompanying the pyramid in the same bay is the famous Stone Mother rock formation that is central to the Paiute creation myth. The story begins with the father of all Indians who lived on a mountain near Pyramid Lake and married a good woman that bore him many children. The oldest boy was very mean and was sent to the west with another daughter, while the nice children remained with their mother and became known as the "Paiutes." The father returned to the mountains and then to the sky, but the mother grieved for her two lost children and began crying bitterly every day. She sat on a mountain facing west and her tears began to form a great lake beneath her. This became Pyramid Lake and since she sat for so long she eventually turned to stone. There she remains to this day, sitting on the eastern shore facing west, with a basket by her side. In precontact times, the Northern Paiute would paddle out to the bay and leave prayer offerings at the base of the pyramid and next to the Stone Mother.

The most famous Northern Paiute was a prophet named Wovoka, who had a vision that would influence many Native Americans in the latter part of the 19th

▲ The Stone Mother formation in Pyramid Lake.

century. His vision came on New Year's Day, 1889 when he reported having had a vivid dream in which, he said, God told him he must not lie or steal and that he must put away all practices that encouraged war. To achieve this goal his people would have to perform a particular dance—the Ghost Dance—and their reward would be a paradise on earth. Wovoka lived in the Mason Valley near Yerington and Walker Lake, but made many trips to nearby Pyramid Lake. He was called the son of the Great Spirit and performed many miracles for those who came to see him but always emphasized the importance of performing the Ghost Dance. Wovoka soon became revered as a sort of messiah, a prophet who foretold of another world coming where the buffalo roamed free again and all the dead Indians were alive. Tribal leaders and representatives from all across the west came to see him and learn the Ghost Dance. The Ghost Dance swept the traditions of the Plateau people and significantly influenced the Plains Indians as well. At first the theme was peaceful, but it progressively changed to satisfy the differing needs of the last lawless tribes. As the dance spread, more and more homesteaders and the U.S. Calvary became uneasy with the practice of native people performing the Ghost Dance. The last Plains Indians outside of a reservation who performed the Ghost Dance in 1890 supposedly precipitated the death of their esteemed leader Sitting Bull. The Ghost Dance and other circumstances also gave the U.S. Calvary a justification for their genocidal massacre at Wounded Knee, South Dakota.

## Getting to Lake Lahontan sites

The Lovelock Cave is located 18.7 miles (30 km) southwest of the Nevada city Lovelock, just off Interstate 80. From Lovelock city center travel east to Amhurst Street, turn south and continue under the Interstate where Amhurst turns into South Meridian Road (Nevada 397). Follow S. Meridian to the very end, then turn left (east). The road becomes a grated dirt track at the end of S. Meridian and continues for 11 miles (18 km) to the cave. After crossing the Humboldt River, take only right turns heading roughly southwest and parallel with the river and mountains. The Lovelock Indian Cave is just up the hill from an old windmill at the end of the dirt road. Normal cars can make the trip as long as the road is dry. There is a small display on the Si-Te-Cah in the Lovelock Museum today, but it ignores the evidence which indicates that the Si-Te-Cah were not Native Americans. The Nevada State Historical Society in Carson City also has some artifacts from the cave.

Pyramid Lake is considered an open lake for visitors fully surrounded by Paiute tribal land. The Pyramid Lake Paiute Indian Reservation, encompassing 475,000 acres (190,000 ha), is located 35 miles (56 km) northeast of Reno, Nevada. From Interstate 80, take the Wadsworth exit to Route 447 north. The 8-mile (13-km) dirt road turnoff to the Fremont Pyramid and Stone Mother is at mile marker 23. All visitors to the lake must purchase a camping / day use permit available at the Nixon General Store, Sutcliffe Marina, or the Pyramid Lake Museum / Cultural Center in Nixon. The Needles area of the lake is closed due to vandalism.

# NEW MEXICO

Arrowheads removed from large mammal skeletons near the towns of Clovis and Folsom affirm the continued presence of humans in New Mexico for 10,000 years or longer. The first nomadic Indians lived primitively in caves or underneath cliff overhangs. The advent of farming techniques imported from Mesoamerica corresponded with the progression of architectural sophistication. Simple pit houses became well-constructed cliff dwellings and multi-storied pueblos. The scattered houses, apartments, and whole villages remain as a testament to the high living standards achieved by these prehistoric people. The ancestral Puebloan legacy lives on in pictures too, especially at the Petroglyph National Monument near Albuquerque which features some 15,000 images across a 17-mile (27-km) escarpment. Contemporary Tiwa Native Americans can trace the founding of their farming town, Isleta Pueblo, back to the 1200s. Equal antiquity has been determined for the "Sky City" of the Acoma, and the Zuni Pueblo south of Gallup. The Tiwa consider Taos Peak rising above the Taos Pueblo as ultra sacred, especially Blue Lake near the summit. Blue Lake is off-limits to non-Indians because it is the Tiwa *Sipapu,* or their entrance portal into the spiritual underworld.

Among the contrasting energy spots of New Mexico are continuously-occupied ancient pueblos, sacred mountains, breathtaking landscapes, atomic energy centers, top-secret military bases, and allegations of a crashed UFO near Roswell. Although the silver, gold, and copper booms were short-lived, they brought thousands of immigrants into this desert territory. New Mexico became a state in 1912 just before Arizona, indicative of its reputation as a backwater region. Its isolation was a key reason why New Mexico was chosen as a center for top-secret government nuclear and military research. The Atomic Age appetite for uranium brought a brief period of mid-century prosperity to a state that remains largely rural and sparsely populated.

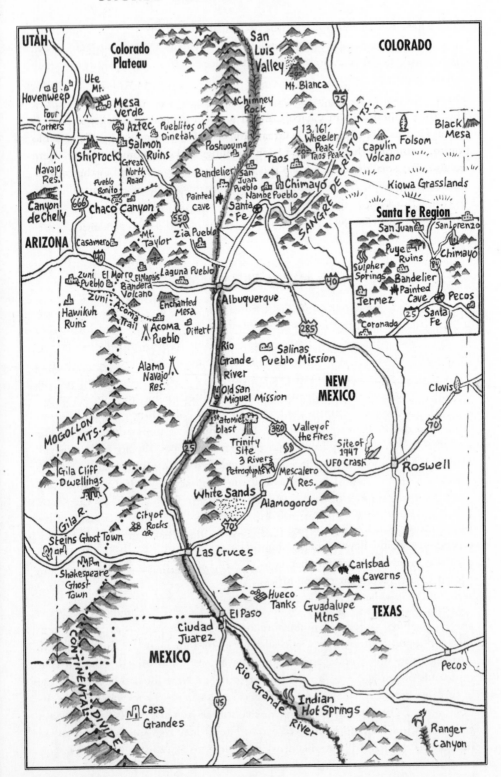

# Chaco Canyon

Called the "American Cradle of Civilization," Chaco Canyon represents the most important concentration of archaeological remains in the United States. The 12-mile (19-km) long and one-mile (1.6-km) wide canyon was a thriving urban center 900 years ago, and home to approximately 4,000-6,000 people. The stone-built towns in Chaco Canyon were individual complexes known as "Great Houses." The largest of 11 Great Houses in Chaco Canyon is called Pueblo Bonito, a complex that contained both dwellings and ceremonial centers. There are also 400 smaller ruins, among the 2,000 total sites recorded in the canyon. The ancient people that inhabited Chaco Canyon are commonly known as the Anasazi—a refined people who designed intricate irrigation systems, outstanding earthenware pots and a city laid out in the manner of modern apartment blocks.

The canyon was first inhabited around 100 CE when a nomadic people settled here and began planting maize and other crops. A thousand years saw this ingenious people go from hunters and gatherers to sophisticated urban dwellers. Chaco's most active building period began around 1020 CE and continued at a rapid pace for several decades. By 1110, this power was manifested at several of the outlying communities where a Chacoan Great House would preside over smaller farming domains. For hundreds of years Chaco influence dominated northwestern New Mexico, and beyond. The Anasazi most certainly had trade and spiritual contacts with their Toltec/Maya cousins to the south. Chaco inhabitants were known to keep macaw parrots imported from Central America.

Evidence of archaeoastronomy at Chaco has been discovered with the "Sun Dagger" image. This spiral petroglyph near the top of Fajada Butte in Chaco Canyon is carved behind three upright slabs of rock, which cast a different interplay of light to denote calendar markings for the equinoxes and solstices. The petroglyph on Fajada Butte, as well as the orientation of certain architectural features, was likely produced to serve as a seasonal calendar. Large seasonal ceremonies would have attracted hundreds of "pilgrims" to the canyon along a ritually used road system that connected Chaco to distant communities, and to the sacred landscape. Oral traditions relate stories of clans migrating from Chaco to the surrounding Four Corners area. Ten Hopi clans trace their ancestry to Chaco. As a result, modern Pueblo people share a strong physical and spiritual connection to Chaco and revere the canyon and all its ruins as extremely sacred. Modern Southwest Indians believe that the spirits of their

Pueblo Bonito reconstructed at CHACO CANYON, NM

▲ Casa Rinconada kiva at Chaco Canyon.

ancestors still inhabit Chaco Canyon, and thus it is a location to be deeply honored and respected.

In its heyday, Chaco Canyon was the administrative, political, spiritual and ceremonial center of the Anasazi people and nation. Scattered across Chaco Canyon and especially in the Great Houses were several round *kivas*, a Hopi term for ceremonial chambers. The scale of the Chaco kiva ceremonies was immense; 400 people could attend each of the 15 great kivas, while 100 smaller kivas could accommodate 50-100 others. The largest kiva in the Southwest, the Casa Rinconada, incorporated a special window for viewing the summer solstice on June 21st and included a series of antechambers, two stairways, wall crypts, and a sub-floor passageway. Kivas were an architectural holdover from Basketmaker pit houses and were usually entered by a hole in the roof that served also as an escape for hearth smoke. Climbing down the smoke-hole ladder was part of the purification ritual for participants in a kiva ceremony. Almost all kivas featured a small hole in the floor behind the hearth, called a sipapu, which acted as a symbolic entrance to the underworld from which the Anasazi believed they once emerged. Other common kiva features are wall niches used for keeping ceremonial objects, foot drums, and wall benches. The tradition of holding ceremonies in a large round room passed on to the Pueblo Indians, most notably the Hopi, Ute and Zuni tribes. Many clans still trace a direct relationship with Chaco, including the Athapaskan speaking Navajo who are not even Pueblo Indians.

Chaco Canyon was home to the first central-
ized civilization in North America, and for
the Anasazi inhabitants, Pueblo Bonito was
the center of their universe.

The largest Chaco Canyon Great House is a "D-shaped" complex called Pueblo Bonito. The name *Pueblo Bonito* means "pretty village" in Spanish, but like all the ruins in the valley, the original Anasazi names are unknown. From Pueblo Bonito, trails and stairways crisscross Chaco Canyon to a dozen other major ruins in the canyon. Designed for communal domestic life, its other functions probably included religion and ceremony, storage, hospitality, trading, signaling, celestial observation, and burying of the dead. The complex had more than 600 rooms, numerous two- and three-story buildings, several kiva complexes, and supported a year-round population between 100 and 400 persons. Some of the alignments that can be made from the structure of Pueblo Bonito itself are impressive. For example, there are two intersecting walls dividing the pueblo, exactly aligned to north, south, east, and west. The east-west wall divides the seasons at the fall and spring equinoxes. Elaborate lunar and solar alignments are featured in the construction of other Chaco Canyon pueblos, including many that integrate high noon solar alignments. But what happened to this advanced culture? From tree-ring dating, it is known that a period of severe drought came upon the Four Corners region in 1250 CE, causing the abandonment of Chaco Canyon. Rediscovered in 1849 by U.S. Army soldiers on military reconnaissance, the site was severely vandalized for 70 years until it was made a national monument in 1907.

### Getting to Chaco Canyon

Chaco Canyon is located in northwestern New Mexico, about 100 miles (160 km) northwest of Albuquerque and approximately the same distance from Santa Fe. Pueblo Bonito and the 12 other main archaeological sites are collectively known as Chaco Culture National Historic Park. From Albuquerque, take Highway 44/550 north and west to the turn off at County Road 7900. This exit is at mile marker 112.5 and 3 miles (5 km) south of the town Nageezi. County Road 7900 will lead to another turn off on a maintained dirt road. The route has many signs and is not difficult to navigate. Rain and snow can make the roads impassible, so it is best to call ahead for park information: (505) 786-7014.

## Chacoan Outlier Great Houses

Outside of Chaco Canyon are several dozen other clusters of Great Houses, the most accessible being Aztec, Casamero, Escalante, Salmon, Lowry Ruins, and Village of the Great Kivas. The expertly designed buildings characterizing the larger Chacoan complexes did not emerge until around 1030 CE when Chaco Canyon was already a thriving metropolis. The outlier villages were built in the 11th and 12th centuries when a period of ample rainfall allowed Chacoan culture to expand. The outlier Great Houses combined pre-planned architectural designs, astronomical alignments, sacred geometry, landscaping, and engineering to create an ancient urban center of unique public architecture. Researchers have concluded that most of the Great House complexes may have had a relatively small residential population, with larger groups assembling only temporarily for annual events and ceremonies, linked by a highly sophisticated network of roads.

Radiating out from Chaco Canyon like spokes on a wheel is a mysterious arrangement of straight lines and wide roads that extend for many miles into the desert. Most of the roads, some as wide as 30 feet (10 m), connect with most of the 75 other Chacoan outlier Great Houses, all within a day's walk, while a few seem to go astray. The longest northbound roadway extends for 42 miles (68 km), leading to the prehistoric communities of Salmon and Aztec. The Great North Road is arrow straight and wide enough for eight men to walk shoulder to shoulder. In fact, most of the outlier roads are arrow straight regardless of terrain. Stairs are carved directly over mesas (table-top mountains), up and down vertical cliff faces, and along courses that oftentimes make them impractical for travel. Aerial photographs reveal more than 400 miles (644 km) of roadways, visible almost exclusively from the air in the early morning or late afternoon when the sun casts deep shadows. Inspecting the roads at ground level it is evident that they were expertly engineered, planned, and involved a significant amount of labor in their construction and maintenance. The extensive link of roads demonstrates that the Anasazi people had a well-developed network for the distribution of goods. Some researchers suggest another purpose, such as a charting of the region's ley lines. The direction north is a known point of origin to most Pueblo people, and the Great North Road is almost perfectly straight and astronomically aligned. Others argue that the markings represent an out-of-the-body experience familiar to ancient native shamans. Archaeological research does confirm that a few of the roads lead to small shrine-like structures where evidence of religious and shamanistic activity took place. It seems reasonable to suppose that these roads, prior to recent erosion, could have been followed across great expanses of land, thereby delineating an enormous grid or map of shamanistic geography. These mysterious lines, often apparently between no particular places, are found in many parts of the Anasazi realm. The roads certainly provided open communication between communities and reveal an advanced social structure.

Two of the finest Chacoan outlier Great Houses remaining in the Southwest are preserved at the Salmon and Aztec ruins in northwestern New Mexico. The large dwellings of the Anasazi—termed *pueblos* by the Spanish—consisted of terraced apartment houses, each self-contained, and having populations from a few families to several hundred residents. Frequently set into cliffs, some of these remarkable habitations towered five stories in height. Both the Salmon and Aztec ruins were freestanding Great Houses in the distinct architectural style of the Chacoan Anasazi. The Salmon pueblo consisted of 300 rooms, situated on the alluvial terrace above the floodplain of the San Juan River. The Aztec pueblo had an estimated 405 rooms on three levels, and 28 ceremonial kivas. Aztec is situated on the banks of the Animas River, located a mere 12 miles (18 km) from the Salmon ruins. Striking similarities between these two sites and the Chaco Canyon ruins suggest a long-lasting interaction in such matters as architecture, ceramics and ceremonial life.

The Salmon and Aztec Ruins were originally Chacoan outlier communities, abandoned once, then reoccupied by the Mesa Verde Anasazi.

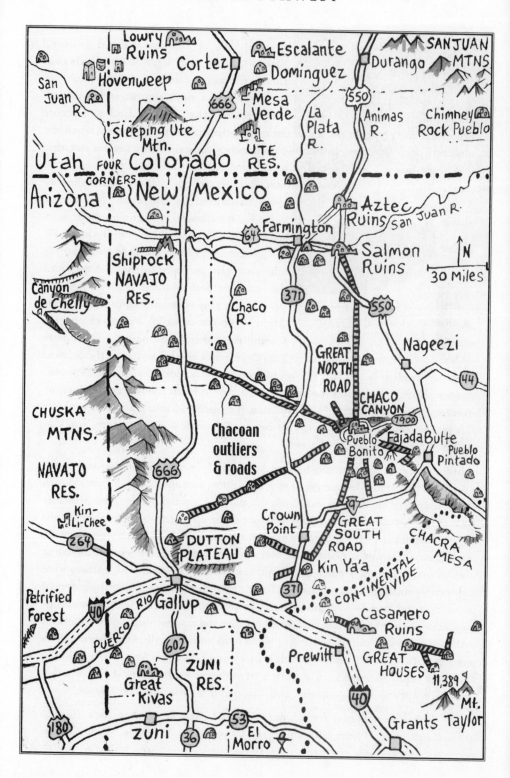

▲ Doorways connecting the
Aztec Ruins.

Salmon and Aztec stood midway between two distinct centers of Anasazi culture, Chaco Canyon and Mesa Verde. Both cultural centers introduced unique building techniques and new artistic styles during two separate inhabitations. Under Chacoan influence the Salmon and Aztec northern communities prospered for several decades as administrative, trade, and ceremonial centers. But by 1150 CE activity diminished as the Chacoan social and economic system waned. An extended drought in about 1130 may have contributed to the decline and abandonment of both sites. About 1200 CE the area saw renewed activity. Aztec and Salmon were both re-inhabited with Anasazi people, but this time they came down from Mesa Verde, 40 miles (64 km) to the north. During the Mesa Verde period, in the year 1263 CE, a major fire broke out in the Salmon pueblo, spreading out of control. 35 children and two adults fled to the kiva rooftop for safety, but the roof collapsed. All perished in an inferno reaching 1,500 degrees Fahrenheit (800° C)—so hot that it fused sand into glass. Shortly after this blaze Salmon was abandoned forever, and about 35 years later Aztec was also deserted for reasons still unknown.

In their heyday, the centrally located Aztec and Salmon communities were ideal crossroads for trade. In one room at Aztec alone, archaeologists uncovered tens of thousands of shell beads, hundreds of quartzite arrowheads, mosaic pendants of abalone shell, a 75-foot (22.5-m) necklace made up of 40,000 beads, 200 bushels of charred corn, and quantities of pottery vessels and effigies. Extensive trade with Chaco Canyon is evident, as well as much farther away regions including the Mesoamerican high cultures of southern Mexico. Tropical bird feathers were especially prized among the Anasazi. Some of the most telling artifacts uncovered at Salmon and Aztec—turquoise jewelry, tropical shells, macaw feathers and copper bells—illustrate a robust trade with Mexico and far-reaching North American tribes. Simple and elaborate burials, along with animal skulls, have been uncovered at both sites. The most famous burial was a 6.2-foot (1.85-m) man found in an Aztec tomb adorned with jewelry, a large decorated basketry shield, wooden swords, numerous bowls and jars, and wrapped in a turkey feather blanket.

The Anasazi originated from Utah's Great Basin and reached their cultural pinnacle a thousand years later during the Chacoan era. The Mesa Verde Anasazi were successors for a century before the entire culture dispersed, died off, or relocated along the Rio Grande River. DNA extracted from Anasazi burials at Chacoan outlier pueblos genetically matches that of contemporary Pueblo Indians. The first Navajo Indians came down from Canada in 1385 CE as a separate linguistic group to settle where the "Ancient Ones" once lived. The Navajo have strong cultural ties with the Anasazi whose ruins scatter across their reservation. The Anasazi certainly influenced the religious practices of the Pueblo Indians, as well as their Hopi cousins who were descendants of Kayenta Anasazi. To the Navajo and Puebloans, spiritual life is an integral part of day-to-day living, a belief that incorporates a symbiotic relationship with humans and all living things. There is no word in the Pueblo language equivalent to "religion." But in their worldview all things are interconnected and form a part of the whole—sharing in the essence of life through endless cycles of birth and death. They believe where the sky and the earth touch, such as across the majestic Colorado Plateau, the boundaries are set for all things to live. The Chacoan outlier Great Houses are considered extremely sacred ancient sites by the Puebloan people of New Mexico, the Hopi in Arizona, and the Navajo of the region.

### Getting to Chacoan Outlier Great Houses

The Casamero Ruins can be found about 4 miles (6.5 km) north of Prewitt, New Mexico. Escalante is located in southwestern Colorado between Cortez and Dolores. The Lowry Ruins are in southwestern Colorado near the town of Pleasant View just off U.S. 666. Village of the Great Kivas is located on the Zuni Reservation in west-central New Mexico. Permission and guides can be arranged at the Zuni Pueblo located along New Mexico route 53, about 17 miles (27 km) north of the ruins. The Salmon ruins and museum are located on U.S. 64 between the towns of Bloomfield and Farmington, in northwestern New Mexico. Aztec Ruins National Monument is on Ruins Road, about a half mile (0.8 km) north of U.S. 550 on the north side of the town of Aztec, 14 miles (20 km) north of Farmington. There are self-guided pathways through both the Aztec and Salmon archaeological sites. Aztec has the largest fully reconstructed kiva on the North American continent.

## Chimayó

The heavily Spanish-influenced town of Chimayó in northern New Mexico surrounds the distinctive Plaza del Cerro, one of the few 18th-century fortified squares remaining in the American Southwest. But even more renowned is an adobe chapel in a small sanctuary deemed the "Lourdes of America" because of the many spontaneous faith healings that have occurred at the site, similar to its legendary counterpart in southwestern France. During the Holy Week, especially on Good Friday, as many as 73,000 pilgrims congregate at El Santuario de Chimayó. The Plaza and chapel attract up to 300,000 visitors per year. Yet the Tewa Indians considered the land sacred long before the Spaniards constructed the first church.

The name Chimayó comes from the Tewa Pueblo Indian term *tsi mayoh,* meaning "obsidian rock." The Chimayó Valley was a chosen site to prehistoric Indians who were attracted to the region by small rivers, trees, natural springs and the rich alluvial soil for planting maze and other crops. The Tewa recognized the potency of the soil and its' healing properties. The basis for the sacred soil is a long revered mud pool which dried up when a nearby volcano erupted and spewed obsidian and ash across the land. The Tewa left Chimayó Valley around 1400 CE, and Spanish settlers arrived in 1692. The Spaniards built several chapels in the valley, including one on the site of the healing soil. As is common worldwide, the earliest settlers recognized the power of place and built their chapel right on top of the indigenous people's sacred site. As time went by another chapel was constructed in 1816 to replace an older one, which is the El Santuario de Chimayó as it stands today. The official brochure of the sanctuary affirms the older Indian heritage as a "tradition passed from one generation to another." A letter written in 1813 by friar Sebastian Alvarez to the Episcopal See of Durango (about the time work started on the present sanctuary) confirms visitors were already "coming from afar to seek cures for their ailments, and the spreading of the fame of their cures induced many more faithful to come in pilgrimage." Close to Chimayó is la Capilla de Santo Niño de Atocha, built in the 1850s. Other private chapels in northern New Mexico are also built on sites associated with healing earth, such as la Capilla de Talpa. Interestingly, most of these chapels overlay religious icons revered by indigenous peoples of Mexico and Central America found at the healing sites, which became sacred to the converted native population of northern New Mexico.

> El Santuario de Chimayó has been described as the "Lourdes of America" by the many faithful who have been relieved of their ailments. For centuries, miraculous cures have been attributed to the soil where the chapel stands.

The pilgrimage focal point of Chimayó is a small room adjoining the chapel called *El Posito,* meaning the "Little Well Room," but it is alternately known as the "Room of Miracles." Inside the room is a round hole in the floor through which people can reach in and scoop out handfuls of soil. Some anoint the sandy clay onto their bodies or apply the medicinal soil to photographs of family members too ill to travel. Many people supplicate themselves on the floor and pray, others kiss the earth or collect samples to take home. Some pilgrims even eat a little of the sacred soil. Approximately 25-30 tons (22,500-27,000 kg) of dirt are brought into the chapel every year and taken away by thankful visitors. A separate room next to El Posito is adorned with used crutches, braces, votive offerings, letters, and photographs' affirming the faithful's healing experience.

▲ The Chimayó adobe chapel and sanctuary.

The nearly two-century old El Santuario de Chimayó is filled with many legends and miracles. The origination story takes place on Good Friday in the early 1800s, when a man named Don Bernardo Abeyta saw a "burst of light" emanating from a hill near the Santa Cruz River. Going to the spot, Senór Bernardo started digging with his hands and claimed to have found a dark green cross with a darkened Christ figure. The artifact was the Crucifix of Nuestro Señor de Esquípulas, a religious icon associated with the indigenous people of Guatemala. He supposedly left the wooden *santo* on the spot, went to the village where he told his neighbors, and they organized a ceremonial procession to carry the crucifix to a church in nearby Santa Cruz where it was enshrined upon the main altar. But the next morning the crucifix was no longer in the church. Miraculously, it was found to have returned to the same Chimayó hillside where it was again unearthed. After a second and third unsuccessful procession to bring it back to the larger church in Santa Cruz, it was decided to leave the crucifix in Chimayó and build the present chapel where it would remain. El Santuario was built over the exact spot where the crucifix was found, also a site of "holy earth," termed *tierra bendita* in Spanish. The practice of bringing forth miraculous cures of ill health through the application of holy earth is called geophagy. Such miracles have inspired many faithful to make a journey with tall crosses of their own or to willingly trek hundreds of miles across the desert to Chimayó.

## Getting to Chimayó

The small town of Chimayó is located 24 miles (38.4 km) northeast of Santa Fe, near Española and Santa Cruz villages along Highway 76. Approaching Chimayó on Highway 76, turn south on Juan Medina Road (County 98) and follow the signs to the famous chapel. The adobe complex was designated a "National Historic Landmark" in 1970 by the U.S. Department of the Interior. El Santuario de Chimayó is open for visitors from 9:00 a.m. to 4:00 p.m. October through April, and 9:00 a.m. to 6:00 p.m. June through September. Catholic mass is held at noon every Sunday. Weekday masses are held at 11:00 a.m. from June through September, and at 7:00 a.m. from October through May.

# Roswell and the White Sands Region

On July 8th, 1947 the headlines of the *Roswell Daily Record* announced "RAAF Captures Flying Saucer On Ranch in Roswell Region," and so began the legend of a crashed UFO near this sleepy southeastern New Mexico town. However, the investigation and debris recovery was handled by the local Roswell Army Air Field. The day after the *Daily Record* headline, military brass changed the story and dismissed the entire affair as a downed Russian weather balloon. The official story of exactly what crashed and the items recovered has changed several times over the years. But the U.S. military and the U.S. government has to date resolutely denied anything extraterrestrial had been recovered at Roswell or anywhere else in the nation for that matter, especially anything like alien bodies, which the government explained away as human test dummies. Since the crash in 1947, however, hundreds of townspeople and military personnel involved in the recovery of the craft have come forward to declare the UFO crash to be a very real event. The small city of Roswell has become famous for having its name attached to what is now called the "1947 Roswell UFO incident," even though the actual crash site was about 75 miles (120 km) northwest of Roswell, near the town of Corona.

> The Roswell and White Sands area hosted the first atomic blast, a widely publicized UFO crash, and spectacular gypsum sand dunes. It is also one of the least populated regions in the United States.

Located in south-central New Mexico are the world's largest dune fields of gypsum sand. The spectacular white sand dunes cover an area of nearly 230 square miles (596 sq km), with many dunes dramatically rising over 60 feet (18 m) in a seemingly stormy ocean of cresting sand peaks. The gypsum sand dunes had been a fabled site of Native American vision quests for various tribes from throughout the American Southwest and northern Mexico. Most of the dunes extend into the White Sands Missile Range, which is administered by the U.S. military and closed to the public. In the northern part of the expansive base is the Trinity Site where the world's first atomic explosion took place on July 16th, 1945. UFO researchers attribute the early nuclear testing at White Sands, and the subsequent crash near Roswell, to the original mass sightings of UFO's in North America. Some would believe that the atomic blasts sent a warning signal throughout the universe to all advanced extraterrestrials signaling that the earthlings had finally entered the Atomic Age. While National Park and government officials will resolutely deny their existence, hundreds of UFO's have been sighted over White Sands during the past 60 years.

The discovery on how to release the enormous energies latent in the nuclei of atoms was developed at the ultra-secret Trinity Test Site at White Sands.

Some of the greatest scientific minds came together during World War II to master the military technology of nuclear fission before Nazi Germany could. As it turns out, Germany had hardly begun a bomb research program, and once the Soviet Union mastered the technology after 1949, the new weapons became essentially obsolete. Perhaps the proper genre for the Manhattan Project story is one of irony, not tragedy. Either way, the deadliest weapons on earth, along with nuclear power, emerged from the desolate New Mexico desert in the mid-1940s. After nuclear bombs completely obliterated two cities in Japan to end World War II, the brilliant minds behind the technology began to see themselves as responsible. In order to comprehend the blinding terrors of the Atomic Age, many of the scientists working on the Manhattan Project turned to philosophy and classical literature to justify the consequences

▲ A sign near Roswell.

of their actions. By creating weapons so powerful that no sane person would ever use them, the scientists ensured themselves that atomic bombs would almost always be "fictions," that is, symbols of a horrific reality rather than reality itself. Several of the scientists suspected that history had already repeated, citing that in order to understand the future, one must first know the past. Many of the investigators related that someone had already expressed their half-formulated discoveries centuries before, not with scientific formulas but with metaphors. The lead scientist responsible for overseeing construction of the first atomic blast at Trinity, the brilliant Dr. J. Robert Oppenheimer, grappled with the moralistic consequences of this new device of mass destruction. Just seconds after the first nuclear explosion in the New Mexican desert, Oppenheimer quoted the many-armed Hindu deity Vishnu from the 2000-year-old *Bhagavad Gita:* "Now I am become Death, the destroyer of worlds." Oppenheimer rationalized his conflicted beliefs by stating "I think it is for us to accept it as a very grave crisis, to realize that these atomic weapons which we have started to make are very terrible." With all the consequences of its potential danger the Atomic Age was born, ushering in the most controversial advance of modern science.

## *Getting to Roswell and White Sands National Monument*

White Sands National Monument is 15 miles (22 km) west of Alamogordo, and about 100 miles (160 km) away from Roswell. The White Sands Missile Range nearly surrounds the park and is strictly off limits, but the Trinity Site is open for tours. The best time to visit White Sands National Monument is on a warm winter day when there are fewer tourists compared to the large numbers during the summer months, and the winter light can be absolutely beautiful on the shimmering sands. The character of the dunes has been known to fill visitors with an expansive sense of calmness and serenity. After the closure of Walker Air Force Base in 1967, Roswell capitalized on the curiosity of the alleged UFO incident, and in more recent years the business community has deliberately sought out tourists interested in UFOs. Roswell has two museums devoted to the UFO phenomenon, and hosts the UFO Encounter Festival every summer.

## Shiprock

The pinnacle called Shiprock is the stand-alone neck of an ancient volcano core located on the Navajo reservation. Its dramatic appearance resembles a clipper ship floating across the flat desert floor near the Four Corners region. Shiprock has long inspired the Navajo people who have several legends and various interpretations of its meaning. Geologists tell us the rock was formed 12 million years ago during the Pliocene epoch. The peak reaches an elevation of 7,178 feet (2,153 m) and soars nearly 1,800 feet (550 m) above the high-desert plain. The jagged peak is at the center of three volcanic pressure ridges that pushed the rock skywards many millennia ago. Two of the pressure ridges extend away from the central peak in a prominent fashion. Navajo legend identifies the two ridges with the wings of a giant bird, while the Shiprock itself is the tail plume of the bird after it crashed into the earth and became preserved in stone.

The peak and surrounding land are of great religious and historical significance to the Navajo people. There are many stories about Shiprock relating to the Navajo people, who uniformly regard the pinnacle as a giant bird who harmed, but also assisted the Navajo. Foremost is the peak's role as the agent that brought the Navajo to the Southwest. This ancient Navajo folk myth tells how the rock was once a great bird that transported the ancestral Navajo to their lands in what is now northwestern New Mexico. The Navajo ancestors had crossed a narrow sea far to the northwest, perhaps the Bering Strait, and were fleeing from a warlike tribe. Tribal shamans prayed to the Great Spirit for help. Suddenly the ground rose from beneath their feet to become an enormous bird. For an entire day and night the bird flew south, finally settling at sunset where Shiprock now stands. This version of the Shiprock legend seems more like a metaphor, hinting at the site's inspirational power to lift the human soul above the problems of daily existence into a higher awareness with the Great Spirit. According to the legend, after being transported, the Navajos lived on the monolith, "coming down only to plant their fields and get water." One day, the peak was struck by lightning, obliterating the trail and leaving only a sheer cliff, and stranding the women and children on top to starve. This legend supports one reason why the Navajos do not approve of anyone climbing the peak, "for fear they might stir up the *chį́idii* (ghosts), or rob their corpses."

Shiprock, as Anglo settlers named this
mighty sand-colored column, is known to the
Navajo as "Tsé Bit'a'í," meaning the Winged
Rock.

Other variations of the Shiprock legend place a real thunderbird living at the summit, or see the mountain as the manifestation of this giant bird turned to stone. The story of a Bird Monster, or *Tsé Nináʼálééh*, nesting atop Shiprock and feeding on the hapless Navajo is the most gruesome. Long ago, a pterodactyl-like bird hunted the people of the area. To appease the monster, children were fed to the bird, but it stole away with grown people too. The Navajo became concerned with their dwindling population and decided that the bird must be killed. Two brave Warrior Twins set about the task of risking their own lives to save their people. One of the twin brothers allowed himself to be swallowed by the giant bird, and when he passed down the throat he pulled out a hidden knife and began cutting up the birds' innards. Seeing the second twin, the giant bird swooped down but was soon overcome with pain caused by the first twin cutting his innards and crashed into the earth. The rock formation of the two ridges represents the bird's wings, while the tall eroded volcanic plume is the back end of the beast's tail feathers. Some time later, a mythical giant spider took many feathers of the giant bird for his bag. One day going home to his web, the spider left the bag open and the feathers flew away into the wind. Each feather transformed into a different bird species, which the spider named for the Navajo people.

With all the lore surrounding it, the Navajo consider Shiprock to be in a category far above most other mountains in the region. From ancient times until today, *Tsé Bitʼaʼí* was a pilgrimage location of major importance, the destination of young men engaged in the rigors of solitary vision quests. The peak is mentioned in stories from the Enemy Side Ceremony and the Navajo Mountain Chant. It is associated with the Bead Chant and the Naayee'ee Ceremony. Shiprock is governed by the Navajo Nation. Although discouraged, the first recorded climb was in 1939. Since 1970, Shiprock has been off limits to climbers, accorded once again the respect due to a special Navajo sacred site.

▲ The solitary formation of Shiprock
dominates the horizon in the Four Corners
region.

## Getting to Shiprock

The monument rises prominently off the desert floor and is visible from four states up to 100 miles (160 km) distant. The mountain is located about 12 miles (19 km) southwest of the northern New Mexico town of Shiprock, which is named for the peak. There is a good turnoff on State 64 into a Navajo subdivision of homes indicated by a Shiprock sign and the Navajo name *Tsé Bit'a'i*. Turn south and drive on a grated dirt road for 4 miles (7 km) to the subdivision and look for a turnoff with good views of Shiprock. Another approach from the south allows closer access, but on a rougher dirt road. From the town of Shiprock travel south on Route 666, then take the westward turnoff at Road 13. There are no facilities, but there is a rest area with picnic tables near the volcanic pressure ridge that extends south of the peak.

# UTAH

Nomadic bands of Paleo-Indians searched for big game across what is today Utah as early as 14,000 years ago. For thousands of years these Ice Age hunter-gatherers lived in caves overlooking a vast freshwater sea, an aquatic ancestor to the Great Salt Lake. About the time of Christ, Utah's northern two-thirds was the domain of the enigmatic Fremont Culture. Throughout Utah there are over 3,800 rock art depictions, mostly drawn by the Fremont, a people long vanished when the first white explorers arrived. Utah is an anglicized word deriving from the Ute Indian name for their tribe, "Noonché." Some of the native Utah Paiutes claim the Fremont as their ancestors. The Anasazi were another prehistoric culture of Utah, living around the vicinity now called the Four Corners. The Four Corners region, high atop the Colorado Plateau, is the meeting point of Utah, Colorado, New Mexico and Arizona. The Colorado Plateau encompasses most of Utah. This high desert upland is roughly circular and approximately 350 miles (565 km) wide. It sits within a ring of volcanic mountains, which are known to experience a high concentration of lightning activity every year. In fact, the Colorado Plateau receives more lightning strikes per year than any other place in the United States. Along with thunderstorms, the Four Corners is known for high solar activity, mysterious "halos" around high peaks, extraordinary static electrical fields, underground water and radioactive minerals. Such natural wonders would have amazed the Anasazi, who farmed around southern Utah's canyon country. When the Anasazi abandoned their villages around 1300 CE, other tribes then arose: the Paiute, Goshute, Shoshone and Ute. Last to arrive were the Mormons who embraced the arid and desolate region as a haven from persecution. Their faith and determination to prosper created a modern culture of astonishing resourcefulness.

# Canyonlands

Around the confluence of the Colorado and Green Rivers is a spectacular wilderness of strangely eroded, multicolored stone. Three distinct districts divide Canyonlands National Park, which include The Maze, The Needles, and an isolated 6,000-foot (1,800-m) mesa separating the two rivers called Island in the Sky. Each district is named after its distinctive landscape. The Maze district contains no paved roads, and requires backcountry use permits. The Needles is the most accessible district, named for its profusion of red rock spires and narrow fan ridges. The many strange landforms in the three districts also contain fossilized sand dunes, soaring pinnacles and precipitous box canyons. After the two rivers converge, the Colorado empties into a narrow chasm called Cataract Canyon. The canyon has 28 sets of rapids, some of which have a Class 5 raft rating. Cataract Canyon has the steepest incline of cliff walls anywhere along the course of the Colorado River. As a further enhancement, Cataract Canyon has a high concentration of uranium in the soil. This radioactive element is a powerful generator of negative ions known to induce human ecstasy states, yet long-term exposure to uranium can be deadly. As the Colorado River flows outside the park it becomes the Glen Canyon National Recreation Area and Lake Powell.

79

The confluence of the Colorado and Green
River in Canyonlands offer stunning scenery
and some of the most unusual prehistoric
rock art galleries in the Southwest.

At least 2,000 years ago, Canyonlands and several outlaying ravines were utilized as sacred ceremonial centers for successive prehistoric cultures. Hunter-gatherers continued to use the area well after the appearance of agriculture about 500 CE. At that time, archaeologists believe the soil in the region was deeper and the area had a higher rainfall and more moderate temperatures than it does today. The fertile valleys, especially along the Colorado River, were reserved for semi-permanent settlements. Indian Creek Canyon is a 16-mile (26-km) side canyon connecting to the Colorado just above the confluence with the Green River. It was utilized by prehistoric farmers as a growing corridor between the basin and the two rivers. Indian Creek Canyon is just outside the park boundaries, but contains hundreds of artifacts, ruins, petroglyphs, pictographs, and Anasazi granaries. Traces of Anasazi can be found in almost every canyon in The Needles. The "Formative" Anasazi and Fremont people, two of the earliest recognized settled cultures inhabiting the Southwest, passed down many legends in the form of rock art. The most peculiar are the large anthropomorphic (manlike) forms characterized by hallowed eyes or missing eyes, the frequent absence of arms and legs, and the incidence of vertical body markings. What's most unusual with the anthropomorphs is the presence of antennae, elongated ears, snakes in hand, and larger than life bodies apparently covered by long robes. They are usually painted high on hanging rock faces as if presiding over ceremonial areas. Most of these tall, "ghost-like" figures are believed to date from the late-Archaic period, painted by the Fremont sometime between 1,500 and 2,500 years ago. These strange images likely represent shamanistic art associated with ritual activities. Barrier Canyon has some of the finest anthropomorphic paintings, but the Great Gallery in Horseshoe Canyon and the Bird Site in The Maze district are equally fascinating. Most require a strenuous hike to reach. These haunting life-sized forms are a fitting reminder of the otherworldly spirit of the back canyons, an arid place where humans came for ceremony, but rarely stayed for too long.

▲ Sego Canyon anthropomorphic pictographs.

The aptly named Newspaper Rock on the way into Canyonlands contains perhaps the highest concentration of petroglyphs at any single site. It features hundreds of figures and designs from several Native American cultures—the

Archaic, Basketmaker, Fremont, Anasazi, Ute, and Navajo—along with Spaniard and Anglo contributions. Newspaper Rock is among the finest examples of successive-era petroglyphs dating from around 2,000 years ago until the first European explorers passed through the region. The glyphs were carved by scraping away the darker "desert varnish" to reveal the lighter colored stone underneath. The dark sandstone slab with the petroglyphs is protected from the elements by a rock overhang. The etched designs depict various wild animals, footprints, wheels, undulating lines, and human hunters on horseback. One giant being with strange antennae on its head is thought to be a stylized representation of a sky god or a shaman wearing an elaborate hat. The meaning of the many figures, faces, handprints and other images of Canyonlands largely remain a mystery and open to interpretation.

### Getting to Canyonlands National Park

Canyonlands is Utah's largest national park, established in 1964. It encompasses some of the least explored regions of North America in a wild desert atmosphere. Canyonlands National Park is world-renowned for its challenging 4WD vehicle routes, bike trails, and whitewater rafting. Major entrances to the park are accessible from US 191, 22 miles (35 km) north of Monticello (Needles), and 35 miles (56 km) northwest of Moab (Island in the Sky). The only other access routes are by unpaved roads and jeep trails. There are no road connections between the districts within the park and traveling between them may take two to six hours by car. The Great Gallery pictographs are in the separate Horseshoe Canyon Unit, 49 miles (79 km) south of the town Green River on the road into The Maze district. Newspaper Rock Recreation Site is located on route 211 alongside the road leading into The Needles section of Canyonlands National Park. Newspaper Rock can be viewed from an overlook off a short side road just south of Indian Creek Canyon and the Visitor's Center. Signs direct motorists to all pertinent turnoffs. Other famous anthropomorphic rock panels can be found at Courthouse Wash just north of Moab in Arches National Park, and Sego Canyon, located 3.9 miles (6.3 km) north of Thompson Springs along Interstate 70.

## Hovenweep

A sophisticated stone building culture developed in the Southwest concurrently with the advent of corn cultivation introduced from Mesoamerica. The Ancestral Puebloan Indians, or Anasazi, became prudent farmers and advanced village dwellers in the dry and rugged country near what is today the Four Corners region. On the Cajon Mesa where Hovenweep is located, population density varied through time. By the mid-1200s, increasing numbers of people concentrated at the heads of small canyons where precious water was available. Along with corn, they planted beans, squash, cotton and various grains in small irrigated fields and terraces. They became experts at utilizing the limited resources of this environment, which was adequate for high-desert agriculture. Up in the valleys they constructed pit-houses, pueblos, kiva ceremonial rooms, and the exquisitely built stone towers that are Hovenweep's trademark. Water "checkdams" were also constructed, possibly to stop flashflood damage or to preserve topsoil wash-out, but more likely they were created as reservoirs to ensure an adequate supply of moisture for their crops. Yet nothing lasts forever. By the late 1200s climatic changes, overuse of resources, overpopulation and perhaps pressure from other tribes forced the people to leave their villages and journey south to the Rio Grande Valley and as far west as the Hopi villages of Arizona.

> The poetic-sounding Hovenweep means
> "deserted valley" in the Paiute/Ute languages,
> although the multiple clusters of pueblo
> ruins were abundantly populated by the
> Anasazi more than 800 years ago.

The Hovenweep archaeological park consists of six groupings of ruins, four in Colorado and two in Utah, all situated at the top of canyon draws. All the creek canyons drain into lower McElmo Canyon that feeds into the San Juan River. The four clusters of ruins in Colorado are named Horseshoe, Holly, Hackberry, and Cutthroat Canyon. The Cajon and Square Tower Canyon clusters are in Utah, the latter being the largest grouping of ruins in the monument. The stunning Square Tower group, an intriguing collection of well-preserved ruins, is clustered along the "Little Ruin Canyon" near the Visitor's Center. Next to Square Tower, a kiva ceremonial room has been excavated, and both structures are situated near the life-giving spring at the head of the canyon. The towers stand like sentries on the canyon rim protecting the precious water sources. Unlike many tower-kiva associations elsewhere, Square Tower and its kiva were not connected by a tunnel. The larger pueblos at Hovenweep date primarily to the 12th and 13th centuries and are distinctive for the high frequencies of multi-story masonry towers within or near each village. All six of the Hovenweep pueblo clusters are within a day's walk of each other.

The earliest Hovenweep towers constructed were square and round buildings, but as time went by they became more elaborate—multi-storied, rectangular, oval, or D-shaped in plan, all the work of expert masons. The Anasazi building engineers did not level the foundations for their structures, but adapted construction designs to fit the uneven rock slab surfaces. Similar to their Chacoan cousins, the Anasazi builders at Hovenweep also tracked the solstices and equinoxes. Several structures have windows to admit sunlight on important alignment dates, which may have indicated planting and harvest times to the prehistoric farmers. The light falls in a predictable pattern on interior openings. The best solar calendar example is at Hovenweep Castle where the doorway and portals of "D Tower" ingeniously integrate the winter and summer solstices, as well as the spring and fall equinoxes. The Unit Type House in Little Ruin Canyon incorporates its own kiva, as well as two openings in the east room wall that mark the summer and winter solstices. Near the Holly Group, under a sandstone cliff, are a series of petroglyphs that illustrate the summer solstice by connecting shafts of light to the pictures. Planetary and solar cycles obviously played an important role in the religion and agricultural practices of the Anasazi. It is suggested that the Hovenweep towers served as astrological observatories, allowing Anasazi priests to forecast weather and celestial cycles for planting and

▲ One of the Hovenweep round towers.

ceremonies. Other guesses are that the towers served strictly religious purposes, or were used as lookout towers to spot approaching enemies. Their mysterious functionality aside, the towers at Hovenweep remain among the most remarkable structures in the Anasazi world.

### Getting to Hovenweep National Monument

Hovenweep National Monument extends across the Utah and Colorado border, 42 miles (68 km) west of Cortez, Colorado. Sage covers the plains of Hovenweep to hide 20 square miles (52 sq km) of farms and fields cultivated by the early inhabitants. Barely over the border in Utah is the Visitor's Center, located just above the Square Tower Group in Little Ruin Canyon. Six different Anasazi ruin groupings are located at Hovenweep, but only the Square Tower site is easily accessible. To visit the other sites requires back-road travel and hiking, which may be difficult or impossible on rainy days. The modest Monument headquarters is on the road between Pleasant View, Colorado and Hatch Trading Post, Utah. Directions to Hovenweep are well-marked at intersections coming from Four Corners via Route 262, or Route 35 through Montezuma Creek. Shiprock is visible from various high points near Hovenweep.

## Salt Lake Temple

Late one night, in 1823, an angel named Moroni visited an impressionable 17-year-old Vermont farmer named Joseph Smith. The spirit gave him directions to a mountain near Palmyra, New York where four years later the young man would unearth several gold plates inscribed with ancient, mysterious writings. Moroni directed Joseph Smith in a vision to the location of the plates. Smith, a former diviner, used his "seer stones" to translate the buried plates. Without looking at the plates or knowing a word of the language he was able to interpret the plates

▲ A fountain mimics the shape of the Salt Lake Temple in the "City of the Saints."

in three years, supposedly through the power of the stones and his own visions. The plates dictate the tenants of an ancient religion, yet new in inception, and tell the story of a Jewish tribe who fled the tyranny of Jerusalem for America 2,500 years earlier. Smith asserted that the plates were abridged by the Israelite clan's historian, a man named Mormon, and later buried by his son. Smith self-published the result as the *Book of Mormon*, and less than a week later he founded the Mormon Church.

Mormons assert that evil forces overtook the Catholic Church in its early years, and that the true inheritor of Jehovah is the lost tribe. Smith's story tells of the Israelite tribe coming to America around 600 BCE and receiving divine instruction to build earth forms, including the great mound cities of the Mississippian Culture. Following the Mormon example, Smith had a vision to establish a true city of God on earth, a blend of heavenly and earthly kingdoms. He and his early followers built a community in Ohio, then Missouri, but were forced to settle in Nauvoo, Illinois. There, in 1844, Smith declared polygamy an official Mormon revelation, which angered many church members, especially the church fathers of whom Smith had relations with about 50 of their wives and daughters. A splinter group printed a letter attacking Smith as a fallen prophet because of his insistence of having several "celestial" spouses at the same time. Smith ordered their printing press smashed, resulting in the governor of Illinois demanding Smith arrested. Joseph Smith had one final vision in jail, this time of his own death and martyrdom. The vision came true when 150 angry Masons swarmed the prison and shot him dead.

Despite Joseph Smith's premature death, Mormonism lives on with over 11 million members worldwide. The Salt Lake Temple in the "City of the Saints" is the most recognized symbol of the Mormon Church, the largest native Christian denomination in North America.

In 1847, pilgrims led by Brigham Young trekked west from their former colony in Nauvoo, Illinois to continue searching for a long-sought refuge from torment. What they found was Utah's desolate Salt Lake Valley, where, from a basin over-look, Young proclaimed, "This Is The Place!" Although dry and arid, the Mormons found the region's isolation a safe haven from religious persecution. Their faith and determination to prosper in such an inhospitable terrain made the Mormon people astonishingly resourceful with what little they had brought along to this desert land—a land that closely resembled the Dead Sea near Jerusalem. Salt Lake City was designed on a grid pattern proposed by Young, with Temple Square in the center representing the spiritual and cultural heart of the city.

The Salt Lake City temple was announced in July 1847, when Brigham Young stuck his cane into the ground and said "here we will build a temple to our God." Ground was broken and construction begun on February 14th, 1853. The cornerstone was laid two months later by Young himself. The Salt Lake Temple took exactly 40 years to complete and was dedicated in April, 1893. A 12-foot (3.6-m) tall golden statue of the angel Moroni is depicted playing the horn atop the temple capstone. The towering temple is Salt Lake City's most recognizable landmark, also one of the oldest structures in the city and certainly the longest in the making. The temple is central to over 120 others around the world, and is designed to house Church administrators as well as worshipers. In its role as directive headquarters, the Salt Lake Temple has an entire floor dedicated to offices and meeting rooms for Church leaders including the Holy of Holies. These are not present in other temples. The inside of the temple is closed to non-Mormon visitors because it is considered sacred by the Church and its members. The temple itself is surrounded by Temple Square, which is the most popular tourist attraction in the state, hosting several million visitors annually. High walls surround the complex, with wrought iron gates providing entrance on all four sides. Within the square is the grey quartz monzonite Mormon Temple, the Mormon Tabernacle and Assembly Hall, as well as various monuments, assorted statuary and two visitor centers. Temple Square and the adjacent conference cen-ter, museums and administration buildings occupy several city blocks in the heart of downtown Salt Lake City. Members of the Church of Jesus Christ of Latter-day Saints (Mormons) consider their temple a sacred site, and those who enter must live according to certain standards. Inside, religious instruction and ceremonies such as baptism and marriage take place. Because of its role as the Latter-day Saints Church headquarters and its historical significance, the temple is visited by Mormons from many parts of the world.

## Getting to Salt Lake Temple

Temple Square occupies a full city block in downtown Salt Lake City, centered within North Temple, South Temple, West Temple and Main Streets. Entering the square, expect to be greeted by eager, cheerful, young Mormon missionar-ies at every gate, and anticipate hearing some polite Mormon proselytizing.

Tours of the square depart from the flagpole every 10 minutes. Temple Square is open from 9 to 9 daily. Call 800-537-9703 for more information. The temple is the only building closed to the general public. This Is The Place Heritage Park where Brigham Young chose the site of his future city is located at the mouth of Emigration Canyon, just north of Hogle Zoo, at 2601 E. Sunnyside Avenue.

## Zion National Park

The seemingly gentle Virgin River flows like a placid creek most of the year, but can turn into a raging torrent during heavy rainstorms. It is the strength of this inconspicuous river that has carved the profound rock gorge of Zion Canyon. It began shaping the valley more than 13 million years ago and continues to this day. Feeder streams of the Virgin create zigzag paths as they follow jointed planes in the rocks. The headwaters of the Virgin River begin at about 9,000 feet (2,700 m), and the river empties into Lake Mead about 200 miles (320 km) to the southeast after flowing 8,000 feet (2,400 m) downward. This gives the Virgin a stream gradient that ranges from 50 to 80 feet (15-24 m) per mile (0.9-1.5%)—one of the steepest stream gradients in North America. Beyond the Virgin River, other box canyons and surprises await visitors around every corner. The park is a geologic showpiece, featuring sandstone cliffs which are among the highest in the world. Zion features stunning scenery found nowhere else on

▲ The majestic Zion Canyon.

earth. The resulting monoliths, soaring towers and arch-shaped rock formations offer a quiet grandeur in Utah's most visited park.

The various canyons of Zion were settled extensively by the Anasazi, or Ancestral Puebloan People, beginning about 2,000 years ago. Human occupation by the Archaic and Basketmaker people predate the Anasazi by several thousand years. The original Archaic settlers may have come to Zion Canyon as early as 6000 BCE. The Parrusits and several other Southern Paiute subtribes were the last Indian settlers in the canyon, first arriving about 800 years ago and staying until the first Anglo explorers arrived in 1840. Evidence suggests the Parrusits held a profound reverence for the large monoliths and turbulent waters in Zion Canyon. They communicated with the rocks, animals, water, and plants in the valley because they believed the monoliths were responsible for the life-giving streams and springs. All of the original riverside pithouses used by the Archaic and the Anasazi peoples have long been washed away. Only the ruins built by the Anasazi high above the canyon floor remain intact. A scenic Anasazi granary survives under an alcove at Weeping Rock where spring water seeps through the porous rock walls to nourish lush hanging gardens. Parunuweap Canyon contains the largest concentration of Anasazi ruins in the park, but they are currently not open to the public. Modern bands of Southern Paiute still visit certain locations within the park to perform rituals and collect plants.

> Among the stunning landscape of Zion National Park are hundreds of petroglyphs spanning several Native American cultural affiliations.

Zion National Park is renowned for its abundant petroglyphs (scratched or incised images), mostly carved by the Anasazi but also created by the Archaic, Basketmaker, Fremont and Paiute Indians as well. Two canyons are especially rich in rock art—Petroglyph Canyon and the Southgate Petroglyph site—featuring a rich array of styles and subjects. Petroglyph Canyon includes two panels containing over 150 images, including a single pictograph (painted image) of a small red triangle. Also in the canyon are several circular spiral designs, which have been determined to interact with sunlight or shadow effects in particular ways during a solstice or equinox. These calendar markings are remarkably similar to the Fajada Butte designs and yearly alignments at Chaco Canyon, New Mexico.

The deep canyons and towering cliffs of Zion were almost beyond description to the first white explorers, but word soon trickled out. Some refused to believe such a place existed, just as others had scoffed at the first reports of Yellowstone. But the massive multi-colored vertical cliffs and narrow canyons were real, and in 1909 the area was added to the National Park system. The Mormons came to ranch and farm in the 1860s and wasted no time naming many of the prominent features after themes from the *Book of Mormon*. The names Altar of Sacrifice,

Kolob Canyon, Towers of the Virgins, Prodigal Son, Tabernacle Dome, Court of Patriarchs and Mount Moroni testify to the reverence the Mormons felt for Zion. The Temple of Sinawava was named after the Coyote God of the Paiutes. The Mormon names stuck and certainly contributed to the spiritual aura of Zion, whose biblical name means a place of peace or sanctuary.

### Getting to Zion National Park

From Kanab in the east, drive 17 miles (27 km) north on U.S. 89, then 24 miles (39 km) west on Utah 9 to Park Headquarters. Beyond the Visitor's Center is the spectacular Zion Canyon. Interstate 15 touches the northwest quadrant of the park, but does not access Zion Canyon. Directional signs lead motorists from Interstate 15 to the Kolob Canyons section of the park. The Great Basin, Mojave Desert, and the Colorado Plateau all converge at Zion and the Kolob Canyons. A number of Anasazi sites have been excavated, but none have been prepared for the public. Perhaps as a precaution to overexposure from Zion's nearly three million annual visitors, Petroglyph Canyon and the Southgate Petroglyph site are not listed on Zion National Park maps. Directions and permission are granted exclusively by park rangers in the Zion Canyon Visitors Center. Otherwise, a fine archaeological diorama in the Visitor Center museum depicts prehistoric settlements in the park. From April through October, the scenic drive in Zion Canyon is closed to private vehicles. During high season visitors must ride the frequent shuttle buses to access the valley and most of the trailheads that access over 150 miles (240 km) of maintained footpaths.

# WEST COAST STATES

*Only after the last tree has been cut down*
*Only after the last river has been poisoned*
*Only after the last fish has been caught*
*Only then will you find money cannot be eaten*
**-contemporary Native American belief**

THOUSANDS OF MILES AWAY FROM WHERE THE NATION WAS born, the West Coast states were America's final frontier. The rugged terrain, coupled with the long sea journey to arrive there, delayed development until the discovery of gold attracted the worldwide attention of fortune seekers. Unlike the flat Atlantic coastline on the other side of North America, the Pacific coastal mountains tumble downward to an abrupt halt when they meet the sea. The dramatic 2,700 miles (4,350 km) of coastline in California, Oregon, and Washington, teeming with wildlife, was a paradise on earth waiting to be discovered. The spectacular scenery of steep-sided cliffs rimmed by giant redwood trees impressed the first European explorers. West Coast modern history began in 1542, when the Portuguese navigator Juan Rodriguez Cabrillo sailed into California's San Diego Bay and claimed the area for the Spanish crown. By 1579, the British dispatched Sir Francis Drake to investigate the West Coast, who may have been the first historic European explorer to discover the San Francisco Bay. After Drake, not much happened for the next 200 years. Spain decided to fortify its California possessions in the late 1760s, when the Russians and British were pursuing their own land claims

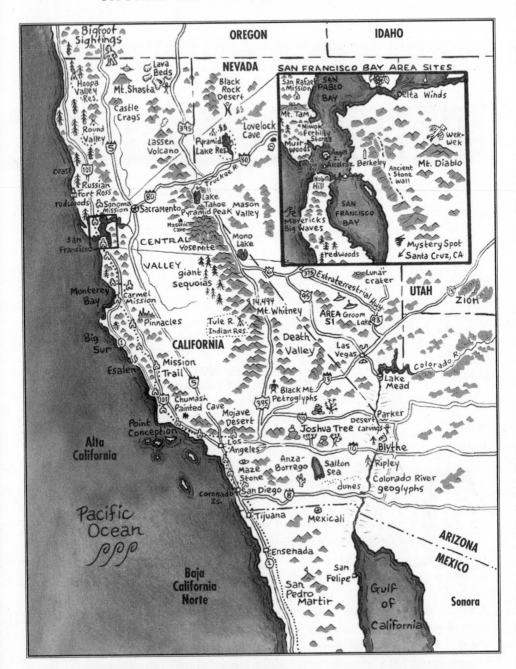

on the Pacific Northwest. By constructing military installations and 21 Catholic missionaries the Spanish devoted considerable resources to shoring up their territorial claims in California. New European sacred places developed alongside ancient indigenous locations. By 1846, American settlers had made new claims to San Francisco and Monterey for the United States, with little resistance from Mexico. When gold was discovered in California two years later, the greatest migration in human history was underway. The ensuing Gold Rush and the developing philosophy of Manifest Destiny brought hundreds of thousands of people into the region from all over the world. The West Coast was soon on its way to becoming a thriving economy, but at the expense of destroying the age-old Native American lifestyle.

Another kind of sacred site, somewhat unique to the West Coast, are the geological anomaly locations known as mystery spots. Animals don't seem to like them, suggesting there is something strange taking place underground. Magnetic anomalies, vortex energies, and electric pulsations are some of the explanations of mystery spots. Similar to its over-commercialized sister destinations, with more than its fair share of kitsch, "The Mystery Spot" in Santa Cruz, California is certainly a sensational wonder with still no uniform scientific explanation. Otherwise, according to the scripted tour guides, it would simply be called "The Spot." Upon a steep incline at a nondescript location in a redwood forest, the forces of The Mystery Spot become apparent as some visitors report feeling tired or dizzy after walking only a few steps up the hill. A trail leads to a tilted shack, which stands at the center of the 150-foot (45-m) diameter magnetic field. A long time ago, the tour guides report, the shack slipped down the hill right into the vortex center of The Mystery Spot, hit a tree and stayed put. After time, the structure became tilted under the mysterious bending forces found at the site. The trees all tilt in the direction of the apparent force field, and balls appear to roll uphill. The most recent theory of the phenomenon is from a German physicist who believes there may be a large metal deposit underground, of a material more dense than lead. This causes gravity to bend around it, causing the visible irregularities that many thousands of visitors experience every year. The Mystery Spot is about three miles (5 km) north of downtown Santa Cruz, on Mystery Spot Road off Branciforte Drive. Bright yellow signs lead the way to the popular tourist attraction, open every day of the year. Other identified West Coast mystery spots include the Oregon Vortex near Gold Hill, Confusion Hill near Garberville in northern California, and San Dimas Canyon in southern California.

# CALIFORNIA

At the end of the last Ice Age, some 14,000 years ago, California was a much different place than it is today. As vast glaciers slowly melted in the Sierra Nevada Mountains, huge quantities of water filled valleys and low depressions in the land. Enormous freshwater lakes that are now extinct covered the landscape. Eventually, due to water seepage and evaporation, the inland lakes dried up but the land remained rich in resources. Massive flocks of birds blotted out the sun when they flew overhead and large mammal herds roamed freely as the first Paleo-Indians arrived to hunt. The various Native American cultures recorded by Spanish explorers were hunter-gatherers in a lifestyle barely changed over the course of 10,000 years or longer. Days were spent harvesting the abundant sea life, trapping mountain animals, or gathering wild grains and berries. Perhaps because of the vast amount of food readily available, California Indians rarely grew their own crops like their neighbors in the American Southwest. Since there were enough resources to go around, no single California Indian tribe dominated the other. While there were indeed occasional skirmishes and hostilities, the general picture drawn by modern archaeologists is one of peace and tranquility among the various native peoples for many millennia.

Upon Spanish exploration of the California coast, the Ohlone and other tribes became the victims of their own hospitality. In December 1602, Sebastian Viscaino sailed into Monterey Bay for supplies and repairs. The Ohlone were right there to help in any way they could, and Viscaino's account of contact is as follows: "The land is well-populated with Indians without number, many of whom came on different occasions to our camp. They seem to be a gentile and peaceful people; they say with signs that there are many villages inland. The sustenance which these Indians eat most of daily, besides fish and shellfish, is acorns and another fruit larger than a chestnut, that is what we could understand of them." Indian remains at Big Sur conclusively date settlement at 3,000 years, but more likely the Ohlone lived in the region for some 10,000 years without interruption. In 1770, the Spanish constructed a mission in Monterey and coerced the peace loving Ohlone to join with them in declaring Catholicism as the true faith. Eventually the Indians who entered the various California missions learned a new language, dressed in different clothes, and were not allowed to practice the ancient traditions they once knew. These baptized and converted Indians worked as indentured laborers, many dying under harsh conditions and restrictive treatment by the missionaries and settlers. Others escaped the missions to unreachable villages in the California interior. Eventually all assimilated into the white man's world, without a single U.S. reservation being set aside for the Ohlone nation.

## Bay Area to Point Conception

Certain locations along the central California coast, especially around the Bay Area, have been cherished by different kinds of people. Early European explorers prized Monterey and the San Francisco Bay for their natural harbors and the riches to be exploited from the bountiful land. Various people from all around the world descended upon central California during the 19th century Gold Rush, most were opportune fortune seekers hoping to declare "Eureka!" The 20th century saw the arrival of the beatniks, hippies, Silicon Valley technology enthusiasts and New Age adherents. Some New Agers claim that San Francisco had originally been an ancient worship site devoted to the Pleiadian star cluster built by an advanced civilization on earth, perhaps the Atlantians or Lemurians. The many Indian tribes living along the central California coastal region identified several power points on the landscape before it became blemished by development in modern times. Such a diverse population in such a beautiful region naturally leads to a fine selection of sacred sites.

▲ Mount Tamalpais as seen from Ring Mountain.

Just north of San Francisco's Golden Gate Bridge is Mount Tamalpais, one of the most visited sacred mountains in the world. The mountain was a spiritual healing site to the coastal Miwok Indians who lived in the area for thousands of years before European contact. Spanish explorers named the peak *La Sierra de Nuestro Padre de San Francisco* in 1770, but it was later changed back to the Miwok name Tamalpais. To Native Americans and New Age spiritual seekers, "Mount Tam" is noted for its powers to heal, purify, and inspire the imagination. Also called the "Sleeping Lady," from a distance Mount Tamalpais does resemble the shape of a reclining woman on her back. Over 6,300 acres (2,520 ha) of redwood groves and oak woodlands surround the mountain as it rises up to its spectacular 2,571-foot (771-m) summit. On a clear winter day, when viewing conditions are ideal, it is possible see the Farallon Islands 25 miles (40 km) out at sea, the Marin County hills extending to Point Reyes, San Francisco and the East Bay communities, Mount Diablo, and even the Sierra Nevada's snow-covered mountains. After the Gold Rush population boom of 1849, more and more people began to use Mount Tamalpais as a place for recreation. Trails were developed and a wagon road was built to the summit. Later, a railway was completed and became known as "The Crookedest Railroad in the World." The railroad was abandoned in 1930 after a wildfire damaged the line, yet several decades later those same roads became the "Birthplace of Mountain Biking." Local cycle enthusiasts Gary Fisher and Charles Crow began riding a new kind of bicycle on the fire roads of Mount Tam in the early 1970s and a sporting institution was born. Mount Tamalpais was utilized as a Nike Missile installation to defend the Bay Area against nuclear attack during the early Cold War years. The out of commission nuclear silos still blemish the landscape near the summit.

Even better views are afforded from the 3,849-foot (1,155-m) summit of Mount Diablo, rising alone at the eastern fringe of the San Francisco Bay Area. With ideal viewing conditions it is possible to see west past the Golden Gate Bridge to the Farallon Islands, Mount Hamilton and the Santa Cruz Mountains to the southeast, the Sierra Nevada Mountains due east, along with both Mount Saint Helena in Wine Country and Mount Lassen in the Cascade Range visible to the north. With binoculars on a clear day, it is possible to see Half Dome in Yosemite

▲ The dramatic Big Sur coastline of central California is the meeting point of the Santa Lucia Range meeting the Pacific Ocean.

National Park and at least 35 of California's 58 counties. Because the mountain stands alone on the edge of the Central Valley, there is virtually nothing to block the sighting from the summit. The Mount Diablo panorama is regarded as the best 360-degree view in North America. Worldwide, the outlook from Diablo's summit is ranked second only to Tanzania's Mount Kilimanjaro. Such stunning views and the commanding location certainly impressed the California Indians living in its shadow for over 5,000 years. Although various Native American tribes worshipped and lived near the sacred mountain, they all regarded it as a bad medicine site to be avoided. Some Indian shaman ventured up the mountain to accumulate the bad medicine, some never returned. In the plains Miwok creation account, Mol-luk (Condor man) lived on the north side of Mount Diablo. His wife gave birth to Wek-wek (Prairie Falcon-man) who wanted to preside over the Miwok in the Central Valley. Back in the Dawn of Time, according to the Miwok creation myth, Mount Diablo was surrounded by water. Wek-wek and his grandfather Coyote-man created all Indian people from the summit of Mount Diablo, and cast them off into the world when the water receded. The bad medicine of the mountain kept most Native Americans away for good, even after European contact. The Spanish adopted the Indian translation *Diablo,* meaning devil, and the name stuck. Today, geomancers claim to follow old shamanistic trails up Mount Diablo, a noted power point to Native Americans and modern New Agers.

Before European contact, the coastal Miwok used to enact a fertility ritual on Ring Mountain in Tiburon. Apart from being a strategic vantage point for viewing most of the San Pablo and San Francisco Bays, Ring Mountain is unique for several serpentine rock outcroppings, one of which displays art markings from an elaborate fertility rite once performed here by young Miwok couples. When an Indian woman wanted to bare a child, she and her lover would visit one particular rock believed to procure a safe and healthy pregnancy. The garage-sized fertility stone is located slightly below the 602-foot (180-m) ridge crest on the southern face of Ring Mountain. Marked on the stone are many full circles and paired semi-circles carved out by the Miwok men and women. Some of these petroglyphs are said to resemble a woman's vagina. The couple would then carve their own groove and rub the tiny stone particles from the soft greenish rock on her body, which would supposedly ensure her maximal fertility and ease her childbirth. As a result of vandalism to the fertility stone and in an effort to save the open space surrounding it, most of Ring Mountain is now a natural sanctuary preserved by Tiburon's Nature Conservancy.

The San Francisco peninsula north of the San Bruno Mountains was a Native American pilgrimage destination and sacred site. No settlement was allowed or desired—the hill was reserved exclusively for pilgrimage. The top of Nob Hill, the present location of Grace Cathedral, was an Indian healing spot and source of a spring. Chinese *feng shui* masters recognized Nob Hill and identified it as the "eye of the dragon for San Francisco." Many great cathedrals worldwide are built upon tribal or pagan worship sites, and most of these have wells underneath that are still tended. Grace Cathedral on Nob Hill is the largest house of worship west of the Mississippi and is modeled after Notre Dame in Paris. New Age enthusiasts claim that long before the Indians came to the peninsula, San Francisco was a temple site called Tlamco with seven hills, including Nob Hill, to denote a map of the Pleiades star system. The Tlamco "Temple of the Sun" reportedly stood at the present location of Haight and Shrader Streets.

> The sacred Mount Tamalpais and Mount Diablo are two polar opposite peaks, both renowned by native people. South of the Bay Area, the spectacular California coastline from Big Sur to Point Conception is noted for its powers to heal, purify and inspire the imagination.

Contemporary authors have portrayed Big Sur as "the greatest meeting of land and sea," but the rugged California landmark went largely unexplored until the last century. The name Big Sur derives its name from the one-time unmapped and unexplored wilderness that lies along the coast south of Monterey. Spanish cartographers named it *El Sur Grande*, meaning "The Big South." Specifically, Big Sur is the 90-mile (145-km) stretch of coastline from the Monterey Peninsula southward to San Simeon. Coast Highway 1 connects north and south, flanked on one side by the majestic Santa Lucia Mountains and on the other by the rocky Pacific coastline. Among the towering redwood groves of Big Sur are several spiritual centers and retreats. The famous healing center Esalen is on the coast, which describes itself as an alternative education center famous for its blend of Eastern and Western philosophies. Buddhist monks live in the mountains above the Carmel Valley at the tranquil Tassajara Zen Center and Hot Springs. The Immaculate Heart Hermitage is home to several Christian monks of the Camaldoli Order, who live a life of retreat and prayer devoted to Jesus Christ based on the rule of Saint Benedict. Interspersed between the

▲ The Transverse Range begins at Point Conception, pictured above. It is one of the few mountain ranges in North America that runs east and west.

mountains and sea are the coastal redwood trees that only grow in a very narrow strip of land from southern Oregon to the Soda Springs drainage of Big Sur. This growing region is about 500 miles (805 km) long and rarely more than 20 to 30 miles (32-48 km) inland from the nourishing coastal fog. Redwoods are a rapidly growing tree, and some individual trees have been measured at more than 360 feet (108 m) in height, making it the tallest measured tree species on earth. The majestic trees offer a cathedral-like canopy of their own, and at one remote Big Sur location very rare albino redwoods can be found.

The indigenous people of Central California were the Miwok, Ohlone, Carmel and Chumash Indians. The name Esalen, a sub-tribe of the Ohlone, derives from *Ex'seien* which means "The Rock." It specifically refers to the land of Big Sur: *Xue elo xonia euene,* an Ohlone declaration meaning "I come from The Rock." While some linguistic terms are still known by contemporary Ohlone members, the last fluent speaker died in 1939 and the language is now considered dead. Many surviving Ohlone members refer to the mountainous interior of the Carmel Valley, an area of profound spiritual and historical significance, as Cachagua, a name derived from the Ohlone word *Xasiuan.*

Point Conception is 100 miles (160 km) south of Big Sur and was regarded as the ultra-sacred Chumash Indian entrance for departing or arriving souls. It was a hallowed realm of the dead where only initiates and shaman would dare venture. The mythical gateway was not just for Chumash Indian souls entering or leaving the planetsphere, but for all beings, hence the name Point Conception. A Chumash village was located at what is now called Jalama Beach County Park, where the unexcavated settlement still remains. The village lasted for many centuries until the Indians were rounded up and taken to La Purisima Mission during the Spanish rule of California. The name Jalama comes from the Spanish spelling of the Indian name for the village, "Halam." Whale watching is popular on this part of the coast in the spring and fall, as well as a world class surfing and windsurfing destination.

## Getting to Bay Area to Point Conception sites

Mount Tamalpais State Park is north of San Francisco's Golden Gate Bridge. From Highway 101 take to the Stinson Beach exit to Highway 1 and follow the signs up the mountain.

Mount Diablo State Park is located on Diablo Road, 5 miles (8 km) east of Interstate 680 in Danville. Mount Diablo can also be reached from Walnut Creek via Ygnacio Valley Road.

Ring Mountain is an open space preserve located about 5 miles (8 km) south of San Quentin in Marin County. Access to the Miwok fertility stone on Ring Mountain is best approached from the north via Tiburon's famous Paradise Drive, turning off just before the Marin County Day School and parking uphill at the end of the road.

Grace Cathedral on top of Nob Hill is surrounded by the oldest neighborhoods in San Francisco and is easily located on any city map.

Big Sur is located along the picturesque Coastal Highway 1, approximately 150 miles (242 km) south of San Francisco, and 250 miles (403 km) north of Los Angeles. Highway 1 was declared California's first Scenic Highway shortly after it was completed in 1937. The famous route provides a driving experience unsurpassed in natural beauty and scenic variety. Esalen Institute is located 17 miles (27 km) south of the town Big Sur.

Point Conception is a 5-mile (8-km) walk down the beach from Jalama Beach County Park, which is 14 miles (23 km) off Highway 1 just south of Lompoc and Vandenberg Air Force Base. Point Conception is on private land as part of the Cojo Ranch and is not accessible by public road. It is only accessible via walking a treacherous beach route at low tide, or by watercraft.

# Blythe Intaglios

The Blythe Intaglios are located alongside one of the most famous waterways in North America just before it enters Mexico and empties into the Sea of Cortez. Along both sides of the Colorado River are numerous enigmatic geoglyphs, or "earth carvings." These intaglios feature images of gigantic humans, animals and geometric figures, created by scraping away darker surface debris to expose the lighter colored soil underneath. Prehistoric geoglyphs are found only in the American Southwest, South America and New Caledonia. There are over 300 recorded intaglios in the Southwest and adjacent Mexico. The Blythe Intaglios are the most popularly known and most easily accessible set of giant desert figures along the lower Colorado River. The Blythe grouping includes different species of animals, several "giant" human or anthropomorphic beings, and random geometric shapes all etched onto the desert floor. The largest human figure at Blythe is 171 feet (52 m) in length, and the smallest is 95 feet (29 m) long. These figures may have represented powerful individuals in an Indian clan, or depict humans interacting with their natural environs. Most of the human figures are etched next to or near animal figures.

Not far from Blythe, at an associated site in Parker, Arizona is a different set of intaglios, similar in their abstract nature. A serpent glyph near Parker, complete with eyes and rattles, sprawls for almost 150 feet (45 m) across the desert floor. Some of these giant figures are associated with nearby dwelling sites about 2,000 years old. Both the Blythe and Parker figures are very similar to those figures carved on the Nazca Plains in Peru. Like the Nazca figures, both cover a vast area, include animal figures, and were made by scraping off the top layer of sun-baked rocks.

> Similar to the Nazca Lines in Peru, the massive Blythe Intaglios are best viewed from the air.

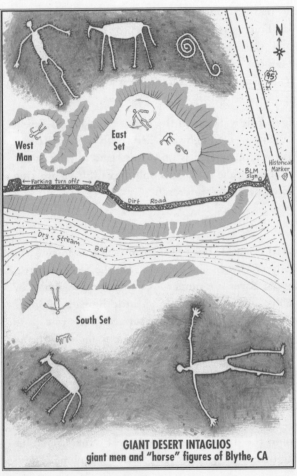

**GIANT DESERT INTAGLIOS**
giant men and "horse" figures of Blythe, CA

The figures are estimated to be anywhere between 450 and 10,000 years old. According to the Mohave and Quechan Indians, the two tribes who inhabited the lower Colorado River area, the human figures represent Mastamho, the creator of all life. The animal figures represent Hatakulya, one of two mountain lion/humans who assisted in the creation. Sacred ceremonial dances were held in the area in ancient times to honor the creation legend. The most famous geoglyphs drawn on the desert floor at Blythe are three abstract human shapes, a coiled serpent, various geometric lines, a dance ring 140 feet (43 m) in diameter and two animals resembling a horse. The long-legged animals, if they are horses, are both about 36 feet (11 m) in length. These animals present a major dating problem because the geoglyphs must have been carved either a long time ago before horses went extinct, or more recently after the Spaniards arrived. Native American horses died off 10,000 years ago and its successor did not reach California until 1540. Another theory holds that some modern horses did exist in North America before the Spaniards, but were regarded as food sources rather than beasts of burden. Either way, the age of the geoglyphs cannot be dated accurately, only theorized.

### Getting to the Blythe Intaglios

The small town of Blythe is located in southeastern California near the Arizona border, about 200 miles (320 km) east of Los Angeles. The ground drawings are situated on two low mesas or terraces east of the Big Maria Mountains. The "Blythe Intaglios" are located just off Highway 95, about 18 miles (29 km) north of the town Blythe. A closer exit on Interstate 10 intersects Highway 95, and is 15.5 miles (25 km) from the site. There is a historical marker on the east side of Highway 95 and a dirt road with a BLM sign accessing the intaglios on the west side. The first dirt road turnoff is .4 miles (.64 km), and the second turnoff is .8 miles (1.3 km) off Highway 95. There are six figures in three locations. 4WD vehicles are recommended. From each turnoff it is a relatively short hike to each set of intaglios—just look for the low chain link fence surrounding each figure.

## Death Valley

The bleak Death Valley in southern California is one of the least populated and hottest areas in the Western Hemisphere. Superstition and mirages, perhaps fueled by heat hallucinations, have filled the minds of many people who have ventured into this inhospitable terrain. To early settlers, Death Valley was the very manifestation of a medieval hell, a River Styx inferno whose temperatures could rise up to 130 degrees Fahrenheit (54° C). The valley received its name in 1849 during the California Gold Rush from emigrants who sought to cross the valley on their way to the gold fields. Pioneers making their way from Utah to California sometimes ventured across this scorching desert instead of risking the snowy Sierras and the infamous mountain pass where the Donner Party was lost. During the 1850s, gold, silver and borax were discovered in the valley.

During the late Pleistocene, the valley was inundated by prehistoric Lake Manly. Nestled between the Panamint Range and the Amargosa Range, the dried lake bed that is Death Valley is 130 miles (210 km) long and between 6 to 14 miles (10-23 km) wide. Death Valley National Park today encompasses more than three million acres (1.2 mil hectares). The bottom elevation of 282 feet (86 m) below sea level marks the location called Badwater—the lowest point in North America. Despite the scorching temperatures more than 1,000 species of plants, dozens of mammals and reptiles, and a unique species of fish called the pupfish thrive in Death Valley.

▲ Charcoal kilns in Death Valley.
(Photo courtesy National Park Service)

The Shoshone Indians lived in Death Valley for over a thousand years before the arrival of the white man. They were of the Shoshone Comanche stock, dark and thickset, and very superstitious. All Death Valley Indians felt that a house should be built with its entranceway facing the rising sun. They also believed that every home must have a side door. In the event of a sudden death, the body could be removed quickly through the hidden door before the spirit could rush back. Petroglyphs are found in a number of Death Valley caves and canyons. Most depict animals such as deer, sheep, lizards, and turtles, some feature humans, and others are undecipherable. The modern Shoshone do not understand the pictures, nor do they know who created them. Death Valley remains home to the Timbisha tribe, who have inhabited the valley continuously for at least 1,000 years. Some families still live in the valley at Furnace Creek. The name of the valley, *tümpisa*, means "rock paint" and refers to the valley as a source of red ochre paint.

Death Valley is the lowest point below sea level in the Western Hemisphere. It is also the rumored home to such paranormal activities as teleporting rocks, UFOs, and underground cities.

Paiute Indian legend relates the story of a city they called Shin-Au-av that exists deep below the desert floor in Death Valley National Park. The people who live in the city dress in leather and speak an unknown language. Several first-person accounts from individuals who claim to have ventured into this city describe it as a fabulously wealthy wonderland. Such stories inspired Charles Manson, the convicted ringleader of the Manson Family who was prosecuted for the brutal Tate-LaBianca murders in the early 1970s. Charles Manson believed that Devil's Hole in Death Valley was an entrance to another level of existence. Manson planned to lead his family through the portal when the war he foretold between the whites and blacks began. On several mesas at the edge of the Panamint Mountains bordering Death Valley are carefully placed lines of rocks stretching for hundreds of feet. These were probably the "ceremonial mesas" of an unknown people, perhaps dating back thousands of years when the valley was a freshwater lake. Several arranged megalithic rock formations located atop high these remote mesas add further mystery to this surreal desert landscape.

### Getting to Death Valley

Death Valley National Park is best accessed from the south, via Interstate 15 connecting Los Angeles and Las Vegas. Route 127 leads to Death Valley Junction and the Badwater Basin. Motorists should be prepared for extremely harsh weather conditions. A ceremonial mesa with circular cairns on its summit is accessible at the southern end of Death Valley, south of Shoshone and near State Highway 178 in Inyo County.

## Joshua Tree

The immense southern California desert, seemingly devoid of life, is in reality an intricate living system dependent on each fragile segment to support the whole system for survival. In this harsh environment where life seems so frail, the creamy white blossom of the Joshua tree in the springtime unleashes a beautiful desert spectacle. The blooming season is from February to late April. Joshua trees do not branch until after they bloom, nor do they bloom every year. Once they bloom, the trees are pollinated by the female yucca moth, which spreads pollen while laying eggs inside the flower. The moth larvae feed on the seeds, but enough seeds remain to produce more trees. Joshua Tree National Park encompasses two large distinct ecosystems primarily determined by elevation: the Colorado and the Mojave Deserts. The Colorado Desert is below the 3,000-foot (900-m) elevation mark and features natural gardens of spidery ocotillo and jumping cholla cactus, located in the eastern division of the park. The Mojave section is slightly higher, cooler and wetter, and is the special habitat of the Joshua tree, or *Yucca brevifolia*. Joshua trees are found only in North America in the states of California, Arizona, Utah, and Nevada, confined mostly to the Mojave Desert between 2,000 and 6,000 feet (600-1,800 m) elevation. A third minor ecosystem consists of the scattered fan palm oases dotting the park, providing dramatic contrast to the arid surroundings. In these few areas where water occurs naturally, flora and fauna abound.

The undisciplined-looking Joshua tree, which gave the park its name, was named by Mormon visitors when they crossed the Mojave Desert in the mid-19th century. Upon seeing groves of immature two-armed plants, a group of Latter Day Saints likened them to human arms reaching up to God. The tree's unique shape reminded them of a biblical story in which Joshua reaches his hands up to the sky to stop the sun by God's command. Ranchers and miners who were contemporary with the Mormon immigrants took advantage of the Joshua tree by using the trunks and branches as fencing, or to fuel ore processing steam engines.

▲ The exotic and surreal landscape of Joshua Tree National Park.

Unfortunately most of the old growth trees were harvested, but if they survived they can live for two hundred years. The tallest trees reach about 50 feet (15 m) in height.

Joshua Tree National Park is rich in cultural and historical resources harking back to the advent of Paleo-Indians in the region. There are over 3,000 Native American sites in the park and almost all are associated with water. The most famous Indian location in the park is called Barker Dam and had once been an ancient initiation site surrounded by a high concentration of petroglyphs. The Cahuilla Native Americans have lived in the Southwest for generations and still identify with the Joshua tree as a valuable resource. Their ancestors used the leaves of *Yucca brevifolia* to weave sandals and baskets in addition to harvesting the seeds and flower buds for nutritious meals. Earlier Paleo-Indians who came to the area were seasonal travelers following age-old migration routes. During the Pleistocene era, one of the Southwest's earliest cultures, the Pinto people, lived here and hunted and gathered food along a slow-moving river that ran through the now-dry Pinto Basin. Later, other American Indians traveled through this area at times when plants yielded maximum food and animals were most abundant. They collected seasonal pinyon nuts, mesquite beans, acorns, and cactus fruit, leaving behind rock paintings and pottery ollas as reminders of their passing. Rock overhangs and caves provided shelter and places to store pottery containers and stone tools. Occasional flash floods continue to wash out ancient pottery shards.

> The boulders of Joshua Tree are some of the most interesting geological displays found in the southern California deserts. About 1.5 million people from all over the world visit the park every year.

Joshua Tree National Park offers a bonanza of opportunities for the outdoor enthusiast. Sport rock climbers from all over the world flock to the park, particularly in winter, to challenge the naturally sculpted granite shapes in an activity known as "vertical adventuring." The spectacular rock formations, unique landscapes, starry skies, and seasonal blooms make it a photographers' dream. Late spring brings vibrant coloration to the desert floor, as wildflowers paint the scenery in a profusion of colors. Joshua trees and yucca plants bring forth their creamy blossoms, interspersed by blooming ocotillos with their flaming tips. Five oases dot the park's 794,000 acres (317,600 ha), rising like islands in a stormy sea. The best known, the Oasis of Mara, was inhabited first by Indians and later used by prospectors and homesteaders, and is now the site of the main Visitor's Center. These oases once served as gathering places, often life-saving, to all prehistoric people who passed through this scorching hot desert. Beyond spectacular scenery, park literature pledges to "provide a space for finding freedom from everyday routines, space for self-discovery, and a refuge for the human spirit." No wonder Joshua Tree National Park was selected as one of the New Age sites for the 1986 Harmonic Convergence. Like Sedona, this area is known for its power to convey serenity and a feeling of peace.

### Getting to Joshua Tree National Park

Joshua Tree National Park is located 140 miles (215 km) east of downtown Los Angeles, and 195 miles (315 km) southwest of Las Vegas. The National Park may be entered from three park gates: Park Boulevard is a few miles east of the adjoining town of Joshua Tree, or 15 miles (23 km) further east is the city of Twentynine Palms and the main Visitor's Center. The third entrance is off Interstate 10 on the other side of the park, serviced by the Cottonwood Springs Visitor Center. The park is open all year round. Between the towns of Yucca Valley and Joshua Tree is the Institute of Mentalphysics and Spiritual Retreat Center "where the prophets of the future can commune with the eternal," according to Founder Dr. Edwin Dingle who claimed to have been an incarnated Tibetan Lama. The Institute is open to all religious faiths and encourages clients to visit the park to help them better commune with God and nature. Also near Joshua Tree National Park is the Integratron, an unfinished health rejuvenation center in the town of Landers reportedly positioned upon several major ley lines. Also in Landers is Giant Rock, the world's largest freestanding boulder.

## Lake Shrine

Every few decades a spiritual educator emerges who makes an impact on an entire generation. Religious movements to this day continue to value the teachings of Krishna, Buddha, Jesus Christ, Moses and Mohammed. More recently, the nonviolent teachings of Henry David Thoreau influenced Mahatma Gandhi, who in turn inspired Martin Luther King Jr. The Indian spiritualist Paramahansa Yogananda can be included in this elite grouping as well. Yogananda has been called one of the most prominent spiritual figures of the 20th century. Hailed as the father of introducing Eastern spiritual yoga practices to the West, Paramahansaji ("ji" is a respectful suffix added to names in India) attributes his experiences and training with modern-day saints and illuminated masters of India. In his writings and lectures he beautifully wove his personal accounts of the yogi masters with scientific clarity and subtle but definite laws by which Indian yogis performed miracles and attained self-mastery.

▲ Portions of Mahatma Gandhi's ashes reside at the World Peace Memorial on one side of the Lake Shrine.

After decades of spiritual study under the tutelage of yogi masters throughout India, Yogananda embarked on his first journey to North America in 1920. His lectures struck a cord almost immediately and many Americans assisted in the establishment of the Self-Realization Fellowship (SRF). Several SRF hermitages and shrines were founded in the United States, especially in southern California where Paramahansaji spent the final decades of his life. The Lake Shrine was dedicated on August 20th, 1950 by Paramahansaji, a date that corresponded with the 30th anniversary of the SRF being established in North America. While supervising the planting and construction work in 1949, the year the Lake Shrine was donated, Yogananda stayed at times in the houseboat, still docked on the lakeshore. He desired the Lake Shrine to be used by spiritual seekers of all religious persuasions: "This SRF shrine is given to you for your use, for your meditation, that you may be able in kind to self-realization teachings and yoga, be able to resurrect the dead body into an immortal body, and keep it ever intoned in the heart of God."

In prehistory, the Chumash Indians of southern California utilized the spring-fed lake as a source of fresh water and food. A movie studio executive owned the property in the 1940s, constructed the Dutch windmill replica, and donated the property to the SRF. When construction began on the Lake Shrine, Yogananda envisioned the placement of two artificial waterfalls to cascade down on opposite shores. The nonsectarian gardens surrounding the lake are filled with flora from six continents. There are tropical palms and ferns, Mexican weeping bamboo and Japanese black pines, cypress and ginkgo trees. There are coastal redwoods, desert cactuses, impatiens, pampas grass, wisteria, passion flowers, and water lilies.

Within this beautiful setting, Paramahansaji also envisioned the Lake Shrine to be representative of all religions. Upon arrival, the visitor enters the "Court of Religions" where each of the five principal religions of the world is represented by a monument that bears its symbol: the Sanskrit symbol of *Om* for Hinduism, a Wheel of the Law for Buddhism, a Star and Crescent for Islam, a Star of David for Judaism, and a Cross for Christianity. "We must recognize the unity of mankind," he said, "remembering that we are all made in the image of God. There must be world brotherhood if we are to practice the true art of living. This shrine is dedicated to all religions that all may feel the unity of a common faith."

▲ The lake side windmill is now a chapel for quiet meditation.

Further around the lake, behind the Golden Lotus Archway, is a "wall-less temple" open to the sky, called the Mahatma Gandhi World Peace Memorial. A brass coffer containing a portion of Gandhi's ashes, sent from India, was enshrined in a 1000-year-old sarcophagus when the Lake Shrine was dedicated. While on his travels in India, Yogananda was befriended by Mahatma Gandhi, and eventually received the only portion of Gandhi's ashes shipped outside of India. The carved sarcophagus that enshrines a portion of Gandhi's ashes is directly across the lake from the Windmill Chapel where Paramahansaji delivered some of his final lectures.

> The verdant gardens surrounding the Lake Shrine offer the visitor a refuge of serenity and harmony. Paramahansaji designed it to represent a universal experience of all religious faiths under the divine kinship that unites all people as God's children.

Paramahansa Yogananda hailed the Lake Shrine as "one of the most beautiful estates in the world, a floral wonderland." The 10-acre (4-ha) site is a natural amphitheater, surrounded by verdant hills. A large natural lake, a blue jewel in a mountain setting, has given the estate its name the Lake Shrine. Two marble statues from China adorn the site—a statue of Lord Buddha and Kwan Yin, the Chinese personification of the Divine Mother. A life-size statue of Jesus Christ stands on a hill above one of the waterfalls. Another statue of Krishna playing the flute is located near the other waterfall, within a little garden.

In one of his last sermons, less than a year before his passing, Paramahansaji recognized the potency of the Lake Shrine. He praised the location as being surrounded by ocean, mountain, and lake. He eulogized it as a place where Jesus Christ and the yogi masters are reflected in every blossom, in every fish in the pond, in every little flower, in every true soul who visits. He suggested to the listeners at his 1951 Easter Sunday sermon: "May you all make it a Mecca and a place of pilgrimage. ... All those who come to this wonderful shrine will feel it. I have left my spirit here, in the ether, and all those who have true devotion will feel it."

Paramahansa Yogananda entered *mahasamadhi*, a yogi's final conscious exit from the body, on March 7th, 1952 in Los Angeles. Weeks after leaving his body Yogananda's unchanged face shone with a divine luster of incorruptibility. The mortuary director of Forest Lawn in Glendale where he was laid to rest has commented that: "the absence of any visual signs of decay in the dead body of Paramahansa Yogananda offers the most extraordinary case in our experience ... no physical disintegration was visible in his body even 20 days after his death ... this state of perfect preservation of a body is, so far as we know from mortuary annals, an unparalleled one." There are people who say Paramahansaji is constantly sending his love to the Lake Shrine. According to the monks on site "he always said that after he passed away he would be watching over this place and sending his blessings."

### Getting to the Lake Shrine

The Self-Realization Fellowship Lake Shrine and Gandhi World Peace Memorial are located in the Pacific Palisades community of Los Angeles, near the western terminus of Sunset Boulevard. The SRF Lake Shrine Retreat is at 17190 Sunset Boulevard, about a quarter mile from the Pacific Coast Highway 1. Self-Realization Fellowship services, meditations, and classes are held weekly at the Lake Shrine, which is open free to the public every day of the week except Monday, but the grounds are rarely crowded. Several SRF monks live full time at the Lake Shrine and the Temple complex located at the top of the hill. For those who believe surfing is their religion, one of the most popular surf breaks in southern California is called "Swamis," named after Paramahansa Yogananda. The Swamis break is located in southern Encinitas, just below the SRF hermitage where Paramahansaji completed his epic book *Autobiography of a Yogi*.

## Lava Beds

Over a quarter million years ago, violent eruptions deposited enormous amounts of volcanic debris over large areas of northeastern California and southern Oregon. Successive eruptions left behind lava tubes, molten rock formations, and a blanket of ash coating the landscape. Much later in time, approximately 12,000 years ago, the last glaciers in the Sierra Nevada were retreating and enormous freshwater lakes covered much of northeastern California. Like neighboring Lake Lahontan in northwestern Nevada, huge flocks of migratory birds and now-extinct land mammals roamed around the lakes and adjacent lava fields. The first Paleo-Indians came to the region in search of the abundant game. The Klamath and Tule Lake basins were occupied by the first inhabitants at least 9,000 years ago, but perhaps as far back as 11,500 years ago. Even as Tule Lake was drying up, it still provided essential foodstuffs for long-term habitation. The hard-stemmed tule plant is also called bulrush (*Scirpus acutus*), which still grows in the marshy areas of Tule Lake. The early inhabitants wove the plant into mats, shelters, boats, baskets, clothing, and sandals.

On the southeastern periphery of Tule Lake is a volcanic tuff-mound that had been an island when the lake level was much higher. The exposed section of the point resulted after a widespread drought over 6,000 years ago lowered the lake level enough for a large undercut section to crack off. The early inhabitants paddled out to what is now called Petroglyph Point to carve strange symbols into the soft exposed rock. Petroglyph Point features over 5,000 mysterious symbols

▲ Petroglyph Point was once an island in a vast lake covering much of northern California.

107

▲ Hundreds of petroglyphs are protected behind a fence at Petroglyph Point, a remote section of Lava Beds National Monument.

along a wide cliff face. The ancient sculptors choose this recently exposed section of the island as their canvas beginning at least 4,500 years ago and continuing for another two thousand consecutive years. Many generations of Native Americans came to Petroglyph Point to carve anthropomorphic beings, animal-style images, geometric patterns, and random lines—oftentimes overlapping older pictures. Although large areas of the cliff face were available to the Indian artists, only certain sections were utilized for their strange etchings. The petroglyphs appear to be related to hunting magic or used to describe an event in the tribe's history. The thousands of carvings at Petroglyph Point, as well as those found on nearby boulders and in cave shelters, make Lava Beds one of the largest rock art concentrations in North America.

Lava Beds National Monument contains over 400 lava tube caves, but only a few were chosen by ancient shaman as special enough to paint archaic symbols and patterns. Modern Modoc people continue to travel across the country every year to experience the sacredness of these caves.

Lava tubes are formed when molten magma flows down a pathway and splashes in different directions to form walls and eventually a roof. Hot lava continues moving along inside until it hardens at its source and is blocked. Subsequent lava flows cover over the tubes, burying them even deeper. Such caves must have truly impressed the first visitors who ventured into them, especially when light shafts or percolating water drips were present. The Catacombs Tunnel at Lava Beds, for example, is nearly 7,000 feet (2,100 m) long and links to adjoining passageways. Rock art was most likely an integral part of the rituals and ceremonies performed by the Native American people. Certain lava tubes became special areas of worship, especially among young men who ventured into the underworld on their adolescence vision quests. By fasting, dancing, meditating, or swimming underwater to another cave, young Modoc braves would seek a guardian spirit to guide them through life. It oftentimes took many days before the spirit entity would reveal itself to the young initiate. As a result, there are many cave associations in the legends of the Modoc tribe. Big Painted Cave features several faded pictographs at eye level, with a secret opening down to a large pond of ice that was probably a favored water source. Symbol Bridge Cave is a wide tunnel opened at both ends, hence the reference to a bridge, with beautifully painted symbols on both sides. Fern Cave is a tube with a collapsed ceiling, giving access to a rich collection of hundreds of wall paintings. These three pictograph sites are the most favored caves for returning Modoc pilgrims who come here to recall the stories and legends of their inherited legacy.

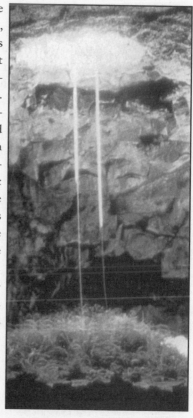

▲ A light shaft in a lava tube. (Photo courtesy National Park Service)

The name Modoc is derived from the original name *Moadoci*, given to them by their powerful neighbors and traditional enemies—the Klamath tribe of southern Oregon. Archaeologists believe that the Modoc and their ancestral lineage had lived in the region for 9,000 years or longer. Before white settlers arrived the Modoc lived relatively peaceful lives, aside from the occasional skirmish over food, women, or hunting grounds with other tribes. Increasing hostility in the 19th century with white homesteaders over land and resources precipitated the Modoc Indian War. The Modoc were forced to defend their homeland against the United States Army in a five-month war in 1873, deftly avoiding capture time and time again by escaping through the familiar lava tubes. The Modoc War was the only major Indian conflict fought in California and the only occasion when a full rank general was killed in action. The Army eventually defeated the warriors and in the process destroyed the cultural identity of a people. The surviving Modocs were denied their request for a reservation on the Lost River and forced to relocate to an Oklahoma reservation.

## Getting to Lava Beds National Monument

Three entrances into Lava Beds National Monument access Route 139, all connecting via Tionesta and Hill Roads. Petroglyph Point is 3 miles (5 km) on the unpaved Country Road 120 from the intersection of Route 139, about a half-mile (.7 km) south of Newell. Big Painted and Symbol Bridge Caves are accessible by footpath, about a mile north of the Visitor Center. A dozen other lava tubes are located off the Cave Loop Road, just south of the Visitors Center. Fern Cave is only accessible by prior reservation with a park ranger every Saturday. Captain Jack's Stronghold fortress, where the Modoc fighting force of less than 60 men held off an Army force 20 times their size, is located roughly between Petroglyph Point and the eastern entrance to Lava Beds. There is a well-marked turnoff to the Stronghold, and a self-guided trail.

# California Indians

The original native people of California were ancestors of the Great Plains Indians, who likely crossed the Alaskan land bridge from Siberia during the last Ice Age. The largest tribes from north to south were: the Modoc; Shasta; Nongatl; Washoe; Yahi; Maiduu; Yuki; Miwok; Ohlone; Yokuts; Salinan; Chumash; and the Serrano. The California tribes seem to have traveled over the inland barriers centuries later, then established themselves in relatively isolated groups throughout the region. On the coast there was no long distance pattern of contact or communication among them, unlike their Central and South American brethren. For many centuries, the California tribes lived in isolated harmony with the land and made pilgrimages to localized sacred sites. Hot springs and wells were particular favorites of the native people.

▲ The Native American named Ishi was considered the "Last Wild Indian." As the final survivor of the Yahi tribe, he emerged from the woods in August, 1911 near Oroville, California. Photo circa 1914.

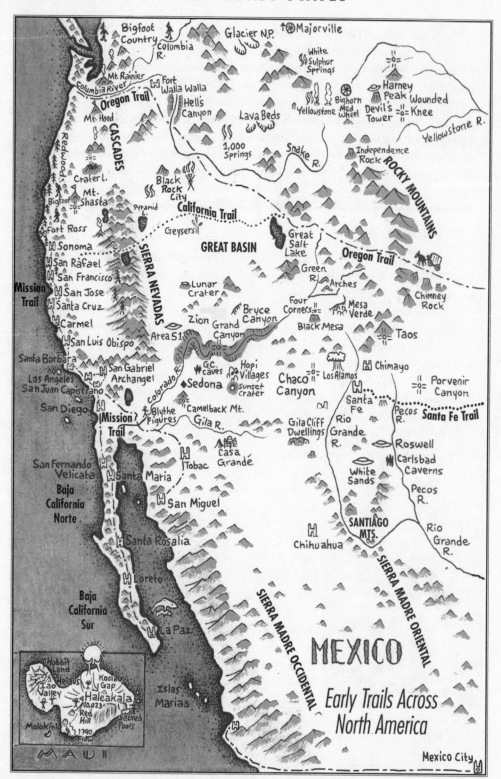

Bigfoot Country
Columbia R.
Glacier N.P.
Majorville
Mt. Rainier
Columbia River
Fort Walla Walla
White Sulphur Springs
Oregon Trail
Hell's Canyon
Yellowstone
Bighorn Med Wheel
Harney Peak
Devil's Tower
Wounded Knee
Mt. Hood
CASCADES
Lava Beds
Yellowstone R.
Redwoods
Crater L.
Mt. Shasta
Bigfoot
1,000 Springs
Snake R.
Independence Rock
ROCKY MOUNTAINS
Pyramid
Black Rock City
California Trail
Fort Ross
Sonoma
Geysers
GREAT BASIN
Great Salt Lake
Oregon Trail
San Rafael
San Francisco
SIERRA NEVADAS
Green R.
Arches
Chimney Rock
San Jose
Lunar Crater
Santa Cruz
Bryce Canyon
Four Corners
Mesa Verde
Carmel
Zion
Grand Canyon
Black Mesa
Taos
Mission Trail
San Luis Obispo
Area 51
Santa Barbara
Los Angeles
San Gabriel Archangel
G.C. caves
Hopi Villages
Chaco Canyon
Los Alamos
Chimayo
Porvenir Canyon
San Juan Capistrano
Colorado
Sedona
Sunset Crater
Santa Fe
Pecos R.
Santa Fe Trail
San Diego
Mission Trail
Blythe Figures
Camelback Mt.
Gila R.
Gila Cliff Dwellings
Rio Grande R.
Roswell
Carlsbad Caverns
San Fernando Velicata
Tobac
Casa Grande
White Sands
Pecos R.
Baja California Norte
Santa Maria
San Miguel
SANTIAGO MTS.
Rio Grande R.
Santa Rosalia
Chihuahua
SIERRA MADRE ORIENTAL
Loreto
Baja California Sur
La Paz
Islas Marias
SIERRA MADRE OCCIDENTAL
MEXICO
Early Trails Across North America
Mexico City

Hobbit Land
Heiau
Koolau Gap
Iao Valley
Haleakala
10,023
Red Hill
Molokini
1790 Flow
Sacred Pools
MAUI

The single most destructive element to California Indians was the discovery of gold. Hundreds of thousands of immigrants from around the world descended upon the gold fields of California to seek their fortune. Nothing would block their way, especially native people who were viewed as more of a nuisance than anything else. Few California tribes were fortunate enough to retain even a small fraction of their land, let alone their way of life. The missionaries also played a large role in subjugating the Indians and encouraging them to forget their cultural ties. Most California tribes died of disease, genocide, starvation, warfare, or were relocated far away from their native homelands.

## Mission Trail

The first sea explorers to reach California visited briefly, primarily seeking supplies and safe harbor before setting off again. The Spanish were the first to make land claims on California, soon to be followed by the English explorer Sir Francis Drake near the San Francisco Bay, and later the Russians at Fort Ross in northern California. In order to shore-up their possessions, the Spanish needed to establish a land trade route to link their permanent settlements. The Spanish referred to Mexico's northwest peninsula region as Baja California, and the region north of Baja was called Alta California, almost all of which today is the state of California. Under Spanish rule, the California Mission Trail was established in 1769 to connect the inland and coastal religious communities from southern Baja to the Bay Area in northern California.

▲ A Chumash Indian poses in traditional clothes.

Before the Mission Trail, several isolated Catholic colonies were established on the west coast of California, some as early as the 15th century. The Mission Trail in Alta California, known as *El Camino Real* or "The Royal Highway," connected each colony to be within a day's travel by horseback, or two on foot. To facilitate overland travel on the 600-mile (966-km) long El Camino Real, mission settlements were rarely separated over 30 miles (48 km) apart, so that each mission was accessible by a single strenuous day's ride on horseback. Heavy freight movement was practical only via water. Tradition has it that the Spanish padres sprinkled mustard seeds along the trail in order to mark it with bright yellow flowers.

Visitors to California are often amazed by the abundance of Spanish saints among city names throughout the state. The names of the saints of the day were often applied to newly discovered localities, whether

112

rivers, bays, mountains or valleys. Spanish saints' names were also chosen for presidios or forts, pueblos or towns, and of course, the Franciscan missions. Today, most of these early missionary settlements are thriving urban communities. From north to south, visit the old missions in the modern city centers of: Sonoma, San Rafael, San Francisco, San Jose, Santa Cruz, Carmel, San Juan Bautista, San Luis Obispo, Santa Barbara, Los Angeles,

▲ The Carmel Mission was home to Father Serra for most of his life in California.

San Juan Capistrano and San Diego. In the Bay Area, modern El Camino Real was one of the first state highways in California, now designated Route 82. Given the lack of standardized road signs in 1906, it was decided to place distinctive bells along the route, hung on supports in the form of an 11-foot (3.3-m) high shepherd's crook, also described as "a Franciscan walking stick." Hundreds of these cast metal bells can still be seen along the route.

## The Mission Trail unified California in the name of proselytizing Christianity.

Most missions were instrumental in California's early development. Perhaps the most significant was the Los Angeles mission called San Gabriel Archángel, located just south of Pasadena. San Gabriel was the first land link with the capital Mexico City in 1774, and became the chief point of contact with Mexico for many decades. Its strategic location made San Gabriel the wealthiest of all the missions. The prosperity of San Gabriel resulted in the building of a beautiful church, peaceful gardens and the acquisition of an expansive art collection. The founder of the Mission Trail, Father Junipero Serra lived most of his life and died in the Carmel mission, one of the most scenic and best-preserved missions in this historic chain. Father Serra is currently being considered for canonization. If he becomes a saint, Catholic pilgrims could soon be flooding the Mission Trail in record numbers.

## Getting to the California Missions

The old missions are a proud and historic part of every California community where they reside. Most are located in the middle of the oldest sections of town, and roads with names like El Camino Real, Dolores and Mission Street usually lead right to their doorsteps. An unpaved portion of the original Spanish road has been preserved just east of Mission San Juan Bautista—this road actually follows part of the San Andreas Fault. The country missions are equally fascinating. From north to south roughly paralleling Highway 101 between Carmel and San Diego look for: Mission Nuestra Senora de la Soledad Ruins near Soledad; Mission San Antonio de Padua on the Hunter Liggett military base; Mission San Miguel Archángel near San Miguel; La Purisima Mission State Historical Park near Lompoc; Mission San Buenaventura near Ventura; and Mission San Luis Rey de Francia near Oceanside. Sunday masses are held in some of the old basilicas, or a nearby Catholic church on the grounds. All have become museums of sort, and a small donation is always appreciated.

# Mount Shasta

Towering Mount Shasta is the prominent centerpiece of northern California, rising like a glimmering diamond in a field of evergreens. Mount Shasta is situated at the intersection of three western mountain ranges: the Sierra Nevada to the southeast, the Cascades extending north to British Columbia, and the western Klamath Range. At 14,162 feet (4,249 m), Shasta is the second highest of the Cascade Range volcanoes and is home to California's five largest glaciers. Mount Shasta rises more than 10,000 feet (3,300 m) from its base, soaring abruptly over a landscape of relatively level ground. Because it is physically unconnected to any nearby mountain Shasta is visible for a hundred miles in all directions on a clear day. This cone-shaped stratovolcano is relatively young, as is evident by the lack of extensive glacial erosion. Tiny sulfur vents just below the summit suggest this dormant volcano is merely taking a geological nap. Long regarded as a place of intense energy, the "Gentile Giant" Mount Shasta possesses a visible and majestic presence. New Age mystics believe it represents our planet's version of the human being's first or root chakra, located near the base of our spine. This theory then expounds that the mountain connects to our collective survival.

To the Modoc Native American people, Mount Shasta was the center of the universe. "Before there were people on the earth," begins a Modoc legend, "the Chief of the Sky Spirits grew tired of his home in the Above World because the air was always brittle with an icy cold. So he carved a hole in the sky with a stone and pushed all the snow and ice down below until he made a great mound that reached from the earth almost to the sky." Today it is known as Mount Shasta. This lengthy creation story goes on to explain how the Chief named Skell formed the trees, rivers, animals and rocky hills, bestowing all the features of the mountain with spiritual significance. The towering volcano was located in the southwest corner of Modoc territory before part of the tribe was displaced in the 1850s, corresponding to the time when gold was discovered in the region. The Modoc have prophesied that when Shasta loses all its glaciers and snow, it will again erupt. When Shasta erupts, according to tribal elders, the world will go through major reformations and climatic changes. During interspersed California drought years, Mount Shasta comes close to being devoid of glaciers. Could the Modoc have foreseen today's global warming and changing weather patterns?

Any Indian tribe who came into view of Mount Shasta held the mountain in very high esteem. Tribes such as the Karuk, Klamath, Modoc, Yurok, Shasta, Wiyot, Yuki, Okwanuchu, Achomawi, Atsugewi, Wintuand and the Wintun revered the mountain as a spiritual center. Others would travel great distances to catch a view of *Wyeka*, or "Great

▲ Mount Shasta rises above Tule Lake in northern California, and is visible for a hundred miles in all directions on a clear day.

White." The dormant volcano is believed to contain powerful Earth spiritual energy where the Great Spirit himself was thought to reside. Native peoples were reluctant to climb large mountains like Shasta because the power of the Great Spirit was too strong there. Since the lodge of the Great Spirit is on peaks such as Shasta, he demands respect and only those of a pure heart can climb to the summit and not be harmed. That is why most native people today still do not climb to the peak, although on the lower slopes, such as Panther Meadows, purification rituals and sweat lodge ceremonies continue every year.

Mount Shasta is a very powerful beacon to the indigenous peoples of northern California and southern Oregon. It is also the rumored home of Bigfoot, citizens of Lemuria, The Great White Brotherhood, and regular UFO sightings.

The energy of Mount Shasta is so powerful that it has been described by New Agers as the "Epcot Center" of sacred sites. Shasta is said to be the abode of many different spirits and beings, both present and past. Almost all metaphysical

115

▲ Among the many mysteries of Mount Shasta include clusters of mounds that appear to have moats surrounding them, and appear like crop circles when viewed from above.

stories relate to the mountain's interior, which is home to several mysterious and legendary beings. Inside Mount Shasta is supposedly a massive cavern with gold-lined offshoot caves. Here can be found the legendary city of Telos with gleaming gold temples. Although they will flee at the sight of a human, keep a lookout for Bigfoot, the Lemurians, the Yaktayvians, and one white-robed character named Phylos who can materialize himself at will. The Lemurians are said to be a peaceful pre-Atlantian race believed to have lived on the now-submerged Pacific continent of Lemuria some 14,000 years ago. The Lemurians were survivors of a great flood who migrated to the safety of the Pacific Northwest. The Yaktayvians are another mysterious race said to be living inside Shasta who can supposedly use their magic bells and force fields to keep humans away from their "doorways" into the mountain. These extraterrestrials reportedly utilize the summit for entering the caverns inter-dimensionally with their spacecraft. Although these entities are of an ancient race, they would rather not interact with or be seen by humans. In their view, we are a primitive people who are ruled by fear and violence. They prefer to disguise their activities and not overtly influence the course of human civilization.

Also included in the extensive list of Shasta mysteries are unexplained mound clusters at different locations around the mountain. Some mounds near Goose Lake were created by Ducks Unlimited for birds to nest, but others defy rationalization. Archaeologists and geologists are in stark disagreement with one another, each claiming the other must explain the mounds. Large boulders are oddly found at the top of some mounds, rather than rolling down over time by the forces of gravity. Many of the mounds do not show signs of deterioration or erosion. What's more, no Native American group claims responsibility, nor do any such groups have a history of creating mounds in this part of the world. At a twin cluster of mounds near the small town of Tennant there are mounds surrounded by interconnected moats. Although the moats are usually dry it is clear that water somehow interacts with the two clusters. Seen from above, the Tennant Water Mounds take on the appearance of crop circles because of their unusual geometric shapes. Nature certainly does not create anything this perfect. It is possible that an eccentric rancher with a penchant for sacred geometry created the mounds with a bulldozer as a watering hole for his livestock. By why go to so much trouble? Those who believe in the underground city of Telos offer another explanation. When the dew point reaches an optimum level, the moats around the mounds are filled by a channel connected to an underground water source. When filled, the water molecules are excited to the point that they can self-regulate the mounds by clearing the moats of any debris. Once in operation the water mounds serve the purpose of creating lenticular cloud cover for entering or exiting spacecraft. It wouldn't be the most far out Shasta theory. After all, unexplained sightings of ape-men, UFOs and hooded phantoms are reported every year. Such stories only enhance the mystery and legend of this powerful mountain.

## Climbing Mount Shasta

Mount Shasta is not a technical ice climbing mountain, and several routes to the summit make the ascent relatively accessible for those lacking mountaineering experience. This is not to say the ascent is easy, because it certainly is not. Weather and season often determine difficulty and, on average, half of those attempting the summit turn back. Altitude sickness is a primary reason for not reaching the summit, second only to foul weather. Since the mountain is so huge, weather patterns develop here, and it is not uncommon to be caught in high winds and/or heavy snowfall. If there are large, rounded lenticular clouds forming over the summit, a storm is likely brewing and it may be time to start descending. Lenticular clouds are the least common cloud in the world, but they are the

▲ Mountain climbers approaching the summit of Mount Shasta.

most common cloud in Nevada and the Shasta region of California. The ideal months for climbing Mount Shasta are July and August, although the potential to climb exists from late spring to middle autumn. Consult the ranger's station in the town of Mount Shasta for permits and updated weather forecasts. Also, there are several places to rent crampons, boots and ice picks in the towns of Mount Shasta or Weed connected by Interstate 5. All are essential for any summit climb no matter the season. To acclimatize in higher elevations, spend at least one day and one night on the mountain, either at Sierra Club's Horse Camp, or at the 10,000-foot (3,000-m) Helen Lake campsite.

# OREGON

The first human migrants established themselves in the Pacific Northwest over 15,000 years ago, but the first known human artifacts in what is Oregon date to 11,200 BCE. In 1938, archaeologist Luther Cressman discovered sage bark sandals near Fort Rock Cave, suggesting a wide dissemination of human activity during the last Ice Age. By 8000 BCE there were Native American settlements across the state, with the majority concentrated along the lower Columbia River, in the western valleys, and near coastal estuaries. Native Americans lived sustainably in the diverse Oregon landscape among the tall, dense forests, below the rugged, glaciated Cascade volcanoes, and around semiarid scrublands, prairies, and deserts until the arrival of the white man.

The "Oregon Country" was opened to the European era after the 1804-1806 Lewis and Clark expedition down the Columbia River. Before that, it was a vast wilderness inhabited by several native tribes. Upon arriving at the mouth of the Columbia River, Lewis and Clark were astonished to find "an Indian with freckles and reddish hair" and the area tribe using beeswax. After the expedition, fur trading, mineral prospecting, and homesteading on native lands greatly reduced the indigenous population of Oregon. The once mighty Klamath and Modoc tribes of southern Oregon were all but exterminated or driven away forever. Smaller native tribes in the north managed to survive and two reservations exist in the high desert region, far from the prized fertile Willamette Valley in the west.

## Crater Lake

The symmetrical Crater Lake actually occupies a caldera, which is the collapsed cone of a volcano, rather than a crater. A latter forming cinder cone is found on top of Wizard Island. The volcano containing Crater Lake was once a large conical mountain towering over 12,000 feet (4,000 m), called Mount Mazama. In a tremendously powerful explosion about 7,700 years ago a violent eruption discharged copious amounts of lava, yet at the same time cracks opened beneath the volcano and drained away several cubic miles of molten lava inside. Mount Mazama, drained by these internal fissures, was without a base to support its

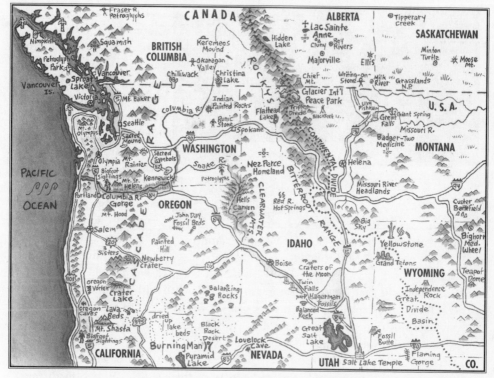

cone. The mountain collapsed into the hollow middle creating a deep basin. Eventually the caldera cooled and the basin filled with rainwater and snow, filling the lake in approximately 720 years to its current level. Some hydrothermal activity remains along the lake floor, suggesting that Mazama may become active again in the future. The spectacular eruption was witnessed by the Klamath people of southern Oregon, and became a focal point of their religion and awe of the mystic lake.

For thousands of years before the white man's arrival, Crater Lake was the focal point of Klamath mythology. The tribe had lived near the lake for so long that Klamath oral history accurately recalls the volcanic eruption that eventually formed Crater Lake. The Klamath people considered the lake so sacred that no one would visit it except for the most practiced shaman, or those in training. The Klamath used Crater Lake for vision quests, which often involved climbing the caldera walls and performing other dangerous tasks. Those who were successful in such quests were often regarded as having increased spiritual powers. An oral history was passed down, but directions to the lake, and the trail to sacred Wizard Island, were kept as a closely guarded secret within the tribe. Thus, over time, the lake was forgotten by non-shamanic Klamath members, and it wasn't until many years after the white man's arrival that the lake was finally discovered, and then only by accident. Prospector John Wesley Hillman stumbled upon Crater Lake in 1853 as he searched for a rumored gold mine.

▲ Hikers marvel at the sight of Wizard Island in Crater Lake.

The Klamath legend of Crater Lake relates the story of a powerful deity named Llao, or the "Chief of the World Below," who lived under Mount Mazama before the eruption. The Chief emerged on the surface one day with a mission to secure a bride from the Klamath people. He found the beautiful and beloved Loha, who rebuffed the Chief and his promises of eternal life. The Chief was so enraged that he swore to destroy the Klamath with a "curse of fire." A great battle of all spiritual deities took place with the Chief of the World Below spewing rivers of molten lava and red-hot rocks upon his enemies. The surrounding countryside was engulfed in flames and the tribe had to flee to Klamath Lake. Desperate to survive the ordeal, the tribe sent its two wisest elders to sacrifice themselves as deliverance for the wickedness of their tribe. The two medicine men climbed the mountain and threw themselves into the fiery pit. The Chief of the World Below retreated to his subterranean home and the mountain fell upon him. Soon the rains came and filled in the hole where the mountain had been and the curse of fire had been lifted. The story of these terrible events was passed for many generations, and few ever dared approach the place that caused the tribe so much fear.

> The depths of Crater Lake belong to a wrathful spiritual deity, so powerful in fact, that no person except the most experienced Klamath shaman would risk venturing to its shores. Even today, the deep sapphire-colored caldera lake is considered by New Agers as one of holiest places in North America.

Crater Lake is the 2nd deepest lake in North America at 1,949 feet (594 m), slightly less than the deepest lake, Canada's Great Slave Lake at 2,015 feet (614 m). It is the 7th deepest lake in the world, but on the basis of average depths, Crater Lake would be the deepest in North America and the 3rd deepest in the world. There is a direct relationship between the lake's brilliant blue color and its remarkable depth. All color emitted on a sunny day is absorbed by the deepness, where only blue is reflected upwards. The remarkable clear water also contributes to its blueness. It is claimed to be among the purest water in the world, with some measurements putting it 20 times purer than most bottled drinking water. Crater Lake is fed solely by falling rain and snow, with no inflow or outflow at the surface, which contributes to its pristine state.

The relatively young lake has an even younger companion, named Wizard Island. After the volcano collapsed, a final eruption created a cinder cone inside the caldera, which became an island when the lake filled with water. Wizard Island rises 760 feet (230 m) above the lake surface and an astounding 2,250 feet (675 m) above the caldera floor. Klamath shaman regarded the crater atop Wizard Island as the ultra-sacred entrance to an underworld gateway. Shaman would cautiously make their way over to the island and pay humble tribute. The gateway was a spiritual passageway between the above and below worlds and could only be successfully approached by those who were pure of heart.

### Getting to Crater Lake and Wizard Island

Crater Lake National Park is located in south-central Oregon, accessed off highway 138 to the north (closed in the winter) and highway 62 from the south. The access road from highway 62 to Rim Village is open year round for spectacular winter views. Adding to the tranquility of the region and nearly surrounding Crater Lake National Park is the Rogue River National Forest. Directly across the lake from Rim Village is Cleetwood Cove, which is the only access to the lake shore. There is a boat service at Cleetwood Cove offering a lake tour and drop off at Wizard Island, departing several times a day in the summer months only. Catch the early morning boat and spend the day hiking to the island's summit. The 360-degree view from the top of Wizard Island is among the finest in the park.

# WASHINGTON

Most people perceive the state of Washington as being in the heart of the rain-soaked Pacific Northwest, which it is, however the state is also a land of contrasts. East of the Cascade Range the semi-desert half of Washington has few trees, while the dense forests of the Olympic Peninsula, such as the Hoh Rain Forest, are among the only temperate rainforests within the continental United States. Mount Rainier, the highest mountain in the state, is covered with more glacial ice than any other peak in the lower 48 states. Despite being somewhat isolated from the rest of the United States, Washington's position on the Pacific Ocean and the harbors of Puget Sound give the state a leading role in maritime commerce with Canada, Alaska, and the Pacific Rim. Rather than extensive bridges, Puget Sound's many islands are served by the largest ferry fleet in the United States.

Famous for the ornately carved totem poles, canoes and masks of the Northwest Coast Indians, the spectacular scenery and the abundant sea resources allowed indigenous people to uniquely interpret their role in nature for thousands of years. "The Earth is our mother" and "the Sun is our father" were common expressions among the Indians of the Pacific Northwest. The various tribes of Washington coexisted peacefully until the arrival of European explorers who were intent on exploiting as much of the natural resources as possible. But even during the first hundred years of contact with foreigners, the land remained mostly unexplored virgin territory. Only 300 settlers lived north of the Columbia River in the early 1800s when Washington was part of the Oregon Territory. It became its own territory in 1853. The population boomed after the railroads came through in the 1880s, leading to statehood in 1889. The growth of the timber industry and the lucrative outfitting of the Klondike gold rushers in the late 1890s paved the way for a complete transformation from Native American fishing settlements to the Modern Age. Its economy is dominated today by aircraft manufacturing and technology.

## Cascade Volcanoes

The Cascade Mountain Range extends from northern California to southwestern British Columbia in Canada, a distance spanning over 700 miles (1,100 km). The Cascade Volcanoes, also called the Cascade Volcanic Arc, encompass many peaks held sacred by Native Americans and features more UFO and Bigfoot sightings than any other region in North America. A wide variety of minor sacred sites can be found in nearby caves, waterfalls, rock towers or near the numerous hot and cold water springs or dormant volcano vents. Some native legends allude to enormous, hidden grottos featuring sleeping giants, supernatural apparitions and other marvels within the volcanoes. Externally, the Cascades soar above the other surrounding mountains, standing out like snow-capped jewels in this spectacular volcanic mountain chain. The most renowned Cascade Volcanoes are Mount Rainier, Mount Saint Helens and Mount Baker in Washington, as well as Mount

▲ The tall and rugged Cascade mountains.
(Photo Courtesy U.S. National Forest)

Hood in Oregon and Mount Shasta and Mount Lassen in California. Each is veiled with its own unique Native American persona. One truly amazing aspect of the Cascades is how new the mountain range is, and how steep the slopes rise. The base of Mount Rainier, for example, soars above the sea-level city of Tacoma to

14,410 feet (3,323 m), making Rainier the tallest mountain in the Cascade Range. Most of the Cascade Volcanoes are typified by deep volcanic gorges and some of the loftiest peaks on the North American continent. Because the Cascades form a barrier just east of the rain-drenched Pacific coast, the western slopes are shrouded in dense foliage, while the eastern slopes taper off into high desert terrain.

> Each of the Cascade Volcanoes is cloaked in myth and folklore. Mount Saint Helens is called the Little Sister by tribes of the Pacific Northwest. Mount Rainier is her grandfather.

Native Americans have inhabited the Pacific Northwest for thousands of years and developed numerous myths and legends relating to the Cascade Volcanoes. According to some of these tales, such as the Bridge of the Gods legend, various peaks such as Mount Hood and Mount Adams are alive and act as god-like chiefs who engage in war by hurling fire and stone at one another. Mount Saint Helens (with its pre-1980 graceful appearance) was regarded as a beautiful maiden, or Little Sister, for whom Hood and Adams feuded. Among the many stories concerning Mount Baker, one describes the volcano as a woman who was formerly married to Mount Rainier, living next to him. Then, because of a marital dispute, she picked herself up and walked north to her current position. Other mythology describes Mounts Jefferson, Baker, Shasta and Garibaldi as a sanctuary for various tribes who escaped a great flood long ago. The Cascade Arc includes nearly 20 major volcanoes, among a total of over 4,000 individual volcanic features, including numerous vents, stratovolcanoes, shield volcanoes, lava domes, and cinder cones. Localized native tribes developed their own names and folklore for each of the Cascade Volcanoes and many of the smaller peaks.

Native Americans particularly revered Mount Rainier, calling it *Takoma*, the Lushootseed name meaning "the Great White Mountain" or "the Mountain that was God." They refused to disgrace the glacier-clad peak by climbing it, instead giving it a wide berth when passing nearby. Early European explorers found that the Indians were actually afraid of the mountain—it was one of the few areas the Indians were unable to guide the explorers—and thus the area remained totally unexplored until the mid-19th century. Native Americans also claimed that the mountain was an active volcano with a "lake of fire" at the summit. These legends were dismissed as folklore until the first ascent of the peak in 1870 confirmed numerous steam vents and a lake at the top formed by melting snow. Since then, geologists have verified the Indian legends, dating the last eruption to about 5,800 years ago.

In some of the most remote and deeply forested regions of the Pacific Northwest, particularly around the wilderness regions of the Cascades, there have been hundreds of sightings of the man-ape known as Bigfoot. The creature

▲ The Cascades soar above scenic Route 530.

is described as anthropomorphic, with somewhat human facial features, 8 to 12 feet (3-4 m) in height, between 800 and 1,000 pounds (360-450 kg), excessively hairy, horrible smelling, omnivorous, mostly but not exclusively nocturnal, solitary and essentially gentile. The Chehalis Indians of British Columbia named the creature *Sasquatch,* but the beast is by no means confined to their reservation. Although sightings of the mysterious Bigfoot range from British Columbia and the Yukon Territory in Canada all the way south to northern California, a vast majority of North American Bigfoot encounters are reported in Washington state, with many sightings around Mount Saint Helens. Unfortunately for Bigfoot and those who hope to catch a glimpse of this mysterious creature, sightings have dropped off considerably since the violent eruption of Mount Saint Helens on May 18th, 1980. If ever there was a population of "ape-men" living along the slopes of Mount Saint Helens, they now might be buried under billions of tons of mud and debris.

Another phenomenon of the Cascade Volcanoes is the numerous UFO sightings above the mountaintops. In fact, the modern age of UFOs began on June 24th, 1947 when a reputable businessman and amateur pilot named Kenneth Arnold reported seeing nine silver disc-like objects moving in formation directly in front of his flight path. He checked his watch as they passed Mount Rainier, and again when they passed Mount Adams at a speed, Arnold figured, to be more than 1,700 miles (2,737 km) per hour. Other witnesses spotted the "flying saucers" that same day and the local newspaper printed the story as front-page news. That single day of sightings was the first of many that soon spread across the nation, starting the UFO controversy that persists to this day. Some UFO researchers suggest the reason why volcanoes are frequented so regularly by extraterrestrial vehicles is that they contain large subterranean cavities where the inter-dimensional spacecrafts can take refuge from the outside world. Such reports of paranormal activity only increases the marvel surrounding the Cascade Volcanoes.

### Getting to Cascade Volcanoes

Mount Rainier National Park is located just outside the city of Tacoma, accessed by Route 7 to Route 708. Mount Saint Helens National Volcanic Monument is located halfway between Mount Rainier and the Oregon state border, via Route 504 off Interstate 5. To reach the north Cascade Volcanoes, take Washington State Route 20 from Burlington on the western slopes to the town of Twisp east of the North Cascades National Park. This route is considered the "most scenic mountain drive in Washington."

# Columbia River Gorge

The Columbia River Gorge is one of the most dramatic canyons in North America, extending partway along the north Oregon and south Washington state borders, and providing the only navigable water route through the Cascades. The narrow canyon is the only connection between the Columbia River Plateau and the Pacific Ocean. The gorge itself is about 100 miles (160 km) in length and is the largest National Scenic Area in the United States. Beyond its physical beauty, the gorge was a Native American settlement for at least 10,000 years before the arrival of the first European explorers. Various aspects of the gorge were of deep religious significance to the indigenous people. Native Americans inscribed their stories in the basalt cliffs and caves in hundreds of locations above the river. Ancient symbols such as sunbursts, animals and circles can still be found etched upon the basalt cliffs. Virtually every petroglyph, rock formation, waterfall or cavern had a spiritually connected legend, some tracing back 11,000 years according to archaeological studies. By far the most important spiritual location along the gorge was The Dalles, the most productive salmon fishing location on the river. Indian bands of the Columbia River—the Cascades, Watlala, Wasco, Walla Walla, Umatilla and Wishram—possessed a common understanding of the world. To these tribes, the animal deity Coyote created it, and for everything to be right, each person had to follow established traditions. These practices passed from generation to generation through tales told during the icy times of winter—the months of the long moons. The American Indian way of life quickly changed after Lewis and Clark navigated the Columbia River in the early 19th century, followed by Oregon Trail pioneers who viewed the Indians as a hindrance obstructing their westward expansion.

Scattered along the cliff walls are many indications that the native people held the gorge section of the Columbia River especially sacred. Dozens of petroglyphs illustrate aspects of Indian life and mythology, often depicting the Indians in an interconnected relationship with the land. The most famous petroglyph is called *Tsagaglalal*, which means "She Who Watches," and is located on a cliff overlooking the Columbia River and Horse Thief Lake State Park in Washington. The most visible sacred site in the gorge is Beacon Rock, named by Lewis and Clark who camped at its base in 1805 en route to the Pacific Ocean. The sheer mass of the columnar andesitic basalt rock formation is all that's left from the core of an ancient volcano eroded away by the Columbia River. Standing as a gigantic monolith rising approximately 850 feet (255 m) above the Columbia River, Beacon Rock is the second largest freestanding rock in the world after Gibraltar in Spain. Local Indian clans knew Beacon Rock as *Che-che-op-tin*, meaning "the Navel of the World."

> The Columbia River Gorge has been a recognized sacred place to native people for thousands of years. Near the gorge was discovered one of the most controversial skeletons in North America.

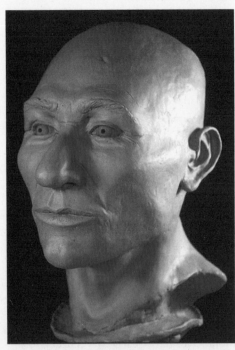

▲ This Kennewick Man facial reconstruction shows a middle-aged man who looked more like a "European accountant than a Paleo-Indian hunter."

About 80 miles (130 km) from the easternmost end of the Columbia Gorge, out on the flats of the Columbia Plateau, a well-preserved skeleton was found near the town of Kennewick on July 28th, 1996, giving rise to the name Kennewick Man. The skeletal remains, complete with an arrowhead lodged in the pelvic bone, were so obviously Caucasian that local police initially thought it was a 19th century settler killed by an Indian arrowhead. Among its features were high rounded eye sockets and a long, broad nose. All the teeth were intact at the time of death. The man was of a tall and slender build. He was also wearing the remains of advanced clothing. Early examination of Kennewick Man's head immediately indicated that the physical features were unlike any American Indian (Mongoloid) skull. Kennewick Man, initially identified by anthropologists as "Caucasoid," is one of oldest, most complete skeletons ever found in the New World. In recent years the

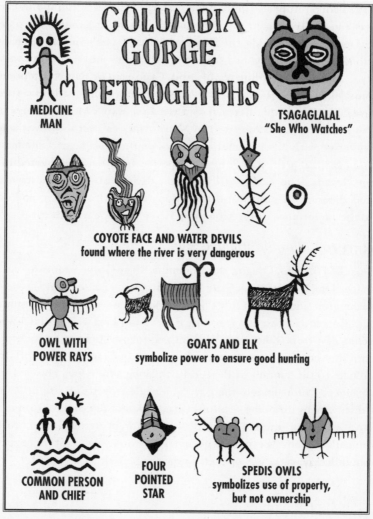

COLUMBIA GORGE PETROGLYPHS

MEDICINE MAN

TSAGAGLALAL "She Who Watches"

COYOTE FACE AND WATER DEVILS
found where the river is very dangerous

OWL WITH POWER RAYS

GOATS AND ELK
symbolize power to ensure good hunting

COMMON PERSON AND CHIEF

FOUR POINTED STAR

SPEDIS OWLS
symbolizes use of property, but not ownership

description of the skeleton as "Caucasoid" has been rejected by most anthropologists who have determined the skeleton's modern ancestry is most closely related to the indigenous Ainu people of Japan. There are now a good dozen sets of more or less complete remains from the pre-archaic period (9,000-5,000 BCE) in the western United States, and none of them resemble modern Native Americans. It would be astonishing if they did, since the world they inhabited, in the waning millennia of the last great Pleistocene glaciation, was totally different environmentally from the world of the last few thousand years.

After radiocarbon dating of a finger bone, it was revealed that the Kennewick Man was at least 9,000 years old, putting him in the Pacific Northwest sometime around the year 7,200 BCE. Such dating certainly throws the conventional Bering Strait land bridge theory into a tizzy, as well as creating a controversy with local tribes who have filed complaints for possession of the Kennewick remains. In

2004, the Federal Appeals Court sided with the scientists, ruling that a cultural link between the tribes and the skeleton was not met. Although discovered on Native American homelands, the Kennewick Man bears none of the characteristics belonging to the Mongolian stock from which all the American Indians supposedly originated. According to this find, Caucasian or East Asian populations were most likely amongst the North American continent's earliest settlers. The only possible scenario that fits well with the Kennewick Man discovery is that a group of Pacific voyagers migrated to North America over 9,300 years ago, and possibly mixed with Native American tribes on the West Coast. Similar ancient Caucasian skeletal artifacts of this time period have been uncovered in northwestern Nevada. The Kennewick skeleton dating calls into question current accepted theories on prehistoric migrations to North America, and certainly adds to the importance of the Columbia River for the earliest arrivals.

## Getting to Columbia River Gorge

Just east of Portland, Oregon the Columbia River Gorge begins to narrow and take shape along Interstate 84. State Route Highway 14 extends along the river on the Washington side. Beacon Rock State Park can be reached by crossing the toll bridge at Cascade Locks, and traveling 4 miles (6.5 km) west on Highway 14, or if traveling east from Vancouver, Washington, follow Highway 14 for 35 miles (57 km) until the spotting the well-marked signs for the State Park turnoff. It is possible to hike to the summit of Beacon Rock along a mile-long chiseled trail that is fairly steep. Unfortunately the government destroyed the site of Kennewick Man's discovery by dropping 500 tons (453,500 kg) of dirt and rock on it because of Native American interest group pressure, prompting researchers to call the government's actions "beyond negligent." In 2006, the East Benton County Museum in Kennewick, WA opened a new Kennewick Man exhibit.

# ALASKA AND HAWAII

*Take only memories. Leave nothing but footprints.*
**-Suquamish Chief Seattle**

T HE INDIGENOUS PEOPLE OF WHAT IS TODAY ALASKA and Hawaii developed their unique cultures in relative isolation for thousands of years before the coming of European explorers. In both locations, British sea captain James Cook was the first European explorer to encounter the native people, and in both cases with disastrous results. Captain Cook had made several voyages in the 18th century to Alaska in search of the fabled Northwest Passage, a route through the southern Arctic Ocean connecting the Pacific to the Atlantic. Incidentally, the Northwest Passage proved impractical as a sea lane, but in the early 21st century it is being considered as a viable summer shipping route due to global warming and the rapidly disappearing Arctic ice cap. Instead of locating the Northwest Passage, Captain Cook encountered the Tlingit, Haida, Aleuts, and Inuit native people of the Pacific Northwest. These were the remote descendants of the first humans to set foot on North American soil. Unwittingly, Captain Cook's crew spread deadly diseases in which these people had no natural immunities, and the result was a near total destruction of their age-old cultures. On another attempt to chart the Northwest Passage, Cook stumbled upon the Hawaiian

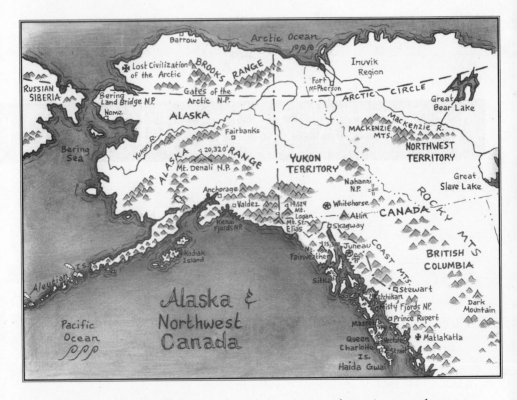

archipelago in the North Pacific. On a return voyage, the eminent explorer was murdered on the Big Island by superstitious natives, including a young man named Kamehameha who went on in 1795 to become the first and only unifier king of the Hawaiian Islands.

Alaska and Hawaii, the 49th and 50th states to join the union respectively, both entered the North American scene as afterthoughts. Alaska was called "Seward's Folly" because the land was deemed worthless after Secretary of State William Henry Seward facilitated the sale from Russia in 1867. This popular opinion would quickly change when gold was discovered near Juneau in 1880. The big 1897 Klondike rush and the even bigger 1898 Nome rush put Alaska on the map, but other resources such as oil deposits, salmon fishing and strategic military bases led to Alaska's statehood in 1959. Hawaii was incorporated into the United States a few months after Alaska, largely because of its strategic military and shipping location in the middle of the North Pacific Ocean. Hawaii has the distinction of being the only state to have once been an independent kingdom nation. Both states retain the aboriginal names given by their earliest inhabitants: *Hawaii* was chosen over Captain Cook's original name "Sandwich Islands;" and the indigenous name "Alaska" is derived from the pronunciation of *Alyeshka*, meaning "the Great Land." Both states hold the distinction of being the northernmost and southernmost extremities of the United States. Each state also has a mountain that can be considered the largest in the world.

# ALASKA

The indigenous Inuit inhabitants of the Arctic coastal regions have had a long and intimate relationship with the harsh climates of northern Alaska. The Inuit, also called the Eskimos, have more than 20 different words for snow, depending on which dictionary is consulted. The *West Greenlandic* dictionary lists 49 words for snow and ice, while the *Kobuk Iñupiaq Dictionary,* used in schools throughout northwestern Alaska, lists 23 words in the Inuit language, known as Iñupiaq, to describe snow in its many different forms. There are three specific words for snow on the ground, while the other 20 describe a myriad of snowy conditions, including melting ice, particular snow to use for drinking water, and a variety of snow descriptions as it is falling. Unlike English, Iñupiaq is a polysynthetic language, meaning that there are dozens of affixes to add nuance to the meaning of a simple noun like snow.

Described as "America's last frontier," Alaska is teeming with wild animals living on boundless expanses of unblemished terrain. It is a rugged outback wilderness featuring several major mountain ranges crossing portions of the state, all running roughly parallel with the Pacific coast. The continuous cordillera that extends from the southern tip of Cape Horn all the way through the Americas terminates in northern Alaska. Between the major ranges are lesser mountains, broad valley, and interior basins. The primary attraction for most visitors to Alaska is the state's stunning natural features and its fabulous wildlife. Alaska is still a place where the ecosystems remain intact and animal migration routes go uninterrupted. For those who live here, out every door is a short route to wilderness. With less than one person per square mile, and almost all residents concentrated in small urban areas, enormous regions of the state are completely free of human activity. For perspective, Alaska is three and a half times larger than California, while having less than two percent of its population. Alaska is also famous for the northern lights, or aurora borealis, primarily visible during the long nights of winter, and the "midnight sun" around the summer solstice.

## Denali (Mount McKinley)

Mount McKinley, named after assassinated U.S. president William McKinley in 1897, is one of the most impressive mountains in the world. Efforts in the 20th century to officially rename the peak *Denali*, the native Alaskan name, have been unsuccessful, yet most people still refer to the mountain by its traditional name (pronounced duh-NAH-lee). As the highest peak in North America, towering almost from sea level to 20,320 feet (6,773 m), Denali has been called "America's rival to Everest." The mountain is regarded as the largest continental mountain in the world, with an impressive 3.5-mile (5.6-km) vertical rise. Denali is surrounded by a closely related grouping of peaks within a larger range, considered the largest massif in the world. The Alaska Range where Denali dominates also contains massive snowy summits that would dwarf the Colorado Rockies, but they appear

▲ Soaring above flowing rivers of frozen ice, Denali is the the tallest mountain in North America.
(Photo courtesy National Park Service)

no more than foothills beside Denali's majestic bulk.

Winter temperatures can plunge to below -75°F (-50°C), and midsummer temperatures on the mountain regularly fall below zero. Denali is such a huge mountain that it creates its own weather around the upper elevations. The Alaskan air is thin, yet superbly clear between storms. Details of the mountain can be seen from afar and Denali is visible from Fairbanks over a hundred miles away. The frequently cloud-covered peak appears in stark contrast to the blue sky and its glacier-clad slopes. The perpetual snow is deep atop the mountain, occasionally hundreds of feet thick in some places. Glaciers carve out deep, trough-like gorges and fill them with ice as they make their slow descent down the slopes of the mountain. The longest glacier in Denali National Park is the 35-mile (56-km) long Muldrow Glacier—extending from the northern flank of Mount McKinley to within a mile of the park road—a virtual river of ice. Each year the Alaska Range slowly grows taller as the southern edge of the Denali fault line continues to thrust itself upwards, overriding the northern plate and pushing the valley floor ever downward. On the slopes of this enormous mountain roam wild grizzly bears, Dall sheep, moose, and caribou.

> With its base nearly at sea level and its summit rising over 20,000 feet (6,000 m), Denali features the earth's steepest vertical relief.
> The mountain is shrouded in Native American mythology.

Native Americans living in the long shadow of Denali proclaim the peak to possess potent supernatural energies. The neighboring Tena and Koyukon Alaskan tribes consider Denali to be extremely sacred. The Athapaskan Indians of Interior Alaska named the mountain *Denali*, meaning "The High One," or "The Great One." In other regions of the state it had different names: *Doleyka, Traleika, Bulshia, Gora* and *Tenada*. New Age adherents ascribe the power of Denali to its location upon on a major global grid intersection. In the tradition of the Great White Brotherhood, New Agers similarly perceive the mountain as a reception point on the earth grid, anchoring and transmitting cosmic energies related to the spiritual evolution of humankind.

The Tena people orally passed down from generation to generation an ancient tale of Denali's creation. The legend spoke of "the world before," the earth as we know it today, which ultimately resulted in the manifestation of our physical world and the beginning of human procreation. In the Tena creation myth a peaceful demigod named Yako lived alone with the animal spirits in eastern Alaska. Yako was told by Ses, the great brown bear, that far to the west is the Raven war chief Totson, where there are beautiful women of Yako's race in his village. Risking the wrath of the war chief, Yako locates the village and sings a song to attract a mate. A young girl is given to him, but Totson is jealous of his song and intimidates Yako, who must escape quickly in his canoe. Totson chases Yako, hurling arrows and spears at the fleeing couple without success. Finally Totson throws his special magical spear, but Yako matches his magical wit, creating the tidal wave of stone that is Denali to block the spear. The magic spear is deflected off Denali into the heavens, while Totson's war ship crashes into the rocks and Totson is transformed back into a raven. Yako, exhausted after the conflict, goes into a long sleep and when he awakes the girl has grown to become a beautiful woman. The two begin an Adam and Eve type relationship, being the first couple to procreate and spawn the Tena people. Their children, taught by their parents to live in peace, justice, and plenty, would in future generations migrate far to the east and south of North America. It is interesting to note that the Apache and Navajo languages share similar lingual roots to the Tena, as well as sharing comparable legends and shamanistic traditions.

### Climbing Mount McKinley

The Sourdough Party made the first successful ascent of Mount McKinley in 1910, but reached the slightly lower North Peak, which is 850 feet (255 m) shorter than the South Peak. The true summit was achieved three years later by the Karstens-Stuck party. Each year the mountain attracts a thousand climbers or more, but only about half actually reach the summit. It is not an extremely difficult climb from a technical standpoint, but it is sufficiently challenging because of unpredictable weather, high altitudes, and avalanche conditions. Independent climbing groups are required to apply for permits with the National Park Service. Permit information and a list of authorized guides are listed in the Appendix. Denali National Park is located 120 miles (195 km) south of Fairbanks along the Parks Highway (AK 3), and 240 miles (387 km) north of Anchorage. The park is accessible by air, rail, bus, or highway. Some roads accessing the park are only open in the summer.

## Sitka

Long before the Russians colonized the rain-drenched Alaskan panhandle as the center of their fur trading empire, several indigenous tribes inhabited the region. The largest and most powerful was the Tlingit, led by the Kiksadi clan, also called the Tlingit Kolosh. These people thrived for several hundred years in Sitka, or

▲ This etching of old Sitka depicts Native Americans living in the shadow of the imposing Russian fort on Castle Hill.

*Shee Atika* as it was pronounced by natives. The native Tlingit Kiksadi clan were known as the "People on the Outside of Shee," referring to the village Shee Atika on Baranof Island facing the calm waters of Sitka Sound. .*Shee* was the original Tlingit name for Baranof Island. Here the Tlingit settled for hundreds of years and developed a rich heritage featuring cultural items such as totem poles, ceremonial dresses, carved masks, petroglyph images and stylized weapons. Designs varied from village to village, with each clan depicting different animals significant to their own tradition. The Kiksadi Tlingit clan of Shee Atika, led by the fierce warrior Katlian, used the raven as the principle motif for their battle attire.

Despite being a hospitable and social people, the Tlingit congeniality did not extend to the Russians who arrived at Sitka in 1799. What could have become an equally beneficial trade arrangement soon led to increased hostility over southern Alaska's fertile fishing and hunting grounds. Mutual suspicion led to outright violence in 1802 when Tlingit warriors attacked a Russian outpost a few miles northwest of Sitka and killed nearly everyone at the settlement, including Aleut Indians allied to the Russians. In September, 1804 the Russians returned in force and demanded that the Tlingit abandon Shee Atika and surrender to the Tsar of Russia. Anticipating such a move, the Tlingit retreated from their village into a nearby fortress to prepare for war with several Russian warships. After a cannon volley did little to destroy the Tlingit stronghold, the Russians and Aleuts advanced on the fort and were bloodily repulsed. Thus began a six-day siege on the Tlingit fortress. On the seventh day the Russians and Aleuts were surprised to find the fort completely abandoned. Out of gunpowder and flints, the Tlingits escaped silently at night and deserted their centuries-old sacred homeland. The Russians lost no time in erecting their own settlement exactly upon the site where Shee Atika had stood, including a new Russian palisade atop "Castle Hill."

For many centuries Sitka was the homeland
and ritual site of the Kiksadi Tlingit Indians.
The settlement was invaded in 1802 by Russian
fur traders who renamed it "New Archangel,"
but the Tlingit name of Sitka stuck.

Four years after being founded, New Archangel became the capital of Russian America and a bustling international port of call. The Russians were busy creating a wilderness empire on the northwestern coast of North America that extended all the way down to Fort Ross in northern California. As headquarters for the Russian-American Company's fur and other trading operations, Sitka became Alaska's economic and cultural capital for over half a century. The opulence of Baranov's Palace, replete with a grand piano and decorations in Saint Petersburg-style, earned Sitka the nickname "The Paris of the Pacific." After the region was nearly denuded of sea otters and fur seals, the remote colony held less and less interest for the Russian government. Embroiled in problems at home and fearing a takeover by the United States or Great Britain, the Tsar finally decided to sell Alaska in 1867 for $7.2 million, thus ending the 126-year Russian New World enterprise following the collapse of the pelt trade. The capital Sitka hosted the ceremony in which the Russian flag was lowered and the United States flag was raised, immediately following the "Seward's Folly" acquisition of Alaska. The flag lowering and raising event is reenacted in Sitka every October 18th, commemorated as "Alaska Day."

The original Tlingit inhabitants of Sitka enjoyed a rich cultural life, both esthetically and spiritually. Surrounded in a world of natural abundance, they reaped most of their food from the ocean but worshipped land and air animals equally. In a subtle way, Tlingit shaman carved rain god images into low lying rocks, knowing that salmon would not enter spawning rivers until a downpour of rain raised the water level. The enduring image of Pacific Northwest Indians is the famous totem poles depicting crest signs of animal and human figures. Totem poles communicate cultural information by portraying the history and greatness of a clan's lineage. They depict legends, ridicule enemies, or provide a mortu-

ary receptacle for cremated ashes. Totem poles cannot be read like a book, but provide insight into the history or legend they were intended to represent. It was largely the exhibition of totem poles at various 19th century expositions that propelled Alaska towards statehood and attracted new settlers into the untamed wilderness.

▲ 19th century photo of the Tlingit Indians near Sitka.

## Getting to Sitka

There are no bridges from the mainland to Baranof Island, so the only way to access Sitka are the regular ferries or scheduled flights from Alaska's capital Juneau. Sitka's location on a remote island makes transportation to the city inherently difficult, inconvenient and expensive. By air, the Rocky Gutierrez Airport on Japonski Island offers regular service from Alaska Airlines and charter carrier Harris Aircraft Services. Flight delays due to Sitka's weather are frequent. The Sitka airport is located on Japonski Island, which is connected to Baranof Island by the John O'Connell Bridge. Many cruise ships dock in the deep-water harbor of Sitka and tourists are allowed an afternoon to explore the town and visit the Sitka National Historical Park just outside of town.

# HAWAIIAN ISLANDS

The Hawaiian archipelago is the most remote population center in the world. The eight main islands are centrally located in the North Pacific Ocean, some 2,500 miles (4,000 km) from the nearest continent or populated island chain. Before the arrival of humans, all flora and fauna on the Hawaiian Islands came by air, on ocean currents, or attached to migratory birds. The odds were against any life form making this long journey successfully, but time is always on the side of evolution. Those species that managed to survive the transition rapidly diversified and flourished due to the equitable climate and few competitors. Species endangerment began when the first Polynesian people stepped ashore with their introduced plants and animals causing some extinctions and near-extinctions, particularly among birds. Many endemic plant species could not compete and became extinct, or are on the verge of extinction today. The State of Hawaii has the most amount of endangered species and threatened wildlife in the United States.

The coming of European sailing vessels in the late 18th century began another era of incredible change not only for the wildlife, but also the indigenous people. Those who followed in Captain Cook's wake—the explorers, whalers, missionaries, laborers, and merchants—introduced a new world of ideas, religions, customs, possessions, diseases, and feral animals to the once-isolated islanders. The introduced microbes of the Europeans arrived as silent and indiscriminate killers. Arriving with Captain Cook in 1778 were syphilis, gonorrhea, tuberculosis, typhoid, and influenza, which the islanders had no immunity. Hawaii's native population was reduced from a half million in 1779 to 84,000 by 1853, the year when smallpox finally reached Hawaii and killed another 10,000 survivors. Such reduction in numbers allowed races of other people to move in, along with the trappings of the modern world. Today nearly all of Hawaii's resources must be imported from the outside world, including: oil, gas, plastics, manufactured goods, building supplies, and most food products. The old Hawaiian tradition had been

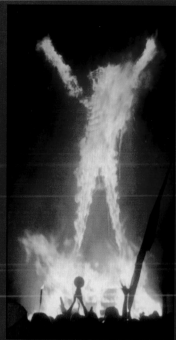

Photo by Brad Olsen, taken in 2007

▲ The David Best Temple at Burning Man is a solemn space for reflection and grieving. Participants commonly create memorials to loved ones inside and around the structure. The Temple always burns on Sunday.

Photo by Brad Olsen, taken in 1998

▲ The iconic "Man" always burns on Saturday night.

Photo by Brad Olsen, taken in 2002

▲ It takes a village to move a pyramid at Black Rock City. Individual theme camps create their own art projects for display during the eight-days of Burning Man.

Photo by Brad Olsen

▲ Canyonlands National Park is a maze of interconnected canyons carved by the Colorado River.

Photo by Brad Olsen

▲ The bizarre anthropomorphic pictographs of Canyonlands appear in areas where complex ceremonial activities once took place ...

... The images ▶ likely represent prehistoric priests interacting with the spiritual realms. It was the task of the shaman to heal, seek animals, entice rain, and create a vision on behalf of the tribe.

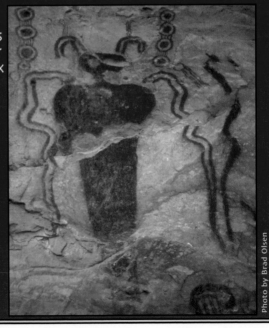

Photo by Brad Olsen

Photo by Brad Olsen

▲ The "Delicate Arch" is the most famous of 2,000 rock spans in Utah's Arches National Park. Its unusual shape certainly inspired Native Americans in the region.

Photo by Brad Olsen

▲ Bell Rock is the most accessible of Sedona, Arizona's four primary vortex locations.

Photo by Jennifer Fahey

▲ The author following the trail to Cathedral Rock on a vortex hunting excursion near Sedona.

Photo by Jain Martin

▲ Situated upon a high-desert escarpment surrounded by sand and mountains, Joshua Tree National Park is perched on the "high" Mojave Desert as it transforms into the "low" Colorado Desert. Wildlife proliferates around oasis environments within the two desert regions.

Photo by Jain Martin

▲ Global warming is altering the sensitive habitat of these oddly-shaped anthropomorphic yucca cactus. Newly sprouted Joshua Tree saplings are becoming rare.

Photo by Brad Olsen

▲ Mount Shasta is the rumored abode of mythological deities including Bigfoot, UFOs, and an inter-dimensional race of beings who supposedly live under the mountain in a hidden city called Telos.

Image courtesy of Google Earth

▲ Mysterious mound clusters with interesting geometric shapes are located in the shadow of sacred Mount Shasta.

Image courtesy of Google Earth

▲ The Tennant Water Mounds resemble the designs of crop circles when viewed from above. Searching for sacred places is taken to the next level when using the powerful Google Earth online resource.

Photo by Brad Olsen

▲ Although dry when this photo was taken, the Tennant Water Mounds show a clear interaction with water. Curiously, the mounds support different vegetation from the grassy meadows.

Photo by Brad Olsen

▲ Chimayo is a famous healing chapel in northern New Mexico. The soil around the chapel is especially prized. The practice of eating or rubbing earthly substances on the body is called geophagy. Crutches and votive offerings attest to the cures wrought by the faithful.

Photo by Brad Olsen

▲ Pueblo Bonito in Chaco Canyon is the largest and most intriguing of all the Anasazi Great Houses. This remote canyon in New Mexico was heavily populated in prehistoric times.

Photo by Brad Olsen

▲ Bighorn Medicine Wheel has been described as a Rocky Mountain Stonehenge. It has been in continuous usage for centuries by several different tribes.

Photo by Brad Olsen

▲ Arcosanti is a prototype city meant to mimic the natural contours of the surrounding landscape.

Photo by Brad Olsen

▲ There are several hot vents on the triangular rock formation rising dramatically out of Pyramid Lake.

Photo by Brad Olsen

▲ The Salt Lake Temple in Utah is a sacred destination to millions of Mormons worldwide.

Photo by Brad Olsen

▲ The ubiquitous totem poles scattered across North America all trace their origin to the family crests of Pacific Northwest indigenous people.

Photo by Brad Olsen

▲ Devils Tower in eastern Wyoming remains a holy mountain to Native Americans.

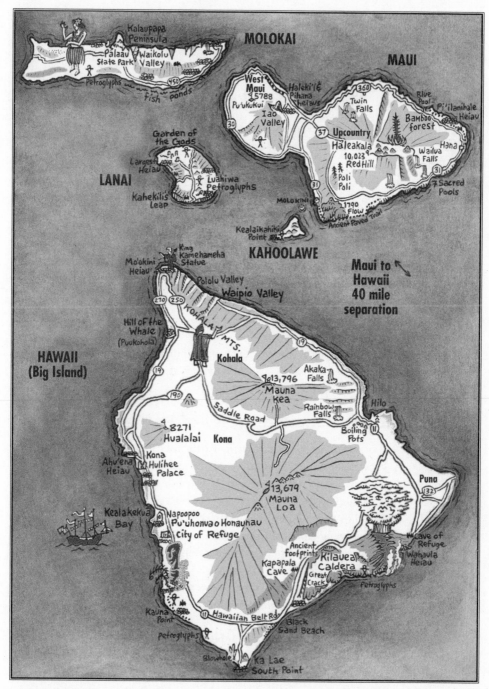

inexorably changed before a new understanding could be formulated. The legitimate Kingdom of Hawaii was a sovereign nation recognized by the international community until a 1893 overthrow of the government. American businessmen instigated the United States annexation of Hawaii to exert their power monopoly over the islands at the expense and total disrespect of the Hawaiian people. Never a people to take conquest lightly, there is a growing political movement today among native Hawaiians and partial native descendants to break away from the United States and again become a sovereign nation.

# THE BIG ISLAND HAWAII

All the Hawaiian Islands were created by volcanic activity, but only on the Big Island of Hawaii are those volcanoes still active and visible. Not only is the Big Island the youngest mass of land in the world, it is the largest single object on earth—that is, if the huge bulk of the underwater mountain is included. By such calculations, Mauna Kea is the tallest mountain on the planet, standing 13,796 feet (4,139 m) above sea level and 20,000 feet (6,000 m) below the ocean. The combined above water and submerged mountain slopes of Mauna Kea far eclipse the height of Mount Everest. As the tallest mountains in the Pacific Basin, Mauna Kea and its sister peak Mauna Loa are the only peaks to have supported glaciers during the last Ice Age. In the shadow of the twin peaks emigrating Polynesians first arrived in Hawaii and erected their villages, sacred *heiaus*, and etched petroglyphs (rock carvings) to explain their existence. The first Polynesian voyagers are estimated to have arrived at South Point (Ka Lae) on the Big Island around the 2nd or 3rd century CE. The progeny of these original Polynesians, along with successive waves of new arrivals, went on to populate the rest of the Hawaiian archipelago.

## Pu'uhonua O Honaunau (City of Refuge)

The name *Pu'uhonua* is an ancient Hawaiian title for "City of Refuge," where those guilty of *kapu* (something forbidden) could be absolved of their misdoing, or the innocent could wait out a violent battle. If a person outside the royal family looked directly at a chief or got too close, it was considered kapu. This strict taboo standard also applied to a commoner walking in the chief's footsteps, touching the chief's possessions, landing a boat on the chief's beach, or allowing one's shadow to fall on the palace grounds. The penalty for breaking kapu was always execution, unless one could escape to a City of Refuge. Everyday activities, too, were regulated by kapu. Women could not eat food reserved as offerings to the gods such as pork or coconut; they could not prepare meals for men; or ever be seen eating with men. Even activities such as gathering wood, fishing or killing animals were all strictly controlled. At the instance of a kapu being broken, suddenly everybody in the community was aligned against the kapu breaker, lest the gods become angered and take revenge on everyone in the form of volcanic eruptions, tidal waves, famine or earthquakes. The only hope for someone breaking kapu was to avoid capture and run to a City of Refuge. Each Hawaiian island had at least one, and the Big Island is thought to have had six, yet only three are known for certain: Pu'uhonua O Honaunau, Waipio Valley and Coconut Island near Hilo.

▲ This small peninsula of jagged black lava rock features the preserved and restored remains of a royal palace, fish pond, beach and private canoe landing, three heiaus, and a pu'uhonua sanctuary that is protected behind the mortar-free masonry of its 16th century Great Wall,

Since only the strongest and the smartest could survive this rigid social system, kapu was the primary way ancient Hawaiians would "weed out the weaklings." Thus, survival of the fittest was a fundamental principle of ancient Hawaiian law, in which might was considered right, unless one could safely escape to a City of Refuge. Inside the heavily fortified sacred precincts were high priests and several *heiau* (meaning "temple" and pronounced hey-OW) surrounded by a high wall. The Hawaiian word *hei* means to summon, capture or ensnare, and *au* implies a vibration, current, or invisible power or energy. Thus, a heiau captures spiritual power (*mana*). Outside the City of Refuge was a fortified compound for the royal chiefs (*ali'i*), which was guarded by armed warriors and a fleet of war canoeists. As noted, condemned criminals had only one option before their summary execution—escape to a City of Refuge—but getting there was the hardest part because every person on the island sought to kill the criminal to avoid catastrophe by the gods. Those who survived the chase and got through the heavily fortified compound were awarded clemency for their crime. Upon arrival, a ceremony of absolution was performed by the *kahuna pule* (priest) and the offender could then return home safely, usually within a few hours or the next day. All islanders respected the spirit of the Pu'uhonua. Since no blood was ever to be spilled within its' confines, non-combatants during war, loaded with provisions, would seek the City of Refuge to wait in safety until the conflict was over. Since the object of war in ancient times was to exterminate the enemy, which included anyone who belonged to the opposing side, women, children and the elderly risked execution unless they could escape to a City of Refuge. Similarly, warriors who were undecided on either battling chief could wait for the outcome and then swear their allegiance to the winner.

A City of Refuge served as safe haven for people wishing to avoid a violet conflict, or guilty criminals hoping to avoid execution and receive a second chance. Pu'uhonua O Honaunau is one of the few that survived dismantling in the Christian era.

The kapu system, however, was to be short lived after the arrival of European explorers, and the City of Refuge stood at the crossroads of immense change within the lifetime of a single person. To most native islanders, the first Europeans in their tall-mast sailing ships came as a big surprise. The islanders had no way of interpreting these arrivals, so they assumed the Europeans were visiting gods and treated them as such. When Captain Cook returned to the Big Island to fix a broken mast after making initial contact, the Hawaiians took this as a bad omen and killed the eminent explorer in a scuffle at Kealakekua Bay, a mere eight miles (13 km) north of Pu'uhonua O Honaunau. An impressionable and ambitious man in his mid-twenties named Kamehameha (pronounced kah-MAY-ha MAY-ha) was present for Cook's first arrival and tragic second landing. It is quite possible that Kamehameha was involved in the brawl that took Cook's life, and present at the ceremony afterward where his body was burned, stripped of flesh, and offered to the gods in exchange for the great navigator's *mana*. Before Cook's death, the young Kamehameha was fascinated by the ship *Resolution*, visiting the vessel several times and even obtaining permission to spend a night on board. What interested him the most were the Western weapons the ship carried, an interest that was to become a determining factor in his successful bid to unify all the Hawaiian Islands under a single regime. He lived his dream and became known as King Kamehameha the Great, but upon his death in 1819 his wife and son dismantled the kapu system forever. Pu'uhonua O Honaunau and all the old pagan temples on the island were either destroyed or fell into disrepair. Fortunately, the temples along the Kona Coast where Kamehameha died were simply abandoned and remain in

▲ Wrathful gods watch over the inner precincts of the City of Refuge.

good condition today. The *pali* (cliffs) above Kealakekua Bay, where Captain Cook met his undignified fate, were a sacred burial location for great chiefs, including perhaps the remains of Kamehameha I and Captain Cook himself. An obelisk on the north side of Kealakekua beach stands to commemorate the spot where the renowned navigator was killed.

### Getting to Pu'uhonua O Honaunau (City of Refuge)

Called the single most evocative historical site in the Hawaiian Islands, the City of Refuge has adopted the name Pu'uhonua O Honaunau National Historic Park. It is located 25 miles (40 km) south of Kailua-Kona via Hawaii Route 11 to Hawaii Route 160 (intersection between mileposts 103 and 104). Information line: 808-328-2288. There are alternative routes near the turnoff for the Painted Church, or via the ocean route past Napo'opo'o. There is a small entrance fee to the historic site, administered by the National Park Service. Just south of Pu'uhonua O Honaunau is a beautiful public beach renowned as one of the best snorkeling locations on the island. Getting down to Kealakekua Bay requires a strenuous hike both ways, but the views are fantastic and dolphins can often be spotted in the bay. There is no entrance fee to Kealakekua Bay. Numerous snorkeling boats congregate at Kealakekua Bay every day, but swimmers are not allowed to swim ashore from boats.

## Pu'ukohola Heiau (Hill of the Whale)

In the year 1790, the Polynesian prince Kamehameha of the northern part of Hawaii had proven his ability to be king through birthright and feats of strength. A war in that year captured Maui, Lanai, and Molokai under the leadership of the young warrior. Upon returning to the Big Island, Kamehameha's aunt delivered to the prince advice from the esteemed prophet Kapoukahi from Kauai who predicted that he would succeed in conquering all of the Hawaiian Islands if he took the precise steps in constructing a *luakini* (war temple) at the Hill of the Whale. The prophet said the new temple was to be built on top of an older temple and be dedicated to his family's war god, Kuka'ilimoku. But this much was clear: if he wished to conquer all the Hawaiian Islands, starting with his as-yet unified Big Island, Kamehameha had to erect his temple by following rigid guidelines prescribed by the priests, which specified there could be absolutely no interruptions at the site during construction.

Hawaiian *heiaus* (temples) were locations of worship that were central to native religious beliefs. From the heiau, the *kahuna* (priest) was able to communicate directly with the gods, and pass this information on to the *ali'i* (royal chief). *Pu'ukohola* (Hawaiian for "Hill of the Whale") was constructed for ceremonies related to war. Heeding the prophet's advice, the Pu'ukohala Heiau was built by Kamehameha himself and thousands of servants in the years 1790-1791. Kamehameha built this temple with care and determination, battling back his enemies who tried

▲ Hill of the Whale temple under construction.
(Image courtesy National Park Service)

unsuccessfully to interrupt construction on several occasions. Upon completion, the purpose of the temple was a place to honor the war god Kuka'ilimoku and perform religious ceremonies dedicated to him. At the opening ceremony for the temple, Kamehameha's cousin and chief rival Keoua Kuahu'ula arrived and was instantly killed upon landing his canoe. With Keoua's *mana* (spiritual power) being offered to his family's war god there was little resistance left to prevent Kamehameha from conquering and uniting all of Hawaii. Kamehameha's native island thus became the name for the entire archipelago. The great king fulfilled the prophecy and became the first Hawaiian king to rule all the islands and establish a Kamehameha monarchy that was to last until 1893. Many heiau once existed throughout the Hawaiian Islands, but their use ceased with the demise of the *kapu* (taboo) system in 1819.

Pu'ukohola Heiau was the last known pagan structure built in Hawaii. The sacred war temple played a crucial role in Kamehameha's ascendancy to unify all the Hawaiian Islands.

How the temple on the Hill of the Whale was constructed, who built it, and how it shaped Hawaiian history is well known. Pu'ukohola Heiau is an incredibly impressive structure made entirely of water-worn lava rocks placed on top of an older temple from two centuries earlier. There was no mortar used in ancient Hawaiian heiau construction, so the whole structure was built of precisely fitted stacked stones. It is believed to have taken several thousand men over the course of one year to build it by hand. There is nowhere in the immediate area to get the specific rocks required, so it is estimated that the workers formed a human chain over 20 miles (33 km) long to hoist the rocks out of Pololu Valley in North Kohala. The temple is 224 feet (67 m) by 100 feet (30 m), with 20-foot (6-m) high walls. Among those helping with construction were two stranded sailors, John Young and Isaac Davis, who became trusted military advisors to King Kamehameha. John Young lived his adult life at a homestead at the Hill of the Whale, first teaching the Hawaiians how to use cannons and firearms, then acting as a sandlewood trade agent for the king. Young was grandfather to Queen Emma and one of only two white men buried in the Royal Mausoleum in the Nu'uanu Valley on

Oahu. When King Kamehameha the Great died in 1819, so did the old religion of Hawaii. His wife Queen Ka'ahumanu and his son Liholiho had both converted to Christianity shortly after his death. Kamehameha the Great ruled according to Hawaiian tradition but outlawed some of the more severe practices such as human sacrifices. The old religion was instantly dismantled and all the pagan temples fell into disrepair upon his son Liholiho's ascension to the throne.

### Getting to Pu'ukohola Heiau (Hill of the Whale)

This massive rock structure is now the main reason for a small National Park meant to preserve the heiau and the surrounding area on the Kohala Coast, popularly known as the dominion of Kamehameha the Great. The Hill of the Whale is located one mile (1.6 km) south of the town Kawaihae via Highway 270, just north of the Highway 19 intersection in Kawaihae. There is no entrance fee to the 77-acre (30-ha) historic site, administered by the National Park Service. The official name is the Pu'ukohola Heiau National Historic Site and includes: Pu'ukohola Heiau, King Kamehameha's Royal Palace, Mailekini Heiau, the underwater Haleokapuni Heiau dedicated to the shark deities, as well as the John Young Homestead. Information line: 808-882-7218.

# Kilauea

The word *kilauea* is Hawaiian for "much spewing" or "much spreading," in reference to the mountain's frequent outpouring of lava. Such displays of fierce volcanic eruptions made a considerable impact on the native Hawaiians. Kilauea Crater is considered the mythical home of Pele, an ancient Polynesian deity whose name means "volcano goddess." Certain unique lava formations around Kiluea are named in her honor. These include the thin, brittle strands of volcanic glass called "Pele's Hair" that often form during a lava flow as it enters the ocean, and the small droplets of lava named "Pele's Tears" that cool in the air and retain their teardrop shapes. Pele was among the most centrally recognized volcano divinities whose worship in Hawaii became widespread in the 13th century as *Pele-'ai-honua*, or "Pele, who eats the land." Hawaiian chants and oral traditions chronologically relate the many eruptions procured by an angry Pele long before the first European arrivals. In addition to manifesting herself as molten lava, she can occasionally appear as a beautiful young maiden, or as an elderly crone. Small acts of charity to her human image were

▲ Bizarre lava formations scatter around Hawaii Volcanoes National Park.

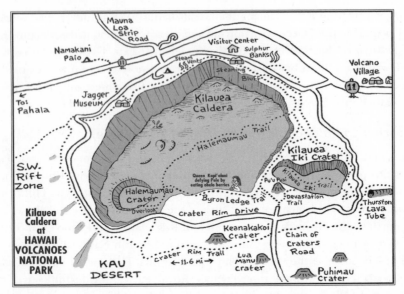

Map labels:
Mauna Loa Strip Road · Visitor Center · Sulphur Banks · Namakani Paio · Steam Vents · Steaming Bluff · Volcano Village · Jagger Museum · Kilauea Caldera · To: Pahala · S.W. Rift Zone · Halemaumau Trail · Kilauea Iki Crater · Queen Kapi'olani defying Pele by eating ohelo berries · Pu'u Puai · Kilauea Iki Trail · Halemaumau Crater · Byron Ledge Tr · Devastation Trail · Thurston Lava Tube · Overlook · Crater Rim Drive · Kilauea Caldera at HAWAII VOLCANOES NATIONAL PARK · Keanakakoi Crater · Chain of Craters Road · KAU DESERT · Crater Rim Trail ←11.6 mi→ · Lua Manu Crater · Puhimau Crater

thought to spare the giver a terrible fate in the form of fire and brimstone. She is said to have resided in all of Hawaii's volcanoes during each island's period of activity. Today, Pele chooses the active Mauna Loa and Kilauea Caldera on the Big Island to call home. According to legend, Pele will sometimes visit other islands in the Pacific, but whenever there is an eruption on the Big Island she is the one responsible for hurling the fiery fumes and fallout skyward. To ancient Hawaiians, Kilauea was the source of all creation and residence of an irate goddess who would sometimes take revenge for human misbehavior.

According to contemporary beliefs of some Hawaiians, Pele is a goddess who punishes people who dare take something that belongs to her. Every year thousands of visitors pass through Hawaii Volcanoes National Park and take home a souvenir rock or a packet of volcanic sand. Locals will warn that Pele frowns on such activity by haunting the guilty persons with bad fortune. After months or years of hard luck, many tourists return the earthen mementos to park headquarters or the local post office. Beliefs were so strong in the mid-19th century that Christian missionaries were perturbed to find most Hawaiian converts refusing to discount the Pele legend. The breaking of the *kapu* system was not enough, even after Queen Kapi'olani defied Pele by venturing into Kiluea Caldera to read her Bible aloud and eat the taboo red ohelo berries previously forbidden for women to eat, let alone spit the pits into the crater. Pele did not punish the queen and the islanders were amazed, yet belief remained strong. In 1881, an eight-month flow from Mauna Loa threatened to wipe out the village of Hilo, much to the dismay of the faithful Christians who prayed daily for the flows to cease. When the lava reached within a mile of central Hilo, Princess Ruth Ke'elikolani was called in from Oahu to help fend off the angry Pele. Under the gaze of missionaries and journalists, the princess chanted and left offerings of pink silk handkerchiefs and brandy for Pele. By morning the flow had stopped.

In geological terms, Kilauea ranks among the
most active volcanoes on earth. In Hawaiian
tradition, Kilauea is where the fire-goddess
Pele tends the fiery furnaces and throws
flaming red lava from the boiling depths.

At a fixed location in the North Pacific Ocean a large opening in the mantle of the earth is called the Hawaiian "hot spot" by geologists because of its prodigious generation of molten lava over many millions of years. As the Pacific plate slowly drifts to the northwest it takes the older islands with it and makes room for new seamounts to form. Kilauea shares the hot spot with its larger active sibling Mauna Loa (13,677 feet or 4,169 m) and the Loihi Seamount, currently growing 21 miles (33 km) southeast of the Big Island at 3,200 feet (960 m) below sea level. The Loihi volcano is not predicted to reach the surface for at least another hundred years, and at the most another 10,000 years. The Hawaii Center for Volcanology and University of Hawaii scientists constantly study the eruptions on Kilauea and Mauna Loa, and gain further insight into the underwater nature of volcanoes by visiting Loihi in a mini-submarine. Unlike most other active volcanoes around the world, Kilauea is approachable and largely predictable. Kilauea has been called the "drive-up" volcano because of its easy access to volcanic activity, especially near the summit caldera. Visitors who are fortunate enough to experience an eruption will certainly remember it for a lifetime. Hawaii Volcanoes National Park is an outdoor museum in volcanology, geology, ecology, meterology, unique scenery and desolate solitude.

▲ The Kilauea Caldera is ringed on two sides by steep cliffs, around 400 feet (120 m) high. Strong-smelling sulphur drifts up from the caldera floor giving the scene an otherworldly appearance. Crater Rim Drive is an 11-mile (18-km) loop tour around the famous caldera.

▲ Walking off marked trails in Hawaii Volcanoes National Park can be life threatening.

The present Kilauea volcanic outflow on the southeastern flank of Mauna Loa has been in a sustained eruption since January, 1983. Known as the Pu`u `O`o Eruption, the current lava flows have added over 500 acres (205 ha) of new land to Hawaii's southern shore. The current lava flows have destroyed nearly 200 houses and covered 8 miles (13 km) of highway with as much as 82 feet (25 m) of lava. It has also destroyed a National Park visitor center, most of Kupaahu town, buried Kaimu Bay, Kalapana Black Sand Beach, and a large section of State Route 130, which now abruptly dead-ends at the lava flow. Near the Kilauea Caldera is the recently destroyed 700 year-old Waha'ula Heiau (temple of the red-mouth), which acted as a *luakini heiau* (sacrificial war temple) devoted to the god Ku. The caldera was the site of nearly continuous activity during the 19th century and the early part of the 20th century. Since 1952 there have been 34 eruptions, and since January, 1983 eruptive activity has been continuous along the east rift zone. There are no signs that the current eruption is slowing or will come to an end anytime soon.

### Getting to Kilauea Crater

The Kilauea Visitor Center is located just off the Hawaiian Belt Road Route 11. When visiting Hawaii Volcanoes National Park always stay on the marked trails and heed all warning signs for volcanic fumes. Visitors with heart or health conditions, as well as pregnant women and small children, are especially at risk in contact with volcanic fumes and should avoid Halema'u-ma'u Crater and Sulphur Banks in particular. There is admission fee per vehicle when entering Hawaii Volcanoes National Park.

## Waipio Valley

When Halley's Comet passed earth in the year 1758, Hawaiian shaman predicted the emergence of a potent leader. In this auspicious year of the white-tailed star a baby boy was born to a princess and a high chief in the Kohala

146

district on the northwestern tip of the Big Island. Many rulers of Hawaii feared the newborn child because the comet omen could only represent a destined leader who would one day challenge their authority. Legend has it that the young boy named Kamehameha was whisked away by priests and taken to the sacred Waipio Valley so the other chiefs could not subjugate him. Living in the valley and teaching the boy were royalty and priests of the *na ali'i koa* ranks, or the chiefly warriors. Kamehameha, meaning the "Lonely One," trained during his adolescence, amassed his prophesied power, and went on to become the first and only king to unify the Hawaiian Islands.

King Kamehameha the Great spent much of his boyhood in Waipio Valley, and returned many times during his adulthood to renew his spiritual power. Kamehameha I, like many Big Island chiefs before him, came to worship in the place where so many great kings were buried. In 1780, the year after Captain Cook's death, Kamehameha received his war god Kuka'ilimoku at Waipio, who proclaimed him the future ruler of the islands. It was off the coast of Waimanu, near Waipio, that Kamehameha engaged Kahekili, the chief of the Leeward Islands and Kahekili's half-brother Kaeokulani of Kauai, in the first true naval battle of Hawaiian history, the so-called Battle of the Red-Mouthed Guns (*Kepuwahaulaula*), so named because it was fought with European naval weapons. Kamehameha routed his enemies and thus furthered his ability to conquer all the islands.

> Waipio is the largest and longest valley on the Big Island. It was known as the "Valley of the Kings," and here King Kamehameha consolidated his power to become the greatest ruler of Hawaii.

Waipio has the remains of four *heiaus,* or Hawaiian temple platforms, located on the valley floor. The most sacred, the Pakaalana Heiau, was also the site of one of the island's two major *pu'uhonua,* or "a Place of Refuge," the other being Pu'uhonua O Honaunau (City of Refuge) on the Kona Coast. The three other Waipio heiaus were once used to make sacrifices to the gods, oftentimes human. Ancient burial caves are located in the sides of the steep cliffs on either side of the valley. Many rulers were buried in the Valley of the Kings, and it is felt that because of their lingering mana (divine power), no harm would come to those who lived in the valley. In fact, despite great devastation in the 1946 tsunami and the 1979 flood, no person died in those valley disasters. The Waipio floor is checkered with abandoned taro patches, and constantly watered by several waterfalls in the valley. Hawaii's highest waterfall, Hi'ilawe Waterfall, cascades 1,300 feet (390 m) near the rear of the valley. Many of the ancient stories of Hawaiian gods are set in Waipio. It is here that beside the Hi'ilawe Waterfall, the brothers of the mighty god Lono found the goddess Kaikiani dwelling in

▲ 19th century drawing of warriors preparing for battle. Waipio Valley was a renowned ancient Hawaiian location of kings and warriors.

a breadfruit grove. Lono descended on a rainbow and made her his wife, only to later kill her when he discovered a chief of the earth making love to her. As she died she assured Lono of her innocence and proclaimed her love for him. In Kaikiani's honor Lono instituted the Makahiki games. These contests were held at a designated period of time following the harvesting season when wars and battles were ceased, sporting competitions between villages were organized, and festive events were commenced.

For many centuries Waipio was the most fertile and productive valley on the Big Island. Located along the Hamakua Coast on the northeast shore of the Big Island of Hawaii, Waipio Valley is the largest and most southern of the seven valleys on the windward side of the Kohala Mountains. *Waipio* means "curved water" referring to the curvaceous nature of the Waipio Stream on the valley floor. This verdant green box canyon is surrounded on three sides by 2,000-foot (600-m) cliffs rising nearly straight up, in a valley six miles deep and a mile wide at the coast. At its cultural peak, around the time of Captain Cook's arrival in 1779, the valley was cultivated with taro and populated with as many as 10,000 laborers. A large number of fish were held in numerous fresh water fish ponds in the valley. In the late 1800s many Chinese settled in Waipio as farmers and fishermen. The conditions were like the Garden of Eden, until 1946 when the most devastating tsunami in Hawaii's history swept enormous tidal waves far back into the valley and destroyed everything in its wake including the four heiaus. After the 1946 tidal wave, most people left the valley and it has been sparsely populated ever since. A severe deluge in 1979 covered the valley floor from side to side in four feet of water. Before the tsunami the valley community supported schools, restaurants, churches as well as a hotel, post office and a jail. Today only about 50 people live there permanently. They remain the taro farmers, fishermen and those who are reluctant to leave their simple lifestyle.

### Getting to Waipio Valley

Waipio Valley is located along the northern Hamakua coast on the Big Island. Beyond Honoka'a town, Mamane Street (Highway 240) continues north for 9 miles (14 km) until it comes to an abrupt halt at the upper crest of Waipio Valley. Getting down to the valley floor is challenging along a steep (25 percent gradient) paved track. The mile-long (1.6-km) road descends from the lookout. Only 4WD vehicles, horseback riders or hikers can make it down. The hike takes about 15 minutes down, and 30 minutes back up. There is a refreshing waterfall for visitors to stand under after the long hike down. The entire valley is lush with vegetation and features an inviting black sand beach.

# KAUAI

Of the eight major islands in the Hawaiian archipelago, Kauai was firstborn. Because of its advanced age, Kauai has thicker soil and is more verdant and lush than any of the others, hence the nickname "Garden Island." Crowning Kauai is Kawaikini Peak, rising 5,243 feet (1,598 m) above sea level. Slightly lower at 5,148 feet (1,570 m) is Mount Waialeale, whose name translates as "rippling water." The northeastern slope of Waialeale draws nearly 500 inches (1,270 cm) of rain per year, making it among the wettest spots on earth. The high annual rainfall has eroded deep valleys in Kauai's central mountain mass and formed spectacular canyons. The spectacular Waimea Canyon, known as the "Grand Canyon of the Pacific," is almost 10 miles (about 16 km) long and more than 0.5 miles (0.8 km) deep. At 19.7 miles in length, the Waimea River is one of the longest rivers in the Hawaiian Islands and is the longest navigable river in the entire state. Kauai is the only island that King Kamehameha was never able to capture by force. Two major naval campaigns to invade were thwarted by inhospitable sea conditions and pestilence. Yet before Kamehameha died, he successfully united all eight Hawaiian Islands by accepting a tribute from King Kaumuali'i of Kauai.

## Waimea Bay

There are traces of the earliest inhabitants of Hawaii landing at Waimea Bay and creating the very first society. The word *waimea*, meaning "reddish water," was a common name in pre-contact Hawaii where a muddy river meets the sea. The mouth of the Waimea River was one of the most important ancient sites in the Hawaiian archipelago. The famous canyon valleys of the Waimea River and its tributary, the Makaweli River, were heavily populated in pre-contact times. The early civilization that grew up around Waimea Bay was distinctly unique from the other islands and may have once supported an entirely dissimilar race of people. In Hawaiian lore, a diminutive group of people called the *Menehune* "black dwarfs" once occupied all the islands, especially Kauai. The name likely derives from the same term given to the first aboriginal people of Tahiti called

▲ A church on Kauai. Some of the earliest missionaries began converting native Hawaiians to Christianity near Waimea Bay.

*Manhune*, a divergent race who were driven away from their homeland by invaders. Like the medieval Irish monks sailing away from the islands in the north Atlantic each time the larger Vikings approached, the Menehune similarly retreated when the taller Polynesians began conquering the southern Hawaiian Islands. Kauai is known to be culturally different from the other islands, supporting the earliest waves of Polynesians, and possibly earlier Melanesian immigrants. If Menehune groups retreated north along the Hawaiian archipelago this could explain why the island of Kauai, as their last holdout, retains the most stories about this small race of people. Legend of the last Menehune king relates the story of him sailing westward from Kauai along with most of his people. The seafarers would have passed the outer Nihoa and Necker islands, where carved stone images have been found which are not typically Hawaiian. Confusion came when Western writers heard stories of Menehune and assumed they were a mythical race of hairy leprechauns who worked at night and hid all day. European images of gnomes spread to the Pacific and a new genre of "Hawaiian" folklore soon developed. Chroniclers received tales of a magically strong little folk working in large numbers, constructing the finest voyaging canoes, huge temple platforms, long aqueducts and large fishponds—in fact nearly all large construction projects in Hawaii are attributed to Menehune builders. Legend has it that each project by the Menehune was completed in a single night, or else left completely undone. They were said to have lived in the forests and were shunned by the Hawaiians. Today, the Menehune are blamed when things go missing like misplaced keys, but the cherished myth of the Menehune as builders continues to live in Kauai. Near Waimea Bay there is solid evidence of an earlier people in the form of rockwork lining called the "Menehune Ditch"—an ancient aqueduct that once brought water from the Waimea River to irrigate dry lands for growing taro. The rocks were expertly shaped and fitted together, using a method of stonework requiring immense labor, and not typical of Hawaiian construction techniques. Most Hawaiians still consider the term reproachful or belittling, meaning a people of small status. But some descendents apparently remained on Kauai, where a census ordered by King Kaumuali'i in the early 19th century recorded 65 persons as being of Menehune ancestry.

Waimea Bay was among the first settlements of Polynesian immigrants in the 4th century CE, and may have been the homeland to an even earlier people. It was also the first known location of contact with European navigators.

In the winter of 1777-1778, on his third voyage to the North Pacific, the English navigator Captain James Cook made the first recorded sighting of the Hawaiian Islands. Lookouts spotted Oahu first, then Kauai. Cook's two ships *Resolution* and *Discovery* sailed along the island's southern shore looking for a place to land and finally dropped anchor at Waimea Bay. Captain Cook went ashore on Jan. 20, 1778 and was welcomed as the returning god Lono. Cook describes the event in his journal: "Several hundred ... were assembled on a sandy beach before the Village. The very instant I leaped ashore, they fell flat on their faces, and remained in that humble posture 'till I made signs to them to rise. They then brought a great many small pigs and gave us without regarding whether they got any thing in return." Along with a small party of Marines and a "tolerable train" of Hawaiians,

Cook hiked into Waimea Valley observing extensive plantations of taro, sugarcane, plantains, and paper mulberry trees, as well as a heiau where a human sacrifice had just taken place. The English ships stayed for only three days at Waimea Bay, until departing north to continue searching for the elusive Northwest Passage above Alaska and Canada.

Kauai was an independent kingdom when Captain Cook visited the island in 1778, and remained so until 1810 when it became annexed to the Kingdom of Hawaii. Shortly after Cook's visit many European ships began arriving at the islands, with the first fur-traders arriving in 1786. Sandalwood was discovered in 1791 on Kauai, and Waimea Bay soon became a principle port of call. Waimea town developed as a provisioning port for whalers and sandalwood traders, until both of those commodities were nearly extinguished. Near the captain's bay a contingent of Russians came in the early 19th century and built a fort to try and gain a foothold in Hawaii. The Russians failed in their attempt to seize the isle, but a ruined Russian fort still occupies a coastal bluff above the Waimea River. It wasn't long before

▲ The Hawaii of Captain Cook was one of superstition and intense fear of wrathful gods.

Waimea was among the first missionary settlements to proselytize the Christian faith to heathen Hawaiians. The first major attempt at agricultural development in Hawaii occurred with the establishment of a sugar plantation in 1835. Sugarcane production was until recently the main industry on Kauai, but tourism is now the major economic draw.

## Getting to Waimea Bay

Kauai is a 30 minute flight to the west of Oahu, and less than an hour's flight from Maui. From the airport town Lihue only one road extends along the south and west shore—Highway 50—to Waimea town and beyond to Mana Point at road's end. Waimea Bay is now the Lucy Wright Beach Country Park, named after the first native Hawaiian teacher at a local school. A small plaque commemorates the exact spot where Captain Cook landed. Highway 550, or Waimea Canyon Road, intersects the main part of town and extends up to the crest of Waimea Canyon, with fantastic views overlooking the "Grand Canyon of the Pacific." A rich sugar-plantation region extends 9 miles (15 km) northwest of Waimea through Kekaha to Mana. Barking Sands Military Reservation is on the coast near Mana.

# LANAI

The word *lanai* in Hawaiian means "hump," and can also be used to describe an outdoor patio. In the case of the island, viewing Lanai from afar at certain angles can resemble a humpback whale about to submerge. In the 1930s, the 6th largest of the Hawaiian Islands adopted the nickname "Pineapple Island" when the Palawai Basin supported the world's largest single pineapple plantation. The ideal 3,000-foot (900-m) elevation growing conditions on the plateau continue to support small pineapple patches, but the grandeur of harvesting a ton of pineapples per day are long gone. Lanai closed most of its production facilities in the early 1990s because high wages made Hawaiian pineapples too expensive in the competitive export market. The new nickname is the "Private Isle" catering to ultra-exclusive holidaymakers. Bill Gates' controversial marriage in 1993 shut down the island for several days. Interestingly, pineapples are not native to Hawaii, but come from Brazil. Pineapples are not a fruit either, but the edible part is an un-pollinated flower.

## The Garden of the Gods

The earliest Polynesians to reach Hawaii never settled Lanai because they thought it was filled with evil spirits. Troublesome Maui islanders of royal descent were banished to die from fright on Lanai, instead of being put to death. Only when one outcast in the 15th century was seen building huge bon fires every night on the eastern shore did other Hawaiians decide to inhabit

Lanai and set up a small subordinate colony to Maui. The population never exceeded 3,000 people, concentrated in small coastal villages subsisting primarily on fishing and raising pigs. These few settlers etched some of the finest Hawaiian petroglyphs in the hills above the Palawai Basin, built small shrines, and watched sunsets from the Garden of the Gods.

The Garden of the Gods is an unusual conglomeration of lava and multicolored boulders with a strange sculptural beauty, considered by most visitors as a "must see" on Lanai. A million years of wind and water erosion has created the surreal landscape on an isolated upland plateau. Erosion at the site has sculpted an array of pinnacles and buttes in a canyon surrounding the open country-side. The scenery resembles the Badlands of South Dakota more than anything typical on Hawaii. The morning and afternoon sun

▲ An old sugar cane train near the Garden of the Gods.

reflection increases the light and shadow of the odd formations, giving them an unusual quality. The rock colors change with the setting of the sun by taking on a rich red and brown hue in the late afternoon. The canyon of red earth and lava rocks is known for the morphing color during sunset when most visitors report having a profound personal experience. Even those who visit in daylight say they have had spiritual moments at this site. Some of the most spectacular views on the island are from the Garden of the Gods. The natural windswept rock forma-tions combined with the distant views of Maui and Molokai is absolutely breath-taking. Perhaps the most obvious trait of the site is the thousands of stacked rock formations called cairns scattered across the landscape. Although most of the cairns have been erected in recent times, the Hawaiians believe they were built as shrines with sincere intentions and should be left alone. The isolated beauty of the Garden of the Gods is a sacred place to many Hawaiians and should be treated with respect.

A sweeping view of several Hawaiian Islands amid a bizarre landscape of multi-colored rocks typifies the Garden of the Gods. Visitors at this remote location have reported a variety of spiritual experiences.

Early Polynesian settlers often depicted their migration and everyday life on Hawaii in the form of etched drawings on rocks called petroglyphs. The earliest examples dating back 500 years show stick figures in various poses, later to evolve into wedge-shaped bodies holding oars or weapons and sometimes superimposed upon each other. The Luahiwa Petroglyph rock carvings, hidden in the hills south of Lanai City from Palawai Basin, aren't easy to find but are considered some of the finest renderings in all of Hawaii. Luahiwa is the site of 20 boulders on a hillside and they are carved with some 400 petroglyphs of human figures, dogs, and European introduced horses. From the west side of the basin a short way up Hoiki Road, walk the hillside towards the peak of Lana'ihale and the petroglyph boulders will soon come into view. Increase the odds of spotting the carvings by enlisting the help of a local guide or getting directions from hotel staff. Palawai Basin is located on Manele Road (HI 441), halfway between Lanai City and the south shore.

### Getting to the Garden of the Gods

The Garden of the Gods borders the Palawai Basin, which is the floor of a volcano that formed Lanai a million years ago. The Garden of the Gods is 7 miles (11 km) northwest of Lanai City on the Polihua Road, an old pineapple track. This rugged dirt road should only be attempted in a 4WD vehicle in good weather. Getting there can be rugged and the road is even rougher past the Garden of the Gods. The dirt track ends at Polihua Beach on Lanai's north coast. Polihua Beach is a wide, white sand strand with good swimming and outstanding fishing. The western tip of the island is Ka'ena Point, also reached by a very rough road branching off just past the Garden of the Gods. Ka'ena Point is another beautiful location, but do not go swimming here because the currents are very strong off the point.

# MAUI

Back in the dawn of time, according to legend, the demigod Maui raised all the Hawaiian Islands from the sea. Native Hawaiian tradition attributes the island's name to the legend of Hawai'iloa, the Polynesian navigator who is credited with discovering the Hawaiian Islands. The story relates how he named the island of Maui after his son, who was in turn named after the demigod Maui. Polynesian mariners, originating from Tahiti and the Marquesas Islands, were the first people to inhabit Maui. The Tahitians introduced the kapu system, a strict social order that affected all aspects of life and became the core of Hawaiian culture. The first chief to unite Maui from centuries of tribal warfare was a chief named Pi'ilani. He not only united all of Maui in the 16th century, but went on to conquer the neighboring Kahoolawe, Lanai and Molokai islands. Together, the four islands are known as *Maui Nui*. Pi'ilani is also credited as the first chief to initiate a road encircling an entire Hawaiian island; wide enough for eight men to walk shoulder to shoulder, and completed by his son Kihapi'ilani. Parts of the modern Pi'ilani Highway follow the ancient route, and near La Pérouse Bay sections of the original road are still intact.

Modern history began in the mid-1700s when Maui was sighted by Captain Cook, who sailed near the shore but never attempted a landing. The first European to set foot on Maui was the French admiral Jean François de Galaup de La Pérouse in 1786, yet he defied orders and refused to claim the island for the French Crown out of respect for the Hawaiian people. The last eruption on Maui occurred four years later, wiping out the village at La Pérouse Bay where the French navigator had just landed. King Kamehameha I took up residence in Lahaina after conquering Maui in 1790, immediately following the decisive Battle of Kepaniwai in the Iao Valley. After uniting the Hawaiian Islands Kamehameha the Great made his capital Lahaina, mainly because it was centrally located in the archipelago where he could keep a lookout for any war canoes coming from the other islands. The Island of Maui is nicknamed the "Valley Isle" because of the large fertile isthmus between its two volcanoes.

## Haleakala

Everything on eastern Maui centers around, or is inside, the massive cone-shaped Haleakala volcano. Rising 10,023 feet (3,055 m) into the tropical sky, from a sea-level base of 33 miles (53 km) in diameter, Haleakala is the world's largest dormant volcano and holds many unusual distinctions. Viewing the huge mountain from top down, Haleakala National Park centers around an enormous crater at the summit—an immense rectangular-shaped bowl measuring 7.5 miles (12 km) long, 2.5 miles (4 km) wide, and .5 mile (.8 km) deep—which could easily accommodate the whole island of Manhattan. Along the upper slopes of Haleakala and inside the crater lives the rarest plant in the world, the silversword. On the south-

eastern slopes lies the area of greatest climatic change in the world. Within one mile it is possible to travel from a tropical rain forest on the windward side to desert conditions on the leeward side.

Significant archaeological remains have been found inside the crater, yet there is no evidence that the

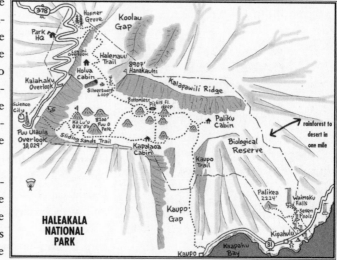

ancient Hawaiians ever made their homes in this hostile environment. In pre-contact times they hiked to the summit to mine basalt for adzes, to hunt birds, conduct religious ceremonies, and bury their dead. Lately archaeologists have discovered traces of an ancient paved road that once crossed the crater floor and led down through the Kaupo Gap. One of the most spectacular sections of the crater is called Pele's Paint Pot, named after the vivid streak of red sand against the view of brown and yellow mounds on either side.

> Haleakala Crater was a very sacred place to ancient Hawaiians, who visited but rarely stayed for too long. The literal translation Hale-a-ka-la means "House of the Sun."

According to an old Tahitian chant, when the earth was discovered by Polynesians in the primordial ocean, the great god Maui set sail in his fleet of canoes and visited all the Hawaiian Islands, building temples wherever he stopped. The legendary demigod Maui has many fantastic tales attributed to his presence on the islands, especially on his namesake island. Within the Haleakala Crater is where Maui captured the sun and demanded the sun take longer crossing the horizon every day to allow his mother's *tapa* (bark-cloth) more time to dry. The trickster god Maui caught the sun in a web of ropes and kept it hostage in the "House of the Sun" for many days. The sun agreed to slow its movement, and Maui let it go. Although clouds usually shroud the lower slopes of Haleakala

▲ A helicopter flying over Haleakala Crater.

and sometimes fill the crater, the summit is often bathed in dramatic sunlight. This magnificent display of light is also attributed to the demigod Maui. The impression everywhere is of dazzling colors, and viewing the sunrise from the summit of Haleakala is one of the most popular activities for Maui tourists.

The crater of Haleakala is not a crater at all, but the collapsed and eroded portions of a once 13,000-foot (3,900-m) tall mountain. The cinder cones inside the crater are the result of minor eruptions long after the erosion process began. Geomancers detect enormous energy coming up through the shield volcano Haleakala. Dowsers believe there is a massive crystal underneath Haleakala; a wedged part of the earth's crystallized core pushed up by the volcano. Maybe this is why there are more New Age healing centers and workshops on the slopes of Haleakala than all the other Hawaiian Islands combined.

### Getting to Haleakala

Winding its way up the slopes of Haleakala to the summit is Highway 378, which is an easy drive for any rental car. Haleakala National Park is open every day of the year. The Hawaiian Islands are serviced by many major airlines from all parts of the Pacific Rim. Most flights land in Honolulu on Oahu, but an increasing number are flying direct from the mainland to the Big Island, Maui and Kauai. Rental cars and accommodations can be arranged at Maui's Kahului airport.

## Iao Valley

Long a place of pilgrimage for the royalty and warrior classes of Maui, the Iao Valley is renowned for its unprecedented beauty. Today it continues to be one of the top tourist attractions on Maui. The valley is the eroded caldera of the West Maui Mountains, an amphitheater where four streams converge. The state park is relatively small, but ample amounts of history and lore surround the area. Mark Twain wrote of his experience in the valley: "I still remember, with a sense of idolent luxury, a picknicking excursion up a romantic gorge there, called the Iao Valley." Dominating the valley is a unique rock formation called the Iao Needle. As the most obvious feature of the park, it towers 1,200 feet (360 m) above the valley floor but is inaccessible for climbing. A path nearby the needle leads to a botanical garden filled with plants brought to the island by Hawaiians who lived in the valley preceding European contact. Before modern farming techniques, the lower portion of Iao Valley was ideal for agricultural production necessary to support a large population. These favorable conditions included a wide valley floor, rich alluvial soils, terraced gardens, and a constant supply of water from Iao Stream. Such factors combined with access to abundant marine resources in Kahului Harbor, made this a prime location for settlement on West Maui before the arrival of Europeans. The lower section of Iao Valley contained some of the most productive taro farming gardens on the island, and as such became a vibrant political and religious center. Fronting the mouth of Iao Stream are two large heiau platforms named Haleki'i and Pihana, the last remaining ancient Hawaiian religious structures in the Wailuku area. Traditional history credits the Menehune with construction of both structures in a single night with rocks collected from Paukukalo beach. Other accounts credit the rulers Kihapi'ilani, Ki'ihewa and Kahekili as the builders of the two lava rock platforms. The Haleki'i heiau was most likely a compound for chiefs, which had thatched huts on top of the stone structure guarded by *ki'i* statues placed around the surrounding terraces. Pihana heiau, the full name of which is Pihanakalani or "the gathering place of the ali'i," was a luakini-type heiau. The luakini war temples were for the exclusive use of male ruling chiefs, and the most infamous religious practice were the frequent human sacrifices made to appease various gods. As such, the upper portion of Iao Valley was the most important location on West Maui for ancient Hawaiians, the equivalent to Egypt's Valley of the Kings: they buried their kings in the long-lost Olopio Cave, and access was strictly forbidden to commoners.

> The word "Iao" is said to mean "supreme light" or "supreme point." Iao Needle was the focal point of religious activity in West Maui and warriors likely used it as a lookout.

The 17th and 18th centuries saw an intensified period of frequent warfare on Maui, first between the chiefs of Maui, and then with the chiefs of Oahu and Hawaii. The most famous was the Battle of Kepaniwai in Iao Valley, where Kamehameha I of Hawaii led his forces to conquer Maui's army in an effort to unite the islands in the late 18th century. Prior to that, the lower Iao Valley was a political center under chief Pi'ilani who had succeeded in unifying Maui by warfare. His two sons, Lono-a-Pi'ilani and Kihapi'ilani fought for political control after his death. Eventually, with the help of warriors from the Big Island, Kihapi'ilani became the ruler of Maui. The last powerful ruler before Kamehameha was Kahekili, the fierce tattooed chief who ruled from about 1765 to 1790. Lower Iao Valley was the site of Kahalelani, his royal residence. He successfully defended his capital in the 1770s when an army of warriors from the Big Island led by Kalani'opu'u invaded. Kahekili's warriors hid behind the sand dunes, surprised the invaders and systematically slaughtered them all. The most famous event in the history of Iao Valley was a battle fought between the forces of Kahekili and those of King Kamehameha the Great, which took place in 1790. Kamehameha arrived from the Big Island in a fleet so huge it was said that the whole Kahului Harbor was filled

with war canoes containing his massive army. Kamehameha brought along a cannon, called Lopaka, and two Europeans, John Young and Issac Davis, who knew how to operate it. The Maui warriors were led by Kalanikapule, the son of the high chief Kahekili, who fought evenly with the Big Island invaders for two days. On the third day Kamehameha brought out the cannon, and a great slaughter occurred, conclusively deciding the fate of the famous battle. Had the fighting been in the usual style

▲ The Iao Needle in Iao Valley.

of hand-to-hand combat, the forces would have been equally matched and the outcome would have likely been a draw. As it was, the Maui army retreated into the narrow Iao Valley and fell under intense cannon fire. The warriors desperately tried to escape by climbing up the steep cliffs. The battle was subsequently called Ka-`uwa`u-pali (clawed off the cliff) and Kepaniwai (damming of the waters), because the Iao Stream had become so clogged with dead bodies floating downstream. The town Wailuku also borrows its name from the battle, literally meaning "bloody river." As devastating as the battle was to the defenders of Maui, most of the important chiefs escaped and proceeded to take refuge on the islands of Molokai and Oahu.

### Getting to Iao Valley

Iao Valley State Park is located 3 miles (5 km) above the sleepy town of Wailuku on Iao Valley Road. This West Maui refuge is a 6.2 acre (2.5 ha) place of uncommon history and beauty. Upon arrival visitors suddenly find themselves in a lush rainforest environment. The air is moist and cool and occasional rainstorms are common. Iao Valley State Park is designated a National Natural Landmark.

# MOLOKAI

The mellow island of Molokai is regarded by most visitors as the most authentic version of what Hawaii must have been like 50 to 60 years ago. There is not a single elevator or traffic light on the island and no building is taller than a palm tree. Yet this sleepy image was not the case in ancient times when Molokai had a bustling population with sophisticated farming techniques and an intricate network of enclosed "aquaculture" fish ponds. Attesting to the richness of the island are the ruins of over 50 separate fish ponds that once extended 20 miles (32 km) along the southeastern coast, and the main reason why Molokai was so coveted by other chiefs. Several heiaus scatter across the island, as well as Molokai's own *pu'uhonua* or a "City of Refuge." Higher up in the mountains is one of the last sandlewood groves and a "sandlewood boat," which is a pit dug in the exact shape of a boat's hull to precisely fill the cargo hold with the fragrant trees destined for export to the Far East. When trade with foreigners began, so did intense servitude of the native Hawaiians. It is said the sandlewood harvesters eventually started pulling out saplings to spare their children from such cruel work.

## Kalaupapa Peninsula

Isolated from the world by rough surf and the tallest sea cliffs in the world, this lonely peninsula was created by a late eruption long after the rest of Molokai was formed. The flat and exposed spit of land, although exceedingly difficult to access, once held an extensive ancient occupation. Just east of the peninsula is the virgin Waikolu Valley, a lush tropical wilderness long considered sacred by the Hawaiians. Although mostly buried in the undergrowth of trees and bushes, numerous shrines, heiaus and gravesites lie hidden on the Kalaupapa Peninsula and Waikolu Valley. With over 1,000 years of native occupation, Kalaupapa has one of the richest and most valuable archaeological preserves in Hawaii. But Kalaupapa was not to remain the pristine homeland to future generations. Once the first shipments of lepers started arriving in the 1860s, the unaffected native population quickly relocated "top side" to avoid contact.

> Kalaupapa Peninsula was the infamous home of Hawaii's only leprosy colony. A Belgian priest named Father Damien devoted his life to easing the leper's brutal suffering.

When the whalers, laborers, and missionaries came to the Hawaiian Islands in the early 19th century, they brought with them diseases completely foreign to the Hawaiian people, including the contagious leprosy, or Hansen's Disease. This hideous disease was likely brought over with plantation laborers from China. The first case was diagnosed in 1835 on Kauai and called *Ma'i Pake,* or the "Chinese disease." Those unfortunate few who contracted leprosy—estimated to be one in fifty by 1865—were sent into permanent exile on Kalaupapa Peninsula, one of the most remote regions in the Hawaiian archipelago. The disfigured Hawaiians suffered immensely upon banishment from their homes and family, as the disease seemingly struck at random with no cure. Upon the first sign of the horrible disease the lepers were rounded up and immediately shipped to the Kalaupapa colony for life. The first few decades at "the Settlement" were complete anarchy as new arrivals were met with the motto "there is no law in this place" and instantly stripped of their possessions and oftentimes raped. The horrendous conditions lasted until 1873 when Father Damien arrived from Belgium and showed his saintly devotion by nursing the sick, burying the dead and befriending those considered untouchable in Hawaiian society. At the earlier settlement of Kalawao Father Damien set to the task of building a church to nourish the poor souls of Kalaupapa. The Saint Philomena's church became the only refuge of compassion available

▲ The "Penis of Nanahoa" rock formation above the Kalaupapa Peninsula.

to the banished lepers. Father Damien finally contracted leprosy himself, died at the age 49, and was buried next to his church until his body was exhumed in 1936 and returned to Belgium. His right hand, however, was returned to his original grave in 1995, just a year after the Vatican beautified him. Surprising to most visitors today is that elderly leprosy patients still live on the Kalaupapa Peninsula. The disease is now controlled and contagion is eliminated by modern drugs, yet these aging patients prefer to live amid the solitude of Kalaupapa.

On a slight hill overlooking the Kalaupapa Peninsula, very close to the trail leading down, is an ancient Hawaiian fertility ritual center at a place called Pu'u Loa knoll. Woman hoping to become pregnant would come to the fertility shrine known as *Ka Ule O Nanahoa*, meaning "the Penis of Nanahoa," to recite prayers and offer gifts. After being directed by the *kahuna* (priests) to the fertility shrine, women would place offerings at the furrowed tip of a large phallic stone, sleep overnight, and then were said to return home pregnant. Their directed prayers were to encourage the latent potency of the stone penis to enter the woman's uterus. The shrine used to be fully exposed to the plains below, but is now shrouded by trees and foliage. A well-worn trail from the lookout parking lot leads visitors to the Pu'u Loa knoll. Ancient petroglyphs are concealed in an overhanging rock nearby, and other phallic images and emblems can be found in the vicinity.

### Getting to Kalaupapa Peninsula

The Kalaupapa Peninsula Lookout is located one mile (1.6 km) north of Kalae via Hawaii 470, then a steep three-mile (5-km) descent by foot trail to the Kalaupapa National Historic Park. Once on the peninsula floor, only guided tours are allowed. Info line: 808-567-6802. Mule rides are available, as well as a small airport where planes can land for pre-arranged walking tours of Kalaupapa.

# OAHU

Being the most populated island in Hawaii, Oahu has adopted many nicknames: "The Gathering Island," "The Meeting Place," and "The Capital Isle." As one of the original islands settled by the first wave of Polynesian settlers it was called the "Heavenly Homeland of the North." The United States government has long held an interest in Pearl Harbor, the deepest harbor in the North Pacific and home of the U.S. Pacific Fleet. Although crowded and sometimes congested, Oahu should not be mistaken for the rampant commercialization of Waikiki or Honolulu. Oahu is rich in culture and history and is every bit as beautiful as the other islands. The spectacular Waianae and Ko'olau mountain ranges spread the island like the wings of a butterfly to open upon an impressive valley. From Waikiki, travel to the windward coast past one incredible beach or scenic bay mile after mile.

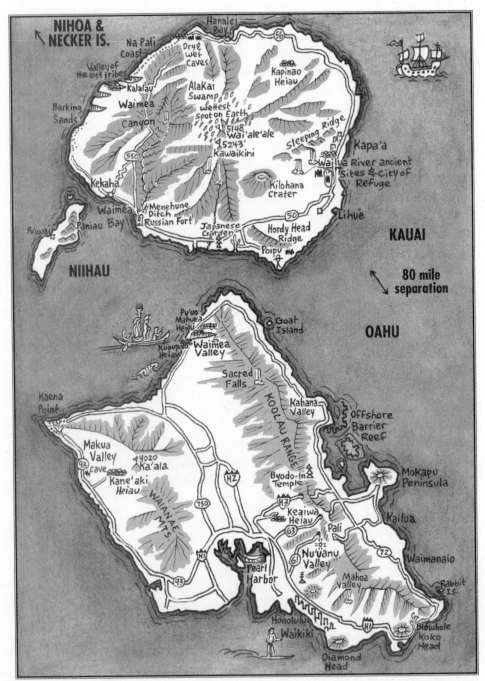

## Kaena Point

The rugged and windswept Kaena Point is the least populated, and least visited, region of the island. Located on Oahu's far northwest corner, the desolate Kaena Point is at the tail end of the Waianae Mountain Range, as well as the confluence of two distinct weather systems—the leeward and windward. Just beyond the point the ocean currents meet in a constant splash of dark water and white foam on jagged rocks. Kaena Point is the winter nesting grounds for many rare Hawaiian birds, including the immense Laysan albatross, which occasionally take to the air to drive people away from their nests if they come too close. The lighthouse at the point offers splendid views. On a clear day the island of Kauai is visible to the northwest. The ten miles (16 km) of dirt road rounding Kaena Point has become an increasingly popular trip for naturalists, hikers, and ornithologists.

## Kaena Point is the legendary "leaping place of souls" for recently deceased Hawaiian spirits.

Ancient Hawaiian mythology describes a colorful array of spirits and dimensions in the afterlife. A Hawaiian euphemistic term for dying was to "travel west," and in the case of people on Oahu it was a journey to Kaena Point on the western extremity of the island. Upon death, or even during a near death experience, a Hawaiian person's soul would first travel directly to Kaena Point to determine if it was ready to continue. As the newly released soul approached the point, it was met by the spirits of deceased ancestors or friends who were waiting for the soul

to arrive. They might send the soul back if the death were not real or if certain earthly obligations were not fulfilled. The spirits could help revive the body if the death was not final. If death was final, the ancestral guides would entertain the soul, comfort it, and begin leading it on its journey off the earthly plane. When the deceased soul was ready to depart, it was guided to *Leinakauhane* (white rock), where the soul would make its plunge into the ocean on its way to eternity. A big white stone on the north side of Kaena Point was the literal leaping place of souls into the land of *po* (heaven).

Another aspect of the departing soul visiting Kaena Point is less tantalizing. Legend also scrutinized how honorable the person had led his or her life. If the newly deceased soul had not fulfilled all earthly obligations to the priesthood, or had been a bad person and disrespected

▲ Kaena Point, where the windward side meets the leeward.

their ancestors, the soul continued wandering around Kaena Point, or was returned to the body. In the event the body was indeed dead and could not be returned, the bad soul wandered for eternity out on the hot and dry western extremity of Oahu. Here the wandering soul would lurk as a ghost, subsist by eating spiders and moths until an *'aumakua* (guardian angel ancestor deity) would take pity on the soul and guide it away. The 'aumakua usually took the form of an animal, such as a sea turtle, an owl, octopus, or bird. The helpful animal guides would eventually escort the bad soul to the leaping stone where the spirit would plunge into "endless night." At this point the guardian angel would guide the soul through sea caves and other wondrous worlds until the soul was then ready to enter the land of po.

### Getting to Kaena Point

Access to Kaena Point can be made from both the windward (northwest) and leeward (southwest) sides. The old dirt road used to be open for 4WD traffic, but time and erosion have closed the road. Both access points are on the same road—the Farrington Highway—yet the roads no longer connect around the point. Old maps may show this road rounding Kaena Point, and indeed it does, but there is no way any vehicle can make it past some of the deep erosion trenches or barrier walls to keep vehicles out. Several side trails lead to remote beaches, blowholes, and exceptional viewing areas along the coast. Look for the parking lots where the pavement ends, at the 42-mile marker on the leeward side, and the 46-mile marker on the windward side.

## Waimea Valley

Before Western contact almost all Hawaiian people lived on the wet, windward side of each island. These rain-soaked regions allowed for one of the most productive farming regions in Polynesia. The word *waimea* in Hawaiian means "reddish water" derived from the red volcanic soil, rich in iron oxide, accumulated from the abundant rains on Oahu's North Shore. "Wai" meaning water and "mea" for the color red was a common name for fertile farming communities on other islands, including large settlements on the Big Island and Kauai. In the case of Oahu's Waimea Valley, a structured and organized work force constructed numerous terraces made of large boulders used for heavy taro farming and enclosed animal holding pens. Waimea was noted for productivity and quality of products, especially the pink taro rootstock that was particularly prized by the chiefly *ali'i* class. The fact that the ancient Hawaiians domesticated animals, cultivated crops from irrigated fields and constructed elaborate fish ponds attest to the high level of agricultural advancement they had achieved.

With intensive food production in place to feed many mouths, the population boomed and elaborate social and political institutions were formulated. Waimea Valley became one of the leading centers for powerful island chiefs, priestly brotherhoods, and highly trained athletes. As early as 1092 CE, Waimea Valley was one of four chosen lands on Oahu to be awarded to the *Kahuna Nui,* or "High Priests of Oahu," in perpetuity. The priesthood of *Pa'ao*—the most powerful kahunas on the islands—was centered in Waimea and exerted substantial control over all Oahu chiefs. King Kamehameha's own per-

▲ A recreated Hawaiian village in the Parks of Waimea.

sonal kahuna, Hewa Hewa Nui, was a direct descendant of the Pa'ao priesthood. Throughout Hawaii, the kahuna were experts in their field of study, whether it was fishing, farming, healing, or consultation with the gods, they played an important role to both the chiefly class and the common classes. In the valley are the remnants of royal burial mounds of stacked rocks, several heiaus dedicated to various gods, family shrines to *'aumakua* (deceased ancestors), and a large platform to indicate the king's residence. The largest platform, the Hale O Lono Heiau, built sometime between 1470 and 1700 CE, was dedicated to Lono, one of four principle Hawaiian gods. Lono ruled the spirits who controlled agriculture, harvests, weather, medicine, and sports. Here the *kahuna la'au lap'au,* or a medical priest practitioner of herbal medicine prayed to Lono for advice, and passed on his wisdom from generation to generation.

> Once a center for the ancient Hawaiian religion of Oahu, today Waimea Valley is a commercially run park, replete with a botanical garden, exotic animals, and footpaths that wander among remnants of temples, homes and entire villages. Within Waimea Valley there are more than 40 historic sites.

The first communication with foreigners on Oahu took place on February 27th, 1779, when the ships *Discovery* and *Resolution* touched at Waimea Bay on their way to Kauai after Cook's death. The *Resolution* stayed anchored for a few days longer to collect water for the long voyage north. The crew instantly took a liking to the valley, calling it "uncommonly beautiful and picturesque." The new Captain Clerke described Waimea as "by far the most beautiful Country we have yet seen among the Isles ... bounteously cloath'd with Verdure, on which were situated many large Villages and extensive plantations." The *Resolution* departed with-

▲ The restored Hale O Lono Heiau is the most prominent historic relic in Waimea Valley. Three stone terraces rise next to the main entrance into the park.

out incident, and Waimea was not again visited by European ships for 13 years, until the *Daedalus* set anchor on May 12th, 1792, headed by Lieutenant Richard Hergest who was a crew member on the *Resolution*. By this time, King Kamehameha's access to European weapons was enabling him to defeat all his rivals. When the Waimea chief and his warriors came aboard the *Daedalus* to trade arms, Hergest ordered them all thrown overboard to the chief's utter humiliation. Thinking the islanders were meek, Hergest took a party ashore to explore the valley while the rest of the crew filled their water caskets. Within minutes Hergest and two men were ambushed below a hill and killed by the fearsome *pahupu*, or "cut-in-two" warriors, so named because half their bodies were fully tattooed. The warriors ran down the steep slope from the Pu'u O Mahuka Heiau, Oahu's largest temple of human sacrifice. The slain seamen were taken as sacrificial offerings to another heiau at Mokule'ia, to be baked and stripped of their flesh in the same manner as Captain Cook had been treated. In this way, the mana could be taken from the foreigners and usurped by those offering the sacrifice.

### Getting to Waimea Valley

The Waimea Valley Audubon Center, formerly called Waimea Valley Adventure Park, is located at 59-864 Kamehameha Highway (Hawaii 83), about 5 miles (8 km) northeast of Haleiwa town. The Waimea Bay Beach Park is on the ocean side of Hawaii 83. Once on the valley floor follow the signs inland to the Waimea Valley Audubon Center. The commercially run valley no longer offers off-road adventures, kayak paddling, horseback riding or the cliff diving show. The "adventure tourism" aspect was controversial to many locals who didn't see these activities as appropriate in a place they consider sacred. Instead, the Center encourages self-guided, leisurely walks through the gardens. Hours of operation are 10:30 am to 4:30 PM everyday, admission fee required. Info line: 808 638-9199. The Hale O Lono Heiau rises on three tiers next to the admission gate parking lot, and the Pu'u O Mahuka Heiau is perched on the eastern bluff above the mouth of the Waimea River. Pu'u O Mahuka can be visited by driving up Pupukea Road and taking the first right after crossing over the cattle guard.

# NIHOA AND NECKER OUTER ISLANDS

Two small northwestern islands beyond Kauai and Ni'ihau had been fishing and hunting grounds to the ancient Hawaiian people for centuries. The two outcroppings are Nihoa and Necker Islands, and like the others, they are ancient remnants of volcanoes. Nihoa Island is about 170 miles (275 km) from Kauai, and Necker Island is another 150 miles (240 km) further west. The truly amazing aspect of these islands is how absolutely small they are in size. While little Ni'ihau offers an environment of 73 square miles (118 sq. km), Nihoa is only 156 acres (62.4 ha) and Necker a mere 39 acres (15.6 ha). Considering that an acre of land is only 1/640 of a square mile, any settlement on either Nihoa or Necker would have been extremely crowded.

It is hard to imagine a colony of people spending their whole lives on these remote nubbins of rock. But the evidence is ample, including 60 archaeological sites on Nihoa and 34 on Necker. Several well-built temples remain, as well as a cave showing human occupation. If the canoes used to reach the island were somehow damaged in the rough surf, the settlers would not have been able to repair their canoes with resources from the islands. They would have been trapped until other canoes arrived from Ni'ihau or Kauai. Partial skeletons of men, women, and children have been found on Nihoa, and two burial sites located. While mystery remains as to what happened to the peoples of Nihoa and Necker, a lack of food sources and fresh water suggest a tragic human drama. Without timber for new canoes and very limited resources to survive upon, it is likely a protracted drought lead to widespread starvation. Whether the inhabitants died off, were rescued, or sailed off on their own, both islands were uninhabited when the first European seafarers arrived in 1789.

> Nihoa and Necker Islands each supported small Polynesian settlements in the 14th century CE, before mysteriously vanishing. The inhabitants erected dozens of heiau platforms and various shrines on both islands.

Since neither island is tall enough to catch the rain, subsisting for any period of time would have been exceedingly difficult. Necker Island is smaller and has even fewer resources than Nihoa. There are no trees and no soil for growing crops on Necker. No springs of drinkable water have been located on either island. The freshwater comes from the estimated 20-30 inches (50-76 cm) of rain that falls annually from passing squalls. Despite these harsh conditions no less that 33 temples have been erected on Necker, and 15 on Nihoa, both attesting to elaborate rituals and ceremonies being performed. Many of the temple sites closely resemble those of the Marquesas Islands and Tahiti, possibly establishing a link between this site and early Polynesian cultures. While it is unclear if Necker ever supported a permanent population, Nihoa was inhabited by the *kanaka*

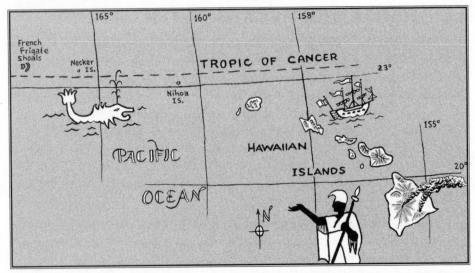

*maoli*, perhaps a version of the Menehune, a people who lived there sometime between 1000 and 1500 CE. About 35 house sites, 15 bluff shelters, 15 heiau, and 28 agricultural terraces have been identified on Nihoa. Various artifacts have also been collected, including fishhooks, sinkers, fiber fishing lines, cowry shell lures, hammerstones, grindstones, adzes, and coral rubbing stones. Remarkable are the unique human images found nowhere else in Hawaii, but are reminiscent of idols from the Marquesas. Several stone statues, the largest around 16 inches (41 cm) high, depict people with outstretched tongues and lacking necks. The images look like flat gingerbread men with expressive round faces. Who or what these images represent is unknown.

The earliest Europeans to visit Kauai and record the ancient lifestyle describe native Hawaiian canoes departing for the northwestern islands on hunting excursions for turtles and seabirds. Oral histories from Ni'ihau residents recall Nihoa as being occupied each summer until the late 1800s as a fishing colony. Nihoa, jutting up from the sea beyond sight of Kauai and Ni'ihau, is the westernmost place in the tradition of Kauai geography. The word *nihoa* has several meanings, including "firmly set," "toothed," or "serrated," possibly a reference to its jagged profile. From one angle the island looks like a molar standing isolated at sea and would have been useful as a navigational checkpoint. Nihoa is a mile long, a quarter mile wide, and almost 900 feet (270 m) high on its east end. In the 1800s and 1900s, Western sailing ships exploited the area for seals, whales, reef fish, turtles, sharks, pearl oysters, and sea cucumbers. The island was formally annexed to Hawaii in 1894, and was designated a wildlife refuge by Teddy Roosevelt in 1906. Today the only inhabitants of Nihoa are insects, monk seals, two species of land birds (the finch and millerbird found nowhere else), and numerous seabirds (terns, boobies, petrels, shearwaters, albatrosses, tropic birds, and frigate birds). The U.S. Fish and Wildlife Service control both islands. Landing on either island is prohibited except for scientific study and cultural purposes.

## Getting to Nihoa and Necker Outer Islands

If permits are secured to visit the Outer Islands, the next hard part is getting there. Ship landing on Nihoa Island is difficult. All landings must be made on a rocky shelf in Adam Bay, and only in ideal weather conditions. High, sheer cliffs prevent landing on the east, north, and west sides. The island slopes down to the south, but the shoreline is rocky and unprotected from the surge of southerly swells. Large vessels anchor offshore, and those wanting to go ashore have to use a small boat or swim ashore. There is no known outfitter that charters trips to Nihoa, let alone Necker, which is 320 miles (515 km) off the coast of Kauai. Both islands are living Hawaiian history and should not be disturbed. Both Nihoa and Necker Islands are on the National Registry of Historic Places.

# WESTERN CANADA

*"How do you design plans to protect sacred places when you are dealing with people who have never held anything sacred? People who probe the earth, probe the sky and oceans, tread upon all the earth, touch everything and all, without feeling the mother earth under them!"*
**-Elders of the Medicine Wheel Alliance**

MUCH OF CANADA IS A VAST WILDERNESS, ESPECIALLY IN the north and western regions of the country. The nation consists of ten provinces and two outback territories. The sparsely populated Yukon and Northwest Territories are the homeland of the Inuit whose name means "the people." Canada is the second largest country in the world—nearly as large as all of Europe—only the Russian Federation is larger. 90% of Canadians live within 100 miles (160 km) of the 3,955-mile (6,379-km) border with the United States. It is the longest unguarded national boundary in the world. The Canadian government is a constitutional monarchy with its capital located in Ottawa, Ontario.

For countless generations the aboriginal natives of the northern Central Plains led a nomadic lifestyle, following the great herds of bison on which they were almost completely dependent. As they moved from camp to camp, all their possessions, including their large hide tents (teepees), were transported on *travois*, tilted sleds made from teepee poles, pulled by dogs and later by horses. Little is known today about these migratory cultures that inhabited the Canadian Plains in the pre-historic period, as some of them ceased to exist prior to the arrival of the Europeans in the 17th century. By the early 1800s, the arrival of the fur traders and missionaries transported the Indians from the Stone Age into the Iron Age, resulting in a complete destruction of their early culture. Since the Plains Indians did not maintain written records, most of their past was soon forgotten. Their abandoned shelters and clothing deteriorated rapidly in the northern climate. What remains today is the relatively indestructible debris of their daily lives, enigmatic evidence of a lost culture. Artifacts from this early society such as arrowheads, rock cairns, pottery and petroglyphs, have been found in many widely separated locations east of the Rockies.

Native Americans in Canada are known as First Nation people, indicative of their status as the original inhabitants. The First Nation people, especially those who remained on Canada's Central Plains, held a deep respect for the Great Spirit and the four directions of power. These four directions also factored into the philosophy of the medicine wheel. In their philosophy, north takes on the color of white which represents wisdom, and buffalo is the deity. South is attributed to the color green, implying innocence or trust and mouse is the token animal. West is black depicting introspection, with the bear featured as the animal symbol. East radiates with the color yellow or gold enhancing the perception of illumination, and eagle is the animal spirit. A warrior who perceives from only one of these areas is merely a partial person. To become a complete person, one must grow by seeking an understanding in each of the four directions to become a full being, capable of balance and decision.

# ALBERTA

Alberta's southwestern boundary with British Columbia is marked by the Continental Divide. Almost this entire western Canadian province is flat prairie, gradually rising in elevation to the Front Range of the Rocky Mountains. Such open land was the historic roaming ground for the North American Plains Indians, including the powerful Blackfeet who demarcated their territory from the Rockies in the west, to the region of Calgary in the north, south to Yellowstone and east more than halfway across Saskatchewan and Montana. The ancestors of the Plains Indians created the enigmatic medicine wheels, some being as much as 3,500 years old. The Blackfeet associate medicine wheels with mortuary practices, and indeed some of the Alberta wheels were used as burial places.

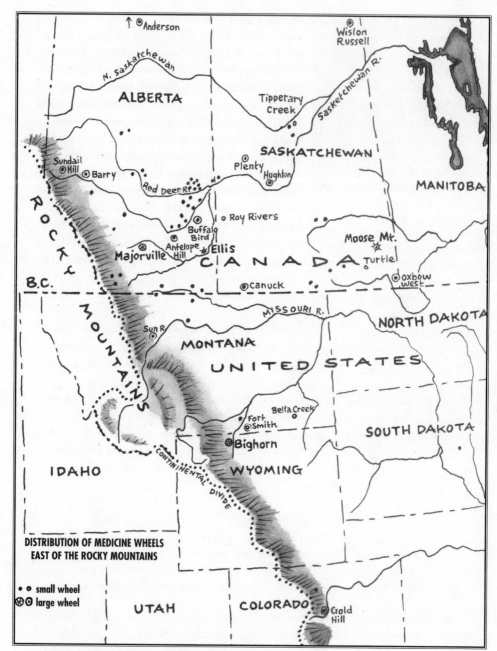

## Ellis Medicine Wheel

Scattered across the plains of Canada, especially Alberta, are thousands of circular stone formations. Most of these are simple stone circles with no internal stone mound or radiating spokes. The most common circles are known as "teepee rings" and they once served the purpose of holding down the edges of animal hide teepees. The larger stone rings with elaborated internal patterns, termed medicine

▲ In the middle of Alberta's Medicine Wheel country is this natural feature of an Indian head in the landscape. (Image courtesy Google Earth)

wheels, are of a more obscure nature. Extremely large stone circles—some greater than 40 feet (12 m) across—may be the remains of special ceremonial centers. Many wheels are simply huge central cairns (mounds of stones), with spokes 100 to 200 feet (30-60 m) across radiating out from these central mounds. The word "medicine" implies a magical, mysterious or supernatural function to Native Americans, through any physical object with spiritual properties. Most medicine wheels are so old that their original use is unknown. It has been verified by the radiocarbon dating of charcoal at the bottom of several Canadian medicine wheels that Plains Indian astronomy began in the north and eventually spread south. This also accounts for the fact that a great majority of medicine wheels are found on the Canadian prairies. Research has indicated a varied and continuous use of the wheels over a long period of time, and has suggested a number of possible functions for the wheels. Medicine wheels seem to be primarily an Alberta phenomenon, or at least appear to have originated in this province. Alberta has many more medicine wheels than do all the adjacent Canadian provinces and United States combined. Researchers determined that a medicine wheel consists of at least two of the following three traits: (1) a central stone cairn, (2) one or more concentric stone circles, and/or (3) two or more stone lines radiating outward from a central point. Using this definition, there are a total of 46 medicine wheels in Alberta. This constitutes about 66% of all known medicine wheels in North America. Alberta, it would seem, was the core center of activity for medicine wheels.

The Ellis Medicine Wheel, also termed the Medicine Man Wheel, is situated on high ground with a clear view of the horizon. The sightings at Ellis depict similar astronomical alignments to other wheels outside of Alberta.

The Ellis Medicine Wheel is located on top of a prominent ridge overlooking the Saskatchewan River. It consists of a circular central cairn with radiating spokes leading to a dozen other outer stone circle rings. Three remaining spoke lines point to the north, south and east. The Ellis wheel has celestial sightings and territorial markings similar to the Moose Mountain wheel in Saskatchewan and the Bighorn wheel in Wyoming. The three wheels may have marked Sioux or Blackfeet territory when these wheels were in prominent use. Testing has determined the Ellis wheel to be a late prehistoric burial lodge and medicine wheel

▲ Ellis Medicine Wheel is located on the high plains overlooking the Saskatchewan River.

in use around the 14th and 15th centuries. New evidence suggests the Ellis wheel was constructed by aboriginal Blackfeet Indians. The central ring was a teepee ring which was used to secure the cover of a burial lodge, and the stone spokes attached to the ring represented honor and respect for the deceased within (indicating that he was probably a renowned warrior or Indian chief). Skeletal and other bone fragments found within the ring revealed the burial spot to be opposite the doorway of the teepee, a place of honor for most Plains Indians. Such death lodge burials were most common among the Blackfeet tribe.

A major excavation and archaeological investigation was carried out at the site on the Stuffield Military Reserve north of Medicine Hat between 1974 and 1980. Several test pits were excavated by troweling and shovel shaving—an archaeological technique similar to the operation of a land surveyor searching for rust remains of old iron posts that originally marked property corners. Arrowheads and stone tools were found, along with human bone fragments under some of the stone cairns. A partially decomposed wooden post found at the site was submitted to radiocarbon analysis, indicating that the site was built or in use between 1270 and 1590 CE. The posthole suggests that they likely held upright timbers so that the original site would have a three-dimensional look, somewhat like Stonehenge in England.

Critical questions remain surrounding the medicine wheels. Why would Plains Indians need to watch the sky? Agricultural tribes in the east and southwest may have needed to keep track of the growing seasons, but the nomadic Plains people lived by tracking and hunting bison herds. Other rock piles point to the seasonal rising and setting of several brilliant stars. Could the people who built the wheels have an association with earlier agricultural tribes who planted crops? Did the solstice mark the summer turning point for them, a time to identify the turning of the seasons and an indication to start counting the days until the start of their summer migration? Such questions may never be answered because those who laid out the medicine wheels have long vanished, leaving later generations few clues to the strange monuments they left behind.

### Getting to Ellis Medicine Wheel

The Ellis Medicine Wheel is located on the eastern fringe of the CFB Suffield military base in southeastern Alberta. Visits must be arranged through Range Control Operations: (403) 544-4310, or (403) 544-4404. Access will only be permitted depending on the extent of military exercises each day. A range awareness briefing and a personnel escort to the site are required for all visitors. The historic site is located on an environmentally protected area of the base just above the Saskatchewan River valley. The entrance to the base is 4 miles (6 km) from the town of Suffield on route 884. Suffield is a small town in southeastern Alberta located 25 miles (42 km) west of Medicine Hat on Canadian Highway 1.

## Lac Sainte Anne

Around the turn of the century in the late 1890s, Alberta was beset by several years of the worst drought in recorded history. The farmers and animals, both wild and domestic, suffered through the sweltering summer months in desperate misery. By midsummer of another virtually rainless year, adverse conditions were becoming intolerable. A Roman Catholic missionary went to a known Native American holy lake to pray and what he noticed was extraordinary. He witnessed an unusually large number of birds and other animals gathering at the lakeshore. The missionary noticed that many of the animals appeared to be suffering from various ailments. Yet after drinking from the lake or splashing the water on their bodies, the animals appeared to be strengthened and relieved. Why this lake the missionary wondered? He shared his observations with his fellow priests who also noticed the peculiar phenomenon. While the priests had been praying for a long time at the mission for an end to the drought, they all decided to renew their prayers on the shores of Lac Sainte Anne, where the animals appeared to seek relief from trouble. After five days and five nights of uninterrupted supplications, rain came in large enough quantities to end the long-standing drought. Ever since, Roman Catholic pilgrimages culminate here on July 26th for the saint's feast day, sometimes attracting as many as 40,000 people.

Sainte Anne is revered as the mother of the Virgin Mary and the grandmother of Jesus Christ. While not mentioned in the Bible, stories of Anne and her husband Joachim are found in early Christian writings. She is often portrayed with a youthful Mary at her side holding a book and teaching her daughter how to read.

In 1876, Pope Pius IX declared Sainte Anne as the Patroness of Canada. Devotion to Sainte Anne has been widespread throughout the world and many thousands of cures have been attributed to her miracle working intercession. French trappers were the first Europeans to pass through Alberta and named the lake in her honor.

> Lac Sainte Anne has taken on the descriptive title "Lourdes of Alberta." Long before Catholic priests recognized its healing powers, the lake was known by the First Nation people as "Big Medicine."

The lake waters are believed by adherents of several religious persuasions to have curative properties, attracting thousands of Native Americans and Roman Catholic pilgrims every year for healing. While the First Nations and Roman Catholics have two very different religious beliefs, it is interesting to note that both are drawn to worship at the same hallowed location. Lac Sainte Anne has been revered by Native tribes for many centuries as "Big Medicine Lake." The history of the lake stretches back to the distant past. Here Native families, who in the fall had scattered to winter camps and trap lines, gathered in the summer for the buffalo hunt. The Crees called the lake *Manito Sakahigan* meaning "Spirit Lake." The Sioux living nearby named it *Waka Mne* or "Holy Lake." Tribal peoples believe it has been specifically set aside by the Earth Mother to nurture all living creatures—animal and human alike. When the Roman Catholic priests were surprised by the restorative effect on animals at the lake, it did not surprise resident Indians.

Although the water is considered curative all year round, only during the five-day commemoration every mid-July do the Roman Catholics take notice of the healing potential regarded as miraculous by more than a century of pilgrimage. Scientific examinations have detected a large mineral content in the water that can explain the basis for the lake's medicinal qualities. From a collective consciousness standpoint, 40,000 people focusing their energy on the lakes' healing properties can create a very real effect on the higher levels of cures that occur at Lac Sainte Anne. Pilgrims from all parts of Canada and around the world descend upon the lake to relieve afflictions of the

▲ A statue of Saint Anne with her daughter the Virgin Mary near the shore of the famous healing lake.

177

body, mind and soul. Many people travel great distances in a solemn pilgrimage with serious health afflictions to seek relief at the lake. Their convocation also commemorates the miraculous events from the late 1890s. The annual appearance of thousands of pilgrims is essentially a celebration of the lake's sacred character. This pilgrimage, which began over a hundred years ago, has become the largest annual Catholic gathering in western Canada.

### Getting to Lac Sainte Anne

Lac Sainte Anne is located 48 miles (75 km) northwest of Edmonton, Alberta. Traveling west on Highway 16 out of the city, turn north on Highway 43. A sign indicating the road to Lac Sainte Anne will appear on the left. A tiny community by the same name resides on the lakeshore, in the Great Plains wilderness northwest of Edmonton.

## Majorville Medicine Wheel

Archaeoastronomy is a relatively new science that interprets the study of astronomical beliefs and practices of ancient or preliterate peoples, combined with verifiable astronomical sightings. In North America, archaeoastronomy has been applied to the interpretation of mound sites and "woodhenges" in the eastern United States, and the curious stone arrangements of the northern Great Plains called medicine wheels. These circular stone patterns were originally named medicine wheels because the word "medicine" suggests a mystical power to Native Americans, and the medicine wheels are not fully understood. Some of these stone structures, found on the high plains and mountains, show consistent astronomical alignments.

Often compared to its counterpart in Wyoming, the Bighorn Medicine Wheel, the Majorville wheel is slightly larger, yet less developed. Both wheels contain 28 spokes and are generally the same shape with similar alignments. Archaeological evidence suggests that the Bighorn wheel was built in stages, beginning probably 300 or 400 years ago. The Moose Mountain Medicine Wheel in Saskatchewan, built about 1,700 years ago, and the Majorville Medicine Wheel were also built in stages. Research suggests that all three wheels served the same function and were built by the same people. Distinctive features of all three wheels are their alignments to the sunrise at summer solstice and to the four brightest stars of midsummer dawn—Aldebaran, Fomalhaut, Rigel, and Sirius. The Bighorn wheel also has cairns outside the circle to establish alignments marking the solstices, as well as the rising of certain stars. The Majorville wheel is built upon a prominent hill, and the Bighorn wheel is constructed at an altitude of 9,640 feet (2,892 m) upon Medicine Mountain near Sheridan, Wyoming.

A designated Canadian Provincial Historic Resource, the Majorville Medicine Wheel consists of a central cairn measuring 29 feet (9 m) in diameter and 5.3 feet

▲ The Majorville Medicine Wheel has the same number of spokes radiating from its center (28) as the number of poles used in a medicine lodge, or a Sun Dance ground, among the Sioux, Crow and Cheyenne.

(1.6 m) high, a surrounding stone ring 88 feet (27 m) in diameter, and 28 stone spokes connecting the two features. The 28 spokes likely represent the 28 days in a lunar month, suggesting this site was a ceremonial center as well as an astronomical calendar. The first excavation of the Majorville wheel started in 1971 and yielded a large number of artifacts that archaeologists can only "date" by style. The style of spear points and arrowheads changed in a regular manner over time, and archaeologists have determined the sequence of these changes. The central cairn inside the Majorville wheel was initially constructed some 4,500 years ago. Radiocarbon dating of bone from the bottom of the central cairn confirmed this date. The dating of the earliest layer at the Majorville wheel makes it 500 years older than the speculated date of Stonehenge in England. It appears that successive groups of people worshipped continually at this site, dropping arrowheads and adding new layers of rock from that early date until the coming of Europeans to Alberta.

> **The Majorville Medicine Wheel is the largest of its kind in Canada. It is also the oldest continuously used sacred site in North America.**

The long period of use, as well as overlapping construction of the central cairn, indicate that the Majorville site served different functions over the centuries. Excavation suggests that ceremonial activities pertaining to hunting successes and fertility of the bison were staged at Majorville. Significant stellar alignments have also been noted at the Majorville wheel, and would have served as a calendar to mark the shortest and longest days of the year, and the timing of important rituals. The small cairns outside the wheel, also called "spirit houses," marked important astronomical alignments and would have been incorporated in the seasonal rituals.

### Getting to Majorville

The Majorville Medicine Wheel has remained relatively undisturbed due to its isolation, but a highway is now being planned within three miles (5 km) of the site. The small prairie town of Milo is about 75 miles (120 km) southeast of Calgary, and the site is located just outside of the town. Most locals in Milo can give precise directions to the site. Milo is located on route 542 at the north end of McGregor Lake. The medicine wheel is located northeast of the Travers and Little Bow reservoirs, with the eastern boundary following the Bow River in Vulcan County.

# BRITISH COLUMBIA

The inland mountains, rivers, lakes and coastline of British Columbia (B.C.) are blessed with an abundance of breathtaking natural wonders. From the deep fjords of the Inside Passage, the Cascade volcanoes and the dramatic Rocky Mountains, to the proud traditions of the Pacific Northwest First Nation, B.C. is an adventure-lover's delight. Despite a temperate maritime climate, winter storms can be severe, bringing in huge amounts of light "powder" snow to the many ski resorts of B.C., which proudly boast of "the world's finest snow." Wildlife abounds in the province, especially in the ocean where killer whales (orcas), dolphins, porpoises, harbor seals, humpback, gray and minke whales make their home. Such abundance greatly influenced the worldview of the indigenous people who held a close interaction with the land and sea.

A new Canadian archeological project is gathering evidence to bolster an emerging theory that ancient seafarers were living in Canada at least 16,000 years ago during the last Ice Age. Federal researchers in British Columbia have begun probing an underwater site off the Queen Charlotte Islands for traces of prehistoric camps on the shores of an ancient lake long since submerged by the Pacific Ocean. Several significant finds have been made in raised caves along the B.C. coast and outlaying islands that were not inundated by the rising Pacific in post-glacial Canada. The new Parks Canada target is now at a site in the Gwaii Haanas National Park Reserve just north of Burnaby Island, near the southern end of the Queen Charlottes. Researchers have discovered evidence of a prehistoric lake and stream bed about 165 feet (50 m) below the surface at a site called Section Cove. The new findings may revolutionize our understanding of when and how humans first reached the New World.

## Queen Charlotte Islands (Haida Gwaii)

On the far western coast of Canada, not far from southern Alaska, the Queen Charlotte Islands (QCI) are among the last remaining virgin forest archipelagos in the world. The 154 isolated islands extend for 180 miles (300 km) along the northwestern coast of British Columbia. The two largest islands—Graham

Island in the north and Moresby in the south—are divided by the narrow Skidegate Channel and separated from mainland British Columbia by the Hecate Strait. Graham Island is the largest and most populated island. Despite only 5,500 residents living in the Queen Charlottes today, the islands once supported thousands more. Hundreds of generations of native Haida people have been nourished by the abundance of the land and sea. This is known because campfire charcoal found on the islands is dated to be over 10,000 years old. For many millennia, the Haida traveled the islands in cedar canoes. When their seafaring skills became refined, they journeyed to the mainland in war canoes to raid other villages. They became so adept at their ability to sack another village and flee that anthropologists have termed them the "Vikings of the Pacific Northwest." After Captain James Cook landed in 1778, and the Christian missionaries that soon followed, the indigenous Haida population was reduced by 90% of their pre-contact numbers by several smallpox epidemics. The lost Ninstints town is an abandoned ceremonial village on the southernmost Anthony Island, designated a World Heritage Site because it contains the largest grouping of original totem poles in the Pacific Northwest.

▲ Only totem poles remain at the abandoned Ninstints village on Anthony Island, southernmost of the Queen Charlotte Islands.
(photo courtesy QCI Department of Tourism)

The native Haida call the Queen Charlottes *Haida Gwaii*, meaning "Islands of the People." The Haida especially prized the southern portion of the archipelago called *Gwaii Haanas*, which translates as the "Islands of Wonder." On Anthony Island is *Sgan Gwaii*, or the "Red Cod Island" town. It is more popularly known as Ninstints, a European version of the word for the village head chief, Nan stins, or "He Who Is Two." Uninhabited by humans since the 1880s, when its population was annihilated by smallpox, the village today is considered by the Haida as the home to honored spirits. This abandoned homeland that once supported a thriving community for thousands of years is now slowly being returned to the verdant mosses of the old-growth forest. The Ninstints ghost town is distinguished by 15 totem poles carved more than 150 years ago by Haida artists renowned for their skills. Totem poles are actually heraldic columns of cedar announcing the crests and lineages of the Haida families. What's left of the old Haida culture can best be seen in the Haida Gwaii Museum in Skidegate, once the Haida village of *Quay'llnagaay*, or "Sealion Town." Old Massett is the northernmost town with a strong Haida culture and an abundance of totem poles. Song and dance remains integral to the ceremonial aspects of this age-old culture.

The egalitarian Haida lived in close harmony with the animals, land, and sea. According to one Haida creation myth, a trickster opened a clamshell near Graham Island that contained the first people and released them to live on *Haida Gwaii*. The oral history of the Haida goes back to stories of the great flood and the Ice Age, when a mythical ice woman swept down from above and wreaked climatic changes upon the mainland. Another creation myth of the first tree on *Haida Gwaii* was adopted as the crest for a prominent Haida family. The Haida believed in thunderbirds, flying animals so powerful that they could literally pick up small whales from the sea. Such a capture by a thunderbird is a common motif in Haida woodcarvings. It is interesting to note that other native populations of North America have thunderbird tales as well, with some tracing the oral and artistic tradition back 10,000 years. The fossil record of the flying dinosaur *Teratornis merriami* may be the root of the legends. Others think some kind of massive flying animals possibly lived in North America until recently.

> The nutrient-rich base and the wide diversity of wildlife on the Queen Charlottes have earned the island chain the title "Galapagos of Canada." Many animal and plant species of the QCI exist nowhere else on earth.

Prevailing southerly ocean currents kept the Queen Charlottes warm and free of permanent ice sheets when the rest of Canada was buried under colossal glaciers during the last Ice Age. Because of the mild Pacific Northwest climate the soil is very nutrient-rich, giving rise to enormous trees and lush moss forests in this unique temperate rainforest. The southern Moresby

Island is virtually uninhabited and is renowned for mushroom picking, lending the Queen Charlottes the nickname "Mushroom Capital of the World." The fresh water rivers are teeming with huge salmon. The entire western coast of the Queen Charlottes is uninhabited, yet is home to an estimated 1.5 million seabirds that nest on the coast from May through August. Japanese fishing floats and massive whalebones can be found washed ashore on the pristine beaches. Verdant forests with huge leaf conifer trees, abundant wildlife, mushrooms, berries and a rich marine environment give the impression that food is everywhere. Yet, however much the Queen Charlotte Islands many seem like a Garden of Eden, the times are changing. Over-fishing is beginning to affect the stable salmon stock and old growth deforestation has become a major problem. We can only hope that this last jewel of wilderness will be saved before modern progress claims yet another irreplaceable unique habitat.

### Getting to the Queen Charlotte Islands

The remote Queen Charlotte Islands (QCI) are very challenging to get to and travel within. If going the overland route it is possible to drive to Port Hardy on the northern tip of Vancouver Island and take a ferry to Prince Rupert, then change ferries to the QCI town Skidegate on the south end of northern Graham Island. The islands are situated 50 miles (80 km) west of mainland British Columbia. Local QCI ferries access southern Moresby Island. There are few paved roads on the QCIs and most overland travel is on gravel and logging roads. Gwaii Haanas National Park and Reserve is a remote area accessible only by aircraft, motorized boat or sea kayak. There are no roads and few services or facilities. For the most part, random camping is the rule in Gwaii Haanas. Only experienced and self-reliant travelers are recommended to explore on their own, otherwise commercial operators may be arranged for tours by calling 1-800-HelloBC, or the Gwaii Haanas office at (250) 559-8818, or the Queen Charlotte Visitor's Center at (250) 559-8316.

# Sproat Lake

For at least 10,000 years, the Pacific Northwest native people viewed the world as teeming with a variety of spirits that dwell within every facet of nature. Animistic spirits occupied all aspects of the material world, integrated in plants, animals, minerals and celestial objects. In the chill waters around Vancouver Island giant beasts like the Orcas swim, along with spawning fish and a myriad of edible sea creatures. In the air were the all-powerful residents of the sky—the raven, the sun, the wind, and the venerable eagle, often symbolic of the shaman. In the mist-shrouded forests the "four-legged" creatures stalked their quarry or sought shelter from pursuit in the dark shadows. Even from the stones that tumbled down the flanks of mountains and the echoes that filled the valleys, a vital force pervaded every fiber of existence. To honor benevolent spirits, the Pacific

183

Northwest tribes would carve elaborate masks, totem poles, and petroglyphs to portray the interwoven genealogies of man, animal, earth, and their supernatural forebears.

> Similar to the famous Paleolithic painted
> caves of Europe, Sproat Lake was a very early
> center for shamanistic rituals, especially
> revered for success in hunting and fertility.

The petroglyphs of Sproat Lake, called *K'ak'awin* by local tribes, are an excellent example of the many rock carving panels to be found along the Pacific Northwest coast. Panels of this style exist from Kodiak Island in Alaska all the way down the west coast to the Columbia River Gorge, bordering Washington state and Oregon. The Sproat Lake petroglyphs were almost certainly carved by the ancestors of the Nootka people who live on what is today Vancouver Island in British Columbia. Sproat Lake is special because of its lakeside location and the wide variety of sea creatures portrayed. Some archaeologists interpret the images as sea monsters living in Sproat Lake, while others view the site as a ceremonial center. It is believed that a shaman impersonating a whale would perform elaborate rituals in front of Nootka tribal members at this location, evoking the spirits of their ancestors, who would assist in propagating their people. Whoever held control over the natural world, such as a shaman holding control over sea creatures, could make recently deceased whales drift ashore near their village.

As with most coastal tribes, fish played an important role in their economy. Some of the Sproat Lake petroglyphs represent salmon, perhaps in a magical context. In the event the salmon were late in returning to their traditional spawning grounds, anxious and hungry Native Americans would call for them with all the ritual and magical powers they could muster. When the first salmon of the year was caught, it was welcomed with prolific thanks as the entrails were thrown back into the river so they could return to the salmon's home and tell how well it was treated. Rituals to prehistoric hunters and fishermen were extremely solemn events, oftentimes with the shaman entering a deep trance through dance where they would appear kidnapped by the spirits, returning to the temporal dimension with helpful information for the tribe. Both men and women were shaman among the First Nation people of the Pacific Northwest.

Petroglyphs are symbolic images inscribed in stone. They do not constitute writing, although they certainly convey specific meanings. Locations for rock art panels were carefully chosen. They were usually places of power or mystery where the forces of nature were believed to be especially strong. They are mostly located near unusual natural features such as caves, waterfalls, or, in the case of Sproat Lake, next to a mystical body of water. Since most sites are near water, they may have been situated along travel routes or near old village sites.

▲ The Sproat Lake "sea monster" petroglyphs represent deities of the water depicted on land for the purpose of shamanistic rituals. Perhaps by controlling the spirits of the water the shaman could control the mysterious forces of nature.

Petroglyph Provincial Park near Nanaimo provides the most concentrated and easily accessible collection of carvings. They are believed to be 10,000 years old, created at a time when the last glaciers melted on Vancouver Island. Perhaps the most interesting image is the beast known as the sea-wolf. Part killer whale and part wolf, this beast lived in his own village under the sea and was responsible for the destruction of the planet in a bygone era. Also in British Columbia, the Stein Valley is a traditional vision quest site, where hikers can still see faded rock paintings from spirit visions of First Nations youth.

## Getting to Sproat Lake

Sproat Lake Provincial Park is located on the north shore of Sproat Lake, 8 miles (13 km) northwest of Port Alberni. Access is directly off Highway 4, or off the Great Central Lake Road. The petroglyphs are located on a trail east of the Lower Campground on the north shore of the lake. Petroglyph Provincial Park is located off the main highway about 2.5 miles (4 km) south of Nanaimo, which is 16 miles (26 km) north of Ladysmith on Highway 1. Both sites are located on Vancouver Island. Camping reservations and general info line: (250) 474-1336.

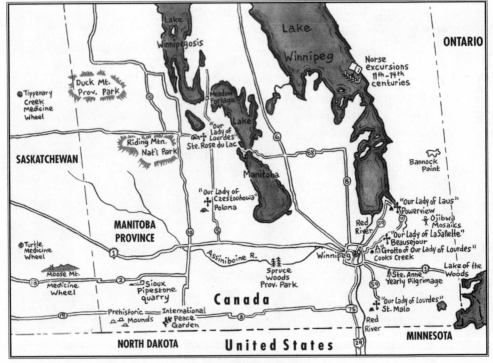

# MANITOBA

Once covered by glaciers, the province of Manitoba features many hundred freshwater lakes, some enormous in size such as Lake Winnipeg, Lake Manitoba, Lake Winnipegosis and Cedar Lake. Middle Age Norse explorers used the lake and river routes in Manitoba to access the Central Plains. They sailed around the Hudson Bay to the Nelson River drainage, down the vast Lake Winnipeg to a south shore feeder river called the Red River of the North that extended hundreds of miles southward into what is today North Dakota and Minnesota. The lake and river routes of Manitoba were considered so strategic that the capital of Winnipeg was built under the auspices that it could become a trade center rivaling the success of Chicago. The fertile soil and northern climates of Manitoba were attractive to the first European homesteaders, especially those from Slavic and Scandinavian countries. "The Forks" is a modern development in the heart of downtown Winnipeg at the junction of the Red and Assiniboine Rivers. This popular gathering place features a river promenade, a variety of international eateries, and unique local shops.

## Grottoes of Manitoba

In the heavily populated Ukrainian region of southern Manitoba there are several pilgrimage and grotto sites deeply revered by Catholics of Canada. Four of the seven large grottoes in Manitoba are dedicated to Our Lady of Lourdes, based on one of the most famous Roman Catholic shrines in Europe. The town of Lourdes, France was hardly more than a hamlet until 1858, the year a 14-year-old peasant girl named Bernadette Soubirous had the first of 18 visions of the Virgin Mary at a location called *Grotte de Massabielle*, by the Gave de Pau. Over a period of several months the young girl and many townspeople gathered at the riverside grotto and viewed an apparition of the Virgin Mary, or the "Immaculate Conception" as she described herself. Once the girl's visions were recognized by the Catholic Church, Lourdes experienced a building boom and is now one of the most visited locations in southern France. Among the multitude of visitors in the last century were priests from Canada who were profoundly impressed with the site and returned home with news of the Immaculate Conception. Several of these priests returned to Manitoba where they were inspired to recreate the Grotto of Lourdes with the help of parishioners. The result of their work is some of the finest recreated grottoes in North America, most built on the 100-year anniversary of the Lourdes' apparitions.

The Grottoes of Manitoba dot the countryside surrounding the capital Winnipeg. Several incorporate Roman Catholic pilgrimages to the shrines take place during various times of the year.

The largest Manitoba grotto devoted to Our Lady of Lourdes is near the small town of Cook's Creek, located adjacent to the Church of the Immaculate Conception. The magnificent Ukrainian Catholic Church of the Eastern Rite was engineered by the priest Philip Ruh in 1930. It replaced an old log church on the site. Its mastery of architecture soon earned it the title "Prairie Cathedral." With the church completed, Father Ruh set forth in 1954 building an immense grotto next door. The grotto was started in that year to be completed in time to commemorate the centenary (1858-1958) of the Immaculate Conception at Lourdes, France. The Grotto of Our Lady of Lourdes is a striking monument. It contains a beautiful altar and cave-like wings housing the Stations of the Cross. The Cook's Creek grotto was intended as a place for prayers, for spiritual solace, and as a pilgrimage destination. More than a monument, Father Ruh intended it to be "a living force for the peace of souls." Father Ruh was devoted to the Blessed Virgin Mary after making two visits to the mountain grotto of Lourdes and being deeply inspired by his experiences there. He intended the grotto at Cook's Creek to become a religious center for the Ukrainians of Canada, but he died before it was fully completed. Father Ruh devoted 32 years of his life to this parish and is buried in the adjacent cemetery. The nearby Cook's Creek Heritage Museum is a tribute to the early pioneers from Ukraine and Poland, eager to make a new life for themselves in Canada. This museum features traditional Slavic clothing, folk art, religious articles and Manitoba's smallest chapel.

▲ Our Lady of Lourdes grotto, Sainte Rose du Lac. This grotto and many others like it in Manitoba were popular places of pilgrimage to commemorate the 100th anniversary of the apparitions at Lourdes, France.

Authentic pioneer homes are located on the grounds and represent life at the turn of the century. "Heritage Day" takes place in August and the festivities include folk music, traditional foods, and pioneer demonstrations.

The second largest grotto devoted to Our Lady of Lourdes is at Sainte Rose du Lac near Dauphin. In 1953, Father Isaie Desautels traveled to France on the occasion of his 25th anniversary into the priesthood. Deeply inspired by his visit, he returned to his parish and immediately set forth building a grotto to commemorate the centennial of the apparitions at Lourdes of 1858. It was designed to be an authentic replica of the Lourdes grotto. Completed in 1961—replete with five Italian statues and a stairway built on both sides of the grotto continuing to the base of the Calvary—the first pilgrimage took place on July 8th, 1962. Pilgrimages continue every two or three years to the shrine. Outdoor mass and marriages are occasionally performed at the Sainte Rose du Lac grotto.

### Getting to the Grottoes of Manitoba

Cook's Creek is located on Highway 212 just outside of Winnipeg. A short distance from Cook's Creek is the Our Lady of La Sallette grotto in Beausejour on Highway 4 from Winnipeg. Further north near Lake Winnipeg in the town of Powerview is the Our Lady of Laus grotto on Highway 11. South of Winnipeg are two Our Lady of Lourdes grottoes, one in Saint Norbert on Highway 75, and the other in Saint Malo on South 59. Also on South 59 is Sainte Anne des Chenes village, destination of the Sainte Anne yearly pilgrimage on July 26th. On the western border of Manitoba is the Czestoohawa grotto in Poloma, off Highway 5. Due north on Highway 5 is the Our Lady of Lourdes grotto in Sainte Rose du Lac. For additional information on directions and pilgrimages to the various grottoes, visitors can call the Archdiocese of Winnipeg at (204) 452-2227.

# SASKATCHEWAN

Second only to Alberta, Saskatchewan contains more medicine wheels than any other province in Canada or in all of the United States. In general, Canadian wheels are less developed, but more frequent, than their American counterparts. Many Canadian sites are simply large cairns, yet not all of them have spokes, rings or other associated features. A common feature of Saskatchewan medicine wheels is that most are located on prairie hilltops with sweeping views of the horizon in all directions. Such locations may have acted as strategic lookouts or consecrated ceremonial centers, but most likely they served as astronomical observatories. The medicine wheels with spokes were used to sight key events, such as equinoxes, prominent summertime stars, the summer solstice sunrise, or the start of the Algonquian New Year. Just outside of the provincial capital Saskatoon is *Wanuskewin*, a Cree Indian name meaning "being in harmony." It is a location of many teepee rings, several prehistoric archaeological sites, and a medicine wheel. All Plains Indians recognized Wanuskewin as a neutral prayer center. The medicine wheel is now within a protected national park, including a sweat lodge still in usage.

## Moose Mountain Medicine Wheel

The highest point on the western arm of the Moose Mountain hills is a long ridge called "The Beaut" because of its sweeping views and strategic lookout vantage points. On the pinnacle of this ridge is where the famous Moose Mountain Medicine Wheel is situated. The name is a bit of a misnomer because the wheel is not located on a mountain per se, but on a wind-swept rise on the open prairies of southeastern Saskatchewan. The 560-foot (168-m) treeless crest where the wheel is located resembles the humped back of a moose. The Moose Mountain Medicine Wheel consists of a central cairn, a middle ring, and five smaller rock piles connected by five stone spoke lines. Although 425 miles (685 km) apart, Moose Mountain bears a strong resemblance to the astrological alignments of the Bighorn Medicine Wheel in Wyoming. The similarity in their construction has led to the speculation that they were built by the same aboriginal culture. With five spokes and an elliptic inner rim, its structure is simpler than the Bighorn wheel, and is most likely an earlier version. It is twice as large as Bighorn in diameter, making it the second largest medicine wheel in the world, second only to

Majorville. Significantly, it contains the same number of cairns placed in similarly related positions with the Bighorn wheel. At the end of the longest spoke, the largest and most prominent cairn lines up with the hub to mark the sunrise on the summer solstice. Just like the Bighorn wheel in Wyoming, the Moose Mountain wheel is aligned to the four brightest stars of midsummer dawn—Aldebaran, Fomalhaut, Rigel, and Sirius. The directions indicated by the star-alignment cairns are a few degrees off their present location, but would have been in direct alignment in an earlier age. Because of the procession of the equinox, time has shifted their relative positions from where they would have appeared 2,000 years ago.

> The northern Plains Indians regarded
> the Moose Mountain Medicine Wheel as
> a spiritual site devoted to the sky. The
> solstice-aligned boulder configurations date
> the wheel to be at least 1,700 years old.

A common feature of most North American medicine wheels are alignments directed to the summer solstice, a date which might have been used for sun worshiping activities or to determine specific hunting or planting seasons. Most of these stone structures, primarily found on high prairie plateaus or mountains, show consistent astronomical alignments. At the Bighorn and Moose Mountain medicine wheels there is one central rock pile and several outlying cairns useful for star sightings. These star alignments are now slightly off. This altered alignment is a result of the slow movement of the night sky called the procession of

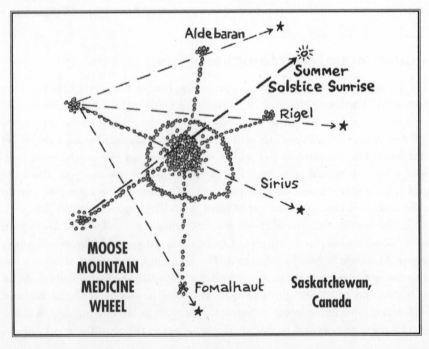

the equinox. The procession is a slight westward shift of the equinoctial points along the plane of the ecliptic resulting in a slight procession of the earth's axis of rotation over a long period of time. For example, the arc is a mere 50.27 seconds per year and any discernible change of the night sky to the naked eye would take more than 70 years. Archaeoastronomers have determined at least two cairns at Moose Mountain align with the solstice sunrise, while the others align with the rising points of bright stars that herald the approach of the solstice when they rose in the pre-dawn sky of 2,000 years ago. Incidentally, one of the cairns would have aligned with the star Capella when it was visible far enough south to rise and set. For several hundred years this star would have been an ideal north sky marker. The sun rising or setting on days near the summer or winter solstice makes an angle of about 30 degrees with a horizontal horizon. There is also indication of a stone "arrow" on another ridge pointing west to the Ellis Wheel in Alberta that could have acted as a directional marking to Ellis, or a domain marker for the Sioux nation.

As important as the Moose Mountain Medicine Wheel may be, it is in serious danger of being lost forever. First documented by Canadian land surveyors in 1895, the original report described the central rock cairn of Moose Mountain as being about 14 feet (4.2 m) in height, yet now the same rock pile is about two feet (0.6 m) high. The problem is people are visiting the site and taking medicine wheel rocks home with them as souvenirs. Moose Mountain is slowly disappearing one stone at a time. As few are protected, many are vanishing and Moose Mountain is not alone in this plight. Theft, vandalism and agriculture have reduced the thousands of original medicine wheels on the northern plains to about 70 intact today. Native Americans and archaeologists both fear the majority of remaining North America medicine wheels may be gone by the next generation.

## Getting to Moose Mountain Medicine Wheel

Moose Mountain Medicine Wheel is located atop the highest hill in the area, just to the southwest of Moose Mountain Provincial Park. The site is on private land within the Pheasant Rump Nakota Reservation, and is still an actively worshipped First Nation sacred location. A Nakota family that lives just below the site manages the wheel and a nearby sweat lodge. Visitors must request permission to enter the property. The site is located 7.5 miles (13 km) north of the town Kisbey on Route 605.

# THE ROCKY MOUNTAINS

*When we try to pick out anything by itself we find that it is bound fast by a thousand invisible cords that cannot be broken to everything else in the universe. ... The clearest way into the universe is through a forest wilderness.* -**John Muir**

THE CONTINENTAL DIVIDE FORMS THE WESTERN BACKBONE of the continent, stretching along the highest peaks of the Rocky Mountains like an imaginary rope. From British Columbia to Mexico, the Divide is the separation of watersheds where many of the great rivers in North America originate. The Rockies were formed about 1.7 billion years ago, but geologists estimate it will take over a million years for the range to erode away. These relatively new mountains were a formidable barrier for the earliest arrivals of humans migrating from Asia. Some groups never made it much farther. The Nez Percé of northern Idaho can genetically trace their descendants to the original hunters who crossed the Bering Strait Land Bridge during the last Ice Age. Unlike the isolated Nez Percé, other tribes around the Rocky Mountains were more transient. The Ute tribe migrated to the southern Rocky Mountain region only a few hundred years ago, while different groupings of Puebloan people in southern Colorado and Utah had been there for thousands of years longer. Of all the native tribes originally living in Colorado, only the Utes were granted a reservation within the state. Some ancient people, like the cliff-dwelling Anasazi, had disappeared long before the first Europeans arrived.

A new national monument in Colorado commemorates and preserves relics of the earliest civilizations. Canyons of the Ancients near the Four Corners region has the highest known archaeological-site density in the nation, but many of the sites are in remote backcountry regions and overgrown by vegetation.

In 1803, President Thomas Jefferson commissioned Meriwether Lewis and William Clark to find "the most direct and practicable water communication across the continent, for the purposes of commerce." Captains Lewis and Clark assembled 26 volunteers and Army regulars, Clark's black slave York, and Lewis's Newfoundland dog, Seaman. Together the expedition was known as the Corps of Discovery. The group departed St. Louis in May, 1804 and by mid-August, 1805 their travels brought them to Three Forks, Montana—the headwaters of the Missouri River. At this point they were beyond the western border of the Louisiana Purchase and for the first time entering a land about which they had no knowledge. It was the Rocky Mountain homeland of the Lemhi Shoshoni, Mandan, Salish, and Nez Percé people, a land that nurtured sophisticated societies with ample resources, where family was foremost and the elderly were valued. Expedition members had no idea how they would be received, but realized with each passing day that their continued success was entirely dependent on Native American goodwill. Lewis and Clark knew that rivers flowed westward from the Continental Divide, but greatly underestimated the expansiveness of the Rocky Mountain wilderness. Even with native assistance, the search for a "Northwest Passage" would prove to be the most difficult leg of their entire journey.

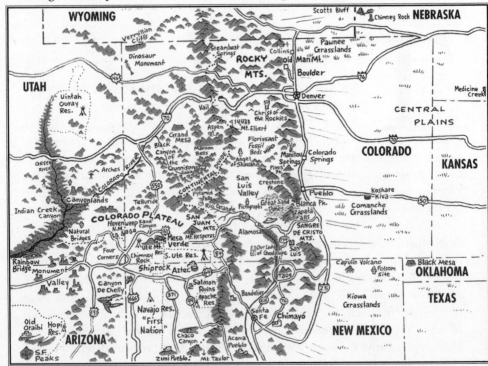

# COLORADO

The "Centennial State" is steeped in a rich history where the buffalo were plenty and Native American cultures once flourished. The eastern Rocky Mountains were inhabited by the earliest Paleo-Indians for thousands of years before the first modern Europeans arrived. The Ancestral Puebloan culture is preserved in the many cliff-dwelling stone buildings, concentrated mainly in the southwestern Four Corners region of the state. The territory that eventually became Colorado was originally claimed by the Spanish, then by the French, before the United States began to acquire it in stages beginning with the 1803 Louisiana Purchase. Colorado became a territory in 1861 and a state in 1876. Considerable growth appeared in the state during an 1859 gold and silver rush in the towns of Clear Creek, Central City and Black Hawk. The influx of settlers greatly disrupted the Native American lifestyle until nearly every tribe was displaced out of state, or confined to a reservation. After the tribes were contained, settlement in Colorado began in earnest and the modern west began to take shape.

## Manitou Springs

Tucked within the foothills of Pikes Peak, Manitou Springs is an ancient network of 26 mineral fountains, some from sources reported to be 20,000 years old. The water originates when rainwater and snowmelt from "America's Mountain" and the surrounding area soaks into rock fractures. As the water penetrates down to the mile-deep aquifer, it becomes heated and mineralized. The warm water then flows back up the Ute Pass fault zone into cavernous limestone and dolomite chambers where it becomes carbonated. When the water percolates up from the subterranean caverns it absorbs high levels of carbonic acid and strong concentrations of minerals. The carbonic acid is what gives the water its' bubbles. Each spring has a distinct mineral flavor, effervescence, or renowned medicinal quality. Because the water takes thousands of years to complete its journey from mountain source to Manitou Springs, it is totally free from the accumulation of industrial and atmospheric contamination acquired in the recent centuries of rampant pollution. Unlike most other mineralized springs, these springs are cool and pleasant to drink.

The sparkling-pure water fountains are located in a verdant box canyon adjacent to the bizarre rock formations called the Garden of the Gods. The whole wilderness area must have been an impressive sight before it became developed. Now removed, large mineral deposits dating back thousands of years had created natural basins into which the soda water erupted and overflowed into a stream. Before the springs were capped, a deep rumbling could be heard as the gasses and water boiled up in dramatic fashion. Large groves of cottonwoods, abundant wildlife and unusual rock formations completed the picture. Such a location made a strong impression on the Native Americans, who viewed the surrounding area as a sacred place where humans and the spiritual world could interact.

> Manitou Springs was a neutral gathering place for many Native Americans. It was recognized that the springs' unusual effervescence was the result of the Great Spirit breathing air into the water.

For thousands of years, various Plains Indian and mountain tribes paid homage to the sacred mineral fountains. The immediate area surrounding the springs was considered neutral territory for every tribe. Manitou Springs, like all natural spring areas in North America, were special locations where anyone could relieve their physical ailments without the concern of having to defend themselves. The Native American diet was especially hard on the digestive tract and the soda water was the perfect tonic. It also had miraculous healing properties for their dry skin. The word *Manitou* comes from an Algonquian term that translates as "Great Spirit," but is not the name given by the tribes who worshipped at the springs. These cool water springs were holy to the Ute, Apache, Arapahoe, Sioux, Comanche, Shoshone, Kiowa, and Cheyenne, who knew them as the "Medicine Fountains." They believed the medicinal properties were bequeathed from the breath of the Great Spirit itself. It was common practice for Native Americans who convalesced at Manitou to leave gifts at the edge of the springs such as beads, clothing, talismans, blankets, robes, knives and other items of gratitude.

Very close to Manitou Springs is a region called the Garden of the Gods, but known to Native Americans as the "Old Red Lands." Various tribes would gather for rituals amidst the elegant spires, jagged pinnacles and spirit faces in the rock. For the Mountain Ute, whose culture dates back hundreds of years and continues to thrive, the towering red sandstone formations were a spiritual site used for

▲ 19th century photo of Indians on horseback descending Ute pass.

vision quest. It was also a destination for the dying. When Ute elders who felt their time in this world was finished they would climb the cliffs and wedge themselves into crevices until they passed over into the spiritual realms. Their bodies would later be removed to a nearby burial site. The Ute Indians used the mountain trail now known as Ute Pass to travel from Colorado Springs to their wintering camps on the western plains. This trail also made a convenient road for early settlers and prospectors. In the mid-1800s, Native Americans became increasingly unhappy with the influx of visitors to their spiritual sites and hunting grounds. The inevitable conflicts didn't end until the U.S. Calvary force-fully removed the Cheyennes and Arapahos to a reservation out of state in 1868. The Utes remained friendly and camped in the area until they too were relocated in 1879 to a reservation in the southwest corner of Colorado.

In the late 1870s, developers created the resort of Manitou Springs to provide popular water therapies derived from Indian remedies. Cultural and medicinal traditions brought prosperity to the resort town, centrally located around the famous springs. The naturally effervescent water was bottled and sold, starting a nationwide trend in Manitou Springs where the first carbonated drinks were introduced. As the town continued to grow, many of the springs were considered nuisances and were plugged or diverted. Many of the original locations became paved over and forgotten. Today, most of the original 26 Manitou mineral springs are capped and some are pumped to the surface in the form of fountains. While the natural ambience is lost, local Utes say the spiritual magnetism of the area still remains.

### Getting to Manitou Springs

The town of Manitou Springs is nestled in a box canyon on the eastern flank of the 14,110-foot (4,233-m) Pikes Peak, also known as "America's Mountain." Follow Highway 24 west about 4 miles (6.5 km), or 10 minutes out of Colorado Springs, then turn off at the Manitou Springs exit. Only nine springs, scattered around the town, remain flowing and open to the public. Entrance to the Garden of the Gods is off the same exit, but located on the other side of Route 24. Admission is free to both the Garden of the Gods and the various parks of Manitou Springs, each featuring a unique mineral fountain. Overlooking the historic town of Manitou Springs is the ancient Anasazi-built Manitou Cliff Dwellings.

## Mesa Verde

Around 2,000 years ago an industrious and creative people were attracted to the forested slopes on the high "green table" plateau of southwestern Colorado. The many deep sandstone canyons and overhanging cliffs provided primitive shel-ter, while the plateau offered near ideal farming conditions. As their culture and farming abilities developed, the people known as the northern San Juan Anasazi started building permanent structures. The finest example of Anasazi construc-tion, aided in their preservation by being under cliffs, is the location known as Mesa Verde. The superbly preserved structures, including multistoried dwellings huddled beneath mesa cliffs towering 2,000 feet (600 m) overhead, became the center of the Anasazi culture that existed in the Southwest and southern Rocky Mountain region for about a thousand years. The term *Anasazi* derives from the Navajo term meaning "Ancient Ones," or "Ancient Enemies." Also regarded as the Ancestral Puebloans, these may be the forefathers of the people who currently live along the Rio Grande River and on high mesas in New Mexico and Arizona.

The modern-day Pueblo, Zuni, Tiwa and Hopi Indians are likely direct descendants of the Anasazi, that is, if the Anasazi never completely dispersed or died out. During the seven centuries the Anasazi inhabited Mesa Verde (550 – 1270 CE), they prospered and developed from a basic hunter and gatherer society into a refined culture known for its advanced agricultural techniques, intricate artistry, and magnificent architecture.

▲ One of the many cliff dwelling settlements at Mesa Verde National Park.

Over a century of archaeological investigation at Mesa Verde has painted a fairly accurate cultural picture of the Anasazi people. Data and artifacts collected from the pioneering Wetherill family's simple record keeping have advanced to extremely detailed excavations and technical reports by the National Park Service and university scientists. Displays in the Chapin Mesa Museum portray a realistic insight into the lifestyles of the cliff-dwellers. Spruce Tree House is considered Mesa Verde's best-preserved structure. The famous Cliff Palace is the most widely recognized settlement largely due to its size, which at 217 rooms is North America's largest cliff dwelling. One obvious sacred structure is the Sun Temple, an oval shaped foundation of stones perched on a 2,500-foot (750-m) cliff with an expansive view to the south. The architecture spans from elaborate stonework masonry to mysterious tunnels, and from towers to ceremonial *kivas*, along with a four-story structure that oddly resembles a modern high-rise. Visitors to Mesa Verde are usually impressed by the abundance of cliff dwellings, numbering over 600 within the park boundaries. Outside the two popularly-visited canyons, other sites in the backcountry held extreme spiritual value to the prehistoric Anasazi. Tucked away in the steep ravines and hidden caves are the native *sipapu* pits, constructed for ceremonies to portray our human origins. In other remote locations are carvings of spirals and petroglyphs indicating prayer niches for native shaman.

"Mesa Verde" is Spanish for green table, describing the high fertile plateau where the famous cliff dwellings can be found. At its peak, the Mesa Verde settlements once supported 7,000 people. It was abandoned around 1300 CE for unknown reasons.

Around 1200 CE the Anasazi culture entered into a century of decline. A combination of overpopulation, crop failure, drought, and possibly warfare or disease played a role in their demise. From Arizona to New Mexico and Colorado, the Anasazi people began migrating south and all but disappeared from their homeland in a hundred years. Their farms were left unattended, their magnificent cities abandoned and their people dispersed. No conclusive reason has been given for their downfall, but an extended drought seems to be the most likely reason. By the time the Navajo arrived from the north, the cliff dwellings had all been abandoned. The Navajo never occupied the ruins, citing the fearful presence of Anasazi spirits protecting the ghost dwellings.

The first mention of Mesa Verde comes from Professor J.S. Newberry in 1859 during the height of the Colorado gold rush. Additional cliff dwellings in the Mesa Verde region continued to be discovered in the decades following the first discovery, and some were looted of artifacts. Concerned citizens in the 1890s urged the government to preserve the ancient ruins. Mesa Verde National Park was established by Congress in June, 1906, enacted by President Theodore Roosevelt, becoming the first national park exclusively devoted to archaeological remains. Mesa Verde contains over 52,000 acres (20,800 ha) in total, and was the first national park in the United States set aside to preserve the prehistoric legacy of Native Americans. Even today, Mesa Verde National Park is the largest archaeological preserve in the United States and contains the largest concentration of cliff dwellings ever found. Today nearly 3,900 individual sites have been located within the park, and over 600 of these are the characteristic cliff dwellings. Mesa Verde is America's first World Heritage Site, designated in 1978 as a "World Heritage Cultural Park," and also holds the distinction of being one of the eight original UNESCO sites. Hundreds of outlaying houses, granaries and crumbled villages are scattered around Mesa Verde, telling the story of a civilization's dynamic growth and puzzling decline, spanning eight centuries.

## Getting to Mesa Verde

Mesa Verde National Park is located in southwestern Colorado, situated high on the Colorado Plateau. The park entrance is 9 miles (15 km) from Cortez heading east on Highway 160, or an hour's drive from Durango, Colorado heading west on Highway 160 to the park turnoff. America's premier archaeological wonder is open every day of the year, but some of the mesa sites are closed during the winter. Spruce Tree House and the museum are open all year round. The Cliff Palace and Balcony House are closed from mid-October until mid-April. The Wetherill Mesa ruins are open only from Memorial Day until Labor Day. Call (970) 529-4465 for more information. Canyons of the Ancients and the Anasazi Heritage Center Museum are both located just outside of Dolores, Colorado along Highway 184.

San Cristobal, NM

Chaco Canyon, NM
Gila Bend, NM
Old Oraibi, AZ

Monument Valley, AZ & UT

Los Alamos, NM

# Kokopelli

St. Johns, AZ

Cieneguita, NM

Peterborough, CANADA

Sand Island, UT

## Kokopelli

Nearly everywhere that primitive people roamed in western North America, they left an enduring record of their culture in the form of pictures etched on rocks. One of the principal rock art symbols of the Four Corners region is the hunchbacked flute player called Kokopelli. This anthropomorphic being's frequent and widespread appearance on pottery and pictography suggest that he was well-traveled and a universally recognized deity of considerable potency. Symbolizing variously as a water sprinkler, a wandering minstrel, a fertility enhancer, or an inspired musician, Kokopelli in all these variations has come to be known as the "Casanova of the Ancient Ones." While his name certainly varied over the centuries among the different cultures that depicted him, the modern name "Kokopelli" derives from the northwestern Arizona Hopi people who have a *kachina* god named after the humpbacked flute player. Regardless of the other names this traveling pied piper may have gone by, his image spreads far beyond his original Four Corners homeland.

## San Luis Valley

The picturesque San Luis Valley in southern Colorado is surrounded on three sides by soaring 14,000-foot (4,200-m) mountains. The Continental Divide extends along the San Juan Mountains to the west, the Saguache Mountains form the northern boundary, and the Sangre de Cristo Mountains enclose the valley to the east. Despite such formidable obstacles, the San Luis Valley has long been a crossroads to many different people at many different times. North America's earliest Paleo-Indians wandered deep into the expansive valley in search of game. These prehistoric hunters, called the Clovis Culture by archaeologists, killed long-extinct mammoth, bison, and giant sloth in the San Luis Valley over 10,000 years ago. Their characteristic projectile points, ancient rock quarries and the bones of their prey have been discovered in various locations around the valley. From the Sangre de Cristo watershed the Arkansas River flows east, and from the San Juan Mountains the Rio Grande flows south. The unusual Great Sand Dunes dominate the eastern side of the basin and several sacred mountains rim the valley. Many Native Americans considered the San Luis Valley a holy place, and made yearly migrations. In more recent times, some of the earliest European settlers in the Southwest migrated to the valley and stayed. The "Hispanic Southwest" extends from Mexico northward up the San Luis Valley, where it culturally blends into the Anglo-influenced Rocky Mountain west.

Neatly tucked below Blanca Peak in the northeast corner of the valley are the Great Sand Dunes, the tallest sand dunes in North America. To the Tewa Puebloans of New Mexico, the Great Sand Dunes were called "Sandy Place Lake," where their ancestors along with all earthly plants and animals emerged from the World Beneath. The Tewa people—now relocated to six villages near Santa Fe—believe that upon death all beings return to the dunes to reenter the Pueblo spirit world through this symbolic passageway. Taos Pueblo people similarly believe that their people emerged from a lake called *Sipapu*, thought to be high on the slopes of Taos Peak, located in the southern San Luis Valley. The warm colors and smooth, wind-shaped dunes glow beneath the rugged backdrop of the Sangre de Cristo Mountains. Dominating the Sangre de Cristo range, Blanca Peak is known by the Navajo as *Sisnaajini*, the sacred mountain of the east. Navajo people mark their ancestral boundary with four such mountains—denoting a home for their Holy People, and a vital source of medicinal herbs and spiritual power. It is considered the "leader mountain" to the Navajo, because it stands as the holy mountain to the east, the place of beginnings, and the source of dawn's early light. The Navajo, Ute, Jicarilla Apache and ten other tribes once considered the peak and valley as extremely sacred. Before the breakdown of Native American traditional ceremonies in the last few decades, Navajo elders ventured over 500 miles from Arizona to perform their blessings on *Sisnaajini* the holy mountain, or "the place where all thought originates." Ute men used Blanca

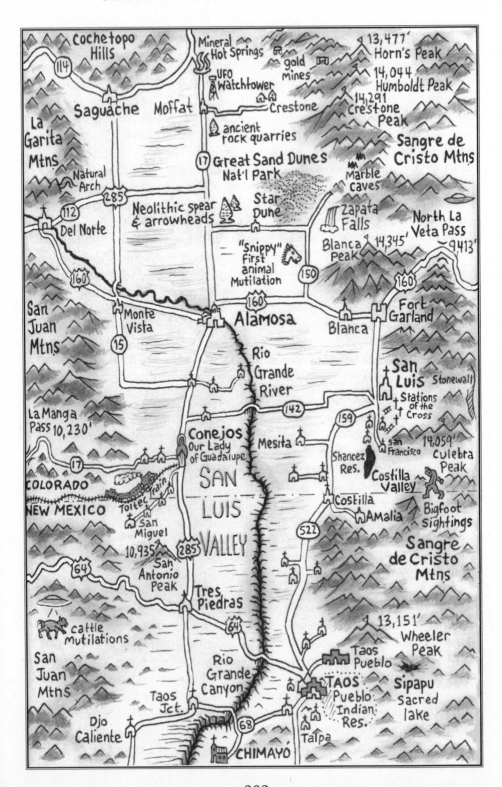

Peak during their meditative vision quests, trained their buffalo ponies in the dunes, and performed certain rituals in the valley. A few Jicarilla Apache continue to collect sand from the Great Sand Dunes for their ceremonies.

> Towering over the Great Sand Dunes in San Luis Valley is Blanca Peak, a mountain held sacred by the Navajo, Ute, Taos Pueblo and Jicarilla Apache for thousands of years.

In the decades following Mexico's independence from Spain in 1821, Mexican and Spanish ranchers migrated north to settle in the San Luis Valley. Huge land grants were given to individual citizens by Mexico, later to be recognized by the United States. Spanish colonists who arrived from northern New Mexico in 1851 established the first town in Colorado they named San Luis. Colorado's oldest church stands in Conejos, about 40 miles (65 km) from San Luis town. Named for its patron saint, *Nuestra Senora De Guadalupe*, Our Lady of Guadalupe Catholic Parish was selected in 1863 as the first permanent church in the state. Even in the 21st century, the San Luis Valley retains a strong Spanish-influenced flavor. Overlooking the town of San Luis is a mile-long trail depicting the Stations of the Cross—a series of graphic statues depicting the final hours of Christ's life.

In the last few decades the San Luis Valley has achieved a new kind of notoriety. The world's first reported animal mutilation case called "Snippy the Horse" occurred in September, 1967 on the King Ranch near the Great Sand Dunes. As a result of this case, the San Luis Valley is regarded as the publicized birthplace of the highly unusual livestock mutilation phenomenon. Since then hundreds of animals, mostly open-range cattle, have been found bizarrely slaughtered in the valley. Nearly all the mutilated animals are found devoid of blood, eyes or other facial features removed, and indicate signs of being dismembered by precise heat laser incisions. Almost every mutilated animal has its "soft tissue" anal passage cored out and the genitals surgically removed. The fetus is usually taken from pregnant cows. There are never tracks found near "authentic" mutilation sites, either predatory animal or human, but many have been found near burned ground with detectable levels of radiation. Some of the dead animals appear to be dropped from above (broken branches, cracked animal bones from impact). There are very few, if any, additional clues available at an animal mutilation site. As a result no one has ever been officially charged or convicted of perpetrating an animal mutilation. As the largest alpine valley in the world, the San Luis Valley sits like an altar at the apex of the continent. At least one researcher has compared the valley to the high altars atop Mesoamerican pyramids, describing the valley as "America's sacrificial altar" because of all the animal mutilation reports.

The San Luis Valley is also a location of frequent UFO and paranormal encounters. The UFO sightings include unidentifiable aerial craft, flying metallic orbs,

and mysterious floating lights or "cheap fireworks" as the locals call them. The San Luis Valley is considered America's premiere unsolved mysterious "hot spot" because no other region in North America features the variety or intensity of unusual phenomenon that can be found here. The other North American hot spots, Area 51 in Nevada and White Sands in New

▲ Mount Blanca and the Great Sand Dunes rise in tandem along the eastern periphery of the San Luis Valley.

Mexico, all have a top secret military presence nearby. On the eastern slopes of the Sangre de Cristo range is the NORAD base located deep within Cheyenne Mountain. It is one of the most secretive and defensively secured military bases in the world. Reports of clandestine underground base used by extraterrestrials, or an inter-dimensional portal within the Sangre de Cristo range and the Great Sand Dunes have also been claimed. Even Native American legends speak of a "doorway" in the Sangres that implicitly leads to another world or dimension. From the ancient past until today, strange phenomenon has been a constant feature in the valley. The San Luis Valley town of Crestone has hosted several UFO and mysterious phenomenon conferences. New Age adherents continue to flock here, calling the valley a "sacred song," a place where the Earth resonates with a symphony of harmonious chords.

### Getting to the San Luis Valley

The San Luis Valley is located in southern Colorado and also extends into northern New Mexico. Spanning 8,000 square miles (12,880 sq km) in two states, the San Luis Valley is the world's largest alpine valley. The average altitude is 7,500 feet (2,250 m). Highway 285 bisects the valley north and south, while Highway 160 cuts across the valley from east to west. San Luis is located in the southeastern part of the valley and holds the distinction of being the oldest town in Colorado.

# IDAHO

Idaho is the state that almost foiled the Lewis and Clark expedition upon their second attempted westward crossing of the Continental Divide. Unable to paddle down the Salmon River, the expedition hastily crossed the Bitterroot Mountains at Lolo Pass and nearly succumbed to starvation and the elements.

The friendly Nez Percé, or *Ni Mii Pu*, upon their first contact with white people, welcomed the party into their village. A year later Lewis and Clark returned the same way after reaching the Pacific, and had a much easier crossing, even stopping for a soak at the Lolo Hot Springs. Today, the rugged terrain offers the same challenges as the olden days. Over two-thirds of Idaho is public lands, mostly mountainous terrain not suitable for urban sprawl. The result is a spectacular mountain state ideal for year-round recreation.

## Nez Percé Homeland

Human occupation along the Snake River uplands of Idaho is regarded among the oldest in North America. Early migrants crossing the Bering Strait Land Bridge during the last Ice Age left weapons and other artifacts in caves where they lived, hunted, and practiced early forms of religion. Bones show that they hunted large game, most of which are now extinct, including camels, ancient horses, and ground sloths. In the millennia after the first human arrivals, the climate steadily grew extremely dry, much drier than it is today. Through these dramatic climatic changes humans were able to adopt and remain in the region. Radiocarbon dating indicates that the earliest visitors left their crude stone tools and bones in the Weis Rockshelter between 12,500 and 13,000 BCE. The Paleo-Indian hunters who made these tools almost certainly became the ancestors of the Nez Percé (pronounced 'Nee-Me-Poo') tribe of historic times.

> Native Americans have lived in the Nez Percé homeland for about 11,000 years. Many tools, needles, animal bones and projectile points found in regional rock shelters trace nearly the entire evolutionary saga of North American indigenous people.

For thousands of years the valleys, prairies, and plateaus of north central Idaho and adjacent Oregon and Washington have been the homeland to the Nez Percé people. Their primary settlements were in the valleys of the Clearwater and Snake rivers and its tributaries. They fished the streams, hunted in the woodlands, and dug edible roots on the plateaus. They worshipped various deities in nature and adopted animal spirit guides. For thousands of years the Nez Percé lived a virtually changeless existence. In the early 1700s the tribe acquired the horse, and their increased mobility added new dimensions to their age-old traditions. The Nez Percé received the Lewis and Clark expedition graciously, provided them with supplies, and told them about the river route to the Pacific. A decade later fur trappers and traders followed in their wake. In the 1840s settlers and missionaries began to make their way westward along the Oregon Trail, and in 1846 the Nez Percé found themselves part of the United States. Rapid change was inevitable and sudden.

▲ Heart of the Monster earth formation in the Nez Percé Homeland.
(Photo courtesy National Park Service)

The Nez Percé and Shoshone tribes, although generally classified as Plateau Indians, made occasional excursions into the Great Plains region. These Indians traveled along the ancient Lolo Trail, generally following the ridge of mountains north of the Lochsa River that extended for 150 miles (242 km) through wilderness. Lewis and Clark followed the Lolo Trail in 1805 on their expedition to the West Coast. The Weippe Prairie is the location where Lewis and Clark first met the Nez Percé Indians, who had never before seen white people. The expedition was exhausted, malnourished and sick from subsisting on local roots when they arrived. The Nez Percé could have easily killed Lewis and Clark and all their men, but they were a peaceful tribe and instead elected to help the foreigners. A sad note in history came some 70 years later when the Nez Percé were forced out of their homeland by the U.S. Calvary and encroaching white settlers. Ironically, several Nez Percé elders could still recall as children befriending the Lewis and Clark expedition. War and disease wreaked havoc on the Nez Percé in the 19th century, reducing their population from 6,000 at the time of Lewis and Clark's visit in 1805, to 1,500 survivors by 1885.

Upon first contact with white people, the Nez Percé homeland spanned from eastern Oregon all the way across Idaho into Montana. Today the roughly 1,300 tribal members live on a small reservation near Lewiston. The reservation is situated on 137.5 square miles (221 sq km) of land, less than three percent of their original reservation size and a microscopic fraction of the land they once roamed. The most famous landmark on the reservation is the Heart of the Monster site near East Kamiah. In the creation myth of the Nez Percé, a popular god named Coyote did battle with a fierce monster devouring all creatures in its path. Coyote saw this and came to the rescue of the animals. He tricked the monster into swallowing him, but when inside the monster's belly, Coyote pulled out a hidden knife and slashed his way out, killing the monster. Once the monster was chopped up into little pieces, Coyote flung parts of the monster far and wide and this site marks where the heart landed. Each piece of the monster became a different tribe, and the Nez Percé were created from Coyote ringing blood from the monster's heart, and the people sprang from the drops. The "Ant and Yellowjacket" and "Coyote's Fishnet" sites also relate additional tales of Coyote's famous exploits. An interpretive trail leads to the large hump of basalt named Heart of the Monster.

### Getting to Nez Percé Homeland

Nez Percé National Historic Park Headquarters is in Spalding, Idaho on U.S. 95, 12 miles (19 km) east of Lewiston. Roughly surrounding the reservation, the Nez Percé Historical Park Driving Tour extends for 200 miles (320 km) in 4 states, and consists of 38 historic sites. The driving tour takes about 6 hours total. Many pull-off sites examine Nez Percé contacts with European Americans, but the park also celebrates traditional culture. From the Idaho-Montana line, the old Lolo Trail parallels U.S. 12 for 4 miles (6.4 km). The Nez Percé National Historical Trail extends for 1,170 miles (1,885 km) along the famous 1877 flight route of Chief Joseph and his band from eastern Oregon to north-central Montana.

# MONTANA

The earliest explorers paddling up the Missouri River to Montana in the 1700s reported encountering the *Ouachipounnes,* or the Mandan, a white tribe. La Verendrye's 1720 expedition described them as "tall of stature, white in colour, with hair light, chestnut, and red ..." Theories about the origin of these "White Indians" include a 12th century Welsh exploration of North America led by Prince Madoc, while others believe they were Greenland Norse who decided to stay. A few decades after they were encountered by French trappers, disease turned Mandan earth lodges into ghostly smallpox hospices.

Without a proper survey or knowledge of the land, the United States acquired from France almost all of Montana in the Louisiana Purchase. Within a year Lewis and Clark were dispatched to map the new territory. They traveled through Montana in 1805, and then retraced their steps in 1806 on their way back to the Missouri River headwaters. Following in the early 19th century footsteps of Lewis and Clark were trappers and miners who viewed the Plains Indians as a dangerous nuisance. The 1860s gold rush in the mountains of western Montana brought an influx of settlers who established the first towns, but the migration also precipitated conflicts with Native Americans, primarily the Sioux. The battles continued through the 1870s and included General George Armstrong Custer's defeat at Little Bighorn in 1876. In time, all the Plains Indians were conquered and confined to reservations. Montana remains one of the least populated states in the United States, a realm where the Old West seems to be preserved in the lifestyle and spirit of modern Montanans.

# Glacier / Waterton International Peace Park

Amid stunning natural beauty is a monument dedicated to fostering peace and cooperation among nations. Canada established Waterton Lakes National Park in 1895 and the United States followed suit with Glacier National Park in 1910. As the years went by, neighboring citizens intimate with the two parks recognized the natural unity and suggested joining them as one. To commemorate the long history of peace and friendship between the United States and Canada, a unified park was established by the United States Congress and the Canadian Parliament in 1932 as a joint international park devoted to world peace. The world's first International Peace Park continues to inspire other nations to open their borders for joint efforts of conservation and goodwill.

The Blackfeet, Salish, and Kootenai tribes knew of the natural splendors and abundant resources of the area long before its exploration by mountaineers and naturalists. In fact, human habitation dates back at least 8,000 years. The diversity of plants and wildlife, along with the distinctiveness of the geographic landscape provided the native inhabitants with both physical and spiritual sustenance. Lake McDonald is known as the "sacred dancing lake" to the Blackfeet tribe, who may have been inspired by a bed of fossil algae on the trail leading down to the lake. The Blackfeet considered the craggy mountain peaks of the Continental Divide as the "Backbone of the World." When the Blackfeet controlled the eastern slopes of the Rockies they fiercely defended the buffalo country from the western tribes such as the Kootenai. Native people climbed the mountains to collect herbs, roots, berries, and special plants for food and medicine. The Glaciers / Waterton region continues to hold special value to Native Americans.

▲ Stunning natural scenery at Glacier National Park.

# THE ROCKY MOUNTAINS

*The soaring peaks at Glacier National Park, especially Chief Mountain, were revered by native people. They would climb the mountains on vision quest, or ascend the high peaks to pick certain flora for medicinal and ceremonial uses.*

Connecting the Blackfeet Indian Reservation to the border of Glacier National Park and Waterton Lakes is the impressive Chief Mountain, towering 9,080 feet (2,767 m) above sea level, dominating the open plains between the two countries. So prominent is this mountain that it is visible anywhere in Blackfeet territory. The summit of Chief Mountain was the most acclaimed vision quest site in Montana to the Blackfeet, Blood, and Piegan tribes. The mountain summit was considered home to the deeply revered Thunderbird deity. According to Blackfeet legend, the butte shaped mountain is the Center of the World. At one time, according to legend, Chief Mountain was the only land left unsubmerged after an immense flood covered the earth. The Creator, also known as "Old Man," looked out from the summit after the flood and created the four-legged animals and two-legged human beings.

Another Blackfeet legend states that when Chief Mountain crumbles it will be the end of all humanity. Carved by glaciers and perhaps ending with glacial erosion, Chief Mountain may be seen as a metaphor for the health of the planet. On the American side of the International Peace Park there are 37 glaciers and all are receding. There are no glaciers anymore in Waterton Lakes National Park in Canada. Jackson Glacier has been documented as receding for over 150 years, yet the rate of melting has been accelerating in the last few decades. It can be argued that the glaciers have been melting at a steady pace ever since the last Ice Age, but the recent rapid melting is clearly an indication of global warming. Incidentally, each person who climbs Chief Mountain is unwittingly crumbling a little bit of the mountain away. Legend told of a brave warrior who climbed the ultra holy Chief Mountain with a buffalo skull on his back as an offering to have a vision that could save his people. This popular story was considered a myth until Teddy Roosevelt's Secretary of State was the first

▲ Chief Mountain borders the International Peace Park.

white man to climb the peak only to discover several buffalo skulls at the summit. Even today the top of Chief Mountain contains many artifacts, including buffalo skulls, attesting to the mountain's continued importance. Along the summit route are many offerings left in prayer fields. Although located on National Park land, it is strongly advised by Blackfeet members that someone from the tribe accompany any climbers of Chief Mountain, and obtain permission by the Tribal Office.

## Getting to Glaciers / Watertown Lakes International Peace Park

The Blackfeet Indian Reservation extends east of Glacier National Park into the Great Plains. The closest town to Chief Mountain is Babb, which is also the road entrance into the Many Glaciers eastern entrance of the park. Highway 2 surrounds the southern part of the park in Montana, while Route 6 in Canada accesses Waterton Lakes in the northeast. The famous "Road to the Sun" bisecting Glacier National Park is closed in the winter. Glacier National Park and Waterton Lakes National Park both straddle the Continental Divide as it makes its way through northwest Montana and then defines the border of British Columbia and western Alberta. Triple Divide Peak is the only watershed in North America whose waters flow to three oceans: the Pacific by the Columbia River, the Arctic by Hudson Bay, and the Gulf of Mexico via the Mississippi system. The first turnout along the Road to the Sun 5 miles (8 km) west of St. Mary offers an excellent view of Triple Divide, but unfortunately there is not a maintained summit trail.

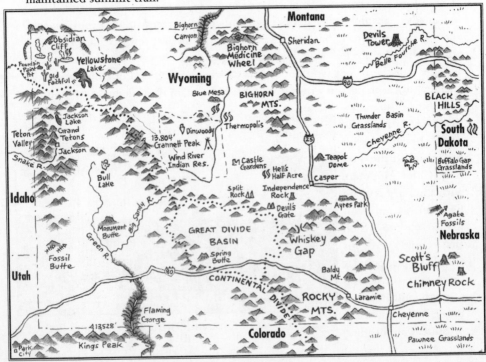

# WYOMING

Claimed at different times by Spain, France, and England, Wyoming fell into the possession of the United States, like most of the Rocky Mountain territories, following the Louisiana Purchase. Fur trappers were the first outsiders to explore the vast region, living with and learning from the Apsalooka (Crow), Lakota (Sioux), Shoshone, and other tribes. The balance of power would turn against the Indians when emigrants following the Oregon Trail poured into the region, then in 1867 when the nation's first transcontinental railroad began to lay track and establish towns across southern Wyoming. During the 1860s and 1870s, Sioux, Arapahoe, and Cheyenne fought for control of the Black Hills and the Powder River grasslands. After the inevitable defeat of the Indian tribes, settlement and ranching helped lay the groundwork for Wyoming's modern economy.

## Bighorn Medicine Wheel

On a shoulder of Medicine Mountain is the most famous medicine wheel in North America. Described as a sort of Rocky Mountain Stonehenge, Bighorn Medicine Wheel was famous with local native tribes as a location for sunrise and sunset rituals, as well as for other celestial observations. This medicine wheel consists of many hundred half-sunken stones resembling the shape of a wagon wheel. The middle cairn (stone pile) is a meter tall with 28 uneven spokes radiating to an outer rim. The 28 spokes likely represent the 28 days of the lunar cycle. Each spoke is about 36 feet (11 m) in length, and the outer ring is about 80 feet (24 m) in diameter and 245 feet (74 m) in circumference. Around the rim are six smaller cairns about a half meter tall and open on one side. The center cairn and one unique cairn situated outside the rim establish an alignment with the rising sun on summer solstice, and another cairn measures the setting sun on the same day. The other cairns line up with the stars Sirius, Fomalhaut in the constellation Pisces, Rigel in the constellation Orion, and Aldebaran in the constellation Taurus. All these star readings fall within one month of the summer solstice. The hollowed out center cairn may have contained an offering bowl, a buffalo skull platform or some kind of lost instrument used for celestial navigating. No one knows how old the wheel is, some estimates date it back thousands of years, but the best guess puts it around 700 years old.

The Bighorn Medicine Wheel near the summit of Medicine Mountain marks the sunrise and sunset of summer solstice, and indicates the rising of prominent summer stars. Its astrological alignments represent a profound understanding of seasonal and celestial navigation.

▲ The summer solstice sunrise alignment on Bighorn Medicine Wheel.

From the impressive elevation of 9,640 feet (2,892 m), the Bighorn Wheel alignments appear to link the distant prairie with the heavens. The site has a long history with the Plains Indians and other tribes in the Rocky Mountains. The Crow, Arapahoe, Shoshone and Cheyenne all have oral histories about important ceremonies being held here. Crow youth came to the wheel as a place to fast and seek their vision quest. Other tribes came to pray for personal atonement, healing, or pay respect to the Great Spirit. Chief Joseph of the Nez Percé came to Bighorn for guidance and wisdom as his people were transitioning from freedom to reservation life. For North American native people the circle represents the cycle of life. The circle is seen as a symbol of eternity—with no beginning and no end—denoting the interconnectedness of everything. The medicine wheel could also represent a microcosm of life, a sort of starting point for all otherworldly aspects. Along with astrological alignments, the circular pathway includes the four cardinal compass points. The four compass points can also be seen as the four seasons, where spring would represent the east, summer the south, autumn the west, and winter to the north. The number four also corresponds to the four sacred elements of earth, wind, water, and fire. Today a circular fence surrounds the Bighorn Medicine Wheel, with prayer offerings tied to the wire.

Since many of the Plains Indians migrated into the region after the supposed construction date of the Bighorn wheel it cannot be directly connected with any individual tribe—rather it seems to predate them all. Crow mythology accounts for the construction by a young brave named Burnt Face, who was scarred as a baby when he fell into a fire. When he reached maturity, Burnt Face traveled to Medicine Mountain for a vision quest and that is when the first medicine wheel was built. During his fast he helped an eagle protect its chicks from a predator, and in thanks the eagle flew Burnt Face to a place where his face was made

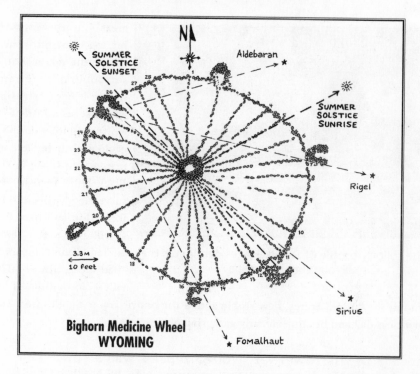

**Bighorn Medicine Wheel
WYOMING**

smooth. The famous history of fasting and vision quests at Bighorn Medicine Wheel has attracted New Age adherents in recent years. These latest enthusiasts view the site as being connected to the power of celestial bodies above, and from earth energy below. However, the influx of visitors is resented by some within the neighboring Native American communities. A few refuse to go to the wheel because of the presence of white pilgrims.

### Getting to Bighorn Medicine Wheel

The archaeological mystery and sacred Native American site is located high atop Medicine Mountain within Bighorn National Forest, 25 miles (40 km) east of Lovell, Wyoming. The nearest city is Sheridan. The Medicine Wheel National Historic Site is located just west from Burgess Junction, on US 14A, open from June until October. The site is inaccessible most of the year due to snow pack and winter weather.

## Devils Tower (Mateo Tepee)

Dominating the skyline of northeastern Wyoming is Devils Tower, one of the most famous rock formations in North America. The soaring stone shaft is the solid core remnant of an igneous intrusion that occurred underground about 60 million years ago and was eventually exposed due to river erosion. Rising 1,267 feet (380 m) above the nearby Belle Fourche River, and reaching 867 vertical feet (260 m) from base to summit, the tower served as a beacon to early settlers on their

▲ The solitary profile of Devils Tower dominates the surrounding landscape.

great journey westward. Jutting magnificently out of the relatively flat surrounding terrain, the volcanic extrusion was first seen in 1875 by white explorers during a geological survey to confirm a gold strike in the Black Hills. Instead, the surveyors discovered the formation and named it Devils Tower after a local Indian name, meaning "Bad God's Tower." The tallest formation of its kind in the United States, it is visible across the prairie for 100 miles (160 km) on a clear day and became an early gathering place.

> Devils Tower, or "Mateo Tepee," was a spiritually bestowed vision quest site to Native Americans since prehistoric times. Several different tribes worshipped at the "Bear Lodge" and continue pilgrimage to the site today.

Known to Native Americans as *Mateo Tepee* or "Grizzly Bear Lodge," Devils Tower has long been a pilgrimage destination to numerous Indian tribes. Many come to leave offerings or chant Native American prayers. The Lakota tribe continues to conduct their Sun Dance every summer solstice at the base of the tower. Various Indian legends relate a similar story about the origin of the tower. The popular tale, common to the Arapahoe, Crow, Cheyenne, Kiowa and Sioux tribes, relates the story of seven little girls pursued by a giant grizzly. According to legend, the seven young Indian girls were one day at play in the woods when an enormous bear came upon them and chased them through the forest, farther and farther away from their home. Slowly the bear closed in on them and there was nowhere else they could turn. Recognizing the hopelessness of their situation, the girls climbed upon a low rock and prayed loudly to the Great Spirit to save them. Immediately the small rock began to grow upwards, lifting the seven girls higher and higher into the sky. The angry bear jumped up against the sides of the growing tower and left deep claw marks, which can be seen as the shafts upon the tower walls. The rock continued to soar towards the sky until the girls were pushed way up into the heavens, where they became the seven stars of the Pleiades. Coincidently, in Greek mythology, the Pleiades are represented as the seven daughters of Atlas (Maia, Electra, Celaeno, Taygeta, Merope, Alcyone, and

Sterope), who also were metamorphosed into stars. Another legend claims that during summer storms thunder is created by the Bad God. The Devil himself beats his drum on the summit of the Bad God's Tower, and the surrounding land trembles in fear.

Devils Tower was popularized by Stephen Spielberg's film, *Close Encounters of the Third Kind*, which may reflect real life extraterrestrial activity. Locals living in the region and tourists to Devils Tower National Monument have reported seeing strange light phenomena and UFOs flying around the towers' summit for many years. UFO researchers propose that active, dormant and extinct volcanoes contain deep hollow shafts into the center of the earth, which may be conducive to inter-dimensional UFO flight, or harbor vast underground bases. It is reported that most of the UFO sighting worldwide appear at, or very close to, volcanic summits.

## Climbing Devils Tower

Devils Tower National Monument is conveniently located in northeastern Wyoming about 35 miles (56 km) north of Interstate 90, Exit 185 to Route 24. It was first climbed using a long wooden ladder, on July 4th, 1893. Proclaimed the first National Monument under the new Antiquities Act by President Theodore Roosevelt in 1906, the tower today is a popular climbing site and registers over 20,000 successful ascents up 220 possible routes. Climbers must register with National Monument headquarters before ascending. There is a voluntary climbing closure in June out of respect for Native American beliefs.

# Yellowstone

The intensity underfoot at Yellowstone National Park testifies to the unsettling power of Mother Nature. When an ancient volcano blew for the last time 600,000 years ago, nearly 240 cubic miles (386 cubic km) of debris spewed all across the western and northern prairie states. What is now Yellowstone's central portion then collapsed, forming a 28- by 47-mile (45- by 76-km) caldera, or a wide basin rimmed by hills and mountains. As one of the world's most active volcanic "hot spots," as well as being the location of the thinnest layer of earth crust, the massive caldera basin of Yellowstone is among the most geologically active regions on the planet. Over 10,000 geysers, hot springs, mud pots, and steaming fumaroles scatter across the vast pine-covered plateau of Yellowstone and throughout the park. Geyser concentrations exist only in Iceland, Russian Siberia and New Zealand, but Yellowstone has the highest density of geysers and hot springs in the world. The three necessary elements for geysers are heat, water, and a porous rock layer where the heated water percolates and then erupts, such as the famous Old Faithful geyser. Although lava does not flow in Yellowstone the heat from the hot spot creates formations that give the region an otherworldly impression. Such impressions certainly awed Native Americans and countless other explorers who passed through the region.

The newness of Yellowstone in geological years, as well as its turbulent history, features the world's thinnest earth crust where heated water erupts in dramatic fashion. Such displays of nature intrigued Native Americans who hunted in the region and prayed to the Great Spirit.

For thousands of years native tribes came to Yellowstone to hunt the abundant wildlife, gather precious stones including obsidian and collect materials for clothing, weapons, and decorative items. The seclusion of Yellowstone also served as a refuge from hostile tribes. Certainly it is untrue that prehistoric tribes avoided the region because they feared the geysers, as arrowheads and other hand-crafted items have been discovered near the thermal features. Also found were deep-rutted Indian tracks intersecting Yellowstone, remnants of old teepee encampments, and elongated fences to direct wild animals into traps. There is an oral history suggesting the geyser basin was a spiritual site, as well as the Lower Falls of the Yellowstone River, which was considered sacred and known as the place of "Big Thunder." The Lower Falls of Yellowstone drop into a golden gorge called the Grand Canyon of Yellowstone, where ospreys nest on rock pinnacles and several small geysers spout. All of the active geysers, almost uniformly, were believed by Indians to contain spirits, some evil yet others enhancing. These spirits held tremendous powers that could work in favor or against the visitor at the whim of the spirit. Thus, though many feared this power, others eagerly sought to gain it and ventured into the geyser regions to commune with the Great Spirit and request help in hunting or with shamanistic practices. The geysers may have acted as a magnet for the most ambitious. Only one tribe, the nomadic "Sheepeaters," were indigenous to Yellowstone when the first explorers arrived. The name was adopted from an Indian term for their hunting of bighorn sheep. The Sheepeaters were known to have used the hot springs of Yellowstone for religious and medicinal purposes.

▲ Boiling mud pots at Yellowstone.

It is now recognized that most tribes who ventured into Yellowstone, including the Blackfeet, Crow, Shoshone, Bannock, and the regional Sheepeaters, were here to collect the prized obsidian stone. Obsidian, or volcanic glass, is formed when molten lava cools quickly. Obsidian was highly regarded by prehistoric people because it is easily worked and sharpened into cutting tools, projectile points and used for decorative items due to its lustrous beauty. There are several sources of obsidian in Yellowstone, with the most famous being Obsidian Cliff in the northwest section of the park. Among the many Indian mounds and gravesites excavated in the Midwest were found artifacts of obsidian long thought to have originated from Yellowstone. This speculation was confirmed when recent tests proved that obsidian artifacts

▲ Yellowstone Indians typically left gift offerings near the spouting geysers.

from 30 sites in Ohio, Illinois, Indiana, Michigan, and Ontario, Canada could be conclusively traced back to Obsidian Cliff and one other site in Yellowstone National Park. Yellowstone obsidian has also been found in the intermediate states of Iowa, North Dakota, and Oklahoma, suggesting an elaborate trading system stretching across much of the North American continent.

## Getting to Yellowstone

Yellowstone was the first National Park created in the United States. Dedicated in 1872, Yellowstone remains the largest national park in the U.S., encompassing a huge section of northwestern Wyoming, but also including portions of Idaho and Montana. Three of the five entrances into Yellowstone are in Montana, the busiest being the portal town of West Yellowstone, which hosts more than 1.2 million visitors per year! Three highways from three states, the 287, 191, and 20, all converge on West Yellowstone town, conversely known as the "Snowmobile Capital of the World."

# CENTRAL PLAINS

*When I was young, I looked at the land and the rivers, the sky above, and the animals around me and could not fail to realize that they were all made by some great power. ... In order to honor (the Great Spirit) I must honor his works in nature*
**-Brave Buffalo, Sioux Medicine Man**

IN AGES PAST, INDIAN TRIBES LIVED, TRADED, FOUGHT AND DIED on the Central Plains. The only vestiges of their existence are arrowheads, pottery, strange effigies and conical mounds. While conical burial mounds are scattered across much of the plains, the mysterious animal and half bird-man effigies are less frequent. A high concentration of effigies can be found along the high bluffs of the western Mississippi River in northern Iowa. Sometimes the old Indian trails which once led to sacred burial grounds are preserved in modern parks. But the real transportation networks were the rivers. The Rio Grande, Mississippi, Arkansas, and Missouri river systems were efficient travel routes into the Central Plains. Most of the Plains Indians were displaced tribes from the eastern woodlands and the rivers provided an exit, as well as sustenance. The Dakota, as the Sioux were known before being renamed by the French, lived along the northern Mississippi and St. Croix rivers long before the European arrival. Then, about 1500 CE, the Ojibwa moved in from the east, driven out of their ancestral lands by the warlike and powerful Iroquois. Outside of small surviving bands, most of the Sioux moved west or north onto the plains to escape their Ojibwa conquerors, only to be banished at last by the white man.

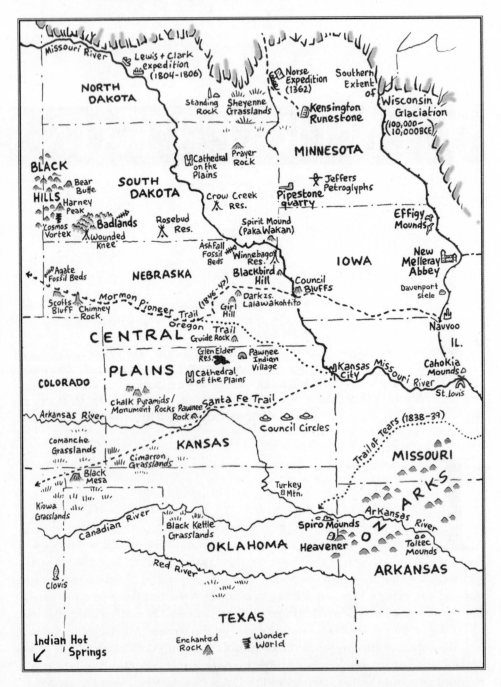

Upon European contact, the Plains Indians were mostly migratory hunters who practiced some horticulture and lived in semi-permanent villages. All would walk to follow the buffalo in the summer hunting season then return to their favored homelands. Horses were not introduced until Spanish explorers scoured the southern plains in the mid-1500s looking for their fabled golden cities. They did not find any, but the Plains Indians took an instant affinity to riding horses captured from the Spanish. The various hunting cultures on the sweeping grasslands were in contact with tribes spanning from the Rocky Mountains to the eastern woodlands. Because of the diversity of languages, an ingenious sign language was developed and understood throughout the plains. It was invaluable for effective communication in the complex intertribal trade network of exchanging goods. Each native grouping identified with their original homeland in the expansive Great Plains. These are now divided up as states and provinces. From north to south the main tribes in central Canada and northeastern Montana were the Blackfeet, Cree, and Assiniboin. On the prairies of North Dakota, southeastern Montana, eastern Colorado, South Dakota, and Nebraska were the Sioux, Cheyenne, Arapahoe, Crow, Mandan, Arikara, Wichita, and Hidatsa. Dominating the southern plains in Kansas, Oklahoma, and Texas were the Pawnee, Omaha, Kiowa, Coushatta and Comanche. There were seven "council fires" or bands of Sioux scattered across the plains. Within the Sioux confederation there were three dialects: Dakota, Lakota, and Nakota—the term "kota" meaning friends or allies.

# IOWA

The historic period of mapping the Midwest began in 1672-1673 when French explorers Father Jacques Marquette and Louis Joliet arrived to chart the Great Lakes and the river routes that could access the western region of the continent. When the expedition reached the breathtaking convergence of the Wisconsin and Mississippi rivers, they encountered their first Plains Indians, including the Ioway for whom the state of Iowa was named. Other French explorers followed in the wake of Marquette and Joliet, exploring different river routes, building forts, and developing trade. After failing to locate a river passage to the Pacific, early French explorers became primarily interested in converting Native Americans to Christianity and trading with them for exotic animal furs. As French influence waned in the mid-1700s, homesteaders came to Iowa for the fertile soil, to avoid religious persecution, and to escape the turmoil in Europe or the American Civil War. The serious agrarian settlers established Christian religious communities far removed from the bustle of eastern industrial cities.

Located above the high bluffs and lowlands along the northern section of the Mississippi River are numerous prehistoric animal-shaped mounds of a type completely unique to North America. Although Marquette and Joliet were the first modern explorers to see the impressive bluffs within the upper Mississippi Valley, they did not notice the prodigious number of mounds lining the inland waterways. Their desire was to find a river route that might access the Pacific Ocean and the riches of the Orient. During the early historic period, the lowland and bluff top mounds went largely unnoticed. Gradually, word of thousands of Indian mounds located in the upper Mississippi Valley began to spread, and in 1881, two men named Theodore Lewis and Alfred Hill began an ambitious survey of the various mound groupings along the entire length of the Mississippi Valley. Among the groups they mapped in 1892 were numerous mounds named "effigy mounds" because they were shaped like animals, humans and abstract objects. Many are preserved within Effigy Mounds National Monument, including the distinctive Marching Bear Group.

## Effigy Mounds Monument

Pre-contact native people on the eastern fringe of the Central Plains constructed large earthen structures called effigy mounds. The builders are known as the Effigy Indians, who lived from the Hopewellian period until historic times. The advanced Hopewell originated in the Ohio woodlands and influenced the latter Mississippian Culture and Effigy Indians among others. The refined Hopewell culture dates from 200 BCE to 600 CE, while the period the effigy mounds were built dates between 500 CE to 1600 CE. The Effigy Indians copied their mound building techniques from the Hopewell, but constructed their mounds in effigy form and buried their dead with fewer grave items. Both cultures enjoyed extensive trading partnerships across the continent. Buried within Iowa effigy mounds were found mica from the Appalachians, obsidian from the Rocky Mountains, seashells from the Gulf of Mexico, and copper from the Lake Superior region. As mysterious as the effigy shapes are, the mound building tradition had all but vanished by first contact, possibly as a result of an advance wave of disease introduced by the Spaniards, or from continued tribal warfare and famine.

Long before the construction of effigy mounds in the Midwest, other mound building people where burying their dead in conical mounds. The oldest mounds in the northern Mississippi Valley belong to the Red Ocher Culture. One single Red Ocher burial site in Effigy Mounds National Monument links this area with the older culture. Excavation of this mound uncovered a burial bundle with a Carbon-14 date to approximately 2,500 years ago. The body had been placed on an earthen floor covered with red ocher and ceremonial offerings, including large chipped spear blades, arrow points, and spherical copper beads. All burials began as shallow pit graves and to finalize the funeral a conical mound was built over it. Oftentimes successive burials were added to existing mounds. A typical burial treatment used in all three cultures featured one (or several) bodies bundled in hides and accompanied with a sack full of essential items for the spirit's journey into the afterlife.

▲ Effigy Mounds National Monument extends along the high bluffs of the upper Mississippi.

To consecrate an effigy ceremony, a shaman would perform a solemn ritual alone or before members of the tribe. These ceremonies appealed to the gods to keep the clan safe and well fed, and attempted to bend the forces of nature in favor of the tribe. Shaman would conduct ceremonies to bring success in hunting by increasing the availability of animals. They also worked to prevent natural disasters by divining earth energies. Circular fireplaces, often located in the "head" or "heart" of the effigies, may have acted as an altar during funeral rites—ceremonies of death through which the people could express their concern for the dead as well as say goodwill prayers for the still-living tribe. The mammal or bird shaped mounds probably had a mystical meaning associated with the self-identity of the builders. Shaman would take special care dressing themselves before a ceremony according to exact rituals. They wore tanned hide breechcloths and moccasins, and jewelry of bone, shell, or copper. They painted their bodies for additional adornment. In a series of rites not completely understood, prehistoric Native Americans carefully formed each earthen effigy to receive the spirit of the departed by selecting the most appropriate bird or animal form, and erecting the effigy in a strategic location.

Some earthworks at Effigy Mounds Monument are so enormous that their shape is difficult to discern at ground level.

Effigy Mounds National Monument

MARQUETTE, IOWA

Great Bear Effigy

Little Bear Mound Group

MISSISSIPPI RIVER

Yellow River Mound Group

Compound Mound Group

Marching Bear Group

Effigy Mounds National Monument was established in 1949 to preserve one of the highest concentrations of earthen mounds remaining in northeastern Iowa. Within the borders of the monument are 191 known prehistoric earthworks—29 in the form of bears and birds. The remainder (and majority) of the earthworks are conical or linear mounds, or a combination of both types called "compounds." Nearly all the conical mounds at Effigy Mounds National Monument contained burials, whereas no animal effigy mounds in the monument have been found to contain human remains. Some effigy mounds in the surrounding region, however, were used for burials. The largest effigy in Iowa, the Great Bear Mound, is 137 feet (41 m) long from head to tail, 70 feet (21 m) from shoulder to foreleg, and 3.5 feet (1 m) high. The Great Bear also has the distinction of being the only effigy facing to the right, while the Marching Bear Group faces the other way. When record keeping of the effigies began in the upper Mississippi, it is documented that in the late 19th century there were at least 10,000 mounds of all types and sizes in northeastern Iowa alone. A hundred years later, fewer than 1,000 survived.

### Visiting Effigy Mounds National Monument

Effigy Mounds National Monument is located 5 miles (8 km) north of McGregor and 3 miles (4.8 km) north of Marquette, Iowa on Highway 76. The Visitor Center has museum exhibits and an audiovisual presentation explaining the prehistory, modern history, and natural history of Effigy Mounds National Monument. The Visitor Center is open daily, except Christmas Day, from 8 a.m. to 5 p.m. (7 p.m. in summer). The park is divided into north and south units, with 11 miles (18 km) of interpretive hiking trails. If going overnight, plan a stay at the Pikes Peak State Park campground, a few miles south of McGregor on Highway 340. Included in Pikes Peak are the bluffs overlooking the junction of the Wisconsin and Mississippi rivers where Marquette and Joliet became the first known Europeans to touch ground west of the Mississippi.

## New Melleray Abbey

On the eastern Iowa prairie is a quiet Catholic monastery still following a tradition of solitary living based on the 6th century instructions of Saint Benedict. The Cistercian tradition of monkhood, of which New Melleray Abbey abides, traces its roots back to the Middle Ages of Europe. In 1098 CE at the New Monastery of Citeaux, near Dijon in eastern France, a reform in the monastic order motivated several monks to return to the silent and simplistic rule of Saint Benedict. The new Cistercian Order spread rapidly, leading to hundreds of monasteries being founded across Europe during the 11th and 12th centuries. In 1539, all things Catholic were outlawed in Ireland under the rule of England's Henry VIII, including 40 Cistercian abbeys, with Oliver Cromwell carrying out the king's edict with unrestrained brutality. Many Irish monks fled to France and lived a peaceful life for many centuries until the French Revolution suppressed all religious houses there, and by 1830 all monks were forced out of Brittany at the point of bayonets. After much hardship, the outcast monks of France started reorganizing a new monastery in 1832 on virgin soil near Ireland's south coast at a place called Mount Melleray.

Only a decade after the founding of Mount Melleray Abbey, starvation and disease would claim nearly a million Irish lives in the dark years between 1841 and 1851. This period was known as the "potato famine" where millions of desolate Europeans, mostly Irish, would immigrate to the United States with hopes of a better life. Several thousand miles away in the wooded hillsides and tall grass prairies along the Mississippi Valley of Iowa and Illinois waves of immigrants, many of them Irish Catholic famine refugees, began establishing subsistence farms and a new life. Among these new settlers were several monks sent over in 1849 by Abbot Dom Bruno of Mount Melleray in Ireland. Out of desperation, Abbot Bruno wrote in 1849, "I want to send the brothers (to America) so as not to see them dying of starvation." Bishop Mathias Loras of Dubuque, Iowa offered the Irish monks a refuge on some Church land only 12 miles (20 km) southwest of Dubuque. New Melleray Abbey in Iowa's hinterland was established that year by the monks of Ireland's Knockmealdown Mountains, home of the "motherhouse" Mount Melleray Abbey. With the land secured, the Cistercian tradition came over from Europe, and once again the brothers started a thriving monastery beginning with nothing but backbreaking labor and the power of prayer.

New Melleray was granted monastic status
by Pope Pius IX in 1862, making it the third
Cistercian abbey established in the United
States, only a year after the first was founded
at Gethsemani, Kentucky.

The monks of New Melleray are devout Catholics, professing the rule of Saint Benedict in the spirit of the founders of Citeaux, France. This tradition has been handed down from the Order of Cistercians of the Strict Observance. All Cistercian monks and nuns live their entire lives within a

▲ The New Melleray Abbey in Iowa is modeled after the Mount Melleray Abbey in Ireland.

community wholly orientated to a contemplative life of prayer. They follow the book *The Rule of Saint Benedict,* which is a set of guidelines and principles for a monastic life written by Saint Benedict in the 6th century. Saint Benedict wrote his "little rule for beginners" as he called it at a time in history when life was barbaric and uncivilized. In his writing, for example, Benedict cautions his monks to remove their knives before going to bed so they would not accidentally cut themselves during sleep. Despite its age, Cistercian monks still find the *Rule* relevant for 21st century monastic living. For them the *Rule* has a status second only to the scriptures. It is the primary focus of study for new initiates into the Order. Monks and nuns make their professions according to the *Rule*, have frequent public reading of the *Rule*, and refer to it often for guidance and decision making in the community.

The American Civil War brought prosperity to the New Melleray Abbey, despite several young monks being forced into the draft. To keep the brothers out of the war, the monastery had to pay the Union Army $500 for every monk aged 21 to 45. In return, the monks worked singularly on grain farming, timber harvest, and livestock production to support the Union war effort. The frugal saving habits and devotional work ethic of the monks paid off handsomely. With a surplus of funds after the war, construction began on a long-planned Gothic style monastic enclosure. The limestone slabs were quarried on site to build a larger church and the impressive quadrangle. An additional guesthouse wing was added to accommodate the increasingly popular demand for outside individuals and small groups; a practice that continues to this day. Although the numbers of monks and their financial resources have fluctuated wildly, the monastery carries on its spiritual tradition into the 21st century with a solid population of Christian monks devoted solely to a quiet yet constructive existence.

### Getting to New Melleray Abbey

New Melleray Abbey is located 12 miles (20 km) southwest of Dubuque, Iowa. Dubuque is located on the Mississippi River, directly across from the Wisconsin / Illinois border. From Dubuque, follow Highway 61 south to Route 151, and take the D41 road exit northbound to the abbey. About the same distance from Dubuque there is also an exit on Route 20 at Peosta on the Y21 road heading southbound. Signs will direct motorists to the abbey. General information and room reservation line: (563) 588-2319.

# KANSAS

The first known Europeans to pass through Kansas were Spaniards under Francisco Coronado in 1541 on their quest to find a fabled gold city called Quivira. The expedition failed to locate any fabulously wealthy cities, but they did see broad prairies where unimaginable numbers of bison roamed. The biggest change to Kansas came at one minute past midnight on January 1st, 1863, when the Homestead Act went into effect. Signed into law by Abraham Lincoln the previous May, the Homestead Act was designed to give nearly every citizen an opportunity to live the American Dream of "ten acres and a mule." It brought thousands of immigrants into Kansas practically overnight and transformed a vast prairie state into an agricultural empire. Conversely, the Homestead Act displaced nearly all Native Americans out of state and contributed greatly to the loss of their unique culture. Homesteading was all but over by the time of the Great Depression, as the best properties were taken and indications of overtaxed land began to develop. By the 1930s farming was seen as too difficult a life, especially after the wretched weather that swept across Kansas during the desperate Dust Bowl years. Kansas' status as the leading wheat-producing state would have astonished the earliest Spanish explorers who called its treeless plains "the Great American Desert." The Flint Hills tallgrass region in central Kansas remains a mostly wild prairie.

The absence of trees in the gently rolling grasslands of the Great Plains has long been an enigma of sorts. While the rocky soil has kept large-scale farming at bay, the grass itself—along with grazing—helps keep the trees out. The grass roots grow deep (20 feet / 6 m), thick and fast, soaking up all available moisture and leaving little space for tree seedlings to flourish. Geologists know that drought and fire also contributed to the dominance of grass over trees on the prairie. Trees cannot survive many years of drought, but the native grasses require much less moisture and are thus better adapted. For centuries before the white man came, any tree seedlings that managed to sprout were wiped out by the wildfires that regularly swept across the plains.

## Pawnee Spirit Sites

The Pawnee were among the strongest of all the Plains Indians. Their influence stretched west into present-day Kansas, Nebraska, and parts of the Colorado prairie. They lived half the year in semi-permanent villages consisting of earth-covered habitations. A short passage entrance led into the rounded, dome-shaped lodges. Entire Pawnee families, along with their favorite dogs and pet animals

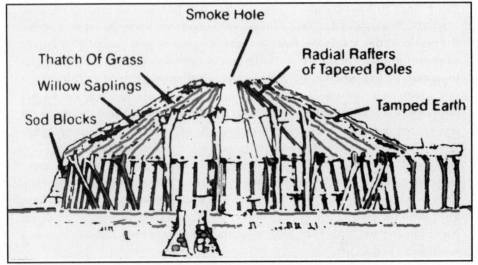

Smoke Hole

Thatch Of Grass

Radial Rafters
of Tapered Poles

Willow Saplings

Tamped Earth

Sod Blocks

▲ An illustration of the Pawnee earth lodge habitation.
(Image courtesy Kansas Historical Society)

shared the inside of the lodges. Horses were kept in corrals outside the village, ready for battle. Under an open-air roof the elders would smoke their pipes, make decisions for the tribe, and pray to their supreme god *Tirawahat*. The most important gathering of the Skidi band of Pawnees was the fertility ritual called the Morning Star Ceremony. This ritual placed a strong emphasis on astronomical phenomena and occasionally permitted human sacrifice, usually a captured female. The Pawnee Indians held a deep reverence for the stars and thus were considered the "Astronomers of the Great Plains."

> Pawnee Spirit Sites were natural features on
> the landscape that resembled their earthen
> lodges, usually taking the appearance of
> prominent hills or artesian springs.

To Plains Indians, a natural spring was considered a shrine in which offerings of various kinds were thrown in for good fortune. One such spring, *Kicawi'caku*, whose name translates "spring on the edge of a bank," was a large artesian pool occupying the top of a limestone mound that vaguely resembled a Pawnee earthen lodge. The water level fluctuated depending on the season, but sometimes overflowed the rim. It was highly revered as a sacred source of mineral water. When the pool was cleaned out during its years as a modern health spa it yielded numerous Native American relics. Beads, weapons, moccasins, and assorted artifacts were deposited as offerings by passing bands of Indians, including the Pawnee and many other tribes of diverse linguistic affiliations. When white settlers moved into the region, they renamed it *Waconda*, based on the name "Great Spirit Spring." As early as the 1870s, bottled water was sold under the name *Waconda Flier*, and in 1884, construction of a health spa was begun. Today, the entire spring and surrounding spa is submerged under the waters of Glen Elder Reservoir.

The Pawnee considered certain natural mounds on the prairie to be "animal lodges," a place where their four-legged relatives held councils of their own. Most of the animal lodge openings were orientated to the Morning Star in the north by northeastern night sky. One such mound, *Pa-hur*, or "the hill that points the way," had a large hole in its side where the miraculously endowed animals would gather and discuss various topics, just as their Pawnee two-legged kin did in their earthen lodges. *Pa-hur* has been renamed in English as Guide Rock, a town across the Republican River in Nebraska about a mile north of the animal lodge. Another famous site, also in Nebraska, is *Curaspa ko*, or "Girl Hill" and it too is shaped like an earth lodge, even featuring a vestibule entrance. Girl Hill derives its name from a time when young Pawnee girls gathered on the hill to watch the men of their village hunt buffalo.

### Getting to Pawnee Spirit Sites

The Pawnee Indian Village State Historic Site and Museum is located 7 miles (10 km) north of U.S. 36 on Kansas Highway 266 near the town of Republic, and 22 miles (37 km) north of Belleville. The Pawnee Village is on the site where 2,000 Pawnees lived in the 1820s. At its height the village contained more than 40 lodges. The museum encloses the excavated floor of one of the largest lodges, with the remains of other houses dotting the ground. *Pa-hur* lent its name to the town Guide Rock, just over the Kansas border, but the hill itself is very difficult to locate because much of it has been torn down for road and canal construction. The Girl Hill animal lodge is located roughly 2.75 miles (4.5 km) between the towns of Hordville and Clarks, Nebraska, along the southern bluff of the Platte River. *Kicawi'caku*, also known as Waconda Spring, was located on the banks of the Solomon River, just southeast of Cawker City, Kansas. Similar to the Aswan High Dam in Egypt, the Glen Elder Reservoir flooded the site and Waconda was lost forever.

# NEBRASKA

The people known as the Omaha, meaning "those going against the wind or current," migrated in prehistory from the Ohio woodlands down the Mississippi, then up the Missouri River to their present homeland. Ever since their arrival, the Omaha were traditional enemies with the Sioux. Encroachment of hunting grounds led to many skirmishes on the Great Plains. As with all Plains Indians, the buffalo was essential to the people's survival and livelihood. Almost every part of the sacred buffalo was utilized: awls, needles and ornaments were made from bone; skins were used for clothing and teepees; rope was made from buffalo hair and buffalo fat was used for hair dressing and hand lotion. As the large herds of buffalo vanished from the prairie, the plains cultures had no choice but to abandon most of their self-supporting lifestyle and become dependents on the white man's government. Canvas replaced buffalo skins for shelter, rifles replaced the bow and arrow, wooden bowls and cups were replaced with copper utensils. Only the skill of creating handicraft items for sacred tribal ceremonies passed down through the generations.

Nebraska had been a major crossroads for the early explorers and settlers as they made their way across the vast Central Plains. The westward-bound pioneers generally followed trails paralleling the Missouri and Platte rivers, which were called the "Coast of Nebraska" trails. Immigrants followed the trails past Scotts Bluff and Chimney Rock in the northwest part of the state before the arduous journey across the Rocky Mountains. When the migrants saw these two landmarks they knew they had made it one third of the way to the West Coast. Eventually Indian trails became wagon wheel tracks, which led the way to railroad lines and interstate highways.

## Blackbird Hill

The prominent rise along the Missouri River known as Blackbird Hill had long been a Native American power point and vision quest site. The mound was also used as a strategic lookout and ritual burial location for powerful Omaha chiefs. In a gorge near the bottom of the hill is a natural outflow of fresh spring water. Nearby the spring is a sandstone bedrock exposure displaying a fascinating collection of indigenous rock carvings. The petroglyphs depict human and animal figures, as well as supernatural beings. The carvings have no tribal or chronological affiliation, yet one petroglyph resembles a human on a horse, suggesting they were created after 1700 CE.

▲ An early 20th century photo of two girls near the petroglyphs at the base of Blackbird Hill.

During the early era of European contact the Omaha tribe became very powerful through trade with the white man. Their village was situated at a strategic location where pelts from the Central Plains and the Rocky Mountains could be exchanged for exotic wares. The Indians eagerly awaited the coming of white traders atop Blackbird Hill. Conversely, as the traders paddled against the current they welcomed the summit with joy, for they knew cold water springs gushed from the sand-stone rock at the foot of the hill, and there was food and friendship for the white man in the lodges of the Omaha village. During this time there was a powerful Omaha chief named Blackbird who was both deeply respected and feared. He traded with the white man tactfully and acquired a high status among all Plains Indians. His cunning in battle and trade was unrivaled. Finally, around 1780, an enemy came against the Omaha tribe that not even Blackbird with all his medicine and mystery could withstand. This was smallpox, a white man's disease that the Omaha had never known. It swept through them like a vengeful curse. They could not under-stand how it could move from lodge to lodge or from village to village. The fever and the dreadful blotches drove them insane. Some Indians left their villages and rushed onto the prairie to die alone. Others set fire to their houses and killed their wives and children. It was estimated that in 1780 there

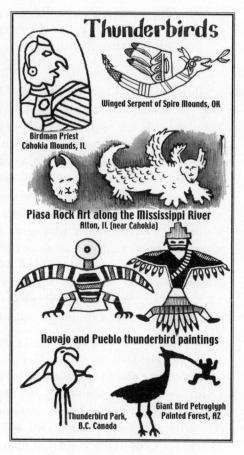

**Thunderbirds**

Winged Serpent of Spiro Mounds, OK

Birdman Priest
Cahokia Mounds, IL

**Piasa Rock Art along the Mississippi River**
Alton, IL (near Cahokia)

**Navajo and Pueblo thunderbird paintings**

Thunderbird Park,
B.C. Canada

Giant Bird Petroglyph
Painted Forest, AZ

were 2,800 Omaha people alive, reduced to a mere 300 by 1802. The Omaha tribe never recovered their old strength or prestige. Even the omnipotent chief Blackbird was himself finally stricken. His friends gathered by his side to hear his last dying words. He ordered them to bury him on top of Blackbird Hill, seated on his favorite horse so that his spirit might overlook the entire Omaha country-side and be among the first to see the white men as they paddled up the river. The dying chief's command was carried out. The horse was led to the summit with the dead chief firmly fastened upon his back. The horse was strangled, followed by a burial of sod and dirt to create an artificial mound until both were buried from sight. Blackbird was also laid to rest with his favorite personal belongings. A pole was set into the mound and upon it were hung scalps that Blackbird had taken in battle. A fire, according to tradition, was kept burning on the grave for a period of four nights. After the funeral, food for the spirit was placed at the mound by the few Omaha people who had survived the smallpox scourge.

Blackbird Hill served as an important landmark and meeting place for early European

> explorers as they traveled along the Missouri
> River. Several prominent Omaha chiefs,
> including Blackbird and Big Elk, were buried
> on the promontory.

When Lewis and Clark traversed the Missouri River in August 1804, Blackbird's artificial mound and pole were still in place. Captain Clark wrote of Blackbird Hill: "after the rain was over, Capt. Lewis myself & 10 men ascended the Hill where the Mahars King Black Bird was buried 4 years ago. A mound of earth about 12 feet Diameter at the base, & 6 feet high is raised over him turfed, and a pole 8 feet high in the center on this pole we fixed a white flag bound with red, blue & white ..." Many other early writers mentioned the mound, as it became a well-known navigational landmark along the Coast of Nebraska. In 1832 George Catlin, the famous painter who spent many years among the western Indians capturing their image on canvas and learning about their life, came down the Missouri and climbed Blackbird Hill. He reported a gopher hole in the side of the burial mound. When he dug into the softened soil a skull dropped down. He quickly wrapped it in a blanket and eventually carried it to Washington D.C. where it was placed in the Smithsonian Institution.

Blackbird Hill towers alongside the mighty Missouri River as it has for many millennia. The springs continue to flow from the sandstone cliffs at its base. A stone fireplace and a keyhole-shaped altar are all the artifacts that remain of the once grand Omaha settlement. Upon the cliff walls are deeply cut petroglyphs of wild animals and strange Indian signs, mingled with the names of early explorers. The artificial mound seen by Lewis and Clark has long since vanished, yet some believe the spirit of Blackbird continues to gaze in vain for his fur trading friends beating up the river in their canoes.

### Getting to Blackbird Hill

Blackbird Hill is located within the Omaha Indian Reservation in northeastern Nebraska, just west of Highway 75, near the small town of Macy, host to the annual Omaha Tribal Pow-Wow in mid-August. Unfortunately, Blackbird Hill cannot be accessed by the general public. The best viewing platform is the Blackbird Scenic Overlook along Highway 75, about 2 miles (3.2 km) north of Decatur. The Interpretive Center is modeled after a circular Omaha earth lodge, featuring historical exhibits based on the Omaha tribe and the mighty Missouri River. The restoration of prairie flora and fauna has developed from the efforts of the Blackbird Scenic Overlook. The overlook offers fantastic views of the river in both directions, and the summit of Blackbird Hill can be seen poking above the Missouri River flood plain. Blackbird Hill is 8 miles (13 km) north of Decatur, and 50 miles (80 km) north of Omaha. The Omaha Reservation connects with the Winnebago Indian Reservation extending along the western banks of the Missouri River.

**THE TEN INDIAN COMMANDMENTS** by White Cloud Talatawi

Remain close to the Great Spirit

Show great respect for your fellow human beings

Give assistance and kindness wherever needed

Be truthful and honest at all times

Do what you know to be right

Look after the well being of mind and body

Treat the Earth and all that dwell thereon with respect

Take full responsibility for your actions

Dedicate a share of your efforts to the greater good

Work together for the benefit of all humankind

# OKLAHOMA

The Sooner State has a long history of settlement by Native Americans and the name *Oklahoma* derives from the Choctaw words meaning "red people." During the early years of America's expansion, Oklahoma was originally the "Indian Territory" for the existing tribes and the multitude of displaced tribes who came from the east after the Louisiana Purchase. Politicians of the newly formed United States designated the territory as a place of "removal." Hopes of an independent Indian nation were dashed after fierce Plains Indians attacked immigrating tribes from the east, a split Indian consensus over the Civil War, and railroads and white settlers encroaching on lands already granted by treaty. Consequently, the nickname Sooner State derives from the first land grabbers who arrived "sooner" and claimed the choice properties before the legal newcomers.

## Heavener

Located in several remote wooded areas near the Arkansas River were found at least five finely cut texts, written in an old runic language reminiscent of the Middle Age Norse alphabet. The inscriptions were located near the small towns of Heavener and Poteau, and another in Shawnee, Oklahoma. The centerpiece is a prominent slab of rock—12 feet (3.6 m) high, 10 feet (3 m) wide and 16 inches (41 cm) thick—jutting from the ground. It features eight runic letters in a straight line, six to nine inches in height, and despite extensive weathering, approximately one-fourth of an inch in depth. This is the famous Heavener Runestone, with

▲ The Heavener Runestone is now protected behind glass.

one side determined by the Smithsonian Institution to contain Scandinavian runic writing. These carved stones are believed to be the work of Vikings who sailed up the Poteau River via the Arkansas and Mississippi River to establish a land claim. It is likely these wayward Scandinavians traded with, and possibly influenced, the Native Americans living near the Spiro Mounds.

Decipherment of the various Oklahoma runestones, according to the late Harvard epigrapher Barry Fell, is difficult because after the 11th century the shapes of the runic letters used in Scandinavia underwent great change with a significant number of letters in the alphabet being reduced. The style of the various runic texts date to around 1050 CE, according to Fell, but cannot be conclusively dated because there is no test to determine the antiquity of an inscription on stone, such as the Carbon-14 test used on organic matter. Yet it is possible to assign approximate dates to runic inscriptions simply by examining the type of letters used. By using the 11th century runic alphabet the Heavener inscription reads, "Gnr medaa" whose meaning is uncertain, along with the Poteau inscription, "Gnng i, eajth" which is also undecipherable. The Shawnee inscription however, is uniformly believed to be a headstone reading "Madok." The Poteau stone was found by two teenage boys in 1967 about 10 miles (16 km) from the Heavener Runestone, and the Shawnee stone was found face down in a stream in 1969. The three famous Oklahoma runestones are in an alphabet not exactly matched elsewhere, and thus have been the subject of varied decipherment.

The first known discovery of the Heavener Runestone was in the 1830s when a Choctaw hunting party stumbled upon it. The Choctaw were likely astonished when they saw the eight mysterious symbols carved into the mossy face of the huge slab of stone. In a bygone era of enormous old-growth trees on Poteau Mountain, early records indicate that there was little underbrush and a deer could be seen from a great distance under the virgin timber. Poteau Mountain was a name given by French trappers, who apparently didn't know of the hidden runestone. The mountain was part of the Indian Territory ceded to the Choctaw Nation when they were removed from present-day Mississippi to Oklahoma. The stone itself stood in a picturesque deep ravine, protected from the wind by overhanging cliffs. The weathering of the edges of the carving in relation to the hardness of the stone and the exposure to the elements provide a guide to its antiquity. In time, American hunters and loggers came across the monument-like stele and referred to it erroneously as "Indian Rock."

> Heavener Runestone is a giant rock slab
> inscribed with Old Norse writing, possibly
> indicating a boundary marker called "Glome
> Valley."

The most recent research of the runic inscriptions on the Heavener Runestone indicates that it might be four hundred years older than first interpreted by Fell. For many years, academics in America and abroad had been stumped because the runes seemed to be the mixture of two ancient runic alphabets: six from the oldest Germanic (Old Norse) Futhark which came into use around 300 CE; the second and last runes from a later Scandinavian Futhark used about 800 CE. Using these combined alphabets, the Heavener stone reads GLOME DAL, which translates as "Valley owned by Glome" denoting a boundary marker or land claim. If this interpretation is correct, it means the Vikings came to North America much earlier than Leif Ericson in 1000 CE. It would also be the first instance on the North American continent when a stone demarked a parcel of property. Several other large slabs with similar inscriptions were known to exist on Poteau Mountain until the 1930s and 1940s, but were wantonly destroyed by souvenir hunters. In the last century, as many as 70 inscriptions were reportedly discovered in the area.

Similar surviving inscriptions and the Heavener Runestone have been the subject of much debate for over a century. The controversy arises both in the decipherment and the pre-Columbus declaration that the Vikings made ambitious incursions deep into the North American continent. The latter challenge of the Heavener Runestone is the reinterpretation of history to include the Vikings, among others, as being the first Europeans to explore and colonize portions of North America. As such, the area around Heavener was a prized location where an individual or some Viking group went to great lengths to mark their territory.

### Getting to Heavener

Heavener Runestone State Park is located 2.5 miles (4 km) east of the small town of Heavener, in eastern Oklahoma. The 50-acre (20-ha) park features the famous "Glome Valley" runestone on Poteau Mountain in LeFlore County. Four more similar runestones are known to exist in the surrounding area. The Poteau and Shawnee inscriptions are in the Robert S. Kerr Museum in Poteau, Oklahoma, and the other two are inaccessible on private land. There are rumors of still more runestones in the general area.

## Spiro Mounds

Situated on a narrow bend of the Arkansas River, the location of Spiro Mounds was a natural meeting place for societies who traveled between the wooded southeast and the western rolling grassy plains. Although various groups of native people had camped in the Spiro region for thousands of years, the location did not become a permanent settlement until sometime around 600 CE. Because the settled Spiro people maintained such practices as truncated mound construction, a leadership of priest-kings, and a religious tradition called the "Southern Cult" common to the southeast, they were an example of what archaeologists termed the mound builders of the Mississippian Culture. The people of Spiro practiced horticulture, primarily consisting of corn, bean and squash cultivation, and gathered other wild food resources. At its peak between 900 and 1450 CE, Spiro's influence stretched from the Gulf Coast to the Great Lakes and from the Rocky Mountains to the Atlantic coast. The 150-acre (60-ha) Spiro site was the center of culture to approximately 60 tribes and 30 language groups. Spiro Mounds was the center to one of the most complex and sophisticated prehistoric cultures in North America.

Dominating the extensive religious complex were 12 large pyramid mounds where elaborately dressed priest-kings would officiate. One burial mound was set apart, and was rumored to be haunted. A remarkable collection of huge pipes and exquisite ceremonial items excavated from the mounds indicate that the Spiro people created a sophisticated trade network termed

▲ The reconstructed Craig Mound as appears today. It was destroyed by treasure seekers in the 1930s when it was discovered to contain a rich array of artifacts.

a "prehistoric gateway," and was one of the farthest western locations of an advanced culture based on the Mississippi River system of waterways. Besides trade, a highly developed religious center emerged at Spiro, along with a political system that exerted control over an expansive region. Unlike other temple mound centers along the Mississippi, Ohio, and Tennessee rivers, Spiro was never fortified by either moat or defensive wall. The assumption is that the priest-kings felt secure with their military control of strategic outposts. The mounds of Spiro are unique for two reasons. There were two locations constructed, one on an upland ridge which contained a ring of nine mounds built over the remains of burned or dismantled ceremonial buildings, and another set on the bottomlands where three mounds were erected. The position of the central temple mound aligns with several mounds to accurately determine both seasonal equinoxes and the summer and winter solstices.

> The Spiro people exerted influence over many people, produced artesian crafts, held an advanced knowledge of the seasons, and planned their city according to celestial observations. Yet no clear reason exists as to why the Spiro empire declined and disappeared.

As Spiro became a prominent Native American political and religious center, influential inhabitants became commercial entrepreneurs. To help identify their growing status in the community, these leaders accumulated a rich array of exotic goods imported from many parts of North America. Influential tribal members collected adornments used as status symbols in the community or worn during special ceremonies. Among the most favored exotic commodities were conch shells from the west coast of Florida, pottery from northeast Arkansas and Tennessee, copper from the southeast and the Great Lakes region, lead from Iowa and Missouri, quartz from central Arkansas and flint from Kansas, Texas, Tennessee and southern Illinois. Spiro artisans fashioned many of these materials into elaborately decorated ornaments, such as ceremonial cups, batons and other symbols of status and authority. Among prehistoric societies such items were a sign of wealth and power, and Spiro's priestly leaders were among the most affluent in their time. Elaborate artifacts of conch and copper were more numerous at Spiro than at any other prehistoric site in North America. The artistic style of Spiro influenced the ideas and works of many other surrounding people. They used a variety of techniques including engraving and embossing, depicting elaborate scenes of dance, gaming, warriors, and mythological creatures, such as winged serpents, antlered snakes, spiders, and catlike monsters that later became important in the mythologies of historic

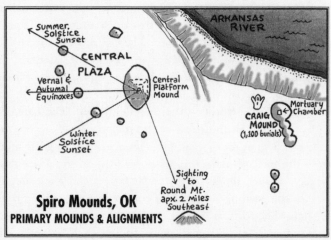

Spiro Mounds, OK
PRIMARY MOUNDS & ALIGNMENTS

▲ The feathered serpent was an important symbol found on several Spiro artifacts.

southeastern tribes. At Spiro, however, the animal figures favored by early artisans were later replaced by humanlike figures.

For reasons unknown, the Spiro complex was abandoned as an inhabited village, yet the priest-kings of newer settlements would periodically visit the mounds for burial rituals or ceremonies. Mound construction continued at Spiro after the village was abandoned, especially burials in Craig Mound, where hundreds of individual graves were uncovered. Their diverse burial affiliations attest to a highly developed hierarchy of religious or political leaders who placed a priority in taking personal items into the afterlife. By 1450 CE, the existing tribal members were no longer visiting the site and ritual mound construction at Spiro had ended. From the mid-16th century until the first Europeans arrived, Spiro's descendants were living in hamlets scattered along the Arkansas River who viewed the mounds as haunted. The descendents of Spiro are believed to have become the Wichita, and possibly the Caddo tribes. The Choctaw, a relocated tribe from Mississippi, also had a tradition of building mounds. The Choctaw recognized Spiro as a sacred site and provided protection for the structures when the region was ceded to them in a land treaty.

Around the late 19th century, Spiro was known locally as a prehistoric Indian site with rumored associations to a Middle Age Viking trade. The mounds lay relatively undisturbed until 1933 when the site attracted national and worldwide attention after a group of opportunistic treasure hunters called the Pocola Mining Company leased the land and began a reckless excavation of the mounds. They brought in dynamite and huge equipment and leveled the mounds, destroying more artifacts than they removed intact. Before excavation, Craig Mound had an Indian affiliation with the lair of jaguar spirits, and early settlers reported seeing an eerie blue light emanating around the mound at night. The Craig Mound was originally 33 feet (10 m) high and 400 feet (120 m) long. It was a work in progress for nearly 600 years, first as four joined mounds, then as a singular mound to cover the graves of the society's most important leaders. A tunnel was dug that led into a mortuary chamber supported by cedar beams and enclosing an enigmatic large male skeleton wearing a full suit of copper armor, polished beads, and engraved conch shells. The fortune seekers discovered rich troves of spectacular artifacts, including objects of wood, pearl, cloth, copper, shell, basketry and stone. In the 1930s, an eager market of buyers was ready to acquire mound objects, and the Spiro Mound goods were among the very best. Over one million artifacts were retrieved from Craig Mound alone. Unfortunately, the diggers were only concerned with finding and selling the relics, not with preserving the past or recording their significance. Consequently, extremely important prehistoric artifacts were looted and sold out of Oklahoma and irreplaceable information about the most colorful Central Plains culture, with possible ties to a Viking outpost, were lost. Years later two amateur archaeologists managed to track down most of the best artifacts the Pocola Company had sold to collectors. They repurchased the remaining items and donated them to the state, where they are among Oklahoma's richest cultural assets. The recreated archaeological site includes the remains of a village and 12 earthen mounds.

### Getting to Spiro Mounds

Spiro Mounds Archaeology Center is a state park located about 7 miles (11 km) east of the small town of Spiro, on Lock and Dam Road, very close to the Arkansas border. Further south on highway 59 in Oklahoma is Heavener Runestone State Park where several Viking runestones were found as outdoor markers, and one still exists, in a deep sheltered ravine. Visitor hours at Spiro Mounds State Park are from 9-5 Wednesday through Saturday, 12-5 on Sunday. Guided tours are by appointment only. Contact Dennis Peterson Rt. 2, Box 339AA, Spiro, OK 74959 (918) 962-2062. Spiro Mounds is Oklahoma's only National Historic Landmark and archaeological center.

# SOUTH DAKOTA

With the stroke of a quill pen plucked from a North Dakota eagle on February 22nd, 1889, President Benjamin Harrison created Washington, Montana, and the "twin" states, North and South Dakota, capping the northern frontier with Canada. The geographic center of the United States is marked close to the town of Belle Fourche, South Dakota, while the geographic center of North America is closer to the Canadian border, just outside of Rugby, North Dakota. The western portion of South Dakota between the Black Hills and the vast open prairie was an important gateway to both animal and human. At one time millions of bison roamed the prairie and provided subsistence for countless generations of Native Americans. The buffalo was the most sacred animal to almost every tribe of the Central Plains. Every part of the animal was utilized. Not only was the meat their primary source of protein, but the Indians also used the blood

▲ The ultra sacred white buffalo has been reborn in South Dakota.

for paints, the hide for clothes, the hoofs for glue, the bones for tools, and the organs for containers. Little was wasted. A white buffalo spotted within a heard was always considered auspicious. An old Indian belief prophesized the appearance of a white buffalo in the future would signal a period when world peace will engulf all good people of all races. The prophecy also stated that the white buffalo would be born to white people in the center of the nation. A mother and daughter white buffalo live just outside the town of Custer in the Black Hills of South Dakota. The mother buffalo was born near Belle Fourche.

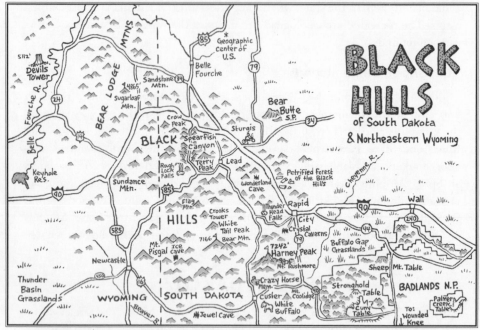

## Badlands

The Lakota Sioux and other Plains Indians have long considered the broad expanse of rugged terrain called the Badlands a place of deep spiritual significance. The saw-toothed ridges and parched canyons inspired many generations of Native Americans, especially young men who came on vision quests to pray for a good life enriched with fruitful hunting. Surrounded on all sides by prairie, this eroded wasteland of layered mineral deposits is a harsh and formidable environment. A vision quest would typically last four days and nights of fasting and sleep deprivation on a lonely hill. In this life-changing test, a young brave would chant and meditate until the vision of an animal spirit arrived. This animal token acted as a protector for the rest of his life. After this spiritual meeting, the brave would return to his village where the elders could interpret the circumstances surrounding his vision and grant him his adult name. Still today, the Stronghold and Sheep Mountain Tables in the Badlands are favored sites for young Lakota men to visit, fast, pray, and seek a vision for their future.

# CENTRAL PLAINS

*The Badlands name derives from the Indian term "mako sica" meaning land bad, a forbidding terrain at "the edge of the world."*

Some migrating Plains Indian tribes would avoid the area at all costs, considering it taboo, or bad medicine. Others would find profound spiritual meaning in the harsh conditions, enabling them to communicate directly with the Great Spirit. The earliest evidence of human usage dates back 12,000 years when the "Plains Archaic" people ventured into the Badlands to hunt wholly mammoth and other large mammals. The night fires of nomad hunters flickered in the badland darkness for thousands of years. By 1000 CE, forebears of the Plains Indians camped on the bordering plains. French trappers, pushing down from Canada, were the first Europeans to visit the area. They called the country *les mauvaises terres à traverser,* which, like the Indian mako sica, translates as "bad lands to cross." The water in the badlands may have been "too thick to drink, and too thin to plow," but that didn't stop some homesteaders from trying. Just outside the Northeast Entrance of the Park is the Prairie Homestead featuring cramped cabins dug into the hillsides.

Several famous Native American ceremonies took place in the Badlands, including the enigmatic Ghost Dance of the Oglala Dakota which promised the disappearance of the white man and the return of the buffalo. The last time it was performed was in the late fall of 1890 when several hundred Oglala climbed the Stronghold Table in the southwest district of the park. The Wounded Knee Massacre took place just south of the Badlands only two months later, in December 1890. It is thought that the Ghost Dance and other circumstances contributed to high tensions in the area prompting the indiscriminate massacre of defenseless people. On this infamous winter day nearly an entire Lakota band of 300 men, women and children were ruthlessly slaughtered by the Army in perhaps the worst documented case of genocide on North American soil. Wounded Knee was the final chapter in the long saga for the semi-nomadic Plains Indians, as their future was sealed on this fateful day. The U.S. Calvary sent a powerful message to all remaining renegade tribes to permanently relocate on a reservation or face the same consequences as the Lakota.

The Badlands is renowned for the significant amount of prehistoric fossils located in the numerous strata of exposed earth. An array of extinct animals, ranging from very small to enormous, once ranged throughout the area now included in Badlands National Park. Some of these strange beasts lived in the subtropical forests that flourished after the retreat of the shallow inland seas, while others inhabited the grasslands that came in the millennia afterwards. Such unusual bones would have amazed the Native Americans, who almost certainly interacted with the fossils. Such deposits of dinosaur bones could have led to the multitude of Plains Indian legends about vicious monsters and giant beasts that roamed the land before the coming of *wasichu,* or white people. One popular tale

241

▲ The strangely eroded landscape of the South Dakota Badlands.

speaks about a winged beast called Wakinyan Tanka, the great thunderbird of the Black Hills. At one point the thunderbird fights against the dreaded Unktehi, or water creatures. In this tale, the thunderbird uses his lightning bolts to defeat his enemies in the Badlands where "their bones were turned to rock." Indeed, the lowest stratum is richly studded with aquatic fossil remains, where snail-like ammonites share space with the stone bones of dinosaur alligators and giant sea turtles. Overlying the marine shale, the Chadron formations expose the remains of the fantastic titanothere, a rhinoceros mammal about the size of an elephant. Strange creatures abound in the Brule sediments, where the oreodont, a pig-shaped animal with sheep-like teeth, roamed the once lush country with small saber-toothed cats, fox-sized horses, and the earliest known camels. Judging from the remains, the Badlands were once a haven and a graveyard for these creatures. Erosion has cut deep into the soft soil of the Badlands over the past half million years and left behind an alien landscape of cones, mesas, gorges, gulches, pinnacles, and precipices. And while the extinction story ended millions of years ago, the fossil record certainly inspired all humans who braved this wasteland and happened upon the exposed bones of fantastic beasts.

## *Getting to the Badlands*

Badlands National Park is easily accessed just off Interstate 90 in southwestern South Dakota. Westbound travelers should use exit 131 to Highway 240, conversely known as the 40-mile Badlands Loop Road. Eastbound travelers on I-90 can do the opposite from the town of Wall. There are also several approaches into the park from the south via the Lakota Pine Ridge Indian Reservation. The Stronghold Table is not accessible to the general public. Please be respectful of brightly colored fabric and prayer sticks attached to branches in the Badlands, as these are signs of traditional worship by tribal members and should not be disturbed. The Badlands Loop is an especially enjoyable drive at dawn or dusk, when the interplay of shadow, light and shifting colors develop into a spectacular crescendo.

## Sacred Peaks of the Black Hills

The Lakota's sacred *Paha Sapa,* or "Hills of Black," is a rugged mountain range spanning western South Dakota and northeastern Wyoming. The Black Hills were supposed to be part of the Great Sioux Reservation under an 1868 treaty, but no treaty could prevent gold fever among settlers. An 1874 expedition led by General George A. Custer alerted the world to gold in the hills, subsequently forcing all ingenious people out. The mountains received their name from the dark Ponderosa pine covered hills that rise noticeably above the treeless prairie. Roughly enclosed by the Belle Fourche and Cheyenne rivers, the Black Hills encompass nearly 6,000 square miles (15,540 sq km), and host an extensive network of hiking trails throughout the range. Geologists estimate that these peaks were once more than 14,000 feet (4,200 m) tall, but have now disintegrated to less than half that height. The resulting erosion has left abundant granite stone outcroppings, now popular for rock climbing or scenic hiking. The disintegration also left behind a treasure drove of minerals, including the world's largest working gold mine in the town of Lead. Besides minerals, wood was extracted from the Black Hills for fuel and building material by Native Americans, white settlers, and the resource-hungry mining and railroad companies.

> Plains Indians worshipped and revered the Black Hills for thousands of years. Harney Peak was a legendary mystic location and Bear Butte was used for vision quests.

To the various bands of the Sioux nation, Harney Peak has always been and remains a mythical mountain. A long tradition of praying at the mountain and recounting visions make the peak renowned to all who live in its shadow. At the age of nine, a soon-to-be prominent medicine man of the Oglala Sioux named Black Elk had a profound vision upon the summit. Black Elk was led by his spiritual guides to the summit. These guides showed him that Harney Peak was located at the exact center of the world. For him, it was a place of spiritual rejuvenation where he could commune with his ancestors. In another vision Black Elk was shown good and evil from the center of a stone circle indicating the four directions. Harney Peak is the tallest of the Black Hills and the highest peak east of the Rocky Mountains. The mountain is a beacon with commanding views of the surrounding region, and on a clear day visitors can see Montana, Nebraska, South Dakota and Wyoming from the summit. Harney Peak was named after General William S. Harney, the commanding officer of Lieutenant G. K. Warren, who mapped the peak in 1857 during a military expedition to the Black Hills. Harney Peak, along with the Cathedral Spires and Needles, were originally intended to be the site of a huge national rock sculpture, but the location moved to Mount Rushmore and became the famous sculpture of four president's faces. Mount Rushmore's backside is visible from the top of Harney Peak and the national memorial

▲ Bear Butte remains a potent vision quest site and pilgrimage destination for modern Native Americans.

looks rather small by comparison. The Presidential Trail at the base of Rushmore includes a small detour so people can gaze up at Harney Peak. Just 17 miles (27 km) west is the Crazy Horse Memorial sculpture, a large figure of the famed Lakota warrior on horseback, which has been under construction since the 1950s.

Bear Butte is a high ridge in the northwestern corner of the Black Hills resembling a huge sleeping bear. The stand-alone butte was a vision quest site used by the Plains Indians for many millennia. Vision quests are tests where the individual searches for spiritual power and self-knowledge. The bear had a strong symbolic meaning to Native Americans, oftentimes symbolic of hibernation and dreaming. The Sioux named this peak *Mato Pah,* meaning "Sleeping Bear Mountain," the Cheyenne called it *Noahavose* or the "Good Mountain," and the Lakota name was *Pahan Wakan* meaning "Bear Mountain." It was on Bear Butte that the Lakota warrior Crazy Horse had his famous vision of the future where all Indians would experience hard times ahead, yet would eventually arrive at a period of spiritual awakening and peace on earth. Along with Sitting Bull, Crazy Horse went on to unify the Lakota, the Sioux and Cheyenne in their victorious battle at Little Bighorn, Montana where General Custer and the entire 7th Calvary were killed. In Cheyenne tradition, the butte is famous for a cave where the chief Sweet Medicine spent four years on a vision quest. In the cave Sweet Medicine met the god Maheo, who bestowed upon him the four taboos—murder, incest, adultery, and theft—in the form of four arrowheads. The four arrows would bless and protect the Cheyenne, which made them believe that they were the chosen people. Despite an ongoing court battle preventing Native Americans the exclusive use of Bear Butte for religious purposes, many people come to hike the hill, including 4,000 Native Americans who arrive annually to pray at the peak. There is also an area near the base of the mountain set aside for Native Americans to practice pipe ceremony, sweats, and drumming rituals.

## *Getting to Harney Peak and Bear Butte*

Rising 7,242 feet (2,207 m) above sea level, Harney Peak is the tallest mountain in South Dakota. To reach the Harney Peak trailhead, take U.S. Highway 16A west from the park's Visitor Center to South Dakota Highway 87 (Needles Highway) and go north for about 7 miles (11 km). A sign on the right to Iron Creek Horse Camp indicates the next turn. Follow the dirt road for about a half mile (.8 km), then take the first road to the left and park at the road's end. The trail is relatively easy to hike, and the lichen-covered summit is a rugged granite dome that provides stunning views. Bear Butte State Park is located 7 miles (11 km) northeast of the town Sturgis on South Dakota Highway 79. Another relatively easy graded trail leads to the summit, passing many prayer flags along the way. Sturgis is host to thousand of motorcycle enthusiasts who meet annually during the first two weeks of August.

# TEXAS

Spanish conquistadors first explored Texas in the 1540s looking for the seven fabulously wealthy cities of Cibola. The fabled gold cities didn't exist, but Spain claimed the vast expanse and named the territory after an Indian word meaning "friendly." The missions of Texas were set up in the early 1700s not so much as religious communities, but rather as fortified settlements to counter the French expeditions into the region. In 1821, Mexico broke away from Spanish rule and encouraged settlers to the region by offering generous land grants. The American newcomers soon grew restless of Mexican rule and rebelled, leading to the famous last stand of the Alamo. After their defeat, the U.S. Calvary arrived in Texas and handily defeated the Mexican army. Texas finally achieved its independence and became recognized as the only state that legally broke away from the United States to become its own sovereign nation. Eventually it joined the United States. Statehood was granted in 1845, and Texas entered the modern age when a gusher blew at the Spindletop oil field.

## Indian Hot Springs

The name comes from the extensive usage of the site by indigenous people during prehistoric as well as historic times. In 1884, Texas Rangers were scouting for cattle ranching sites when they came upon 22 artesian springs near the Rio Grande River. The springs were networked by several well-worn footpaths, including several extending across the river into Mexico. Native American artifacts, debris, and offerings from successive camps have been discovered alongside the springs. A waterway carved into the travertine rock deposit adjacent to Chief Spring was likely cut by Native Americans reworking the water flow.

▲ Indian Hot Springs is privately owned but open to the public.

The springs are on a floodplain of the Rio Grande, spread across a plateau at the southern edge of the Quitman Mountains. Being situated over the Caballo Fault, near the Rio Grande, and close to underground uranium deposits, the Indian Hot Springs are subject to electromagnetic field discharges that keep the air rich in negative ions. Included among the water constituents are relatively high levels of boron, lithium, chloride, sulfate, potassium, sodium, calcium, magnesium, bicarbonate, nitrate, and strontium. The thermal springs in this area of Texas and Mexico are replenished by water contained within the immediate area, including the Quitman Mountains. The water seeps into the bedrock, interacts with different minerals as it is being heated, and eventually percolates back up to the surface. The main pools at Indian Hot Springs have been named Chief (or Bath), Squaw, Stump, Beauty, Soda, Salt Cedar, Masons, Itty Bitty and Grass Spring, each with its own unique chemical balance.

The Indian Hot Springs were originally a group of 22 artesian springs renowned for their curative powers. For over a thousand years shaman and folk healers have made use of the springs' mud and water for ritualistic cleansing and physical regeneration.

All the springs except Soda Spring flow from an extensive travertine plateau supplied by an underground source. Only Stump Spring actually discharges water to the surface, at an astonishing rate of 100 gallons (400 l) per minute! All others discharge water through the permeable travertine or alluvium soil above the subsurface strata by flowing up the Caballo Fault to the surface. Temperatures of the springs range from the Stump Spring, the warmest (also the hottest thermal spring in Texas) with a temperature of 117° F (47° C), to Soda Spring with the coolest waters at a temperature of 81° F (27° C). The travertine mounds at Chief, Squaw, and Stump springs are the largest mounds, standing approximately 1.5 feet (0.5 m) above the plateau. The mineral constituents in the different pools are a product of interaction with subsurface strata as the water makes its way to the surface. Around each spring are colorful mosses, clay, mud, and stones. The Indian Hot Springs contain a substantially higher concentration of chemicals than other thermal springs in Texas and northern Mexico. The region also has natural radiation levels 13 times higher than the immediate surroundings. Each individual spring has its own unique mineral content in the water, mud, and mosses, which may be used to relieve certain ailments. Bath Spring is reportedly good for the liver and general body purging; Squaw Spring is beneficial for women with menstrual problems or needing detoxification; and Stump Spring gives relief to those suffering from asthma and diabetes. The mud and mosses have healing properties too. Covering oneself in the black mud supposedly cures insomnia; the mosses relieve rashes; and the particular mud in Sulfur Spring helps clear up skin blemishes. Sitting on certain stones in and out of the pools for a period of time also seems to relieve those with piles or constipation. Others report an occasional "jolt" of energy conducted through the stones, acting as a sort of antennae for transmitting underground energy.

Following the removal of the last nomadic Apaches from west Texas, the area was opened to widespread settlement, ranching, farming and development. Residents of Sierra Blanca first used the springs as early as 1906, and two attempts in the 1920s to commercially develop the site as a health resort failed. In the early 1940s another attempt to build a fancy resort was never completed because of World War II. A very strong "spirit of place" resides at Indian Hot Springs, which some claim have kept the large developers at bay. Visitors enjoy several small adobe bathhouses located around the Chief and Squaw Springs, while smaller rock tubs have been constructed around some of the other pools. People staying overnight at the springs often report having vividly wild dreams of tall dark-skinned Indians and bands of wild horses. Indian Hot Springs is now privately owned, and was listed on the National Register of Historic Places in 1991.

## Getting to Indian Hot Springs

The Indian Hot Springs, a cluster of seven large geothermal springs and several smaller pools, are on the Rio Grande floodplain in southern Hudspeth County, just north of the Mexican border. Access to the springs is along a public dirt road that begins about 25 miles (40 km) south of Sierra Blanca. Follow the signs on Interstate 10 for a turnoff south towards the Rio Grande River. The road is usually passable by 2-wheel drive vehicles, unless there has just been a rainstorm and then the route can be muddy.

# GREAT LAKES REGION

*"We do not inherit the Earth from our Ancestors, we borrow it from our Children."* -**Indian proverb**

AS RECENTLY AS 12,000 YEARS AGO MOST OF THE MIDWEST including eastern Canada and Appalachia were covered by massive glacial ice sheets. As the climate warmed the glaciers melted and the Great Lakes were formed. The retreating glaciers and subsequent runoff left behind some of the most fertile soil in the world. On the western periphery of the Great Lakes were the expansive grass prairies where millions of buffalo grazed and occasionally wandered into the heavily forested eastern half of the continent. Before modern settlers began clearing the eastern forests for farm land it is said that a squirrel could travel along the treetops all the way from the Atlantic Ocean to the Mississippi River without touching ground.

In the woodland area of eastern North America, especially south of the Great Lakes, various people from different cultural affiliations constructed elaborate earthwork structures on the generally flat landscape. The highest concentration of mound cities existed around the middle Ohio River Valley where as many as 1,000 to 1,500 mound complexes once existed in Ohio alone. Most of the earthwork features that were present five centuries ago when the European colonization of

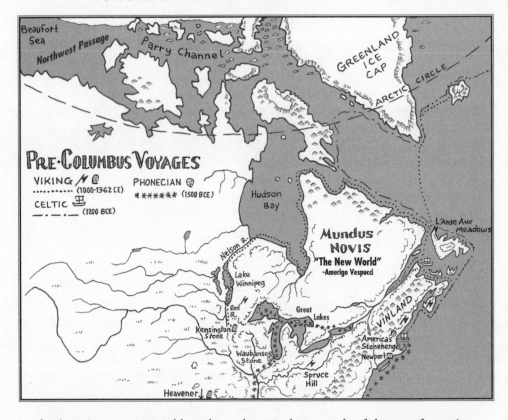

the Americas commenced have been destroyed as a result of the transformation of eastern North America into agricultural, urban, and transportation landscapes. Almost all of the contemporary native people in the Great Lakes region reported that mounds were there when they arrived. The tradition of mound building was all but forgotten when the first historic European explorers came into the area, except for certain effigy mound builders in the Great Lakes region. The only mound building tradition that continued was the Winnebago tribe living near the sizeable Winnebago Lake in Wisconsin. Effigy mounds were shaped into unique land forms, usually based on a favored clan animal, a geometric design such as a straight line, or sometimes a human figure. The largest ancient mounds, the platform mounds with flat tops used for temples or religious ceremonies, typify the Mississippian Culture. Multi-level platform mounds are not found in the earlier Adena or Hopewell traditions of burial mound building. Adding further mystery, many temple mounds were oriented to the east and aligned with regular celestial events.

# ILLINOIS

The name Illinois is a French corruption of *Illini*, meaning the land of great men or warriors. All traces of the mound building Mississippian Culture had disappeared by 1673; the year French explorers Father Marquette and Louis

Joliet traveled and charted the Mississippi River. Returning north up the Illinois River, the French explorers were led by their Indian guides to a strategic portage into Lake Michigan near present-day Lyons, a western suburb of Chicago. A small tributary called Portage Creek flowed into the Des Plaines River just east of Harlem Avenue from Mud Lake, an ancient swamp that accessed the shortest overland portage into the South Branch of the Chicago River. In the spring, especially during a heavy rain year, this was the only total-water route from the Great Lakes to the Mississippi because it was possible to pass through Mud Lake without having to portage a boat. Soon after charting this route into Lake Michigan, the French established several missions and trading posts along prominent Illinois waterways. These early outposts include La Salle, Marseilles and Champaign, where the French assimilated various Indian tribes and converted them to Christianity.

## Cahokia Mounds

Located on an expansive flood plain near the confluence of the Illinois, Mississippi and Missouri rivers is the preserved central section of the largest prehistoric Indian city north of Mexico. As a World Heritage Site, Cahokia Mounds includes 68 hand-packed earthen mounds, a wooden sun calendar, several burial tombs and a central plaza, all spanning across 2,200 acres (880 ha). There are 106 remaining mounds in total, out of 120 known. Among the most interesting excavations, Mound 72 produced nearly 300 burials including a 45-year-old male ruler whose body was placed upon 20,000 shell beads. Next to his body were four men with their heads and hands missing, along with the bodies of 53 women between the ages of 15 and 25 who were sacrificed with their ruler. The city at its height in 1200 CE was home to at least 20,000 residents, but may have been as high as 50,000. At that time Cahokia had a larger population than the city of London, England. Expansive agricultural fields encircling the city supported the citizens. Cahokia is also the renowned birthplace of archaeoastronomy, the science of identifying astronomical alignments within the architecture of prehistoric structures. Archaeoastronomy became a new component of North American archaeology following Warren Wittry's 1964 discovery of several woodhenges at Cahokia. Wittry demonstrated that these wooden features were solar observatories and determined that its builders had an integral understanding of celestial movements.

The Mississippi River and many of its tributaries once supported an advanced early American civilization that mysteriously disappeared. The Mississippian Culture thrived for 500 years, emerging around 900 CE, seemingly as a direct result of the earlier Adena and Hopewell mound builders of the middle Ohio Valley. The cultures' lasting legacy is the variety of mound cities to be found along waterways from Wisconsin down to the Gulf of Mexico. Many of these early settlements were developed later as modern cities; for example, St. Louis, Missouri was originally called "Mound City." The people are known as the "Mississippian

▲ The expansive walled city of Cahokia as it would have appeared in the 11th century CE.
(Image courtesy National Geographic Society)

Culture" mound builders because no recorded name exists. Similarly, the name "Cahokia" is taken from a sub-tribe of the Illini Indians because no knowledge of the original name exists. Like the Mayans in Central America, this advanced culture went into decline, then all but vanished by the time modern Europeans explored the area. Suggestions as to why Cahokia was abandoned include natural resource depletion, climatic change, war, or social unrest. Most likely an outbreak of smallpox or another lethal disease was unleashed in 1541 by Spanish conquistadors led by Hernando De Soto during their ill-fated search for gold across southeastern North America. De Soto and his men recorded some of the mound cities still under construction and occupied, yet never made it as far north as Cahokia. What actually became of the original Cahokia inhabitants remains a complete mystery. Later tribes lacked the oral traditions or knowledge of the site to link them to any actual builders, yet Cahokia was the largest city of the Mississippian Culture. Ceremonial activities such as human sacrifice and sun worship took place at Cahokia. Atop the pyramids were astronomical observatories, sometimes burial crypts, and usually ritual buildings where a priest-king would oversee various ceremonies.

> Monk's Mound at Cahokia is the largest pre-
> historic structure in North America. Originally
> more than four city blocks long, the sacred
> pyramid had a base slightly larger than
> Egypt's Great Pyramid.

At first glance, the layout of prehistoric Cahokia is remarkably similar to the design of Central American sacred cities, carefully arranged in rows of houses surrounding various open plazas. Platform mounds were erected to house leaders in elevated temples and were laid out based on specific solar and other astronomical events. The central precinct facing Monk's Mound was enclosed by a high stockade wall plastered with hardened clay, effectively making it a giant fortress. Bastions were erected at regular intervals to make defense of the walls easier.

Excavations show that the walls were rebuilt at least four times and also uncovered thousands of arrowheads where the walls would have burned under siege. A wooden sun calendar, named "Woodhenge" by Wittry, was erected to determine the seasons and to schedule ceremonial activities, including where various games were to be played. Cahokia is sometimes referred to as "the City of the Sun" because a "Birdman" tablet was found, similar in appearance to Quetzalcoatl, regarded as the high priest of the city. But perhaps the greatest similarity to prehistoric Central American culture lies within the enormous earthen mounds shaped like pyramids. The largest pyramid at Cahokia was erroneously named Monk's Mound after French Trappist Monks who lived at the site in the 1800s, much later than any of the mound builder cultures. Monk's Mound is the single largest prehistoric earthwork in the Americas. This ancient pyramid once had a base of 16 acres (6.4 ha), making it larger than the Great Pyramid in Egypt. The earthen mound once stood 10 stories tall, yet due to soil settlement and erosion it is now only 35 feet (11 m) in height. Important ceremonies were held on two levels of the great mound. At the top, a priest-king lived in a huge wooden temple, dedicated to the sun god.

Recent drilling into Monk's Mound has revealed an unsuspected find. In January 1998, workers broke a drill bit when they struck a hard surface while probing into the mound. According to archaeologists, the find could be the remnants of a ceremonial structure, a burial tomb, a cache of tools, or some sort of drainage system. The structure was encountered at 40 feet (12 m) under the second terrace, where the drill bit broke after boring through 32 feet (9 m) of stone. What makes this interesting is that the Mississippian Culture is not known to have used stone for their construction, at least not at this site. Further remote sensing at the site found three "anomalies"—the original stone structure, a densely packed earth structure above it, and a second earthen structure was identified 70 feet (21 m) deeper into the center of the mound. These finds may be part of an older structure pre-dating Monk's Mound. It is common throughout the world for ancient sites to be located on top of older structures or upon their original foundations.

## Getting to Cahokia Mounds

The expansive 2,200-acre (880-ha) Cahokia Mounds State Historic Park can be found a mere 12 miles (20 km) from St. Louis, MO. In ancient times the mound city would have been just a short canoe trip down a tributary creek to the Mississippi River, only 5 miles (8 km) away. The proximity to the Illinois, Mississippi and Missouri rivers made Cahokia a crossroads for early boat traffic. Yet most motorists today will find the Cahokia Mounds World Heritage Site located just outside of St. Louis, across the Mississippi River, in Collinsville, IL. Interstate 55/70 runs very close to the site, and well-marked signs direct motorists from Exit 6 to the ancient city.

# Waubansee Stone

One of the most fascinating and obscure artifacts in North America is tucked away in a downtown Chicago museum. The Waubansee Stone is a huge glacial erratic granite boulder with a larger-than-life head sculpted upon its upper surface. The expertly fashioned relief carving shows the face of a man with a chin beard, depicted with his mouth open and eyes closed. On the top of the stone, just above the head, is a large drop-shaped bowl that once emptied through the head and out of the mouth, over the lower lip, to another drainage spout below the man's goatee. There are also two connecting holes on either side of the boulder, presumably used as a line anchorage for a sea vessel. All holes and drainage spouts are currently plugged with putty or other additions, suggesting there is no interest in a modern restoration. The mysterious face carving and associated cavities have given rise to speculation about its origins, including one theory that the stone was carved by prehistoric Mediterranean seafarers who used the 3,000-pound (1,350-kg) boulder as a mooring stone.

Originally standing around 8 feet (3 m) in height, the Waubansee Stone is mentioned in early Fort Dearborn accounts as being located just beyond the stockade walls, along the shore of the Chicago River. *Checagou* was an Indian word for "wild onion," a plant that grew profusely along the banks of the river. When the first fort was built in 1803, the Potawatomi Indians of southern Lake Michigan had been trading with white people for well over a century, but were becoming increasingly hostile to the amount of new settlers coming into the region and staking a claim on their land. President Jefferson, who was very interested in the Northwest Territory, was anxious about its security. He felt that an American military outpost should be established to protect the new frontier. He selected the mouth of the Chicago River as the site for a new fort. At that time there were several fur traders and their Indian wives living in the region. The fort was named after General Henry Dearborn, Secretary of War. It was built on the south side of the Chicago River where Michigan Avenue now crosses at Wacker Drive. Skirmishes with the Potawatomi were on the rise, reaching a crescendo in 1812 when 50 settlers and soldiers were massacred and the first fort was burned to the ground by the enraged Indians. The second Fort Dearborn was rebuilt in 1816-1817 and the Waubansee Stone was presumably reduced in size to be dragged into the fort's parade grounds where it remained until the fort was dismantled. After that the stone passed from collector to collector until it found a permanent home at the Fort Dearborn section in the Chicago Historical Society, where it remains to this day.

Historian Henry H. Hurlbut developed the generally accepted theory about the stone's origin in 1881, unsupported by any records or documentation. His belief, admittedly based on no evidence, has the stone being carved in the early 1800s by an un-named soldier stationed at the original Fort Dearborn. Its face was supposedly fashioned after the friendly Native American Potawatomi chieftain, Waubansee, and this appointed name stuck. Hurlbut had only hearsay on which to base his observations, including the presumption that the Indians used the upper recess as a mortar to grind their corn. This accepted explanation has come under fire from several angles. For starters, the recess was intentionally plugged after the Indians supposedly used it, so it would have been an ineffective mortar because the corn would have drained through the mouth. Also, why would a frontier soldier, who was probably suspicious of the Potawatomi in the first place,

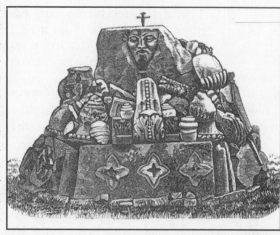

▲ The Waubansee Stone grouped together with artifacts collected after the Chicago Fire. This 19th century etching gives an indication of the relic's scaled-down size. It had originally been much taller.

spend many months to carve the likeness of their tribal leader? Aside from the fact that granite is one of the hardest stones to sculpt, the face is clearly the work of a master stonecutter who must have devoted a considerable amount of time and labor to the job—hardly in keeping with the strenuous daily tasks of a common frontier soldier. Finally, Native Americans were not known to have grown goatees, nor did they ever carve in granite. But if not Hurlbut's anonymous soldier or an Indian sculptor, then who crafted the mysterious features on the Waubansee Stone?

With more source material than Hurlbut had at his disposal, yet with an uncertain date and a possible grisly usage, fragments of evidence can be pieced together using various historical theories to arrive near the truth. An article in the *Chicago Tribune* dated September 22nd, 1903 clearly illustrates the two opposing viewpoints clashing over the stone's origin: "The second school of historians and antiquarians is convinced that the so-called Waubansee Stone dates back hundreds and perhaps even thousands of years before even Father Marquette first visited the site of Chicago in 1673. They see in the tall bowlder (sic), with its deeply top, a sacrificial altar on which perhaps the mound builders of prehistoric America offered even human sacrifices, and they are ready to believe that the face carved on one side of the stone is a representation of an ancient idol—one of the far off gods to whom that mythical people poured libations and offered the sacrificial blood of animals. However that may be, there is no question of doubt that in the early days of Fort Dearborn, as far back as we have any record, that identical stone, practically the same as it is today, lay near the stockade of old Fort Dearborn."

The diffusionist theory of the Waubansee
Stone describes it as a sacrificial altar for
ancient Celtic and Phoenician traders in the
millennium before Christ.

All historians agree that the Mississippian Culture performed animal and human sacrifices high atop their platform mounds, but where this practice originated is unknown. The Aztec or Toltec people from Mexico may have influenced them, or perhaps an earlier seafaring people notorious for infant sacrifices were responsible. It is well known that the Phoenicians (and their Celtic allies) traveled across the ocean to "the Farthest Land" known as Antilla. The precise location of Antilla was a closely guarded secret because it contained the most valuable commodity to Bronze Age people—copper. Michigan's Upper Peninsula is the richest natural deposit of pure copper in the world. It may seem a long way to go for the metal, but in the Bronze Age copper was more prized than gold or silver since it was the primary alloy used in weapon and tool production. With profit as a clear motive for their journey it makes sense that the Phoenicians would travel very far to export copper. It also makes sense that the Phoenicians would spread their religious practices with their voyages. An integral element of the Phoenician religion was infant sacrifice to appease pagan gods and win favor for whatever activity was at hand. At the height of Phoenician power—lasting a thousand years from 1,200 BCE until the Second Punic War—babies were taken to an outdoor sacred site, called a Tophet, where a young child was placed in a carved depression on an altar and had its' throat slit. Both the Celts and Phoenicians were known to sacrifice infant children of their enemies, or barter with their trading partners to acquire a baby for this heinous ritual. In the case of the Waubansee Stone, the sacrificial blood would flow through the sculpture into the Chicago River as an offering to the water gods, thus ensuring a safe passage. The stone's hideous purpose is evident in the closed eyes, an unusual style elsewhere, but recurring in surviving Phoenician art used for infant sacrifices. Moreover, the face depicts a chin beard, a personal grooming style of male Phoenicians. The mouth of the Chicago River was a necessary transition stop before entering the narrow river network leading into the Mississippi and then down to the Gulf of Mexico. The heavily-laden ships would need to be reconfigured from open water safety to narrow river defense. Oars and shields would replace conspicuous sails. After arriving at the mouth of the Chicago River, the ancient explorers may have settled for a brief time, sailed onward, been killed off, or possibly assimilated with the native population. There was likely a small Tophet temple at this strategic crossroad of lake and river, which thousands of years later would grow up to be the third largest city in the United States.

### Getting to the Waubansee Stone

The Waubansee Stone is on display in the Fort Dearborn Section of the Chicago Historical Society (CHS) museum. The CHS is located at 1601 N. Clark Street at North Avenue in Lincoln Park. CHS general information line: (312) 642-4600. Canoe enthusiasts can follow the North Branch of the Chicago River to any number of possible overland Indian portages to the Des Plaines River. The South Branch of the Chicago River is closed to recreational boaters. The Des Plaines River empties south into the Illinois River, which connects to the Mississippi River near St. Louis, MO. Several important mound sites are located along the Illinois River, including the Dickson Mounds and Rockwell Mound, both located near Havana, IL.

# MICHIGAN

A seasonal pilgrimage of sorts occurred for thousands of years in the northern Great Lakes region. Prehistoric sailors traversed the sacred lake *Kitchi-Gummi* to Isle Royale and the Upper Peninsula of Michigan for metal mining. Along the southern shores of Lake Superior, extending for a hundred miles on the northwestern Keweenaw Peninsula, are numerous open pit mines of the "Old Copper Culture." Over 2,000 ancient mining pits have been found on Isle Royale alone. Some pits still reveal the slice marks where prehistoric hammer stones had battered off chunks of the nearly pure copper. What makes the ancient copper mines so intriguing is the question of were it all went. One estimate places 2,000 times the amount excavated to the amount accounted for in North American archaeological finds. Even the most conservative academic will admit that much of the copper went "somewhere else." Also abundant are the rich iron ore deposits concentrated in northern Michigan, particularly along the Menominee Iron Range and the mining community of Iron Mountain, named by a prospector in 1845 after he discovered a nearby "mountain of iron." It is estimated that several million tons of copper and iron have already been extracted in modern times, and much more awaits excavation. The enormous reserves of iron and copper taken from the precambrian heart of Michigan is largely responsible for the steel and automobile manufacturing plants that transformed the state during the Industrial Revolution.

## House of David

Around the turn of the 19th century, starting in 1894, a charismatic husband and wife team traveled the Midwest preaching a unique version of Christianity. Benjamin and Mary Purnell sought to live by the original teachings of the New Testament, professing celibacy, eating only vegetarian food, and encouraging men to follow the example of Jesus Christ by growing their hair and beards long. After a decade of extensive travel, Benjamin and Mary envisioned starting their own Israelite community where they would reign as "king" and "queen." Benjamin suggested divine intervention when a dove perched on his shoulder supposedly declared him the chosen Seventh Messenger of the Faith. The dove also directed Benjamin and his followers to Benton Harbor, Michigan. The Purnell's visions, or "presentiments," led the loyal believers to a lush 100-acre lot (40-ha) in southwestern Michigan where they founded the legendary House of David. Their followers

▲ The Diamond House, where Benjamin Purnell lived his final years in seclusion, is now abandoned.

were mainly from an older Christian community of the same order dating back to 1792. The group claimed to be the nucleus of the lost Biblical tribe of Israel. As the Purnell's popularity spread, membership into the religious community came from distant parts of the world including Australia, Europe and Canada. Arriving at their prophesied destination with little more than the clothes on their back and a strong desire to succeed, the vagabond group began construction on what would become one of the most famous communal societies in North America.

> The House of David is the third oldest practicing communal order in the United States. It is situated around sacred Indian wells termed "Big Medicine" because of the springs' renowned healing properties.

The House of David, founded in 1903 by Benjamin and Mary Purnell, is located on the same property as several sacred Native American fresh water springs. Originally a famous healing site to the Miami Indians of southwestern Michigan, the artesian springs were exalted as "Big Medicine" for their well-known rejuvenating powers. Father Jacques Marquette took a sojourn at the springs to recover his strength before continuing on his 1672 exploratory mission through the Midwest. Following Marquette's visit, the springs became a famous convalescent center for other French explorers. The springs produced the best water in the area and may be the key reason why the Purnell's choose this location. Upon it they built the Eden Springs Amusement Park, replete with caged animals, lush fauna, and picturesque landscapes surrounded by a miniature train track. The zoo began in 1905 with exotic animals from around the world to compliment the elaborate fruit tree gardens. The park would also feature a baseball stadium, two miniature racecar tracks, vaudeville shows, and a bandstand for orchestras. Among its many accomplishments the House of David supported a pennant-winning baseball team, two traveling jazz bands, and ushered in the premiere "pre-Disney" amusement park in Middle America. Walt Disney himself toured Eden Springs in the early 1950s and bought one of the miniature steam locomotive engines for his studio. The manufacturing division at the House of David could produce just about anything they needed, including eight miniature trains and a fleet of diminutive racecars. While the bearded baseball team and band members toured the country, the House of David grounds became a major tourist attraction. The colony was able to tap into a lucrative tourist trade after the World's Fair in Chicago as big steamer ships came

▲ Mary's Israelite City of David is located adjacent to the House of David property.

across Lake Michigan to Benton Harbor. Equipped with their own hotels, hospital, green houses, bus line, trolley car line, cruise ships, vegetarian restaurants, and the biggest tourist plaza in America at the time, the House of David did all they could to capture the imagination of the early American tourism trade. Original patented items of the House of David include the world famous waffle cone topped with ice cream and the automatic pin-set for bowling.

Like other communal orders of the early 20th century, the House of David required all members to pool their personal assets and donate their labor for the collective good. Beginning with a handful of devoted and hard working people, the religious colony grew by leaps and bounds until it had become a small empire. Shortly after Benjamin's death in 1927 the colony was at its peak with over 1,000 members, yet without Benjamin as the central authority figure, internal division came quick. A major battle ensued over the leadership of the community, with Mary on one side and Benjamin's legal team, called the Dewhirst faction, on the other. Basically cut off from the assets and imprisoned in her own compound, Mary Purnell suffered a sore defeat by losing the entire community that she had made her life's work. Mary was further humiliated by the media's defamation of her husband who became a very controversial figure in his latter years. Mary Purnell would eventually settle out of court, walk two blocks east of the House of David properties with 217 faithful members, and reform the House of David as she had originally envisioned it. Mary's City of David followers were committed vegetarians as prescribed in Genesis as the diet of Eden. After the division several in the Dewhirst faction returned to the social practice of eating meat, which the Israelite Faith required them to forsake. Mary was tireless in her elder years, running her community and a vegetarian restaurant until her death in 1953 at the age of 91.

The backbone of the Israelite House of David teachings is called "the Marriage of the Lamb" from Revelation 19, calling for male and female equality and the restoration of the Divine Order that was Eden. Celibacy was a doctrinal feature at the House of David, and to this day is required for membership status in Mary's City of David. Although it has been suggested that celibacy was to blame for the community's loss of members, it was due less to the declining Israelite Faith than to a major power struggle following Benjamin's death. Some left the religious colony disillusioned, but most stayed on and simply died of old age. Since the remaining men and women lived separately there are no children to pass on the control of the properties. The decline was expected and is documented in the prophetic writings of both Mary and Benjamin. To this day the two sides remain bitterly divided, but because of their belief in celibacy, there now exists only a half dozen living members on each side—all in their elder years. Both sides predicted a resurrection in their membership after the millennium, but so far this has yet to occur.

### Getting to the House of David

Both the original House of David complex and Mary's City of David are located on Britain Avenue, off Michigan 139, in Benton Harbor. Coming from the south, take Exit 28 two miles (3.2 km) north of I-94. Coming from the north on I-94 take Exit 33 (Business 94) to M139. Coming from the north on M63, drive into downtown Benton Harbor and go east on Main Street, turn south on M139, two stoplights, go east on Britain Avenue to the property. Britain Avenue is located between Empire Street and Business 94. What remains of the Eden Springs Amusement Park is closed to the public. Mary's City of David Museum and Tours, located next door to the House of David, is open on summer weekend afternoons (June through September). The House of David Museum in the nearby town of Riverside is a museum devoted to securing artifacts from their famous past. This nonprofit "Historeum" seeks preservation of the relics and structures from the House of David, and eventual restoration of the Eden Springs park and recognition on the National Register of Historic Places.

## Sleeping Bear Dunes

At the base of Michigan's Leelanau Peninsula, on the eastern shore of Lake Michigan, are a series of unusually massive sand dunes on a finger of land jutting into the lake. Dwarfed in height only by Colorado's Great Sand Dunes and the sand mountains of Saudi Arabia and the Sahara Desert, Sleeping Bear Dunes rank among the biggest in the world. Native Americans were the first to tell tales of how the dramatic sand dunes were created. In more recent years scientists have carefully studied the 34-mile (54-km) stretch of massive sand dunes and developed a comprehensive theory explaining the complex geologic history. Fossils found in the area indicate that at one time the whole area was a shallow

260

and warm sea inhabited by long extinct animals. During the various Ice Ages the entire state of Michigan was covered in a thick sheet of ice until a global climate change set the glaciers to melting, only to reform again during the next cooling phase. The shoreline, the dunes, the valleys, and the many small lakes are evidence that the powerful forces of ice, wind, and water have been working for eons to sculpt the contours of northwestern Michigan. Finally, 11,800 years ago, the last ice sheets disappeared forever. As the glaciers retreated they deposited huge piles of sand and rock debris, leaving behind the hilly terrain that so intrigued Native Americans and scientists alike.

## Sleeping Bear Dunes was a famous Native American site associated with the legend of three bears swimming across Lake Michigan.

The Ojibwa (also spelled Chippewa) legend of Sleeping Bear Dunes relates the story of a mother bear and two cubs being driven into Lake Michigan by a raging forest fire on the Wisconsin side. They swam farther and farther across the lake until they sighted the Michigan peninsula. Sometime along the journey the mother bear reached the other side, but the two younger bears, exhausted from the swim, drowned just before reaching the Michigan shore. Not aware that her offspring were lost, the mother bear perched herself on top of a bluff and waited for many days and nights. The solitary "Sleeping Bear" dune marks the spot where the mother gazed out into the lake and grieved for her two lost cubs. She can be seen in profile on the largest dune in the park. The two drowned cubs became embodied as the North and South Manitou Islands 12 miles (19 km) offshore. Legend has it that the Ojibwa gave it the name because the dark vegetation atop the great sand massif resembled the grieving bear who had curled up on top of the dunes and went to sleep.

The Sleeping Bear legend is an appealing one, but explains nothing about the true glacial heritage of the dunes. The mammoth line of dunes were created by sand that had been ground down by Lake Michigan and then blown on top of steep bluffs fronting the lakeshore. In this regard they are not normal dunes composed entirely of sand, but rather cover the top of a massive glacial moraine. And while the moraine rock pile

▲ The Sleeping Bear Dunes span for several miles on the northeastern shore of Lake Michigan.

left by an Ice Age glacier never moves, the shifting sand around it certainly does. As recently as the 1800s, three villages located along Michigan's western shoreline succumbed to the dunes' relentless advance. The villages now lay buried in the sand, along with remnants of several ancient forests. Sometimes the haunting remains of dead trees or buried buildings become exposed, only enhancing the lore of Sleeping Bear Dunes.

### Getting to Sleeping Bear Dunes

Several north-south highways approach Sleeping Bear Dunes National Lakeshore, including U.S. 31 along Lake Michigan, U.S. 131 through Grand Rapids, and Interstate 75, which extends the full length of Michigan, from the Upper Peninsula to Detroit, and south to Ohio. U.S. 31 connects to Highway 22, the main road extending through the park and around the Leelanau Peninsula. Two east-west routes, Highway 115 and 72 (through Traverse City), also connect to Highway 22. The Visitors Center is in the town of Empire. A summer ferry makes daily round trips to South Manitou Island, featuring dunes similar to Sleeping Bear but on a smaller scale. Most visitors come to hike the 2-mile (3.2-km) wide sand mesa atop the Sleeping Bear Dunes.

# MINNESOTA

Despite the popularity surrounding Paul Bunyan and his blue ox Babe, there is no historical record that these two mythological giants created the 10,000-plus lakes in Minnesota. Two centuries ago, Minnesota had millions of acres of tallgrass prairie. Today, farms and industry have reduced the prairie to less than 1% of its original acreage. The grasslands of Minnesota on the western fringes of the Great Lakes was the ancestral homeland to the Dakota tribe, only to be encroached by the Ojibwa when they made their historic western migration in the 16th century. The two tribes fought bitterly until the arrival of historic white explorers who used their rivalry to gain a foothold in the area. French fur trappers were the first to establish military posts, followed by the British who ruled the region until losing the territory to the United States after the Revolutionary War. Later in the 19th century, jobs in lumbering, railroading, milling, and especially farming lured many northern European immigrants to Minnesota. These immigrants were mostly Lutheran Germans and Scandinavians who favored the landscape and weather as being similar to their homelands in the Old Country.

## Kensington Runestone

In the fall of 1898, near the small town of Kensington, a Swedish immigrant farmer named Olof Ohman and his son Edward struggled to get a particularly stubborn tree out of the ground as they were clearing a field to plow. So difficult was the struggle that Edward ruined the blade of his father's prized axe trying to free a rock embedded underneath the tree. When the 40-year-old aspen tree was finally overturned, it was found to be growing on top of a large flat stone firmly entangled in the roots. Upon closer inspection, Edward noticed the stone was inscribed with strange markings. News spread quickly about the enigmatic stone with a runic text carved onto the rock's face and one side. Experts were called in, but from the time immediately following its discovery the Kensington Runestone has been the source of an ongoing debate regarding its authenticity. Even before the text could be translated the stone was declared a forgery for a number of flimsy reasons. The strongest hoax theory emphasized the inconsistencies in the style and type of its runic letters, including the mixed language used. After examination, the Committee of the Minnesota Historical Society concluded: "(1) It (the inscription) cannot be the work of some unlettered amateur of the present day. (2) It is either the uncritical record of an exploration of the 14th century, or the fabrication of a consummate philologist familiar with the dialect of Vestgotland in the 14th century." In the mostly-illiterate farming communities of northwestern Minnesota there were no consummate philologists to be found anywhere. In fact, it took several years to correctly decipher and read the following text:

8 : goter : ok : 22 : norrmen : po : opdagelsefard : fro : vinland : vest : vi : hade : lager : ved : 2 : skjar : en : dags : rise : norr : fro : deno : sten : vi : var : ok : fiske : en : dagh : aptir : vi : kom : hem : fan : 10 : man : rode : af : blod : og : ded : AVM : fraelse : af : illy : har 10 : mans : ve : havet : at : se : aptir : vore : skip : 14 : dagh : rise : from : deno : oh : ahr : 1362 :

TRANSLATION:

"8 Goths (Swedes) and 22 Norwegians on a voyage of discovery from Vinland through the west. We had anchored by 2 skerries (rocky islets) one day's voyage north from this stone. We were out and fished all day. After we came home (we) found 10 men red with blood and dead. AVM (Ave Maria) save us from peril. We have 10 men by the sea to look after our ships and 14 day's voyage from this island. Year 1362."

Middle Age Scandinavians used an alphabet based on a crude letter system passed down from their earlier Viking forebears. Runic writing appeared rather late in the history of writing and is clearly derived from one of the alphabets of the Mediterranean area, most similar to the Greek alphabet. Runes appear in the historic record written almost exclusively by the Vikings, usually carved onto metal plating or stones. In the Middle Ages, the runic alphabet was constantly changing and runic letter shapes varied in different countries over several centuries. Three out of place letters on the Kensington Runestone, "AVM," a favored reason for originally declaring it a hoax, actually delivers the sufficient mark of antiquity to prove the stone genuine. The detail around the Latin abbreviation AVM correctly dates its authenticity into a narrow timeframe when the runic alphabet was mixed with Latin text. The letter V in AVM was carved on the stone in a unique way, with a slightly elongated curl on the right part of the V. This is known as a "superscript," an abbreviation style common in the Middle Ages, but long out of use by the 19th century. There were very few medieval epigraphy specialists in the world when the Kensington Runestone was discovered who could verify this abbreviation to be correct. The stone is especially unique because it mixes runic letters with Roman letters to show special respect to the Deity. The Catholic prayer, "Ave Virgo Maria save (us) from evil," was recited at funerals for victims of the plague, which may be what the explorers were escaping from in Europe. Recently uncovered European documents relate the orders of King Magnus dispatching Paul Knutson on an expedition to Vinland in 1354. The number of men returning to Scandinavia after the expedition shows that more than half died during the long trip. Furthermore, the 19th century Lutheran Swedish farmer who supposedly forged the stone would not have known that the 14th century visitors to America would have been Catholic. And even if they knew this, they would have held few sympathies for the Vatican because of long standing resentments dating from the 16th century Reformation. Furthermore, it is extremely unlikely that anyone in 19th century Lutheran Minnesota would have known the medieval abbreviation presented in AVM. The signature of antiquity goes far beyond the abilities of an expert forger. In fact, nearly every scientist and epigrapher who has intimately examined the stone has declared it to be genuine.

The lengthy runic inscription on a dated stone without detection of forgery, and the mixed alphabets on the Kensington Runestone firmly establish its authenticity. It also confirms several centuries of Viking explorations deep into the North American continent.

The Kensington Runestone clearly records a 14th century Scandinavian expedition into the North American heartland. The best way to understand the ill-fated voyage is to reconstruct the story as it is told. The exploratory mission was a summer journey that originated in Vinland (New England), and set out for the west on an *opdagelsefard* (voyage of discovery). While it would have been impossible for the warring Swedes and Norwegians to be on a trip together in the 11th or 12th centuries, it is perfectly feasible that they would be on an expedition together in the 14th century when the stone is dated because they were then allied nations. Scandinavian sailors in the Middle Ages considered "a day's sailing" on inland waters to be about 75 English miles (120 km), placing the sea party in either Lake Superior or more reasonably Hudson Bay, where the stone tells us 10 crewmen stayed behind with the larger ships. The "sea" is more likely to be Hudson Bay than the Great Lakes because "havet" usually refers to salt water. Indeed, the Hudson Bay lies within 14 sailing days due north of Kensington. By this approach, the expedition would have entered the Nelson River and followed it to Lake Winnipeg. From Lake Winnipeg they would have continued southward to the mouth of the Red River of the North flowing south from Minnesota. At the Buffalo River fork the expedition presumably established a camp on the shore of Lake Cormorant based on the discovery of two large boulders with mooring holes in a remote location near its present shore. It is also interesting to note that all along the river route from the Hudson Bay down the Red River of the North have been found Viking-style mooring stones, suggesting several Viking explorations of this particular river route. Before Lake Cormorant was partially drained in the 19th century, the carved rocks would have been close to the original

▲ The mixed runic and Latin text is an astonishing feature of the Kensington Runestone.

lake level and would have fit the definition of "skerries." This evidence suggests that Lake Cormorant is the scene of the massacre, suitably about one sailing day (75 miles / 120 km) north of Kensington where the survivors presumably fled. They wrote their desperate message on a 202-pound (91-kg) graywacke native rock and possibly built a crude shrine. By inscribing their story, the Vikings were keeping with an old tradition of marking the furthest point they were able to reach. Castaways and shipwrecked sailors, finding themselves faced with inevitable death, left similar records of their demise in runic inscriptions. The unfortunate fugitives who survived the Minnesota massacre left their timeless tale for posterity, perhaps dedicating it in a solemn Catholic ceremony.

## Getting to Kensington Runestone

For most of 1948, the Runestone was on exhibit at the Smithsonian Institution, where the Curator and Director publicly praised it as "probably the most important archeological object yet found in North America." The stone was returned to

Minnesota in March of 1949 to be unveiled in St. Paul in honor of the state's centennial. In August. 1949 it came to a permanent home in Alexandria, Minnesota, at the Runestone Museum, where it resides to this day. Alexandria is the county seat where the stone was found locally near the small town of Kensington. From Minneapolis, take Interstate 94 for 120 miles (190 km) northwest to the Alexandria Exit and follow the signs to the museum. Lake Cormorant is located in Becker County, Minnesota. Signs direct visitors to the "Mooring Rocks," situated in a remote location near the present shore of Lake Cormorant.

## Pipestone

The Ioway and Oto people—and many tribes from the Great Plains—came in peace and quarried the exposed bedrock at Pipestone for their ceremonial pipes. Their legends specify that this site was the center of creation. Smoke from pipes made of the stone carry messages to the Great Spirit. 2,000-year-old stone artifacts originating at Pipestone have been unearthed at Mound City in Ohio and other burial mound sites across the Midwest. Many tribes traveled hundreds of miles to this location, sometimes across hostile territory. They considered the immediate land around these quarries as extremely sacred. According to some accounts, warring tribes stopped fighting when entering these neutral grounds. Tribes would not camp near the hallowed quarry grounds, but would set up camp on higher ground to the west and north and entered the quarry area only for the purpose of obtaining pipestone. Every tribal member followed strict formalities. Only men were allowed to enter the quarries, and only after making proper offerings to appease the spirits that protected the valley.

Native American carvers prized the durable
yet relatively soft stone—which ranged in
color from mottled pink to brick red—to
fashion ceremonial pipes. Pipestone,
Minnesota was the most famous quarry for
the sacred rock in North America.

Entrenched Indian tradition, coupled with structured daily routine honoring the spiritual world, were the main features of a pipe ceremony. Not only did peace pipes figure prominently in the ways of village life, but they were instrumental in dealing with other tribes. Ceremonial smoking marked the activities of the Plains Indians. They would be smoked by the leaders before rallying forces for warfare, trading goods and hostages, medicine ceremonies, and ritual dancing. All tribes held the peace pipes in high esteem and had many legends surrounding the origin of the stone. The best-known account of the Pipestone legend was recorded by George Catlin, a noted painter and student of Native American customs. He visited the quarries in 1836 and lived among the Sioux who told him their origin beliefs of pipestone: "At an ancient time the Great Spirit, in the form of a large bird, stood upon the wall of rock and called all the tribes around him, and breaking out a piece of the red stone formed it into a pipe and smoked it, the smoke rolling over the whole multitude. He then told his red children that the red stone was their flesh, that they were made from it,

▲ Native Americans digging at Pipestone.
Photo circa 1885.

that they must smoke through it to reach him, that they must use it for nothing but pipes: and as it belonged alike to all tribes, the ground was sacred, and no weapons must be used or brought upon it." Indeed, the Indians viewed the landscape around the pipestone quarries as spiritually hallowed. Residing in the cliff walls overlooking the quarry are the "Old Stone Faces." These include a leaping rock to test an Indian's bravery and faith, and the "Oracle" stone face where a medicine man (tribal shaman) believed the rock could talk and voices were said to issue from its cold lips. Also featured near the quarries are a scenic waterfall and lake, natural prairie grasslands, and the Three Maidens boulders of granite where traditional offerings were left.

## Getting to Pipestone

Pipestone National Monument is located in southwestern Minnesota, just west of the town Pipestone. Follow signs from Interstate 90 to U.S. 75, or access the site from MN 23, or MN 30. Once at the Pipestone Visitors Center, follow the Circle Trail to the principle points of interest at the monument. Permission to quarry, fashion, and sell pipestone within the monument has been reserved by law to Native Americans exclusively.

# OHIO

The fertile woodland valleys of Ohio supported indigenous tribes for at least 3,000 years before the modern European arrival. The southern lands along the middle Ohio River tributaries formed the heart of an ancient Indian culture, whose earthworks still imprint the landscape. The so-called Adena and Hopewell cultures of southwestern Ohio, and the Mississippian Culture that stretched along the vast waterway, primarily characterized the mound builders. The name Hopewell and Adena come from the two Ohio landowners who leased

their property for mound excavations. For lack of a better term, because we have no way of knowing what they called themselves, the Hopewell and Adena names stuck. The mound builders created an impressive trade network extending from the Great Lakes to the Gulf of Mexico. What is today Ohio was likely both the origin and capital region of the mound builders. The prehistoric population density of Ohio was more than twice of what it is today, with a major set of earthen ruins every few miles. By the European arrival, the mound builders were long gone and an entirely different collection of native people inhabited Ohio. The new tribes (who did not build mounds whatsoever) include the Delaware, Miami, Shawnee, Wyandot, and a few more that overlapped into other states.

Many broken treaties provoked the Ohio Indian Wars, which led to an almost full relinquishment of native lands. In 1790, President George Washington called for the forced removal of all remaining native tribes out of Ohio.

## Newark Earthworks

The enormous Hopewellian earthen enclosures scattered around the town of Newark are among the most compelling and mysterious architectural remains of ancient America. Hopewell culture is characterized by the construction of large geometric earthworks and the establishment of a wide ranging trade network spanning the eastern half of North America. The worldview of the Hopewell is reflected in the orientation and symbolism of the massive earthworks and the exquisite artifacts they left behind. In most cases the Hopewell charnel mounds (buried mortuary houses) were aligned according to lunar events, including Newark where alignments in the Octagon Works demarked the major rising and setting points of the moon. Exploration of Hopewell mounds has produced evidence indicating that the mounds and earthworks were associated with highly developed mortuary rituals including artistic objects of a material culture. Only now is it being understood that many Hopwellian earthworks were specifically designed for pinpointing solar and lunar eclipses, solstices, and the appearance of significant constellations.

The earthworks inside and surrounding the town of Newark is a vast complex of once-interconnecting mounds, built sometime between 100 BCE and 500 CE. Originally the site covered about four square miles (6.4 sq km) before urban expansion and farming destroyed much of the complex. The last remaining earthworks at Newark, including the Great Circle, the Wright Earthworks, and the Octagon and Observatory Circle are all incorporated in Moundbuilders State Memorial. The Hopewell people enclosed places of special importance with earthen walls built in diverse shapes and sizes. The Newark Earthworks included arrangements of circles, squares, octagons, parallel embankments, and circular and elliptical mounds sweeping across the landscape. The largest single earthwork is the Great Circle, which is 1,200 feet (360 m) in diameter and features what appears to be an eagle effigy in its center. The Octagon enclosure and an adjacent circle are specifically oriented to the rising of the moon. The small mounds at

▲ One of the opening gateways into the Octagon at Newark, as drawn by the famous mappers Squier & Davis.

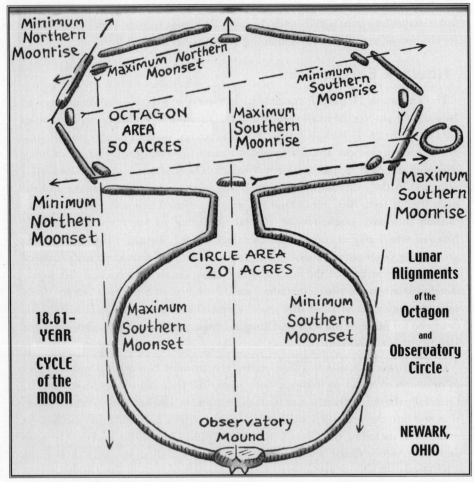

Minimum Northern Moonrise

Maximum Northern Moonset

Minimum Southern Moonrise

OCTAGON AREA 50 ACRES

Maximum Southern Moonrise

Minimum Northern Moonset

Maximum Southern Moonrise

CIRCLE AREA 20 ACRES

18.61-YEAR CYCLE of the moon

Maximum Southern Moonset

Minimum Southern Moonset

Lunar Alignments

of the Octagon and Observatory Circle

Observatory Mound

NEWARK, OHIO

each opening within the Octagon continue to be a highly sophisticated way of capturing lunar alignments, and thus predicting seasons. The Octagon, enclosing 50 acres (20 ha), was the largest single feature in the entire complex. Newark may have included mortuary rituals, but it also served as an astronomical observatory where periodic ceremonies for the living occurred.

> The Newark Earthworks were the single largest complex of joined geometric earthen enclosures ever built. Because of their immense size, the site has come to be known as the "greatest outdoor church in the world."

The Observatory Circle connecting the Octagon at Newark has a duplicate of the exact same dimensions over 50 miles (80 km) away at the High Bank Works just outside the city of Chillicothe. Amazingly, the main axis of these two sites are orientated precisely perpendicular to each other, despite the great distance that separates them both. The two earthworks record in the alignment of their walls the rising and setting points of the moon through a precise 18.61 yearlong cycle. The remarkable symmetry of Hopwellian geometry in form and dimension, oftentimes located great distances apart, can be found at several other Ohio locations. Another example is the outer circle at Circleville with the exact same diameter as Newark's Great Circle. The circles connected to the octagonal enclosures at Newark and Chillicothe were precisely the same size (20 acres) as the inner circle at Circleville. Unfortunately, the two concentric circle earthworks at Circleville have been ruined. Also destroyed was a prehistoric roadway of long, straight parallel earthen embankments that once connected the ancient Newark Earthworks to Chillicothe. These parallel walls running due southwest from

▲ The Decalogue Stone features Hebrew text and an image of Moses.

Newark were recorded in the 19th century as extending "over fertile fields, through tangled swamps and across streams, still keeping their undeviating course." This long "Great Hopewell Road" appears similar to the arrow-straight roadways of the prehistoric Chaco Canyon Anasazi, the Yucatan Maya, and the South American Inca. Pilgrims would have traveled along the road carrying trade items to barter for flint. The prehistoric quarries at Flint Ridge near Newark were the single most important source of flint for the Ohio Hopewell culture. It is possible the Great Hopewell Road extended south to Portsmouth on the Ohio River, the main source of Ohio pipestone. Both flint and pipestone had a deep symbolic and spiritual value to Native Americans.

Adding further intrigue were several inscribed stones found near the mounds called the "Newark Holy Stones." The two most famous stones, the Keystone and the Decalogue, were uncovered a few months apart in 1860 by amateur archaeologist David Wyrick. In his capacity as the Licking County Surveyor, Wyrick was working on one of the most detailed original maps of the Newark Earthworks when he came across the Keystone in one of the wells along the parallel walls east of "Octagon A." The Keystone contains four lines of nearly standard Hebrew lettering with the text: "Holy of the Holies"; "King of the

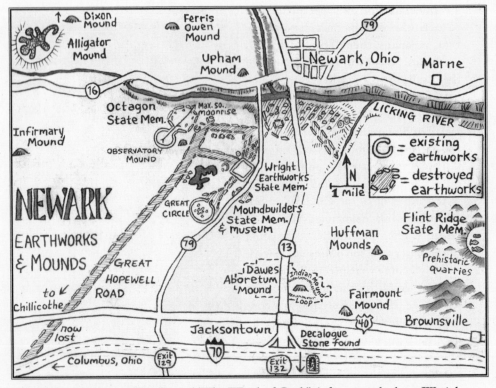

Earth"; "The Law of God"; and "The Word of God." A few months later Wyrick discovered the Decalogue stone fit within a stone holding vessel, and a stone bowl in a burial mound he was excavating about 10 miles (16 km) south of Newark. The Decalogue stone is inscribed on all sides with a condensed version of the Ten Commandments, or the Decalogue, in a peculiar form of post-Exilic square Hebrew letters. In the center of the stone is a robed and bearded figure identified as Moses by letters fanning over his head. Such finds were immediately called a hoax by academic archaeologists, mostly because of the implication that the Adena or Hopewell might be linked to the theory that the Lost Tribe of Israel immigrated to North America. While there is little if any evidence to back up allegations of a hoax, there is ample evidence to prove that the stones are authentic. First off, the Decalogue stone shows considerable wear on its back, suggesting it must have been held for a long time in someone's left hand. Also difficult to fake would be the carrying case and a stone-carved bowl—the bowl being an understandable ritual object of Jews who kept the purity laws in this time period. Secondly, the text of both stones date to the Second Temple Period (20 BCE – 70 CE) when such objects were used commonly in daily prayers, unlike the pre-Exilic "Old Hebrew" text of the Lost Tribes. The post-Exilic script of the Newark Holy Stones is broadly consistent with the Hopewell mound building era. In 1867, several years after Wyrick's death, another stone with similar script was discovered in the same mound group that the Decalogue stone was found.

▲ Saint Joseph's Oratory in Montreal, Canada attracts over two million visitors per year. Some come to marvel at the largest dome in North America, while others are attracted to the healing tradition established by a humble priest named Brother Andre.

▲ The town of Beaupre north of Quebec City also has a healing tradition. This statue of Saint Anne holding her daughter the Virgin Mary stands in front of a Catholic hospital near the massive Saint-Anne De Beaupre Basilica.

Photo by Brad Olsen

▲ The small town of Alexandria, Minnesota claims to be the "Birthplace of America" because of an enigmatic Viking stone found on a local farm. The Kensington Runestone recounts a Norse expedition in the year 1362 venturing deep into the American heartland. The stone describes several members of the party being killed in an ambush, while others managed to escape. The survivors inscribed their message for the ages, possibly consecrated in a primitive Catholic chapel.

Photo by Brad Olsen

▲ A mural depicting the creation of the Kensington Runestone is behind the famous artifact in the Alexandria Museum.

Photo by Brad Olsen

▲ One of several remaining megalithic stone chambers at America's Stonehenge in southern New Hampshire.

Photo by Brad Olsen

▲ The drywall chambers at America's Stonehenge ...

Photo by Brad Olsen

Photo by Brad Olsen

▲ The entrance to the Upton Stone Chamber in Massachusetts is fairly well hidden on private property. A narrow passageway leads to a large internal "beehive" chamber. The passageway is aligned to four cairns on Pratt Hill, doubling its purpose as an ancient observatory and calendar.

▲ ... were easily quarried stone in the 19th century. About half of the original America's Stonehenge was carted away with no regard to the site as an archaeological treasure.

Photo courtesy of Chautauqua County Tourism

▲ Former Supreme Court Justice Sandra Day O'Connor addresses the summer assembly crowd in the Chautauqua Amphitheater.

Photo courtesy of Chautauqua County Tourism

Photo courtesy of Chautauqua County Tourism

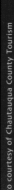

▲ Lily Dale in Chautauqua County is another summer assembly founded in the 19th century. Both the entrance gate to Lily Dale and the Clock Tower at the Chautauqua Institution are famous symbols.

▲ South Cape on the Big Island was the location where the first Polynesians arrived in Hawaii. These simple petroglyphs at Ka Lae may represent this important prehistoric event.

▲ As Hawaiian religion evolved, so did the images of their deities. These statues in the City of Refuge were meant to evoke fear and respect for the priestly caste.

▲ The City of Refuge, or Pu'uhonua o Honaunau, is the best preserved ancient temple complex in Hawaii.

Photo by Edward Taylor

Photo by Edward Taylor

Photo by Edward Taylor

Photo by Brad Olsen

▲ Kaena Point on Oahu was the "leaping place of souls" for recently deceased Hawaiian people.

Photo courtesy of the North Carolina Division of Travel

▲ Pilot Mountain was once a vision quest site and initiation location for the Cherokee people.

Photo courtesy of the North Carolina Division of Travel

▲ Pilot Mountain dominates the eastern landscape of the Appalachian Range in North Carolina. To the Cherokee it was the home of their spirit guide "Jomeoki."

Photo by Brad Olsen

▲ The basic right for all people to have public voting access became a Civil Rights flashpoint in Selma, Alabama.

Photo by Brad Olsen

▲ The Edmund Pettus Bridge in Selma was the scene of a clash with police who halted a peaceful protest march.

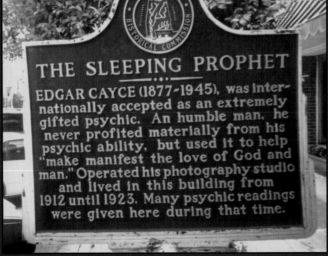

Photo by Brad Olsen

▲ The famous "Sleeping Prophet" Edgar Cayce rose to prominence as a psychic while living in Selma, Alabama.

▲ The Graceland mansion is one of the top tourist attractions in Memphis, Tennessee. To Elvis Presley fans, this home is hallowed ground enshrining the celebrity lifestyle and lifetime achievements of America's most successful homegrown entertainer.

▲ Elvis Presley's former racquetball court at Graceland now showcases his many awards, movie posters, gold records, and performance jumpsuits.

This independent discovery, in a related context, by reputable citizens, of a third stone bearing the same unique characters of the Decalogue stone, strongly confirms the authenticity and context of all three Newark Holy Stones. The third stone has subsequently been lost, but lithograph copies remain.

### Getting to the Newark Earthworks

The town of Newark is located 14 miles (22 km) north of Interstate 70 and State Route 79 in Licking County. Take SR 79 north to Church Street, turn left on 30th Street, to Parkview where the Octagon mounds will come into view. Continue on SR 79 north to Newark and turnouts for Moundbuilders State Memorial featuring the Great Circle and Wright Earthworks will be marked. All remaining earthworks are located in the southwestern section of Newark. In antiquity, the Newark complex covered over 4 square miles (6.4 sq km), but today the State Memorial encloses a mere 26 acres (10.4 ha). These mounds are maintained by the Ohio Historical Society, which also manages the Ohio Indian Art Museum located nearby. An entrance fee is charged for the museum but not for viewing the mound sites, portions of which are now part of a golf course. Flint Ridge State Park is located 3.75 miles (6 km) north of I-70 and the Brownsville exit. The Keystone and the Decalogue Stone are on display in the Johnson-Humrickhouse Museum, at 300 Whitewoman Street, in Coshocton, Ohio.

## Serpent Mound

South of the great freshwater sea, in a land called "O-hi-yo" by Native Americans, is the largest effigy mound in North America. Atop a slightly curved hilltop in a low valley ringed by higher hills is a serpentine mound whose origin, builders, and purpose remains unclear. Unlike other mounds in the region, Serpent Mound was not a burial site, but an enormous earthwork effigy. Three separate burial mounds across a low valley are also included in the Serpent Mound State Memorial. The serpent effigy was built by first laying out a pattern of stones. Packed yellow clay covered the rocks and that, in turn, was covered with soil sufficient to raise the monument to the height of a standing adult. The serpentine body goes through seven major curves and ends with a tightly wrapped tail. The

▲ The Serpent Mound as seen at dusk from the observation tower at the site.

form seems to slither across the hilltop as if it were alive in animated motion. The serpent's open mouth appears to be swallowing an egg, while the body undulates for most of its length until the tail recoils as if in attack. The effigy is so large that it is barely discernable in its entirety from ground level. Similar to the gigantic Nazca Lines in Peru, the shape is best viewed from above. The mound has been described by archaeologists as "one of the most important American artworks," yet exactly who built it, when, and why remains conjecture. The mound could have been started anytime between 1,000 BCE to 1,000 CE, only widening the spectrum of prehistoric builder possibilities. While the mound has long been attributed to the Adena, a 1991 excavation dated charcoal samples to 1030 CE, making the possible builders a Hopewell descendent called the Fort Ancient people. 19th century Christians believed the site to be "a mark of God" denoting the Garden of Eden where the serpent tempted Adam and Eve with forbidden fruit. Mormon founder Joseph Smith claimed the mounds of Ohio were built in 600 CE by a Lost Tribe of Israelites who fled Jerusalem by boat and crossed the Atlantic. Smith claimed the Israelites were divinely inspired to build earthen mounds. Additional influences could have been an influx of serpent-worshipping Aztecs, Southwestern Hopi, or iron smelting Vikings in the region. Conventional archaeologists maintain there was never a "Lost Tribe" or any outside influence, just the Indians themselves.

Serpent Mound is the foremost earth sculpture in North America and largest snake effigy in the world. Several recently discovered geo-astronomical alignments only make the site more intriguing.

Since nothing was left to date the mound with a time or people, the Serpent Mound is most commonly associated with two of the three conical burial mounds found nearby. The third tomb, called the elliptical mound, is attributed to the Fort Ancient culture. The conical mounds include characteristic Adena artifacts placed alongside the burials. The Adena themselves are an enigma of history, with some of their mounds revealing giant skeletons wearing metal armor and buried with hieroglyphic tablets. Eventually the Adena people developed into the Hopewell culture, who gave way to the agriculturally-adept Fort Ancient people. All cultures were prolific mound builders in the middle Ohio River Valley. Whoever built the Serpent Mound directed an inspired team of people to carry thousands of riverbed stones to the hilltop location above Ohio Brush Creek. After laying the foundation of stones, the workers packed yellow clay and may have applied an unknown surface design or texture. The result is the 1,348-foot (400-m) long, 20-foot (6-m) wide, and 5-foot (1.5-m) high effigy, that if unwrapped would extend nearly a quarter mile in length. The long and undulating coils conceal astronomical alignments exactly halfway along each major bend. Most of these correspond to lunar sightings, but two correlate with the winter and summer solstice sunrises.

The Serpent Mound can also predict the spring and fall equinoxes, the summer solstice sunrise, and depicts an orientation with the North Star Polaris. Other mounds in Ohio had astronomical alignments, but none include the complexity of the Serpent Mound.

Adding further intrigue to the Ohio effigy is a similar snake mound located on the shores of Rice Lake in Serpent Mounds Provincial Park, near the famous Peterborough Petroglyphs in southern Ontario. Both serpents are featured on prominent juts of

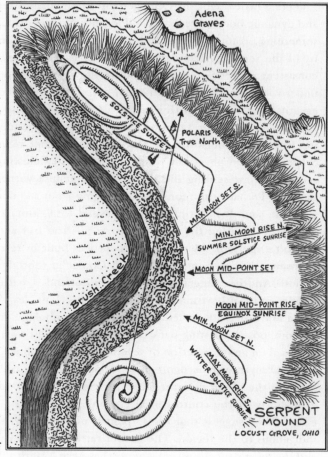

land near water and were constructed with the natural resources at hand. The Canadian snake is not as long or undulating as its American counterpart in Ohio but is still quite impressive, measuring 189 feet (57 m) long by 24 feet (7 m) wide by 5 feet (1.5 m) in average height, situated 80 feet (12 m) above Rice Lake. Near its head is an oval mound, containing five burials. One theory of its origin, relating to the Ohio Serpent Mound as well, is that the Snake Clan of the Hopi visited the region during one of their annual migrations across the continent. It is surmised that the Hopi traveled quite extensively in prehistoric times, teaching knowledge and introducing their settled agricultural lifestyle to various northeastern people. All experts agree that corn originated from the American Southwest, and before that came from southern Mexico. Conch shells from the Gulf of Mexico found with Canadian Serpent grave goods suggests an extensive trans-continental trade network or frequent migrations. One Hopi legend specifically states that if there were no appropriate rock faces to carve their images, the Snake Clan would instead construct a serpent mound. The earliest farmers in the Ohio Valley were the Fort Ancient people who introduced large-scale production of corn, supplemented by bean, squash, sunflower seed and chenopod cultivation.

There is little doubt the Ohio Serpent Mound has given rise to a rich, diverse, and dynamic body of research and legend. No one disputes that it symbolized something profoundly mythical or religious to its builders. The close proximity of the Serpent Mound with nearby caves, sinkholes, and springs would be consistent with the symbolism of the effigy as being a portal, or entrance to the underworld. Native American belief universally regarded creeks, crevices, and caverns as avenues into this mythical realm. The close physical proximity of the Serpent Mound to Ohio Brush Creek may be symbolic of a monster emerging from the underworld via the stream. Another interpretation is that the Serpent Mound physically resembles a snake swallowing an egg-shaped disk, seemingly representing the sun or a solar eclipse witnessed by the unknown builders. Perhaps the monster is emerging from the underworld to do battle with the sun? It is estimated that several total, annular, and partial eclipses were visible during the Adena (800 BCE – 100 CE) and Hopewell (200 BCE – 600 CE) periods. Maybe the serpent was built in reverence to a prolonged eclipse or the emergence of Halley's Comet in 1066 during the Fort Ancient period? Another suggestion is that the mound is patterned after the Little Dipper and may have aided in celestial navigation. New Agers contend this site and a few others identified by the serpent symbol are associated with ancient wisdom, possibly dating back to Atlantis. They also maintain that the mound is placed on an intersection of several powerful ley lines, which in Tibetan and Oriental mythology is signified by a double serpent coiling around the earth. Some of the physical features of the Serpent Mound, such as the overcoat of yellow clay or the controversial embankments located on either side of the effigy's head suggest that the serpent is modeled after the timber rattlesnake indigenous to the region. The timber rattlers are the largest at 6.5 feet (2 m), and the most dangerous snake of northeastern America. Despite the encroachment of civilization, rattlesnakes are still fairly common in state forests within close proximity to the Serpent Mound. The Serpent Mound ridge offered all the natural features sought by the timber rattler in prehistoric times, but identifying the builders and understanding their relationship with the serpent remains the larger mystery.

### Getting to Serpent Mound

Serpent Mound State Memorial is located 5 miles (8 km) north of Locust Grove on SR 73 in southwestern Ohio. State Route 73 is 6 miles (10 km) north of State Route 32, and 20 miles (32 km) south of Bainbridge in Adams County. Visitors can climb a three-story tall observation tower to observe the overview shape of the serpent, or walk a short trail along the full length of the mound. The museum contains exhibits about the burial mounds and the geology of the surrounding area. There is an entrance fee and the grounds have shorter operational hours during the winter months. Call (800) 752-2757 for more information.

## Spruce Hill

One of the most important North American archaeological sites, if not the single most under-reported and misunderstood location, is the "Ancient Stone Work" called Spruce Hill in the Paint Valley of south-central Ohio. At 140 acres (56 ha), Spruce Hill is the largest of the hilltop enclosures typical of the Hopewell or Fort Ancient people. The flat-topped prominence has attracted generations of amateur archaeologists to study the massive wall enclosure made entirely of stone, plus the once abundant vitrified fire pits presumably used for casting metals. The furnace remains were first reported in 1811 by James Foster, a newspaper editor in nearby Chillicothe, Ohio who was led to the site by astonished local residents curious to know more about the ruins. Foster reported seeing "about 30 furnaces" in the stone-pile walls which encloses 140 acres (56 ha) of the hilltop plateau, upon which huge trees were growing. The tree age implied to Foster that the furnaces were at least several hundred years older, perhaps even a thousand. After visiting the site, Foster wrote in a letter that he could not speculate what the furnaces had been used to produce, but he said ashes in the furnaces resembled those of a blacksmith's forge. Because of the huge trees growing along the walls, Foster concluded that the furnaces must be ancient. In 1847, Spruce Hill was mapped by the famous archaeologist team Squier and Davis, who mapped hundreds of other earthworks across the eastern United States. They depicted the narrow neck of the plateau, or "the isthmus," as the spot where many of furnaces were located, and where casting molds were found. At another location within the compound Squier and Davis reported seeing "strong traces of fire" in "two or three small mounds of stone, which were burned throughout." They also said many stone mounds along the wall exhibited marks of intense heat, vitrifying the surfaces of the stones. They noted that "light, porous scoriae are abundant in the centers of some of these piles." Celedon glazes found around Spruce Hill furnace debris are proof that temperatures of 2,300° degrees Fahrenheit (1,260° C) were reached, implying the use of both charcoal fuel and a powerful air blast. The glaze results from the reduction of red clay mortar, which contains iron

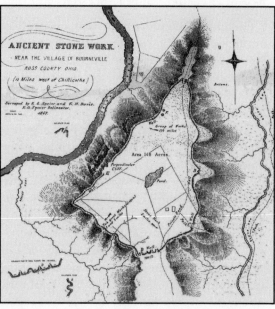

▲ Spruce Hill as mapped by Squier & Davis in 1847.

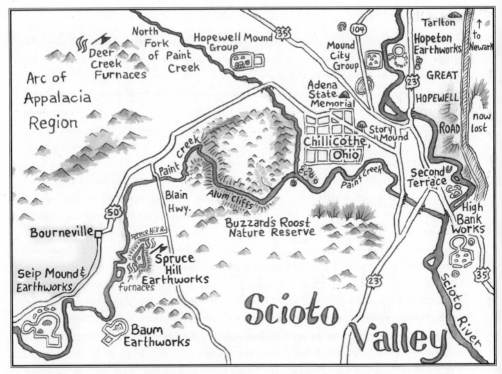

oxide, exposed to extreme heat. It is unfortunate that no intact furnaces remain at Spruce Hill. Destruction of the walls and furnaces took place before and for nearly two centuries after Foster's 1811 visit.

The Spruce Hill furnaces present a major dilemma to historians because modern archaeologists are unwavering in their opinion that no pre-Columbian Native American people ever cast metals, yet some sort of prehistoric metallurgical operation was being conducted on Spruce Hill hundreds of years before the site was discovered. At one time there were truckloads of cinder in the form of ancient slag, obviously subjected to very intense heat for long periods of time. Unscrupulous souvenir collectors have scoured the site clear of many furnace-related artifacts. The ancient hearth-pit furnaces found on Spruce Hill were wasteful smelters and most of the slag to be found retains much of the original iron ore. They represent a wealth of archaeo-metallurgical remains almost unknown to America's community of professional archaeologists. The apparent reason Spruce Hill has not received the widespread recognition that it deserves is because of the historically problematic metal processing features found at the site. Findings of molten slag and glazed bedrock have led to controversial debates as to who was responsible for the metal-smelting furnaces on the property, either in historic or prehistoric times. The local archaeological community does not accept the ancient furnaces idea. It seems quite amazing that such a variety of enigmatic high temperature pit furnaces should exist in a relatively small region of central and southern Ohio. It is no wonder investigators are still confused by this situation. What is accepted by all is that pure copper was abundant in the Great Lakes region and bog-iron could be collected from swamps or moors, so acquiring the raw materials was certainly possible. "The whole theory of all pre-Columbian Native American civilizations being locked in the Stone Age must be rejected," argued metallurgist Arlington Mallery in his book *The Rediscovery of Lost America*, "if only a small percentage of the 10,000-plus copper objects stored in our nation's museums were accepted by academics as being made from cast copper." For example, the 28-pound (12.6-kg) Seip Mound celt on display at the Ohio Historical Society Museum in Columbus is evidence of copper casting, as are many of the copper artifacts of the Perkins collection in the Wisconsin Historical Society. It is obvious to modern metallurgists that not all the recovered prehistoric copper artifacts were pounded into shape by Stone Age Indians—some were obviously created from cast metals. Yet archaeologists and historians are of the unanimous opinion that the mound builders, who supposedly constructed Spruce Hill, or any other Native American people for that matter, did not employ metal casting technology.

All of this has given rise to speculation that not the Indians, but perhaps visitors from the Old World, came over long before Columbus and created most of these works. Despite the enigmatic furnaces, Spruce Hill is attributed by archaeologists to the native Hopewell peoples. The Hopewell culture gave way to the Fort Ancient culture (900 – 1400 CE), who also lived in the Ohio Valley. Since everyone seems to agree that North American Indians did not know how to melt and cast copper at such high temperatures, then who else could have been responsible? When the pit furnaces in Ross County were first reported in 1811, and it was apparent that a certain degree of technology was attained in their manufacture, speculation suggested the ancient visitor theory. Some groups, such as the Mormons, continue to believe the earthworks proved the Lost Tribes of Israel must have reached America and became the mound builders. There is not enough sufficient evidence to establish the exact construction date of many mounded forts in Ohio, nor can the period of occupancy be fixed, so diffusion with an outside group is plausible. The furnaces of Spruce Hill were seemingly imported and designed by expert metallurgists of another civilization, a learned group who likely practiced their craft in other locations of North America. Indeed, Spruce Hill is not the only location where furnaces have been found. About ten miles (16 km) north of Spruce Hill, in the Deer Creek Valley, are 14 additional iron-working sites, and in Mecklenberg and Brunswick counties in Virginia 16 smelting furnaces were unearthed in the 1950s, including 400 pounds (180 kg) of swords, knives, ship's nails and rivets. All of the North American furnaces discovered thus far follow Medieval European designs. If this iron-working technology was premature for the Lost Tribes of the Old Testament, then who else designed furnaces in this style? The closest examples are those discovered at the abandoned Viking settlement of Austmannadal, Greenland, which are virtually identical to those found at Deer Creek. The unusual features of the North American furnaces—an underground flue passing through a cobblestone base under the furnace floor—strongly suggest the Greenland Norse were the designers. One of the biggest mysteries in European history is the disappearance of hundreds of Greenland Norse, who already established several colonies in North America (see *Sacred Places Europe: 108 Destinations* by Brad Olsen). The ability to work iron was perhaps the single biggest advancement of Middle Age Europeans, a technological achievement undoubtedly foreign to the Indians of central Ohio.

> Enclosed by a collapsed wall of loose stones,
> Spruce Hill features evidence of an advanced
> prehistoric metal working site, along with
> the remains of what appear to be Norse
> graves marked by rune stones.

Extending for more than two miles along the Spruce Hill plateau is a prehistoric wall of laid-up stones. The Spruce Hill walls equal some 200,000 tons of cut rock surrounding the hilltop enclosure, including nine Scandinavian style stone-vaulted burial chambers, or "passage graves." Before they were stolen from the site, there were several grave mounds with stones engraved in runic letters from the Norse alphabet. James Foster observed in 1811 something else: "At the bottom of the

hill on the southwest side are the ruins of a town, or rather a city. The cellars and stone foundations of the houses still remain. The streets are in regular squares. ... It was from all appearances the residence of a warlike race." Ever since Foster wrote about the site in the early 19th century, fortune hunters and amateur archaeologists have scoured the site and removed or damaged many artifacts, yet the crumbling walls and some overgrown fire pits can still be seen at Spruce Hill. What is left of the extensive wall, numerous furnace pits and building foundations appear to be the work of expert stone cutters. It is interesting to note that well-fortified stockades like Spruce Hill were used by the Iroquois, one of the most advanced eastern Indian nations, also thought to have been influenced by the Greenland Norse.

▲ The Fort Hill defensive mound complex is similar to several other hilltop fortresses in the Spruce Hill region.

Abundant prehistoric copper mines have been located on the shores of Lake Superior, allowing practical boat transportation through the Great Lakes to Lake Erie, then a short overland trip to the tributary streams of the Ohio River. The location of Spruce Hill near the Scioto River, and dozens of other important earthwork sites around Chillicothe, indicates a sea-faring people who utilized the integral network of rivers and the Great Lakes to transport goods. The Scioto River was important to the early development of Ohio, as it proved to be an instrumental waterway for prehistoric peoples as well as the first pioneer set-tlers. The contemporary Shawnee tribe utilized the river as their primary means of transportation from one village to another. Passing close to Spruce Hill was the Native American Scioto Trail that followed the Scioto River from northern Ohio to the Kentucky hunting grounds. The furnaces on Spruce Hill raise the distinct likelihood that at some stage of prehistory, northern Europeans managed to sail the divide between Europe and North America and eventually settle along the Eastern Seaboard and the Great Lakes region. Unless history is not open to reevaluation, Spruce Hill should be recognized as an important center of an ancient metallurgical industry.

### Getting to Spruce Hill

Spruce Hill dominates the skyline south of the small Ohio village of Bourneville. Spruce Hill is located about 12 miles (19 km) southwest of Chillicothe, in the heart of Ross County. The village of Bourneville is 3 miles (5 km) west of the intersection of the Blain Highway. Take the Blain Highway southbound, over the Shotts Bridge spanning Paint Creek, and take the first right (west) on to Black Run Road, which becomes Spruce Hill Road. Although Spruce Hill was threat-ened to be sold off to developers in 2007, a consortium of nonprofit conserva-tion groups and individuals have successfully saved the archaeological site from the auction block. The long-term vision for Spruce Hill is to manage the site as a nationally significant historical and nature preserve, offering permitted access via hiking trails. The iron smelting furnaces on Spruce Hill and the enclosure wall may soon become part of the larger grouping of prehistoric mound sites surrounding Chillicothe, arguably the cultural center of the Ohio Hopewell.

# WISCONSIN

During the peak of the most recent glacial phase about 15,000 years ago, most of Wisconsin lay under the grip of colossal ice sheets. The result of advancing and retreating glaciers can be seen in the rolling hills and pristine lakes of Wisconsin. Glaciers covered most of the state from about 100,000 years ago to as recently as 10,000 years ago. The last Ice Age is a period known as the Wisconsinan glaciation, which left behind dramatic moraines as far as the ice sheets advanced. Shortly after the ice melted Paleo-Indians roamed into Wisconsin and developed a lifestyle of hunting and gathering that lasted

over 8,000 years. Alongside moraine hills, lakeshores, and riverside cliffs the Winnebago and other tribes built thousands of conical and effigy mounds out of packed soil. The mounds were erected for religious purposes—sometimes as burial grounds, other times as sacred compounds—but the motive for their construction remains unclear. Chief Wapella, headman of the Fox (now called

Mesquakie) tribe of Wisconsin, called his nation the "Red Earth People," possibly referring to their heritage of effigy building. The first modern Europeans, mostly trappers and explorers, arrived via the Great Lakes in the mid-17th century.

## Aztalan

Wisconsin's most popular archeological site was originally discovered in 1836 by a settler named Timothy Johnson. At first the site was named "Ancient City," but a short time later a Milwaukee judge, Nathaniel Hyer, coined "Aztalan" after the legendary northern Aztec homeland, and the name stuck. The famous German traveler and geographer Alexander von Humboldt, who suggested in his books that the Aztecs had migrated to Mexico from North America, influenced Judge Hyer. Unfortunately, most Aztalan artifacts were destroyed or scavenged by souvenir seekers before modern archaeologists could examine them. The fight to preserve the site was long and mostly unsuccessful. In 1838, a conservationist named Edward Everett asked U.S. President Van Buren to withdraw the site from public sale. The preservationist view was ignored and the government sold the land to a farmer for $22 who in turn plowed the site many times over to grow his crops. Even the efforts of Judge Hyer could not prevent the wanton destruction, and he later wrote "We are determined to preserve these ruins from being ruined." Unfortunately work crews, souvenir collectors, or anyone needing "Aztalan brick" scoured the site for several decades before the land was finally secured in 1912. A Smithsonian archaeologist named I. A. Lapham visited the area in 1850 and did a study of the site. While documenting Aztalan, he made a map that now differs somewhat from what is known of the site today. The maps are different most likely because the area had not yet been completely destroyed by the farmer's plow.

The Aztec legend recounts how the people had come from a homeland named "Aztalan," a place of flowing waters far to the north of their Mexican city Tenochtitlán. The former city of the Aztecs in North America featured a pyramid structure and a temple, yet inconsistent with Wisconsin Aztalan, had water on all

▲ The largest platform mound at Aztalan once had a temple at its summit where human sacrifices were performed.

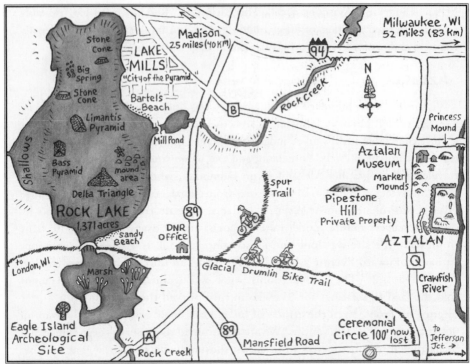

sides. Nearby Madison, however, is surrounded by two lakes on an isthmus and once supported an elaborate mound city where the capital building now stands. Most archaeologists present a strong case that the Wisconsin Aztalan site was merely the northernmost outpost of the Middle Mississippian Culture, with absolutely nothing to do with the Aztecs of Mexico. Yet the Aztec story is somewhat feasible, and certainly compelling. Similar to the Aztec, the Aztalan people practiced cannibalism and human sacrifice rituals. It is known that Aztalan was last occupied sometime between 1200 and 1300 CE, corresponding to the "hundred year" Aztec migration, finally ending in 1325 CE when they reached present-day Mexico City. The Aztecs chronicle their occupation in the Valley of Mexico for two centuries before Spanish conquistadors destroyed their civilization. With the 1519 arrival of the Spanish army led by Cortés, several Mexican cities willingly joined forces with the invaders. These Indian allies, in particular the Tlaxcalans, aided the Spanish in defeating their traditional enemies. Both the Aztec city Tenochtitlán, and Aztalan in Wisconsin were pillaged and burned to the ground after being conquered. If the survivors of Aztalan migrated far enough to the south it is possible they could have been the Aztecs, especially when considering that the whole Mississippian Culture, including the metropolis of Cahokia, also mysteriously vanished around that time. Aztalan has been associated as either a colony of Cahokia or a trading center between Cahokia and its northern periphery. It is a remote possibility that the Mississippian Culture collectively migrated to Mexico after a series of military defeats, or insufficient resources to support its burgeoning populations.

The people of Aztalan were, in many ways, more advanced than other tribes living in southern Wisconsin at the time. Perhaps their refined civilization, their religion incorporating temple mounds, or their fortified city made the Aztalan people feel superior to the surrounding Woodland tribes. In this regard, it is possible that the Aztalan priest-kings subjugated their neighbors and demanded tribute from them in the same way the

▲ The partially restored stockade wall enclosing a temple mound at Aztalan.

Aztec dominated central Mexico and extracted tribute from its subject people. The Aztalan site contains a platform mound where a temple stood, a pyramid, and several earthwork features. The site also reveals evidence of hostilities with its immediate neighbors. As noted, the Spanish were victorious in quashing the Aztec so easily in 1521 because of their alliance with thousands of people in eastern Mexico who had been subjugated by the Aztecs and wanted freedom from their rule. Similarly, it is possible that the power of Aztalan was broken by an alliance of subject peoples in southern Wisconsin seeking freedom from its control. Before destruction, an ancient Indian civilization flourished at Aztalan from 900 to 1300 CE. In its heyday, the city had a population of about 500 people on a 172 acre (69 ha) site. Most people farmed in the outer area and lived inside a fortified and fully-enclosed city—now partially restored—with an area of 21 acres (8.4 ha). Outside the walls were large earth sculptures of birds, rabbits, reptiles and a series of astronomically aligned conical mounds. In one of these mounds the remains of a woman wearing a robe of 1,978 polished beads was unearthed. If the people of Aztalan were driven away from the region by more powerful forces, it is plausible that they would seek the safety of some distant land where they could reconstruct their civilization and reinstitute their dominant rule.

> Before the Aztec settled in Mexico they called their homeland Aztalan, located in "the far north of flowing waters." What happened to the Wisconsin Aztalan people and why their city was destroyed remains a mystery. Adding to the lore is nearby Rock Lake containing several sunken ruins on the lake floor.

The first settlers around Lake Mills in the 1830s heard stories from Winnebago Indians about "stone teepees" submerged in nearby Rock Lake. Over time, especially during periods of extreme drought, fishermen reported seeing large

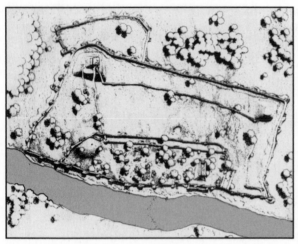

▲ Aztalan contained several defensive walls.
(Image courtesy Wisconsin Historical Society)

geometric structures on the lake floor. At one point the mayor of Lake Mills spotted one of the pyramids himself and the technological search was on. Aerial photos, side boat sonar scans, and underwater divers eventually revealed a complex of at least nine different stone structures, including: two rectangular pyramids, several stacked-rock walls, several "Stone Cone" areas, a conical pyramid and a large "Delta Triangle" structure. There is also a part of the lake floor that supposedly features Indian mounds similar to Aztalan. The largest underwater pyramid, dubbed the Limantis Pyramid, has a length of about 100 feet (30 m), a base width of 60 feet (18 m), and a height of 24 feet (7.2 m), although only about 12 feet (3.6 m) protrude from the silt and mud of the lake floor. The Limantis Pyramid is a truncated tent-like pyramid, built largely out of rounded black stones. The cap stones on the two rectangular pyramids are squared rather than round. The remains of a plaster coating is detectable, similar to the coating used on the Aztalan stockade walls. Murky dive conditions usually make the ruins hard to locate, but scuba enthusiasts continue to report their presence. So what are stone pyramids doing at the bottom of a lake? It seems the ancient Aztalan people constructed a dam at the feeder stream to control water flow into Rock Lake. Apparently they kept the wide lake basin dry but could fill it at will. It is anyone's guess if the structures were funerary, part of a larger construction, or used for ritualistic ceremonies. Researchers call Rock Lake "North America's Most Controversial Underwater Archaeological Discovery of the 20th Century."

## Getting to Aztalan

Aztalan State Park is located on the banks of the Crawfish River in Jefferson County. The park and adjacent Aztalan Historical Museum are about 20 miles (32 km) east of Wisconsin's capital, Madison, and three miles (5 km) east of Lake Mills, which borders Rock Lake. The Museum and State Park can be easily reached from Interstate 94 by using the Highway 89 exit south into Lake Mills, then east three miles on Jefferson County B road. Aztalan is located on County Q road, just past the corner of County B where the Aztalan Museum is located. Aztalan State Park was established in 1952 to preserve what was left of the stockaded Indian village. Some private divers rent scuba tanks in the town of Lake Mills.

# Devils Lake

Towering above Devils Lake on three sides are spectacular crumbled quartzite bluffs formed by the rushing water of a long extinct river. Originally an arm of the Wisconsin River, the valley around Devils Lake was formed at the end of the Wisconsinan glaciation. The glaciers covering much of the area melted and eventually diverted the river by pushing up two moraines of rock and soil that land-locked the remaining water. The spring-fed body of water now called Devils Lake is "trapped" between the quartzite bluffs and the two glacial "plugs." Presumably, if there had not been a series of Ice Ages, the Wisconsin River would still be located in its preglacial course and Devils Lake would not have been formed. Today the lake varies from 40-50 feet (12-15 m) in depth.

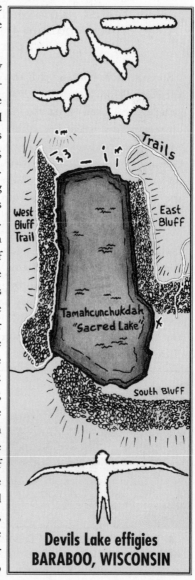

Native Americans in central Wisconsin highly revered Devils Lake and told stories for generations about how the lake was created. The Winnebago (now called Ho-Chunk) believed that water spirits who lived in the lake's depths battled with powerful thunderbirds in the sky, and in so doing threw up the boulders and cliffs. The destruction was caused by the lightning bolts of aerial thunderbirds versus the spouts of the water spirits while fighting each other. The lake is enclosed on the east, west and south by enormous fallen rock piles, the remains of these legendary battles. The Winnebago were the most important tribe in the area, but it is believed the Sauk, Fox, and Kickapoo people also made periodic visits to the lake. Whoever came on a sacred journey, presumably in the summer months, cautiously approached the lake making prayer offerings along the way. When the tribes gathered in large numbers, their ceremonial activities centered around the effigy mounds on the north and southeastern shores. On the north shore of Devils Lake are three types of mounds: those in the form of various animals, the "true" effigy mounds; those which look like ridges, the linear type; and those which look like giant chocolate drops, the round or conical types. In total on the north shore are four effigy mounds, two linear mounds, and two conical mounds, attesting to

**Devils Lake effigies**
**BARABOO, WISCONSIN**

287

its esteemed value as a ritual site. One the south shore near the eastern cliffs is a lone bird-shaped mound, the only mound in the park found to contain a human skeleton. It is possible that this 150-foot (45-m) long "fork-tailed" bird effigy may also represent a "bird-man," combining the wing characteristics of a bird and the legs of a human. In all likelihood the bird mound and the clusters of mounds on the north shore were sacred places for holding ceremonies and rites.

> The Winnebago called the lake Tamahcunchukdah, meaning "Sacred Lake," or "Spirit Lake." Devils Lake is the mistranslated name of the spring-fed lake said by the Woodland tribes to contain underwater supernatural spirits.

Some sources contend that the effigy building tradition lived on in the Siouan-speaking Winnebago tribe of southern Wisconsin, while others argue that the practice was lost at least 750 years ago and soon passed out of memory. Almost all researchers agree that around the time of contact with white settlers most Midwestern Indians had continued to excavate new graves for the recently deceased into previously existing mounds, similar to the way new graves are added to a family plot in cemeteries today. But as Manifest Destiny mandated the spread of the white settlers westward, almost every tribe in the last of the mound building regions were coerced or forced to vacate their land. Most Winnebago were removed from their homeland by a treaty in 1832 to live in the Nebraska "Indian Country," and whatever little was recorded of their unique customs remain vague. By 1838, the Winnebago had relinquished all their lands east of the Mississippi River. Through neglect, prejudice, and contempt for Native American traditions, what may have survived of the effigy building tradition was lost to history. The century-old tradition of Effigy Indians leaving their mark on the land would be forgotten and then rediscovered several hundred years later by Euro-American settlers.

▲ The northern shore of Devils Lake has a high concentration of linear formations and effigy mounds.

The effigy mound building region of Wisconsin, eastern Iowa and northern Illinois seemingly centers on Devils Lake. Effigy mound groupings show an uneven distribution throughout the effigy region, however some general patterns exist. With an affinity for natural beauty the effigy builders typically chose vista points overlooking bodies of water for their creations. The lake region of Madison, Wisconsin once contained over 100 effigies among 1,000 estimated mounds, and several surrounding lakes showed similar densities. Other areas of remarkable effigy group densities occur along the Fox River and the lower Wisconsin River, especially near the confluence with the Mississippi. Water spirit effigies, mostly in the form of lizards, predominate in the eastern part of the state near Lake Michigan. Land animals, especially bears, represent the earth and can be found mostly in western Wisconsin, especially alongside the Mississippi River. Bird mounds signify air and are most commonly found atop scenic valley bluffs or lake view prominences. The Devils Lake effigies represent water spirits, earth animals and birds, congruent with the Winnebago legend of the lake's destructive creation. Wanton demolition by the farmers' plow, ambitious developers, and souvenir seekers has decimated this once-dense concentration of priceless artifacts. For over a hundred years the mounds were plowed down by farmers and regarded as obstacles to cultivation. Records in the State Historical Society of Wisconsin indicate that around 4,000 mounds remain in the state. This figure represents a mere 3% to 4% of the total mounds origi-nally found across the countryside of the Dairy State. The remaining mounds, now protected by the 1985 Burial Sites Preservation Law, are a small fraction of what were once a common characteristic of the Wisconsin landscape.

### Getting to Devils Lake

Devils Lake State Park is located about an hour north of Wisconsin's capital Madison, and three miles (5 km) south of Baraboo on State Highway 33. Several effigy mounds are preserved on both shores of the lake, and there is a self-guided "Indian Mounds Nature Tour" pamphlet available in the Ranger's Station or the Nature Center. There is a nominal recreation fee for motorists entering the State Park.

## Madeline Island (Moningwunakauning)

Jutting into Lake Superior as Wisconsin's northernmost landscape is the scenic archipelago known as the Apostle Islands, numerically yet erroneously named after the New Testament's 12 apostles. Apostle Island National Lakeshore includes 22 forested islands and 12 miles (20 km) of mainland Lake Superior shoreline, featuring pristine beaches, sheltered coves, spectacular sea caves, remnant old-growth forests, resident bald eagles and black bears, and the larg-est collection of lighthouses anywhere in the National Park system. Madeline Island is the largest in the Apostle Island chain and the only island that sup-ports a year-round population. About 175 residents call Madeline Island their permanent home, yet thousands of tourists visit every year. It was named in 1785 after the wife of a son whose father was a famous French Canadian fur trader on the island. The original Ojibwa (also called Chippewa) tribal name of the island was *Moningwunakauning*, meaning "home of the golden-breasted woodpecker."

▲ The "Indian Cemetery" of converted Christians in La Pointe was originally a Native American ritual site.

The Ojibwa people eventually arrived at the 12-mile (20-km) long Madeline Island by divine prophecy, only to abandon it about a hundred years later.

Around the time the Renaissance was blossoming in Europe, the Ojibwa people lived in the St. Lawrence River region of eastern Canada. They battled frequently with the Iroquois and other powerful eastern tribes for land and resources. After a series of bad occurrences, including continued war and famine, the beleaguered tribe started having collective visions of a great white shell in the sky called the "Megis." The Ojibwa seemed to suffer a sort of spiritual malaise before their famous visions led them on a westward migration toward the Great Lakes. From estimations of the Ojibwa's rather vague conception of time, it is believed that the tribe left their home on the Gulf of St. Lawrence, and after a trek of several decades, arrived at the Apostle Islands around 1490. The legend of the tribe attributes the migration to the mysterious presence of the Megis, which appeared several times along the way and "gave warmth and light to the tribe." Each time the shell sank from beyond view of the Great Lakes, "death daily visited the wigwams of our forefathers," wrote Ojibwa historian William W. Warren, who relates the story of the arduous journey. The final apparition of the Megis shell appeared over Moningwunakauning, or Madeline Island, where the tribe finally settled. When the shell rose above "where it has ever since reflected back the rays of the sun, and blessed our ancestors with life, light, and wisdom," Moningwunakauning became a sort of Promised Land, a place where the Ojibwa at last found refuge from their enemies and woes.

Moningwunakauning became the new Ojibwa homeland and central focus of their legends and traditions. The western migration of the Ojibwa had encroached upon the territory of the Fox and Santee (Eastern) Sioux Indians, resulting in several battles on Madeline Island and elsewhere. The Ojibwa eventually prevailed and the other tribes were displaced from Michigan's Upper Peninsula and northern Wisconsin into Minnesota and then onto the prairies. Victorious in battle and strong once again, the Apostle Islands, Chequamegon Bay, and the Bayfield Peninsula became sacred property for the newcomers. Long Island, the site of a pivotal battle with the Sioux, is cited in Ojibwa migration legends as an important resting point. Madeline Island became the tribal center for *Mitewiwin* ceremonies and sweat lodges. The cold and sometimes treacherous waters around the islands teemed with fish, as did the feeder streams and rivers. Wild rice marshes, such as the Kakagon Slough southeast of the Apostles, produced nutritious grain. Maple sugar sweetened the native diet, while birch trees yielded material for baskets, wigwams, and canoes. Abundant deer, elk, bear, and beaver provided food, hides, bone, sinew, and fur in such abundance that it eventually enticed the French from Montreal into western Superior. The Ojibwa believed that their cultural hero, the legendary Wenabozho, invented the canoe for them, and Indians can point to a pile of rocks on one of the Apostle islands, citing these stones as the ones he used in weighting down the form of the first canoe.

> The collective vision of a great white shell
> in the sky led the Ojibwa people to Madeline
> Island. The tribe thrived on the island until
> their episode of fortuitous occurrences unrav-
> eled into a period of haunting darkness.

The Ojibwa lived a happy existence on Moningwunakauning, playing stick games like lacrosse and paddling over to the mainland to hunt or gather wild rice. It is estimated that they lived on the island for about 120 years. There is one estimation that puts their population as high as 20,000 people. However many the Ojibwa came to be, there were evidently so many of them that the island could not support their large numbers. In one severe winter, when food ran short, their medicine men resorted to cannibalism, selecting mostly young females as their victims. They continued their practice for a number of years until the enraged tribe, overcoming their fear of witch doctors, put them to death. Despite this remedy they imagined the spirits of the dead victims stalking forth at night, and they considered this an omen to leave the island forever and resettle on the mainland. Even today the native Ojibwa consider the island haunted and some will not live there. Another haunted island in the Apostle chain is appropriately named Devil's Island, which they named after their evil god or devil, Matchimanitou.

The Ojibwa established the first permanent community on Madeline Island, abandoned it, only to be resettled a few decades later by French traders who named their town La Pointe. Similar to other Woodland tribes, the Ojibwa became fur-trading partners with the Europeans. In exchange for pelts, canoes, snowshoes, ceramic beads, clay pipes and a native knowledge of the land, the French offered guns, alcohol, metal goods, and woolen blankets. Seeking affinity with Indian ritual sites, the first Catholic chapel was erected near a native burial ground at La Pointe harbor. Attempts by Catholic missionaries to "civilize" the Ojibwa were largely ineffective. After the defeat of France in 1763, the Great Lakes trade fell under British and U.S. control. Although the Ojibwa were a non-aggressive tribe who never waged sustained warfare against the U.S.

government, they nonetheless lost most of their land, motivated by the new industrial copper, timber, and fish trades. The tiny Red Cliff and Bad River reservations in northern Wisconsin, including a small portion of Madeline Island, are all that remain of the Ojibwa homeland in this area. At the docks of La Pointe stands the white-shingled post office in a building built in the 1830s as the Protestant mission house, as well as an Indian cemetery of converted Christians. Many claim the island is still haunted and locals know of a secret miniature village hidden somewhere on the island.

## Getting to Madeline Island

Madeline Island is located in Bayfield County, just a ferry ride across from the picturesque Victorian town of Bayfield, Wisconsin. The Madeline Island Historical Museum is open daily from 9 a.m. to 5 p.m., early June until early October. For information on individual and group rates, write to the museum at La Pointe, Wisconsin 54850, or phone (715) 747-2415. During the summer season, a car ferry operates hourly between Bayfield and La Pointe. Casual restaurants and bars spread along the historic waterfront of La Pointe in this popular summer resort town. In the winter, it is possible to drive a snowmobile or car over the frozen Chequamegon Bay to Madeline Island.

# EASTERN CANADA

*"It is the broad approach (to American Ethnology), though often liable to error, is most likely to produce important new ideas." -Smithsonian Director Matthew Stirling*

S PECULATION HAS EXISTED FOR CENTURIES ABOUT WHO THE first discoverers of North America really were, that is, if a continent already inhabited by millions of indigenous people can actually be "discovered" in the first place. While Christopher Columbus receives the lion's share of credit, it is now accepted history that there were previous Old World explorers before 1492 when the Nina, Pinta and Santa Maria first dropped anchor in the Caribbean. After all, crossing the Atlantic Ocean is not so extremely difficult: one man did it in a bathtub and teenagers have sailed across solo. Once past Greenland, the Labrador Current is an especially strong south-flowing current spanning the full extent of eastern Canada. For mariners, hugging the coastline past Newfoundland is practically an ocean gateway to the Eastern Seaboard of the United States.

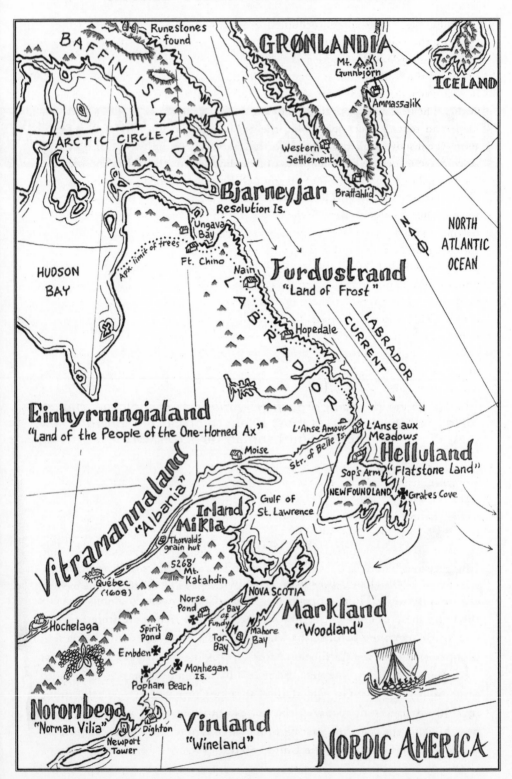

Runestones found

BAFFIN ISLA

GRØNLANDIA

Mt. Gunnbjörn

ICELAND

ARCTIC CIRCLE

Ammassalik

Western Settlement

Brattahlid

Bjarneyjar
Resolution Is.

Ungava Bay

N 40

NORTH ATLANTIC OCEAN

Apx. limit of trees

Ft. Chino

Nain

Furdustrand
"Land of Frost"

HUDSON BAY

L
A
B
R
A
D
O
R

Hopedale

LABRADOR CURRENT

Einhyrningialand
"Land of the People of the One-Horned Ax"

Moise

L'Anse Amour

L'Anse aux Meadows

Str. of Belle Is.

Helluland
"Flatstone Land"

Sop's Arm

NEWFOUNDLAND

Grates Cove

Irland Mikla

Gulf of St. Lawrence

Vitramannaland
"Albania"

Thorvald's grain hut

5268'
Mt. Katahdin

Québec (1608)

Norse Pond

NOVA SCOTIA

Markland
"Woodland"

Hochelaga

Spirit Pond

Bay of Fundy

Mahore Bay

Embden

Tor Bay

Monhegan Is.

Popham Beach

Norombega
"Norman Vilia"

Dighton

Vinland
"Wineland"

Newport Tower

NORDIC AMERICA

Middle Age Norse sailors recounted stories to other mariners of their excursions to the shores of eastern Canada, thus making them the first confirmed discoverers of North America. It is quite likely other Old World explorers preceded the Vikings, but no maps or written records from these people exist. Scandinavian documents from the 11th to the 14th century recount the Norse discovery. The best records of these early incursions come from a series of Icelandic maps and texts, collectively called the Sagas, which describe in no uncertain terms the discovery of continental North America by Vikings. The Norse were an assemblage of people from all parts of Scandinavia, but the Greenland colonies established by Eric the Red and his son Leif Ericson included mostly Norwegian and Icelandic colonists. Beginning with a good start in the 10th and 11th centuries, the Greenland colonies were in decline by the 12th and 13th centuries. Dispirited by the worsening climate, Eskimo attacks, harsh trade restrictions imposed by the King of Norway, and tithing demands of Rome, the Greenlanders completely abandoned their colonies. No mass graves have been found, no human bones showing group starvation, or any sign that they were massacred. In one of history's biggest mysteries, thousands of Vikings simply went missing in the 14th century. The diffusionist theory logically follows the Vikings to their various settlements in North America. The "White Indians" of eastern North America discovered by European explorers following Columbus were the likely descendents of Greenland Viking progeny who were known to make frequent incursions to a place they called Vinland. Along with the written records are abundant Viking artifacts and Indian customs that suggest an extended interaction with the First Nation people of eastern Canada.

French explorer Jacques Cartier is regarded as the discoverer of modern Canada, as well as popularizing the name of the country. As he sailed up the Saint Lawrence Seaway in 1535, the Algonquian greeted Jacques Cartier with the word *cantata*, meaning "welcome." Some historians believe this salutation contributed to the country being named Canada. Another possible origin of the name comes from Spanish *acanada* meaning "nothing there," as they sailed along the coast of the Gulf of Saint Lawrence. Not to be outdone, the Portuguese sailed the Saint Lawrence long before Jacques Cartier, saw the area where the seaway narrows to a river and described it as *canada*, meaning a "narrow passage." Early Basque navigators used the word *canada* to signify a straight or narrow passage.

# ATLANTIC PROVINCES

The often-overlooked New Brunswick, Prince Edward Island, Nova Scotia, and Newfoundland provinces offer exciting opportunities for hiking, sea kayaking, and canoeing adventures combined with nature study and a fair share of Viking history. Along the many inlets, fjords, and rivers of the Atlantic Provinces are water bank mooring holes carved into rocks for securing large ships. These mooring holes were here when the first settlers came to eastern Canada in the 17th century. Another curious item found by white settlers were distinctive wide-eyed Norse cats living with the native population, otherwise found only in Scandinavia, Greenland and Iceland. Canadian Indians, especially the Micmac, played Viking games like lacrosse and practiced Norse funerals. There is an intriguing list of Norse loan words in the widely spoken northeast Canadian Algonquian languages, including Micmac. The word for "bay" in Norse is *bukt,* and *bookt* in the northeast Algonquian languages. Other examples are "boat" meaning *bata* and *pados*; "rope" is *reb* and *lab*; "must" is *mos* and *maa*, all in respective order. From coins to runestones to weapons, abundant Viking relics have been found in the Atlantic Provinces, especially in Newfoundland and Nova Scotia. In Tor Bay, Nova Scotia, a Norse battle axe was found in 1889 with an inscription in old Norse reading "for divine protection." Also at nearby Yarmouth there is a large runestone on display, which reads *Leivur Eriku-Resr,* which translates "Leif to Eric, raises this monument."

## L'Anse aux Meadows

In the summer of 1961, a Norwegian archaeologist named Dr. Helge Ingstad and his wife Annee Stine Ingstad uncovered and excavated a distinctive Norse long house at the northern tip of Newfoundland Island. The dwelling had a hard clay floor with a fire pit containing charcoal in the center. Radio-carbon dating indicated that the fire burned in the decades around 1000 CE, concurrent with the timeframe of Leif Ericson's first voyage to the New World. The discovery of the long house and other artifacts found at L'Anse aux Meadows conclusively place the Vikings on the North American continent nearly 500 years before Columbus.

Continued excavations at L'Anse aux Meadows uncovered a large long house and several smaller dwellings clustered together in a community. A blacksmith's workshop, including an iron smelting furnace and charcoal kiln, were located

▲ The reconstructed Viking settlement at L'Anse aux Meadows.
The grassy shores of Sacred Bay lie a few miles north.
(Photo courtesy Parks Canada)

slightly away from the homes. Most of the buildings contained stone-lined ember pits used for cooking and heating. In all, eight buildings were uncovered that formed three distinct groups. The houses consisted of a large multi-roomed hall that served as a living room, a workshop, and storage area. The structures were made of timber and covered with turf (earth and grass), the same materials used on Viking houses in Iceland and Greenland. Distinctive Norse artifacts were unearthed in or near the house sites. These include a number of iron nails, rivets, a bone needle, a stone spindle whorl used to spin wool, a needle-sharpening stone and a bronze coat pin. Later discoveries by caretaker Birgitta Wallace of three butternuts (a type of walnut) were found at the site, which could only have been brought there by humans. The closest area where butternut trees grow is New Brunswick (bordering the state of Maine), adding another tidbit of evidence that the Vikings traveled extensively into the interior of North America.

> The L'Anse aux Meadows settlement was a
> Viking base camp used for explorations of the
> continent, boat repairs and the last stopover
> for shipment of goods back to Greenland.

Many isolationist historians refuse to believe that Leif Ericson, nor any other subsequent Norse voyager, had ever ventured further south than L'Anse aux Meadows at the northern tip of Newfoundland Island. This perspective is extremely shortsighted considering who the Vikings were, the geographic position of Newfoundland, and basic facts that can be drawn from the Sagas text. "Why would they stop?" queries anthropologist Thor Heyerdahl. The Norse explorers from Greenland and Iceland were fierce warriors, strong seamen and fearless navigators. Inhospitable conditions and a lack of resources drove them from Iceland to Greenland, then from Greenland to the New World within a single generation. Their sheer cunning and curiosity would certainly have motivated them to venture much farther than Newfoundland, which lacks the abundant timber resources and vines, or grapes, which they so ardently desired. L'Anse aux Meadows was strategically positioned for voyagers coming and going from the Saint Lawrence Seaway or the practical coastal route, but was certainly not the "Vinland" so eloquently described in the Sagas. The Vikings would have followed the same "stepping stones" to the New World as the Phoenicians, Celtics, and Irish Monks had used decades and centuries before. The stepping stones are the large landfalls, or islands, those mariners would encounter when sailing down the eastern Canadian coast from Greenland. First there was *Furdustrand,* or "land of frost" on the Labrador coast where the Greenlanders ventured often. With resources becoming more abundant the further south and west the Vikings traveled, they would have bypassed *Helluland,* the "land of rocks," or Newfoundland, for the abundant timber resources on *Markland,* the "woodland" of Nova Scotia. The final stepping stone was the New World, or *Vinland,* where wild grapes grow from Connecticut to southern Maine, but nowhere farther north. The Sagas specifically describe Cape Cod as "a peninsula's sharp elbow" and the "extensive shoals" are reminiscent of the outlying Martha's Vineyard and Nantucket Island. Here Leif Ericson and crew spent a "mild winter" in 1000 CE, where they "found vines and grapes" along with abundant timber to fill their cargo hold. Upon returning to Greenland in the spring via L'Anse aux Meadows, Leif and his crew earned themselves a small fortune because wood and wine were in such great demand. Leif acquired the nickname "Leif the Lucky" and thus began the legend of "Vinland the Good" and subsequent voyages by Greenlanders, then Icelanders, then Scandinavians, to the small colony on the New England coast. A Viking long house, similar to the one found at L'Anse aux Meadows, has been uncovered at Buzzard's Bay on Cape Cod, and another at Norse Pond in Maine.

### Getting to L'Anse aux Meadows

L'Anse aux Meadows National Historic Park is located near a small fishing settlement of the same name. L'Anse aux Meadows is on the barren shores of Épaves Bay, near the town Saint Anthony. The 430 highway is the only road accessing the northern tip of Newfoundland Island. Car ferries access Newfoundland all year 'round from the mainland, and the closest ferry to the site runs across the narrow Straight of Belle Isle from Blanc Sablon in Québec province to Saint Barbe. A reconstruction of a Viking long house is located at the archaeological site.

# ONTARIO

The lakeside capital Toronto is the largest city in the country, yet Canada's national capital is Ottawa, located in the far southeast corner of Ontario along the Ottawa River bordering Québec. The province of Ontario contains all Canadian land access to the northern Great Lakes. The interconnected chain of five ocean-like bodies of water—Lake Superior, Lake Huron, Lake Michigan, Lake Erie, and Lake Ontario—have an international border dividing four of the five lakes. The Great Lakes have a combined surface area of about 151,900 square miles (245,000 sq. km) and are among the biggest and deepest lakes on the planet. Together, they comprise the single largest concentration of fresh water in the world (excluding the polar ice caps) and are the only glacial feature on Earth visible from the surface of the moon. The North American Great Lakes are so huge that they moderate the region's climate—presently ranging from sub-arctic in the north of Ontario to humid continental warm in the south—and effect the movement of major weather systems. The lakes' thermal features heat the surrounding land in winter and slightly cool the region in summer. Because of their immense size, these major water reservoirs rarely freeze in the winter, except for isolated inlets and bays. The Great Lakes help humidify much of Ontario throughout the year.

## Eastern Canadian Great Lakes

To indigenous "First Nation" Canadians, the vast Great Lakes region was called the "Place of Shining Water." The expansive network of waterways played a vital role in the social development of the various tribes who resided along its bountiful shores. Traversing these huge waterways led to a vibrant exchange of goods, ideas, languages, and religious practices for many millennia. Most Great Lake Native American groups belong to language families of either the Algonquian or the Iroquois. At times, large tribal migrations intersected the Great Lakes, such as the Algonquian-speaking Ojibwa from the St. Lawrence River region of eastern Canada, the Iroquois-speaking Oneida tribe from present-day New York, or the Siouxian-speaking Winnebago (Ho-Chunk) from the Great Plains. One of the most powerful tribes in the eastern Canadian Great Lakes region were the Huron people who occupied a land networked by rivers and lakes between Lake Huron and Lake Ontario. French explorers named the people *Huronia* after the tribes' lake of influence. The French considered the Huron people as noble traders. In the 1500s the Huron numbered close to 45,000, yet by the mid-1990s there were only about 2,700 remaining. In the year 1640, the Huron experienced mass deaths by disease and were further decimated by Iroquois attacks. The Huron loss of population is a classic example of the devastating effects of European diseases, especially smallpox, measles and mumps, which pre-contact Indians had no natural immunities. Intertribal warfare and conflicts with European powers also diminished the Native American population around the northern Great Lakes. Unfortunately, almost all of the remaining tribes were eventually displaced far away from their homeland, and most of their vision quest sites were lost from memory.

Those individual sacred sites that are still known scatter across the islands and shores of the Canadian Great Lakes. The most famous is Dreamer's Rock, located on Birtch Island in northern Lake Huron. Here the Anishabec and other tribes worshipped *Gitchi Manitou*, or

▲ The solid white quartzite Dreamer's Rock.

▲ Huron culture in Canada.

the Great Spirit. Adolescent Indian children would go to Dreamer's Rock on a vision quest without parental guidance or provisions. The boys and girls were to fast and pray and learn about their individual spirit guide who would remain with them throughout their lives. Dreamer's Rock was a vision quest site to the Anishabec, Huron, Ottawa, Ojibwa and other tribes. The enormous Manitoulin Island next to Dreamer's Rock was considered spiritually endowed. It is the world's largest freshwater island, situated between northern Lake Huron and Georgian Bay in Ontario. Manitowaning Bay on Manitoulin Island is known as "the Den of the Great Spirit." Manitoulin Island was conversely known as *Mnido Mnis*, meaning "Isle of the Manitou," "God's Isle," or "Spirit Isle." Here *Gitchi Manitou* created the four sacred elements of fire, earth, water, and wind, where all the features of the land developed and he bestowed upon humans the greatest gift of all—the ability to dream.

Another stunningly picturesque location on Lake Huron is Nipissing Bluff, a sheer cliff that drops 185 feet (60 m) into Georgian Bay. Across the water is Giant's Tomb, an island where the spirit *Kitchikewana* resides. At Rock Lake in Algonquian Provincial Park and areas north of Lake Superior are the Puckasaw pits, or vision pits, consisting of deep rectangular stone pits of very early origin, perhaps dating to 1,500 BCE. Puckasaw pits are found on raised cobble beaches along the north shore of Lake Superior, consisting of average 3-5 feet (1.2 m) deep 4-6 feet (1.5 m) wide, although some are larger rounded depressions within the raised cobble beach. The vision pits illustrate the Indians' quest for sacred visions near special bodies of water. In the late 17th century two French priests observed a human-shaped rock near the shore of Lake Erie that had been painted with red ochre to resemble a person. Native Americans about to cross the lake would leave offerings to ensure a safe passage.

> The Algonquian-speaking tribes of the Canadian Great Lakes lived under an egalitarian system where all were treated equally. Elder women were part of the chiefdom, especially because the mother's bloodline determined membership into the clan. This matrilineal organization incorporated their creation story based on a female deity.

Many Native American belief systems feature the goddess in a worldview of interconnectedness. The Huron tribe shared a spiritual relationship with the Earth reflected through their belief in a Divine Woman creator. Huron mythology retraces the beginning of time when there was only water and water animals on the planet. One stormy day the sky ripped open and a woman fell out. The water animals saw that she was Divine Woman and crafted for her a place to rest on top of the Turtle deity, who held the woman on his back long enough until soil was collected to start the Earth. From that day forward, according to the story, Turtle has been holding up the world. On the land Divine Woman created people and animals to keep her company. When she died, Divine Woman was buried beneath the soil. The subsequent plants that grew above her offered all the nourishment necessary to sustain life for generations to come. This creation story of the Huron gives credibility to the long-entrenched matriarchal society of northern Great Lake tribes.

### Getting to Eastern Canadian Great Lake Sacred Sites

The 1,640-foot (492-m) quartzite Dreamer's Rock rises dramatically above Lake Huron, located on the White Fish Indian Reservation on Birtch Island near Little Current. Turn off at the Birtch Island Lodge sign to access Dreamer's Rock, but only after receiving permission from the tribal office in Little Current. Route 6 is the only road to Manitoulin Island, with ferry access from the southern Bruce Peninsula and bridge access north to the mainland. A short distance from the intersection of Routes 6 and 17 is the spring-fed Fairbank Lake, created millions of years ago when a meteorite hit the earth. Nipissing Bluff faces Giant's Tomb Island in Awenda Provincial Park located in the southern section of Lake Huron's Georgian Bay near the town of Midland.

## Lake Superior Sites

The rugged, rocky coastline and the wind-tortured spruce pines of Lake Superior have long inspired Canadian Native Americans. Such striking locations provided Ojibwa vision seekers the solitude necessary for communing with the spirit world. On select cliff and rock faces, as well as along major waterways draining into the lake, are some of the finest displays of rock art in Canada. The rich oral tradition of the Ojibwa tells of powerful supernatural beings, passed from generation to generation through the tribal elders. The Ojibwa believed that tiny spirits called *maymaygwayshiwuk* inhabited certain rocks. These spirits lived in the craggy cliff faces and emerged to play tricks on humans. The painting of rocks constituted a magical ritual of the artist by identifying a location where earth energy from below rises to the surface. The power of the rock combined forces with the painter to enhance a site with perceived spiritual energy. Pictographs do not record history, but rather represent the visions of young men or document significant activities. Ancestors of the Ojibwa are believed to be the painters of

▲ Prehistoric copper miners.
(Image courtesy National Park Service)

the red ocher figures on the rocks, some dating back 500 years or more. The Ojibwa and other Native Americans held the rock art locations in deep admiration, either passing by at a distance or approaching in reverence and leaving offerings of tobacco to propitiate the spirits.

The Ojibwa believed that inside the massive headlands of the eastern shore was the domain of several powerful gods. Although many suitable cliffs were available to early artists, only those places associated with resident spirits were chosen. A rocky peninsula on Lake Superior's eastern shore called Cape Gargantua is regarded as one of the most sacred places on the entire shoreline due to its enchanted atmosphere. The Ojibwa considered it a highly charged spiritual center, and the abode of *Nanaboozhoo*, the trickster god who governed the moods of the water and granted peaceful journeys upon the lake to those who paid homage to him. Nearby is Devil's Chair, a lozenge-shaped rock about 60 feet tall (18 m), rising majestically out of the water. The rock somewhat resembles a chair, surrounded by another small island called the Devil's Frying Pan. Not far away, a small rock island along Cape Gargantua is called Devil's Warehouse, a small island off the cape where the Ojibwa mined the red ocher from hematite. The Ojibwa, perhaps the most influential tribe of Lake Superior, performed most of their rituals at Gargantua Bay until French Jesuits weaned them away from these sites by telling them that they were locations of the devil.

The Agawa Indian Rock in Lake Superior Provincial Park contains several dozen well-preserved pictographs just above the lake level. The figures include the Ojibwa sea monster *Mishipeshu*, four suns, two large serpents, a horse and rider, bears, caribou, and many images of people in canoes. Another panel on Agawa Rock features a depiction of Mishipeshu, also known as the Great Horned Lynx, this time with a long reptilian tail and spikes along its back accompanied by fish. In another panel, Mishipeshu appears to be leading two canoeists safely across the lake as part of an epic crossing. Below are serpents with feet who also live in Lake Superior and hoard the mineral wealth. The images, etched in red ocher, are among the best preserved of about 400 rock art groupings on the Canadian Shield. Agawa Rock is one of eastern Canada's most sacred sites. Such reverence was apparent to the Native Americans, as well as French-Canadian traders, who all kept the habit of leaving offerings of tobacco and small gifts at Agawa Rock.

▲ The sea monster Mishipeshu at Agawa Rock escorting a group of Indians in a canoe across Lake Superior.

"Kitchi-Gummi" was the Algonquian name for Lake Superior, meaning Big Lake. The largest Algonquian tribe, the Ojibwa, considered it their spiritual home.

Some of the interesting sites surrounding Lake Superior are more mysterious, such as the prehistoric open-pit copper mines and associated dolmens. Huge quantities of raw copper were removed from the shores of Lake Superior and Isle Royale in prehistoric times. Conservative estimates put it between 20-50 million (9-22 million kg) pounds. In modern times it is estimated that 500 million pounds (225 million kg) of copper have been removed. Reliable carbon dating on a dozen Isle Royale copper pits place the time period for mining from 2400-1200 BCE. Primitive copper mining was done over a 1,200-year period before coming to an abrupt halt. Most of the prehistoric copper mines surrounding western Lake Superior conform to this consistent dating pattern. Substantiating the prehistoric seafarer theory are many ancient relics near the Lake Superior mines with equally ancient dates. Examples are: the Saw Bill Landing Dolmen in northern Minnesota with an Ogam inscription of "Baal" the Canaanite sun god; another dolmen known as the Huron Mountain Mystery Stone near Marquette, Michigan; the Newberry, Michigan statues and tablet with an undecipherable script that appears to be a cross between the Minoan alphabet and a version of Hittite; a possible calendar site marking the spring equinox on Devil's Island north of Sault Ste. Marie in Ontario; and numerous other monolithic standing stones, some containing Ogam inscriptions or other writings, strategically placed to denote safe anchorages or markers indicating the various river routes leading north to Hudson Bay.

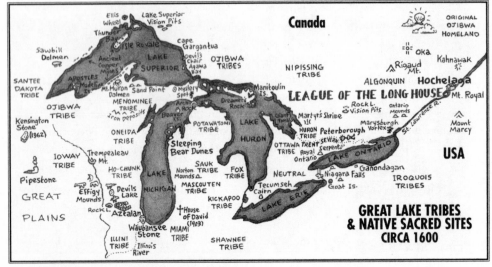

**GREAT LAKE TRIBES
& NATIVE SACRED SITES
CIRCA 1600**

## Getting to Lake Superior Sites

Cape Gargantua and Agawa Indian Rock are both part of Lake Superior Provincial Park, accessed by Trans-Canada Highway 17, and then via coastal hiking trails. Agawa Bay is located 80 miles (140 km) from Sault Ste. Marie. Agawa Rock may be visited by following the well-marked interpretive trail located just north of the park's campground. Do not visit the site when Lake Superior is stormy, as rough waters have been known to sweep people away. It's an overnight hike to see the Devil's Chair but access there and to Warehouse Island must be by boat. Typically a sea kayak is better than canoe, provided the boater has received previous instruction. Canoes are available for rent in Lake Superior Park at the Agawa Bay campground and at Montreal River, but this is too far to paddle. Instead, rent sea kayaks and canoes at the town of Wawa. Guided canoe and sea kayak tours to Lake Superior sacred sites can be arranged with Naturally Superior Adventures, (800) 203-9092. Trips are all-inclusive led by professional guides.

## Peterborough Petroglyphs

One long white crystalline marble outcropping in Petroglyphs Provincial Park features a full array of Algonquian petroglyphs, along with others that seem oddly misplaced for southern Ontario. The out of place markings are remarkably similar to ancient native art found in Scandinavia, while several others are reminiscent of prehistoric images from the American Southwest. The Algonquian people were the latest artists, contributing their style sometime between 900 and 1400 CE. The mammoth stone, at nearly 180 feet (55 m) long and 100 feet (30 m) wide, contains an astonishing 800 images—300 being very distinct, the other 500 somewhat ambiguous. One carving depicts a squatting figure with a natural hole in the abdomen that may be symbolic of death and rebirth. Others represent supplications to the Great Spirit. There are similar figures of Algonquian

304

shaman as well. Perhaps the most intriguing Algonquian image is the "Symbolic Womb" carved above a fissure in the rock, which may be an interpretation of an entrance to the underworld or the symbolic womb of the Earth Mother. The local Anishnawbe people call the slab *Kinomagewapkong*, meaning "the rocks that teach." Native American shaman used the Peterborough site as a blackboard to teach new generations mythology, history and conduct rituals. After ceremonies, the petroglyphs were covered up with moss and branches to protect them from damage due to the freezing and thaw effects of the Canadian winter. Forgotten for centuries, the sacred slab was found again in 1924 by historian Charles Kingam.

The Algonquian petroglyphs, while interesting indeed, do not convey the pre-historic mystique of other carvings with obvious characteristics of far-away cultures. Two clearly evident boat petroglyphs bear no resemblance to the traditional craft of Native Americans, but one solar boat—a stylized shaman vessel with a long mast surmounted by a sun—is typical of petroglyphs found in Scandinavia and northern Russia. Several inscriptions are nearly identical to those found on a rock near Boslund, Sweden. Harvard Professor Barry Fell was convinced that many of the Peterborough carvings were created by a Norse king named Woden-lithi, (Servant of Odin), who was said to have sailed down the Saint Lawrence River from Norway sometime between 1500 and 1700 BCE. This Norseman was a precursor to the latter arriving Greenland Vikings by several thousand years. While in the area trading for copper, Woden and his men made several inscriptions on the rocks depicting Norse mythology. Perhaps the Norse saw some of the Native American spirit canoe images and added their own carvings or modified the originals. The masts on the ships and the Vikings standing on the deck have

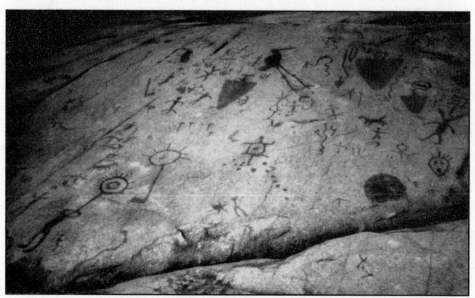

▲ The Peterborough Petroglyphs feature a vast array of artistic styles and images.

305

a double meaning just as they did in prehistoric Europe. Fell interprets these as the Ogam language and the translation compiled at Peterborough does seem to describe a transatlantic voyage and trading expedition. The motivation for travel was copper, which is very abundant near the surface only a few hundred miles away in the Lake Superior region. The Peterborough area is about halfway along the strategic Trent-Severn Waterway connecting Lake Huron and Lake Ontario. The fact that the Peterborough Petroglyphs are located near a known prehistoric trade route certainly reveals much about exotic travel in bygone days right up to colonial times.

> The more than 800 Peterborough Petroglyphs represent one of the best-preserved and stylistically diverse rock art sites in North America. To many successive cultures it was a billboard to commemorate an event, praise a deity, or teach mythology.

Adding further intrigue, two Peterborough carvings look strikingly similar to the Hopi *kachina* flute-player called Kokopelli. This pair of hunchbacked figures, along with long-robed anthropomorphic figures, are misplaced over three thousand miles from their Arizona homeland, where their depiction proliferates in the Southwest. Legend has it that various Hopi clans traveled on multi-year migrations across both the North and South American continents. They left their marks as signposts for other Hopi travelers or to pay homage to their spirit helpers, such as the distinct hunchback figure Kokopelli. No Native Canadian culture depicted any kind of image like Kokopelli. Of the two types of hunchbacks depicted, one is the traditional flute playing kachina portrayed with a phalanx symbol, and the other has a peculiar "antenna" on its head. The latter could be viewed as one of the mythical "Ant People" deities who helped the Hopi through the destruction of the first world and are viewed as very revered spiritual helpers. One of the Hopi kachinas is located near an Algonquian "spirit canoe." In Native Canadian mythology a tribal shaman would take unhealthy people into the spirit world to help them heal by using these special boats. Similar spirit canoes are also depicted in Mayan mythology throughout Mesoamerica. Other Hopi clan symbols represented at Peterborough are the Turtle, Wolf, Eagle, and Crain clans. Yet these can be argued away as common animal motifs of worship that most indigenous cultures used. Another Hopi clan symbol worth noting is a large serpent mound only 60 miles (97 km) away from Peterborough with similarities to the Great Serpent Mound in Ohio, which is also mentioned in Hopi legends. The Hopi kachina symbols at Peterborough, so far away from their Southwest homeland, lends credibility to Hopi legends that the history and trade lines of North America are much more ancient and sophisticated than is commonly accepted. The argument that the Peterborough Petroglyphs reveal proof of Pre-Columbian contact in the heart of North America only adds to the mystique of the site.

## Getting to the Peterborough Petroglyphs

Located 34 miles (55 km) northeast of the town of Peterborough is Petroglyphs Provincial Park. Travel north from Peterborough on Highway 28, turn right on Highway 6, then turn right on Northey's Bay Road. Signs for the Provincial Park mark the way. Petroglyphs Provincial Park is closed in the winter; call 705-877-2552 for hours and days of operation. The two large stones with petroglyph incisions are enclosed by a large greenhouse dome, built to protect them from the elements. The Provincial Park also features excellent hiking and picnic areas in one of the most beautiful areas of Ontario, Canada. When viewing the site, consider it as an outdoor cathedral used by various cultures for many thousands of years.

# QUÉBEC

After a French commissioner traveling with Italian navigator Giovanni da Verrazano sailed into New York harbor and surveyed eastern Canada in 1524, the king of France was notified that there was abundant territory free for the taking. The king sent Jacques Cartier to explore the new lands in 1534 and again in 1542, attributing French names to the places he discovered and lay claim to all the northern territories in the name of France. Cartier was on his way home when he passed the shipload of French colonists under Sieur de Roberval coming to attempt the first, ill-fated settlement. Later Samuel de Champlain, Louis Joliet, Father Marquette, Robert La Salle, and others were to move westward and establish New France in what is today Canada and the Mississippi Valley in the United States. From 1604 until his death in 1635 Champlain was the foremost French colonizer. In 1608 he founded the fortified village of Québec, the first permanent settlement in French America. Although Québec City earned the nickname "Gibraltar of America" because of its strategic hilltop position, the British managed to capture the city and all French holdings east of the Mississippi in the 1756 to 1763 French and Indian War. In a stroke of colonial wisdom, the

British passed the Québec Act in 1774 allowing the French subjects to retain their old laws and the freedom to worship as Roman Catholics. This explains why the province of Québec remains largely New France, with a Catholic majority of French speakers who have yet to lose hope of someday achieving their political autonomy from Canada. In the northeast, the Gaspé Peninsula of Québec is an attractive rural region of small villages that retain strong French traditions. This is where the northern section of America's Appalachian Mountains meets the ocean. In the language of the original inhabitants, the Micmac "Indians of the Sea," *Gespeg* means "Land's End," and the Gaspé Peninsula offers the kind of rugged beauty in a place where mountains collide with the sea.

## Hochelaga

French explorer Jacques Cartier's account of his first visit in 1535 to the Iroquois stronghold of Hochelaga has long captured the imagination of Canadians. Cartier reached Hochelaga on the island of Montreal on October 2, 1535, during his second voyage up the Saint Lawrence River. He visited the settlement (inhabited by some 2,000 natives), observed the local customs, explored the region around Mount Royal, and returned to Stadacona (Québec City) a few days later. Cartier used the name Hochelaga to identify the Native American village, as did most explorers up to the early 17th century. It is likely that this name meant either "Big Rapids" or "Beaver Dam." Upon arrival at Hochelaga, a thousand natives rushed out to greet Cartier with honor and delight. So awed with the newcomer, the Indians thought of him as someone with miraculous powers. Cartier played the role of a Christ figure to obtain more information, while the natives brought their sick and maimed to be healed by his touch. Cartier, not believing the accounts of the previous tribe he met, confirmed the existence of the city of Saguenay on the Ottawa River as well as accounts of the Great Lakes and Niagara Falls. He climbed the highest peak on the island to survey the fertile valley and see the Lachine Rapids and Ottawa River, at which time he proceeded to christen the surrounding land Mount Royal (Montreal).

Most impressive to Cartier and his crew was the highly advanced level of civilization the Indians of Hochelaga had achieved. Their earthen fortifications appeared similar to those of northern Europe. The Iroquois at Hochelaga lived in an orderly society, characterized by well-kept plantations and granaries and three-story fortifications to protect the giant communal houses from outside attack. Nowhere in his native France, except the castles and palaces, had Cartier ever seen dwellings comparable in size and functionality. The city was built in the round with three levels of heavily fortified ramparts leading up to the communal granaries and 50 large two-story long houses set row upon row around a central square. The countryside surrounding Hochelaga was filled with cultivated fields, mainly corn. Cartier was also introduced to tobacco but failed to recognize its market potential.

Discovered by French explorer Jacques
Cartier, the Iroquois capital of Hochelaga was
the most advanced Native American settlement in eastern North America.

How did the Iroquois achieve such a refined state of development? Ethnologists are still unclear on the origin of their culture and readily acknowledge that the Iroquois were an amalgamation, a mixture of several cultural types. It is a strong likelihood that the Iroquois speaking tribes along the Saint Lawrence River and upper New York state were the partial direct descendents of the assimilated Northern European peoples who arrived some 600 years before Cartier. During the golden age of Irish civilization, contemporary with the collapse of the Western Roman Empire, Celtic navigators were known to have voyaged to Iceland and Greenland. That the Celtic Irish settled in North America before the Vikings is almost certain, for reports of traders from Iceland who entered

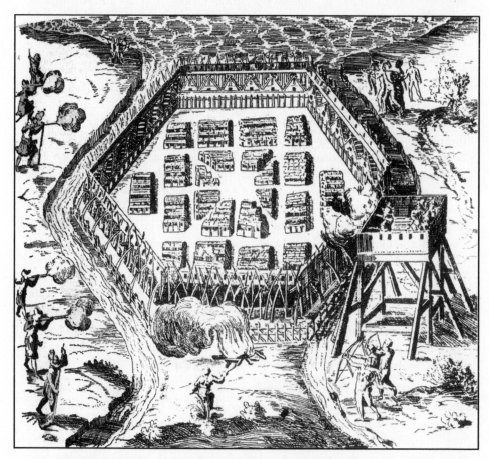

▲ Hochelaga had a similar layout to this 18th century image of an Iroquois
walled city.

*Vitramannaland* "Land of the White Men" were recorded by both early and contemporary historians. Some time later the region became known as *Irland Mikla,* or "Great Ireland," and eventually renamed Albania, also meaning "White Man's Land." Twenty years after Leif Ericson discovered Vinland, as related in the *Eyrbyggia Saga,* a party of Norsemen landed in *Vitramannaland* and discovered a thriving Irish settlement. It seems clear that these settlements along the Saint Lawrence were there long before the Norse excursion in 1020 CE. Subsequent Norse migrations to eastern Canada took place in the 11th and 12th centuries, and again in the 14th century at the conclusion of the Greenland colonies. Although Cartier and later explorers found no Celtic or Norse people per se, after several hundred years it is reasonable to assume that they had assimilated culturally and genetically with the native tribes. Viking invaders were known to quickly merge with the people whom they conquered by adopting the native language without changing materially its structure or inflections. It is interesting to note that there are many Old Norse "loan words" in the various Iroquois and Algonquian languages. Many mythological stories of these tribes could be from the pages of the Old Norse tales of Odin and Thor. Their ancestors, says the Iroquois creation "myth," came from the east or northeast. Apart from similar traditions and social customs, another telling sign of Northern European diffusion was the Iroquois adaptation of the Norse style long house, so prolific in 16th century Québec and Ontario provinces that the unified tribes called themselves the "League of the Long House." The early Scandinavians up to the 12th century, and the Iroquois throughout colonial history, lived in dwellings that were different from all other Native American communal houses. The Iroquoian code for compensation and death, as described in Thwaite's *Jesuit Relations,* was almost identical to the Viking code—the law governing the payment of *baug*—stipulating "an eye for an eye, a tooth for a tooth, a life for a life." To take revenge was not only a right, but practically a religion in both cultures. The Jesuits observed this strict practice with the Iroquois, and like the Norse, both had a fixed scale of atonement levied in regard to the slain person's status. Jacques Cartier had no way of knowing these complex laws when he captured a neighboring chief and several others to bring back to France. All of Cartier's Indian captives died except one young girl. Cartier again visited Hochelaga in 1542, but this time he was met with extreme hostility, forcing him to immediately return to Stadacona (Québec City) with the new chief in hot pursuit. Cartier made no mention on the current state of Hochelaga in his records, probably because this time he was fleeing for his life.

The French coined the term *Iroquois,* a derogatory term meaning "sneaky" or "snakes." Ever since Cartier's second visit to Hochelaga the Iroquois were hostile with the French, mainly because the Iroquois were allied with the Huron tribe who controlled passage through the eastern Great Lakes. Today, the Iroquois Nation consists of six prominent tribes: the Senecas (Keepers of the Western Door); Cayugas (Pipe Bearers); Onondagas (Fire Keepers); Oneidas (People of the Stone); Mohawks (Keepers of the Eastern Door); and in 1722 the Tuscarora

(People of the Shirt) were added. The Iroquois prefer to be known by their traditional name, the *Haudenosaunee*, meaning the "People of the Long House." The Iroquois long house was the dwelling for all members of the same family clan. The longest was known to be 410 feet (123 m) in length, with at least eight long houses (one for each family clan) per compound, all surrounded by a protective palisade. Inside the long house bunks were covered with braided cornhusk mattresses, animal furs and blankets. Two doors on either end of the long house and smoke holes in the ceiling were the only outlets to the outside. The long house also served as a symbol for the "People of the Great Law"—five nations under one protective roof that included northern New York state and portions of the Saint Lawrence Seaway. The Haudenosaunee constituted the most powerful confederacy in eastern North America prior to historic European contact, up until the American Revolution and arguably to the present day. As land speculators realized the potential value of Iroquois territory, they initiated a series of dubious "negotiations" with Indian leaders. By the early 19th century most of the expansive Iroquois territory was lost.

### Getting to Hochelaga

The native village of Hochelaga was located where the present-day city of Montreal stands, at the foot of Mount Royal. John William Dawson discovered remnants of Hochelaga just south of the McGill campus in 1859. The Indian village was completely destroyed during conflicts over the French fur trade. All that's left of Hochelaga in Montreal is the name. There is a West Island voting district called Hochelaga-Maisonneuve, a Hochelaga Street near downtown, and Hochelaga county in Québec province.

## Saint Joseph's Oratory

The world-renowned basilica dominating the southwestern Montreal skyline started out as a small wooden chapel on Mount Royal. The founder was a simple brother who lived a childhood of poverty, and was orphaned at age 12 along with 11 brothers and sisters. His name was Alfred Bessette (1845-1937), a physically frail man with little education, yet with a big heart and healing touch that would one day inspire millions. Growing up a poor French-Canadian orphan he was forced in his teens to be a migrant worker in the textile mills of New England. He returned to his native Québec province in 1867. Three years later he joined the priesthood, but because of his weak condition was relegated to the responsibility of a doorman. Once accepted as a novitiate of the Holy Cross Order at age 25 he was given the name Brother André, a name which took on spiritual consequences when his healing prayers to Saint Joseph for others began to manifest physically. His blessings were most appreciated by the poor and sick that would come to Brother André in a saddened and oftentimes desperate condition. He invited them to pray with him to Saint Joseph to obtain favors, and in a short time many people reported that their prayers were being answered, yet always when

▲ Saint Joseph statue in front of the famous oratory.

Brother André was not present. He was a modest man who took little credit for his efforts, solely attributing all the healing power to Saint Joseph. In 1904, Brother André helped pay for a small wooden chapel by cutting hair at the Holy Cross. The small chapel was crowded from the beginning and too small for the amount of people who flocked to the site. Brother André moved into an apartment over the chapel a few years later to accommodate the steady flow of pilgrims. By 1914, a major basilica was being built near the small chapel, but construction was halted several times due to financial constraints. Brother André died in 1937 at the ripe old age of 91 and was buried in the crypt of the unfinished church. A million people came to his funeral during a bitter winter storm. The magnificent Saint Joseph's Oratory was finally completed in 1955. Brother André was beatified in 1982 by Pope John Paul II, the final honor before being declared a saint. Although the basilica is a powerful tribute to Joseph, devotees from all over North America come as much to honor Blessed André's shrine as they do to pray for sickness cures.

> The massive dome of Saint Joseph's Oratory is the largest in North America, second only in the world to Saint Peter's in Rome. Its prominent location in Montreal and the healing tradition founded by Brother André attract more than two million pilgrims per year.

The Catholic Church regards the Oratory as the most important sanctuary devoted to Saint Joseph in the world. As father of Jesus Christ, Saint Joseph is represented as the model of workers, guardian of virgins, supporter of families, terror of demons, consolation of the afflicted, hope of the sick, patron of the dying, and protector of the Church. Brother André had a strong devotion to Saint Joseph based on their mutual experiences as impoverished exiles and unskilled laborers. Despite the passing of Brother André, the sanctuary still retains its reputation as a healing center. Hundreds of thousands of pilgrims arrive each year to prostrate themselves at the long flight of stairs leading up to the Oratory. The middle staircase is constructed of wood so pilgrims may ascend the staircase on their knees. Canes, crutches and other objects hang between pillars in the Votive Chapel, as well as on the walls of the little wooden chapel founded by Brother André. His loving and ever-optimistic spirit endears the legacy he left as a humble servant to Saint Joseph whose ability to inspire others became legendary.

## Getting to Saint Joseph's Oratory

Saint Joseph's Oratory is located on the slopes of Mount Royal, in the southwest region of Montreal. The address is 3800 Queen-Mary Road, a few blocks from the *Côte-des-Neiges* metro station. Saint Joseph's Oratory overlooks the twin sprawling cemeteries called *Cimetière Notre-Dame-des-Neiges* and the *Cimetière Mont-Royal* on the backside of Mount Royal. Brother André's little wooden chapel is on the grounds next to the massive oratory.

# Sainte-Anne De Beaupré

From the earliest times of Christianity, believers had an interest in knowing more about the historical family of Jesus Christ, especially his mother, father and grandmother. Despite no mention in the Bible, the Virgin Mary's mother has long been regarded as a Jewish woman named Anne. She is first mentioned in a Greek manuscript called "the Revelation of James," probably written around the year 160 CE by a non-Jewish Christian. The James account speaks of Mary and her parents Joachim and Anne. Although the story was most likely fictional, the cult of Saint Anne has nevertheless influenced millions of Christians worldwide.

In Canada, devotion to Saint Anne goes back to the beginning of New France, and was brought to Québec by the first settlers and early missionaries. The original parish on the present site dates from the year 1650 and achieved legendary status when several shipwrecked sailors on the Saint Lawrence River attributed their deliverance to Saint Anne. A few years later, on March 13, 1658, a foundation was dug for a larger stone-built chapel, which by general consent, would be dedicated to the beloved Saint Anne. On the first day of construction the spirit of Saint Anne demonstrated how favorably she viewed the undertaking by healing Louis Guimont, an inhabitant of Beaupré who suffered terribly from rheumatism of the loins. With little strength but for his confidence in Saint Anne, he came forward and placed three more stones in the foundation, at which time he found himself suddenly and completely cured of his ailment. Shortly thereafter the French-Canadian tradition of pilgrimage to Sainte-Anne De Beaupré began for the sick and despondent, making it the oldest pilgrimage destination in North America. By 1707 the site had gained importance with Saint Lawrence Indian

▲ Sainte-Anne De Beaupré is the most popular Christian pilgrimage destination in North America.

tribes, also called "First Nations" in Canada, who came to venerate the one they called "Grandmother in the Faith." Popular for centuries due to the high status they afforded to grandmothers, the Micmac and other tribes make an annual pilgrimage to Beaupré every June. The largest pilgrimages come for the feast of Saint Anne (July 26th) and the Sunday closest to the feast of the Nativity of Mary (September 8th). From July 17th pilgrims make a *novena*—nine consecutive days of private prayer and public worship—ending in a candlelit procession on the eve of the festival. On the feast day the sick are anointed outside the Basilica, then come inside to pray at the Miraculous Statue, an impressive oak carving of Saint Anne and a young Virgin Mary. Over the centuries the miraculous cures have rendered the site comparable with the great pilgrimage destinations of Lourdes, France or Fátima, Portugal. Sainte-Anne De Beaupré has been described as "the Lourdes of the New World." Until 1875 the yearly number of pilgrims did not exceed 12,000, but to judge by the heap of crutches left at the saint's feet, there appears to have been many marvelous cures wrought at Beaupré.

Although the present Basilica at Sainte-Anne De Beaupré dates from 1926, it replaced the older, more endearing church of 1676. On either side of the main doorway are crutches, walking-sticks, bandages, and other offerings left behind by the faithful who have gone home healed.

Pilgrims come to the cathedral not only for miracle cures, but to view the sacred relics of Saint Anne. The oldest is a finger-bone of Saint Anne, which was first exposed for veneration on March 12th, 1670, and has ever since been an object of great devotion. Other relics of the saint have been added in later times to the treasury of this shrine. Perhaps the most visible object in the Basilica is the Miraculous Statue of Saint Anne holding a young Virgin Mary. Pilgrims direct their prayers to God through the intercession of the saint. This important statue stands on a pillar in the north transept, where it can be seen from almost every point in the Basilica. In 1892, Cardinal Taschedreau presented a "Great Relic" to the Basilica, the four-inch (10-cm) long wrist bone of Saint Anne. When the wrist bone was brought over from Rome it was first shown in New York City, where an epileptic was cured on its first appearance, causing a tremendous excitement in the city. Ever since, American pilgrimages have increased to Sainte-Anne De Beaupré. The road from Québec City, the traditional pilgrimage route still walked by many (particularly on the feast days), is marked by wayside shrines and bread ovens.

### Getting to Sainte-Anne De Beaupré

The huge Catholic Basilica and associated religious buildings form their own village just south of the town Beaupré along the shores of the Saint Lawrence River. Sainte-Anne De Beaupré is located 22 miles (35 km) north of Québec City on Canadian Highway 138. The picturesque surrounding area includes Ile d'Orleans between two branches of the Saint Lawrence, the Chute Montmorency (a waterfall twice as tall as Niagara Falls), the Mont Sainte-Anne ski resort and the Sainte Anne River emptying at the town of Beaupré. The official pilgrimage season runs from early June to early September, with around a million and a half visitors each year.

# NEW ENGLAND

*"The Native peoples of this country believe that certain areas of land are holy. These lands may be sacred, for example, because of religious events which occurred there, because they contain specific natural products, because they are the dwelling place or embodiment of spiritual beings, because they surround or contain burial grounds, or because they are sites conducive to communicating with spiritual beings."*
**–United States American Indian Religious Freedom Act, 1934**

THE POPULAR IMAGE OF *MAYFLOWER* PILGRIMS LANDING ON the shores of New England and communing with friendly Indians inspired the late-November holiday of Thanksgiving Day in the United States. The reality was quite different, as over half the original Pilgrims perished in the first year and Indian attacks were a real and persistent threat for over 50 years until the colonists won a decisive battle. Yet the English Pilgrims arriving at Plymouth, Massachusetts in 1620 were merely a continuation of several centuries, perhaps many millennia, of European contact in New England. The distinguishing feature of the English colonists is that they survived and established an unbroken historical line that continues to the present day. Previous European inhabitants such as the Mediterranean Phoenicians, seafaring Celts, Middle Age Knights Templar, Irish monks and the Greenland Norse may have assimilated with the indigenous people, given up any claim on a settlement and sailed home,

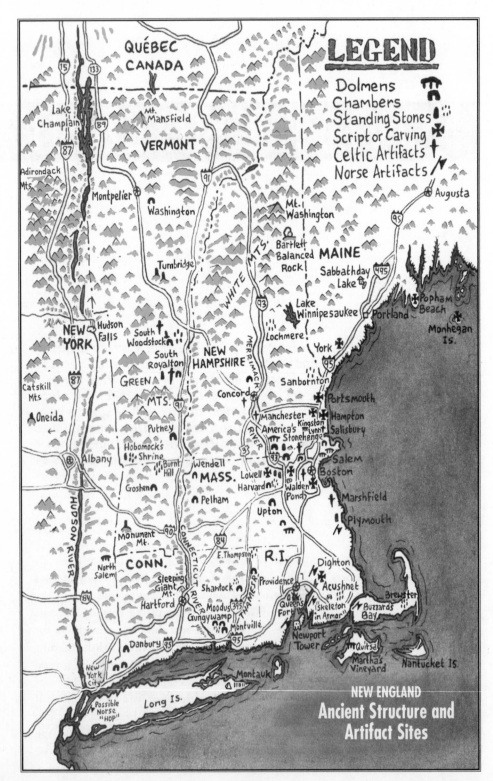

**LEGEND**
- Dolmens
- Chambers
- Standing Stones
- Script or Carving
- Celtic Artifacts
- Norse Artifacts

QUÉBEC CANADA

Lake Champlain

Mt. Mansfield

VERMONT

Adirondack Mts.

Montpelier

Washington

Turnbridge

Mt. Washington

Bartlett Balanced Rock

MAINE

Sabbathday Lake

Augusta

Popham Beach

Monhegan Is.

WHITE MTS.

Lake Winnipesaukee

Portland

NEW YORK

Hudson Falls

South Woodstock

South Royalton

GREEN

MTS.

NEW HAMPSHIRE

Concord

Lochmere

York

Sanbornton

Portsmouth

Catskill Mts.

Oneida

Putney

Hobomock's Shrine

Albany

Burnt Hill

Goshen

Manchester

America's Stonehenge

Kingston

Lynn

Salem

Boston

Hampton

Salisbury

MERRIMACK RIVER

Wendell

MASS.

Lowell

Harvard

Walden Pond

Pelham

Upton

Marshfield

Plymouth

HUDSON RIVER

Monument Mt.

CONN.

North Salem

Sleeping Giant Mt.

Hartford

Moodus

Gungywamp

Montville

E. Thompson

Shantock

R.I.

Providence

Dighton

Acushnet

Skeleton in Armor

Brewster

Buzzards Bay

Queen's Fort

CONNECTICUT RIVER

THAMES R.

Danbury

New York City

Montauk

Newport Tower

Quitsa

Martha's Vineyard

Nantucket Is.

Possible Norse "HOP"

Long Is.

**NEW ENGLAND**
**Ancient Structure and Artifact Sites**

or have been indiscriminately killed off. Like the earliest attempts by the French in the Saint Lawrence region and the English in North Carolina, colonies could be wiped out very swiftly if the wrong enemies were made.

Many of the earliest developments in the historic colonization of North America began in New England. The first successful European settlements in North America, communal religious orders, the struggle for self-rule, and the beginning of the American Industrial Revolution all have their origins in New England. Massachusetts set the pace for New England in homesteading, shipbuilding, agriculture, commerce, and defiance toward the British crown. By 1700 Massachusetts had developed a more secular, less theocratic character and a strong spirit of independence that would eventually lead to the American Revolution. The small farming communities that marked New England during the early decades of independence shifted quickly in the mid-19th century, as sprawling industrial factories began to dominate the picturesque river valleys. The textile mills fell into decline in the early 20th century when many of the factories moved south for cheaper labor. New England has rebounded in recent decades with a new focus on high technology, finance and tourism.

## Prehistoric Stone Buildings of New England

Upon settling on their new farms in New England, colonial homesteaders were surprised to discover curious one story stone buildings embedded into hillsides or completely underground. Scattered across a half dozen states are hundreds of remarkable stone chambers made of dry masonry. Some of these structures are freestanding or sunken into the earth, whereas others are accessed by passageways driven into the hillside. The most elaborate are described as "beehive" chambers, indicative of the conical shape of their ceilings. Some were completely underground and were discovered only years later when a roof caved in or a plow or pick-axe penetrated the chamber. Their age was usually authenticated by trees hundreds of years old growing into their unmortared walls or megalithic roof slabs. Many contained elaborate "smoke holes" to ventilate the chambers, as well as stone crafted recesses built into the walls. It is unfortunate to mention that a vast majority of these original New England stone buildings have been torn down for quarried stone, bulldozed over for modern development, repeatedly vandalized, or otherwise dismantled, destroyed, and abandoned.

Assuming that the structures were built by vanished Indian tribesmen and were free for the taking, the colonial farmers put them to use as extra storage space shelters. These numerous chambers were circular or rectangular in form, up to 30 feet (9 m) in length but usually half that, and up to 10 feet (3 m) wide and eight feet (2.4 m) high or more. The conventional wisdom at the time was that these enclosures were built as "colonial root cellars" or "steam baths for Indians." These dismissive theories conveniently overlooked several basic facts, such as

▲ Interior view of the "beehive"
Upton Stone Chamber.

the passageways being too low and narrow to wheel a cart into, having soil floors that would rot vegetables, or that nowhere else in North America did Indians construct sweat lodges made of stone. If not European colonials or Native Americans, then who could be responsible for their construction? Where else in the world are beehive enclosures of this kind located? Like nowhere else, the chambers closely resemble structures built by Culdee Monks from Scotland and Ireland who adopted the building style from their Celtic ancestry.

The Culdee Monks are known to have been driven from their home countries by Norse invaders around 800 CE, only to flee along the Atlantic "stepping stones" to Iceland and Greenland, where they again hastily retreated from the Vikings in 1007, this time presumably traveling to the New World. Many of the New England beehive stone structures were constructed long before Columbus. They may be as old as the Celts themselves who, along with their Phoenician alliance, were navigating the northern seas in the millennium before Christ. Arriving some 2,000 years later, and perhaps overlapping upon existing structures, the Culdee Monks arrived and required shelter for religious purposes. The monks would have cultivated a friendly interaction with the Indians, and very likely were the first to introduce Christianity to the "savages." The mostly pagan Vikings followed a few decades later, led by the recently Christianized Leif Ericson and his colonization of Vinland. The Vikings would have traded with the Indians or *Skraelings* as the Norse called them, but continued to have bloody conflicts including the death of Leif's younger brother Thorvald. Eventually the various prehistoric European settlers assimilated with the Indians, and over time their descendents reflected their mixed heritage. All up and down the northeast coast there were "white" Indians mixed with darker skinned Indians who incorporated in their culture many northern European traits, including language, writing, peculiar customs and building practices. These similarities amazed the first 14th century European sea captains as they charted the Atlantic Seaboard.

The mysterious stone structures of New England remain as evidence for a long suspected pre-Columbian association with the Old World of Europe.

The Medieval Culdee Monks who lived in monastic settlements in Ireland, Scotland, and the outer islands created beehive dwellings resembling an igloo of stone. Unlike monks of the modern age, the Culdee (Worshippers of God) were married and had families. Their worship practices of 800 CE were a blending of Celtic paganism with Christianity, including older vestiges of Druidism mixed with outward forms of Catholicism. Druid practices, including human and animal sacrifices, continued in Ireland until Saint Patrick drove out all the pagans, also identified as driving out the snakes, in the 6th century. Yet for many centuries the two religions blended. After being displaced by Norse invaders the Culdee Monks took to the sea and headed north to Greenland, west to Labrador, and then south past Nova Scotia. New England has a similar climate to their home countries, yet was free of invasion or religious persecution. With them the Culdee Monks took their religious holidays, such as Easter from the Spring Goddess *Eostre,* and the Druid practice of determining annual cycles of the sun, moon and stars. Of the 275 very distinct drywall beehive chambers in New England, many have been determined to have astronomical orientations or are associated with nearby standing stones or large cairns that may have once supported posts. There are some 105 such chamber sites in Massachusetts, 62 in Connecticut, 51 in New Hampshire, 41 in Vermont, 12 in Rhode Island, and four in Maine.

With such an abundance of stone structures in New England, what follows is a description of the most prominent chambers and associated prehistoric access routes. The Merrimack River valley in Massachusetts and New Hampshire was a seemingly active avenue for ancient voyagers and their riverside settlements, as was Connecticut's Thames River drainage, and the Connecticut River extending north up to Québec, Canada. In the hills surrounding Boston, the Upton Stone Chamber is one of the largest and most precisely built beehive chambers in New England. This chamber is aligned to observe the setting solstice sun and stars of the Pleiades, as marked by cairns on nearby Pratt Hill. The Wendell Beehive Cave in Massachusetts is very similar in size and design to the nearby Pelam Chamber, being about four feet (1.2 m) tall in the main chamber, constructed of mortar-free masonry in the shape of a beehive, and covered with earth. The Thames River mouth in Connecticut has a large collection of ancient chambers, the most extensive being a complex called *Gungywamp*, originally thought to be an Indian word but now translated in Gaelic as meaning "Church of the People." Besides containing two beehive chambers and petroglyphs, Gungywamp has two sets of double concentric circles comprising 21 large quarried stones laid end to end, just north of the chambers. It also boasts a number of megaliths, cairns and marked stones of a bird and carved letters. On the spring and fall equinox, sun rays penetrate an opening in the west wall of one chamber, suggesting Gungywamp was an astronomical observatory. Another prominent ancient observatory site is at South Woodstock, Vermont, consisting of stone chambers, standing stones, and cairns in a natural bowl surrounded by hills and ridges. Besides having close proximity to waterways, the beehive structures would have been interconnected by an intricate network of footpaths.

### Getting to New England's Prehistoric Stone Structures

In Massachusetts, the Upton Stone Chamber is located on private land just outside the town of Upton on Elm Street, about 12 miles (20 km) southeast of Worcester. Across the valley from the chamber is Pratt Hill where several cairns are located near the summit. The Wendell "cave" is located on a hillock known as Mount Mineral, about 12 miles (20 km) north of Pelham in Franklin County. Pelham Chamber is on private land, 2 miles (3.5 km) west of Quabbin Reservoir on Route 202 in Hampshire County. In southeastern Connecticut near the town of Groton in New London County is the enigmatic Gungywamp site, located in a 100-acre (40-ha) area behind the Croyton Ship Yard in a Boy Scout camp. In Vermont, the vast South Woodstock complex is on private land surrounding the town of the same name. Nearby Elephant Valley in South Royalton, Vermont, is home to the famous "Calendar I site."

# MAINE

After Samuel de Champlain's exploration of Maine's rugged coastline in 1604, the French attempted settlements in the area. Soon after, in 1607, the English made their own claims to the territory of Maine, and for the next 150 years the two European powers contested a boundary along the Penobscot River. Only in 1759 was British rule fully established. Since colonial times Maine has been an important source of timber, first as masts for British ships, then as pulpwood for paper mills. Even today in the state's North Woods region timber is king. Along the coast the long-held traditions of shipbuilding, fishing, and lobstering continue. In the past few decades tourism and high technology have become recent additions to the economy.

## Mount Katahdin

The landscape of Maine is very irregular, a result of glacial action. In the northwest a mass of mountains rise to about 4,000 feet (1,200 m), and towering Mount Katahdin, near the center of the state, reaches an altitude of practically one mile above sea level. The rolling Appalachians, in Maine called the Longfellow Mountains, and the state's narrow river valleys join with more than 2,400 small lakes to form a region of unusual scenic charm. The imposing Mount Katahdin is a granite peak rising 5,267 feet (1,580 m) above the North Woods. As the tallest mountain in the state, it is also situated near the northern terminus of the Appalachians as they gently tumble into New Brunswick, Canada.

The grandeur of Mount Katahdin had been a devotional object to indigenous people for thousands of years. Young Indian males seeking to achieve warrior status favored the "Great Mountain" for their vision quests. Worshipped by several regional Native American tribes, including the Eastern Abenaki, Passamaquoddy,

▲ Mount Katahdin reclines majestically on the horizon in northern Maine.

and the Penobscot, Mount Katahdin was the abode of a wide variety of mythical deities and supernatural beings. The most famous was Pomola, a spirit being with the body of a man, the head of a bull moose, and the wings of an eagle. Pomola was fiercely territorial and would attack any unwelcome Indian climbing Katahdin into his lofty realm. His terrible howls, echoing on the strong northerly winds that scour Katahdin, frightened local Indians, some to the point of insanity. Yet Pomola was a winter spirit who flew away with the spring warmth and returned with the fall chill. Pomola presided over local weather activity and was assisted by his spirit helper, "the storm bird," which appeared to humans as a tiny bird that could foretell storms if people would closely observe and listen to its voice. Another deity was the giant man named Katahdin, considered perfect in physical condition and proportions. Penobscot legends relate how he had a fondness for young and attractive Indian women who would visit the mountain and succumb to the giant's sexual prowess. Besides lending his name to the mountain, Katahdin also fathered a son with one Penobscot woman.

> Local Indian tribes refer to Mount Katahdin as the "Greatest Mountain," and believe it was guarded by numerous mythological deities who had the power to control weather systems.

Non-indigenous people have also felt the powerful attraction of Mount Katahdin. In 1797, a group of Voodoo-inspired Africans escaped Halifax, Canada from the chains of slavery. When they learned about a great holy mountain they headed west into the North Woods. The Haitian slaves, also called the Wild Maroons, lived for a while with the Penobscot tribe near present-day Staceyville in view of Mount Katahdin. The Wild Maroons couldn't survive in the wilderness for too long. Some were adopted by Penobscots, others emerged in the neighboring villages begging for food, but most simply disappeared, likely dying of starvation or freezing to death.

Famed author Henry David Thoreau took a trip to Mount Katahdin in the summer of 1846 and climbed it with several fellow explorers. In Thoreau's time there was no mass transportation, so just walking from Bangor to the base of the mountain took them about a week. When his party first saw the mountain he wrote: "had our first, but a partial view of Ktaadn (his spelling), its summit veiled in clouds, like a dark isthmus in the quarter, connecting the heavens with the earth." On the day they climbed the mountain they set off at 6 a.m. and bushwhacked their way directly towards the highest peak. The views "presented a different aspect from any mountain I have seen, there being a greater proportion of naked rock, rising abruptly from the forest." By 4 p.m. the climbing party was too wearied to carry on, but Thoreau wanted to complete his goal. He was profoundly struck by the experience and climbed to the summit alone. Catching up with his friends later, Thoreau and his companions descended the same way they came, expecting few to endure the harsh conditions and physical rigor they had just experienced. "It will be a long time" Thoreau commented, "before the tide of fashionable travel sets that way." He found the country to be "grim and wild ... savage and dreary," fit only for "men nearer of kin to the rocks and wild animals than we." The climbing experience left him, in the words of one biographer, "near hysterical."

### Climbing Mount Katahdin

Mount Katahdin is located in Baxter State Park, in Piscataquis County near the town of Millinocket. Baxter State Park is about 26 miles (42 km) west of Interstate 95. The hike up the tallest peak in Maine is described by Baxter State Park literature as "strenuous," but can be done round-trip in a day by fit climbers who set out early. The main route to the summit is the Hunt Trail along the southwest slopes, following the route of the first recorded ascent of Katahdin in 1804. The rugged 5-mile (8-km) Hunt Trail begins at the Katahdin Stream Campground, follows the relatively flat stream for the first mile, then continues forcibly upwards. Near the top of the mountain the trail leads around boulders to the Gateway, a challenging climb above the treeline. Finally the Hunt Trail emerges onto the Tableland, a relatively flat terrain leading to the rock pile summit known as Baxter Peak. Those who spend the night on the summit wake up to the delight of seeing America's first sunrise, a shared honor with Maine's Cadillac Mountain on Mount Desert Island. The Appalachian Trail to Georgia begins nearby.

## Sabbathday Lake

The United Society of Believers in Christ's Second Appearing, or "The Shakers" as they became known, can trace their founding back to a tiny band of religious enthusiasts in southern France. There, in the year 1689, a strong religious upheaval took place in the form of trance dancing and visions, followed by violent physical movements and "deep utterances of inspired truths." Denouncing the evils of the day, along with their peculiar religious zeal, the French group understandably aroused much opposition and persecution. The group left their homeland and crossed the English Channel in 1706 where they established new roots. Their religious style seems to have become an outgrowth of early Methodism. In England, the group was called in derision the

▲ The communal buildings and farm plots of the Sabbathday Lake Shakers.

"Shaking Quakers" because of their ecstatic bodily agitations in religious worship, but they prospered and new societies were established all over the country. In 1747, several Quakers were forming a sect in Manchester when a young girl named Ann Lee came to the group in search of God's truth. Living through intense hardship that would solidify her religious convictions, Ann Lee had been married and saw all four of her children die. In 1770, Ann Lee had a personal vision of Jesus, accepted by the Shaking Quakers, but rejected by their peers in England. Accused of witchcraft, they were persecuted and had to immigrate to New England. They gave up everything in Great Britain so they could start a new life devoted to "authentic Christianity." The Manchester society departed for North America in 1774 under the leadership of the illiterate Ann Lee, or "Mother" as she became known, to spread their gospel in the New World.

The Shakers overcame resentment by their American peers mainly because of their progressive beliefs, generosity, quality workmanship and intense devotion. They were a Christian sect that preached celibacy and equal rights for both sexes. Their frenzied dancing, they thought, brought them closer to God. In America their wild gyrations were toned down, to be replaced by an orderly and patterned ritual dance. They sang deeply solemn songs as part of their devotional practices. The Shakers believed in collectivism, social equality free from prejudice, and joyful personal worship. They were an inventive group who attributed their ideas directly from God, including their desire for perfection. "Find God from within," is considered the genius of Protestantism, along with "Christ sets his example." They were simple inventors who designed and built their own furniture. Workdays started at 4:30 in the morning during summer, and 5:30 a.m. in the winter. Work was considered worship. Even the most mundane of tasks were an act of God. Carpenters and artists didn't sign their work, because after all, it was God's work. A Shaker belief was "Order is Heaven's First Law."

Arriving in New England with nothing more than their strong religious convictions, Mother Ann and her followers began preaching a unique version of personal salvation. Celibacy was a commitment to God and considered a core obligation. Men and women were kept in separate living quarters. The Shaker faith was open to all as long as they would follow the teachings of Jesus Christ and base their spiritual lives on the three-fold disciplines of celibacy, confession of sins, and obedience to wise elders. Mother Ann believed intercourse was the original sin separating humankind from God, just as it was in the beginning for Adam and Eve. In order to reclaim the Kingdom of God, all Shakers were required to forsake marriage and sexuality so to recapture the original innocence. This morally demanding lifestyle segregated the colonies by sex, yet all shared equally in hard work and leading an austere life. By the late 1770s, Mother Ann's first farm community had been established, and Sabbathday Lake was founded in 1782. When Mother Ann died at the age of 48, she left a handful of inspired leaders, both women and men. No image of Ann Lee exists. New generations grew up without ever knowing Mother Ann. Some of the new generations of Shakers began to have visions of Mother Ann, just as she had envisioned Christ.

After Mother Ann's death, 19 self-supporting Shaker colonies were eventually established in 11 states, with Maine alone hosting three. Colonies expanded out to Kentucky and Indiana, but not farther. The frontier moved on instead. For over 100 years the Shaker communities flourished, housing almost 6,000 permanent residents. The "Winter Shakers" would come during the season of scarcity, and none were ever turned away. People of all races were accepted. It is estimated that 140,000 Americans joined different religious communities in the early 19th century. The Shakers accepted many of these new members and were widely regarded as the oldest and soundest of the American religious communities.

The Civil War draft was against the Shaker's pacifist belief system, making them the first conscientious objectors in America. Respecting their convictions, President Lincoln granted the Shakers clemency from the draft. The Shaker sect started to decline after 1875, and only seven communities remained in 1920. By the mid-20th century almost all of the colonies were closed due to lack of members. Their numbers dropped sharply in the post-Industrial Age with the emergence of population shifts to the cities. Shakers couldn't compete by selling their goods competitively with mass produced goods. Without new members being born into Shakerism, along with the rigorous demands placed on new applicants, the dynamic religious movement of the 19th century was all but dead by the beginning of the 21st century. Yet the Sabbathday Lake Shakers strongly believe a prophecy of Mother Ann that the sect would decline sharply, only to rebound in numbers and fervor.

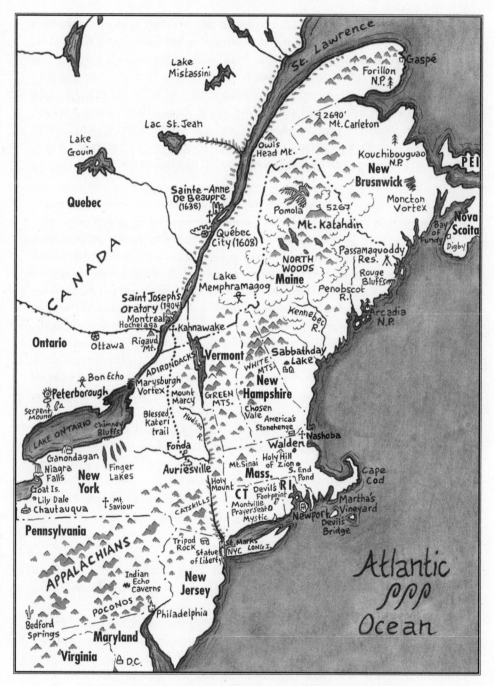

The dozen living Shakers of Sabbathday Lake are the final remnants of a major religious communal movement in the American Protestant tradition.

The stunning rise of the Shakers is due in part to their resourcefulness and ingenuity as a group. Despite their often-ridiculed worshipping style, the Shakers promoted progress and social change. They were devout pacifists and strong supporters of women's suffrage and workers' rights. The Shakers embraced electricity when it was introduced and invented a number of labor saving devices, including the first horse collar and the one-horse wagon, the washing machine, the flat broom, the screw propeller, the circular saw, and many other clever innovations. The Shakers of Sabbathday Lake were the first in Maine to prepare garden seeds in small paper packets for market. The Shakers excelled at taking a good idea and making it better.

At their peak in the early 19th century, Shaker communities were instructed to select sacred hills for their own "feast grounds" or outdoor religious ceremonies. Most of these hills were originally Native American worship sites. Sometimes, it was noted, the Shakers outdoor ceremonies incorporated elements of Indian rituals. In 1842, an edict by the elders went out to all Shakers requesting they hold service twice a year on the highest point of land closest to their community. Thereafter, Mount Sinai in Massachusetts became an outdoor church to the small Shaker community in Hancock, and artifacts found on the hill indicate that the peak was sacred to local Indian tribes before it was utilized for Shaker worship. In nearby Harvard the Shakers claimed the Holy Hill of Zion as their own, flattening the top of the hill and conducting sacred rituals that many claimed induced a second appearance of Mother Ann. In New Hampshire, Mount Assurance was utilized as a sacred peak to the Shaker community in Enfield. Similarly, in upstate New York a nearby Shaker community utilized a hill called Holy Mount. The Sabbathday Lake outdoor worship site was called Mount Horeb, located on the grounds near the present-day water tower. No remnants of the site exist today after the hill was plowed down in the 1890s when a large commercial orchard was planted. A beautiful landscape was visible from all the outdoor worship sites, unquestionably inspiring Native Americans and the Shakers alike.

### Getting to Sabbathday Lake

The last community of Shakers is located a half-mile from the banks of Sabbathday Lake in the town of New Gloucester, in southern Maine. From Portland, take the Maine Turnpike 495 to Exit 11, also the exit for Highway 202, and travel north on Route 26 for 8 miles (13 km) to the Sabbathday Lake Shaker Community located at 707 Shaker Road. The museum shop and Shaker store are open from 10 a.m. to 4:30 p.m. daily except Sunday, from Memorial Day until Columbus Day. Call (207) 926-4597 for a schedule of tours, workshops, and craft demonstrations. The group holds their Public Meeting (worship service) every Sunday at 10:00 a.m. During warm weather months the group meets in the 1794 Meeting House, the rest of the season in the Dwelling House. Public Meeting services are always open to the public.

# MASSACHUSETTS

The second permanent English colony in America (after Jamestown, Virginia founded in 1607) was the Plymouth Colony, founded in 1620. The *Mayflower* sailed out of Plymouth, England in September of that year, with 41 families on board. Only 50 of the first 102 Pilgrims survived the first winter, many succumbing to disease or exposure. In 1621, more settlers came to cast their lot with the courageous surviving settlers. After the small harvest was gathered, the pilgrims celebrated the first Thanksgiving Day. The intense religious devotion of the Plymouth settlers prevented them from abandoning their fledgling colony. In 1630, another group of Puritans founded Boston, which grew to be a thriving commercial center for the British Colonies. Over a century before the American Revolution was fought, Harvard was founded in 1636 at Cambridge, making it the oldest college in the United States. Defiance to the English Crown centered in Boston just before the war erupted, and the first battles were fought at Lexington, Concord, and Bunker Hill. After the war, port towns such as Boston and Salem grew fabulously wealthy, paving the way for the Industrial Revolution. Today Massachusetts continues to be a leader in investment banking, electronics, and higher education.

## Walden Pond

On the shores of this half-mile long pond the transcendentalist philosopher Henry David Thoreau (1817-1862) conducted a multi-year experiment in solitude and self-sufficiency. His friend and mentor Ralph Waldo Emerson owned the land around Walden Pond and invited Thoreau to establish himself there as a writer six years after he graduated from Harvard College. Inspired by Emerson's 1836 essay *Nature,* which advanced the then unique concept that each individual should seek a spiritually fulfilling relationship with the natural world, Thoreau decided to live and work in the woods. Thoreau writes: "I went to the woods because I wished to live deliberately, to front only the essential facts of life. And see if I could not learn what it had to teach and not, when I came to die, discover that I had not lived." Starting in July 1845, he established himself in a single room cabin that he built, keeping a journal of his thoughts and his encounters with nature and society. He continued to collect and revise his observations during the next seven years and published them in 1854 in the now classic book entitled *Walden.* At the time Thoreau's decision to live in the woods was met with skepticism, yet his desire was to live a simplistic life surrounded by nature. Justifying his actions, he commented: "my friends ask what I will do when I get there. Will it not be employment enough to watch the progress of the seasons?" In September of 1847, Thoreau completed his two year experiment in simplicity and returned to the civilized life once again. His essays and poems would make him a famous author, but it was really Thoreau's book *Walden* that made him renowned for motivating the world to value our natural environment.

New England author Henry David Thoreau popularized the concept of living simply in harmony with nature: "Live in each season as it passes, breathe the air, drink the drink, taste the fruit and resign yourself to the influence of each." Walden Pond is regarded as the birthplace of the American conservation movement.

Henry David Thoreau's sojourn at Walden started a long tradition of people coming to the pond and its surrounding woods for recreation and inspiration. The lake is a famous example of a kettle hole, being formed by retreating glaciers about 11,000 years ago. The emergence of Walden as a public park was in keeping with the belief that nature was primarily meant to be left alone and enjoyed by people in its pristine state. "I think that each town should have a park ... a common possession forever, for instruction and recreation," he wrote in his journal on October 15, 1859. Much of the land surrounding the

pond had been clear-cut of trees just a few years before Thoreau lived there. The natural destruction he witnessed compelled him to encourage conservation of natural places like Walden: "All Walden wood might have been preserved for our park forever, with Walden in its midst." In 1922 the Emerson, Forbes and Heywood families granted the land surrounding the pond to the Commonwealth of Massachusetts, with the stipulation of "preserving the Walden of Emerson and Thoreau, its shores and nearby woodlands for the public who wish to enjoy the pond, the woods and nature." In 1990, musician Don Henley initiated The Walden Woods Project to prevent the surrounding area around Walden Pond from being developed. Today, it is estimated that around 600,000 people visit the reservation every year.

▲ American poet and essayist Henry David Thoreau (1817-1862).

Later in his life, Thoreau would become increasingly involved with the social and political issues of his time. He was an outspoken critic of economic injustice and slavery. With other members of his family, Thoreau helped runaway slaves escape through the Underground Railroad to freedom in Canada. His 1849 essay *Civil Disobedience* has influenced countless protesters and eventually brought him international recognition. The key to Thoreau's theory of civil disobedience was his emphasis on the individual conscience, including his own willingness to go to prison (which he did) to protect the purity of his thoughts. In prison, the just person is protected from the biggest threat of evil, that being the loss of integrity that comes from complicity in state sponsored injustice. Prison, Thoreau argued, is actually the place of greatest freedom in an unjust state. His writings have influenced such eminent peacemakers as Mahatma Gandhi and Dr. Martin Luther King, Jr. both of whom relied on *Civil Disobedience* in developing their own ideas of nonviolent resistance. After a prolonged struggle with tuberculosis Thoreau died at the age of 44 near Walden Pond. He is buried on Authors' Ridge at Sleepy Hollow Cemetery in Concord.

### Getting to Walden Pond

Walden Pond State Reservation is located in the greater Boston area near the town of Concord. Motorists should take Route 2 to Walden Street (Route 126) south and follow signs to the lake. Route 126 extends just east of Walden Pond and is clearly visible from the road. The lake itself is a 102-foot (31-m) deep pond, 61 acres (24.4 ha) in size, with a walking trail around its 1.7 miles (2.7 km) diameter. Auto and bus parking and the Thoreau reconstructed cabin are across the street from Walden Pond. The parking lot can fill up early on sunny days in the summer.

---

# The First Recorded European Settlement

One of the most misunderstood and underrepresented parts of North American prehistory is the Greenland Norse settlement of a colony called "Vinland the Good," a region which was reported on for several hundred years by people returning from Vinland to medieval Iceland. *The Greenlander Saga* recounts the adventure of a young Viking named Leif Ericson setting off in the year 1000 CE on a southwest trajectory to find a wooded land known from another excursion 15 years prior. In desperate need of timber for their ships, Leif and his crew set out to explore the eastern Canadian coast, continued south, then spent a "mild winter" at a place where grapes grew wild—"Wineland." The ancient texts specifically recount the expedition departing Vinland the following spring loaded with timber and grapes destined for Greenland. The sagas description of "a peninsula's sharp elbow" near "extensive shoals" would be all that's needed to direct further expeditions, and today fits the geography of Cape Cod. Once at Vinland new arrivals would find Leif's long house surrounded by outlying homesteads and planted fields. The ample natural resources and many safe harbors of Narragansett Bay and Cape Cod must have seemed like a Nordic promised land. News of Vinland spread to Scandinavia, mainland Europe, and eventually to the Vatican in Rome. The pope dispatched 16 bishops to oversee Greenland and associated lands between IIII and the demise of the Greenlandic colony at the end of the 15th century. An earlier Archbishop wrote in 1075, "(settlers) may have found in this great ocean, and which is named Vinland because grapes grow wild there, and yield the best wine. There is also an abundance of self-sown grain, as we know not from hearsay only, but from the sure reports of the Danes." Medieval bills of lading in Bergen, Norway refer to black bear, sable and marten furs, none of which are found in Greenland but were most surely exported from Vinland. In 1355, the King of Sweden and Norway ordered an expedition under the command of Paul Knutson to report on the status of the Christian colonies in Greenland. Learning that the Western Settlement had immigrated to the mainland, Knutson traveled

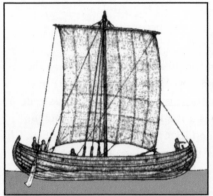

▲ A Viking "knorr" of the type used by the Greenland Norse in the 11th century.

to Vinland, and then on to the Great Lakes region (see: Kensington Runestone) in search of the lost colonists. By 1490 no European ship had called at Greenland for 80 years, and its people had vanished, presumably migrating en masse to Vinland.

Settlers and traders from throughout the North Atlantic trickled into the small colony, a land free of royal tax collectors and powerful bishops demanding tithes. On becoming Vinlanders the newcomers lived primitively, left little trace, and co-mingled with Native Americans, much as the French trappers did centuries later. Eventually, the little colony could not sufficiently defend itself from its enemies, and after three centuries the remainder of the colonists returned to Iceland, were killed off, or assimilated with the native people. Over a hundred years later Italian explorer Verrazano arrived by ship and described the Narragansett Indians as a "handsome and well-mannered people with very white skin (*bianchissimo*)." Subsequent explorers would note that "they excel us in size," had skin "more inclined to whiteness," and were "friendly and generous, beautiful and civilized." The founder of Rhode Island, Baptist religious leader Roger Williams, believed the "white skinned" local Indians of Newport were of "Icelandic origin." The natives commonly were described as having red hair and green eyes. Williams also observed that the Narragansett Indian language contained many Norse loan words, and their Indian shell pendants closely resembled Irish or Norse coins and gaming tokens.

# NEW HAMPSHIRE

The White Mountains of New Hampshire, part of the Appalachian chain, extend southward from the Canadian border to below the center of the state. The White Mountains are the highest, most celebrated, and most impressive peaks in all of New England. Among the several ranges are eight mountains over a mile high (1.6 km), with Mount Washington at 6,288 feet (1,886 m) the highest peak in New England. Mount Washington is famous for having what is probably the worst weather at any permanently occupied place in the world. Hardy workers reside all year long at the noted Mount Washington Observatory and the TV and radio transmitter building. The most prominent of the several White Mountain ranges is the Presidential Range, about 15 miles (24 km) long and five miles (8 km) wide. Mount Washington lies roughly at the center of the range, with mounts Clay, Jefferson, Adams and Madison to the north, and Monroe, Franklin, Eisenhower, Clinton, Jackson and Webster to the south. The mountains give the state its nickname the "Granite State," a useful building material for both ancient and modern homesteaders. Granite rock slabs were used by megalithic inhabitants who sailed across the Atlantic in prehistoric times, and employed as quarried stone in the construction of modern New England.

## America's Stonehenge

On a hilltop near the Massachusetts border are a series of low stonewalls and cobbled rock chambers called America's Stonehenge. The entire complex covers about 30 acres (12 ha) of hills and woodland, around which extends an apparently haphazard collection of walls interspersed with tall, triangular-shaped

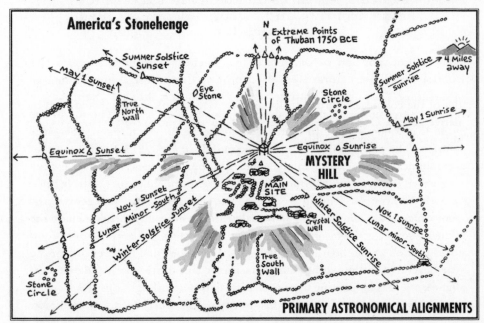

standing stones. The site's central feature is Mystery Hill, situated on a single acre, which contains 22 stone chambers (dolmens) and other megalithic features. Immediately surrounding the central site are upright stone monoliths aligned to predict prominent astronomical sightings.

In the central section of Mystery Hill are several engaging features of curiosity. The centerpiece is a T-shaped chamber with internal structures similar to a chimney and hearth, as well as a "couch" sculpted right into the living rock. From the couch, a pipe-like hole called a "speaking tube" ascends to the surface and runs directly below an enormous rock table weighing 4.5 tons (4,080 kg). The tube may have been used for some kind of spooky oracle because it distorts voices from below, and the table above may have served as a sacrificial altar because of the carved gutters on top to catch the blood. Surrounding the "Oracle Chamber" are more than 20 stone chambers of various sizes, which may have been used as shelter for the presumed Bronze Age inhabitants, or were utilized collectively as some kind of religious ceremonial center. There is evidence that the entire complex is built over a natural cave system, but no entrances have yet been located. Instead, deep well shafts have been discovered, and the most intriguing pit leads not to a cave, but to a natural fault where a cluster of quartz crystals were recovered. The crystals may have been mined nearby, or came from afar with the inhabitants and had been ritualistically placed into the well to indicate the site as a power point. It is known that crystals were worshipped or used for tools by ancient cultures.

> America's Stonehenge has been determined by several independent surveys to be an accurate and astronomically aligned calendar.

The hilltop position of the megalithic "beehive" chambers suggests this location and its structures were used primarily as a village surrounding an observatory. The Summer Solstice Sunrise Monolith is situated where the sun rises over this upright slab of granite on June 21 of each year. The top of the stone is uniquely shaped to match the landscape on the horizon where the sun rises. The place to view this is in the middle of a stone circle, where other astronomical computations can be made. Nearby the stone circle there is a tall rock called the True North Stone, which was determined in 1975 to have lined up with the pole star Thuban around 1750 BCE, and is on the main central axis from which other alignments can be calculated. These alignments include the annual summer and winter solstices (June 21 and Dec. 21) and seasonal equinoxes (March 22 and Sept. 22), as well as specific solar and lunar events of the year. Several of the low stonewalls also indicate true north-south and east-west alignments. It is interesting to note that all astronomical sightings at America's Stonehenge were in a position to accurately predict their events around 1500

▲ One of several megalithic chambers at America's Stonehenge.

BCE. However, due to the earth's changing tilt over several thousand years called the procession of the equinoxes, they can no longer precisely predict astral movement events.

Formerly called the Mystery Hill Caves, America's Stonehenge is more of an academic problem child than a mystery. Professional archaeologists who refute any European contact before Columbus or the Vikings routinely dismiss this sprawling complex as a fraud, ignoring even the most basic evidence. For instance, tree rings from a white pine tree found growing through one of the walls conclusively determined its age to be at least 30 years older than the birth date of farmer Pattee, the first homesteader on the hill. Jonathan Pattee purportedly created this megalithic complex as a hoax in his spare time, then after all his work, turned around and started dismantling and selling the larger slabs for spare change. Yet how Pattee could have erected megaliths weighing 15-20 tons (13,600-18140 kg), dug drainage canals through the bedrock without using modern tools, and aligned markers to indicate solstices and equinoxes was never explained by the stodgy academia. It is known that at least 20% to 50% of the site was devastated by quarrymen in the 1920s who hauled away "cartload after cartload" of the megalithic stones to build sewers and curbstones in Lawrence, Massachusetts. All that's left today are the skeletal remains of a much larger site. Perhaps the most startling evidence indicating the real age of America's Stonehenge is the carbon dating of charcoal debris excavated for analysis. Two separate tests in 1969 and 1971 determined the age of America's Stonehenge to be at least 3,000 and more likely 4,000 years old. In addition, pottery shards found at the site seem unrelated to anything Viking, Irish or Native American, suggesting even older voyagers visiting New England, namely Mediterranean Phoenicians and their Celtic allies from the Iberian Peninsula. Along with the characteristic megalithic stone-slab chambers and associated henge stones marking celestial events, rune-like inscriptions have been deciphered as Iberian Punic and read as a dedication to the Phoenician sun god *Baal*. Other inscriptions identified at the site bearing the Celtic Ogam script refer to *Bel*, The Celtic sun god, long suspected to be the same god as the Phoenician *Baal*. Just the terrifying thought of such pagan deities being worshipped on the Puritan shores of New England has kept the Semitic and Celtic people excluded from their deserved role in prehistory. Nonetheless, the picture of America's Stonehenge emerges as a thriving first century BCE Celtic community, Punic trading post, pagan religious center and Iberian astronomical observatory.

### Getting to America's Stonehenge

Located in North Salem, America's Stonehenge is only about an hour's drive from Boston, and 18 miles (30 km) from the Atlantic Ocean. Boat captains of antiquity would have reached the hilltop location by navigating up the Merrimack River to a tributary that runs just below the site. Today most visitors drive to America's Stonehenge and take Exit 3 off the I-93 to Route 111. Motorists should follow the signs from North Salem. The land around North Salem, New Hampshire is becoming increasingly urbanized by the encroaching urban sprawl of Boston.

# NEW YORK

The Dutch explorer Henry Hudson sailed up the river that now bears his name in 1609, giving the Netherlands an early claim on New York territory. The Hudson River has often been compared to Germany's Rhine, a river whose surrounding landscape varies from ruggedly picturesque to horribly industrial, a river once of strategic importance in war, in commerce, and most recently in battles for conservation. The Dutch traded fur with the Indians until 1664 when the English captured this Dutch colony called New Amsterdam and established a military monopoly in the region. The eventual consequence of British dominance was the American Revolutionary War where one-third of all battles were fought on New York soil. In 1825 the Erie Canal was inaugurated with much rejoicing, as the highway of the Hudson now reached all the way to the Midwest by way of the Great Lakes. By the late 19th century corporate titans such as J. P. Morgan, John D. Rockefeller, and Cornelius Vanderbilt created vast industrial empires, which began the process of making New York City the world's leading financial center.

## Auriesville and Fonda Shrines

Kateri Tekakwitha was born in 1656 to the Mohawk chief of her village and an Algonquian mother. The Mohawk were considered the "Keepers of the Eastern Door," one of six prominent tribes comprising the Iroquois Nation. The site of her birth, Gandaouaga, is believed to be located in present day Auriesville on the south side of the Mohawk River. Auries was the name of the last Mohawk who lived there, and from this name the modern designation was formed. Shortly after Kateri's birth, trouble beset the village and her people. During the ten years she lived in Gandaouaga she was the only member of her immediate family to survive a smallpox epidemic, which started to devastate her village when she was four. Smallpox left her face scarred with pockmarks and nearly blind for the rest of her life. After her parents died, her Mohawk aunt and uncle adopted her. Hardship struck again in 1666 when their village was destroyed by invading French soldiers and their Canadian Indian allies. The next year the surviving members constructed and moved to a fortified village on the north side of the Mohawk River called Caughnawaga, close to present-day Fonda. It was here where Kateri lived most of her life and where she was baptized on Easter Sunday, 1676 at Saint Peter's Chapel in Caughnawaga. Today the village or "castle" of Caughnawaga, where Kateri lived half of her life, is the only intact and fully-excavated Iroquois village. The spring, whose waters were most likely used for her baptism, still flows at the site.

Shortly after her baptism, Kateri was greatly persecuted by her own people because of her Christian conversion. She refused her uncle's repeated attempts to force her into marriage, and soon had to flee the Mohawk Valley for the Jesuit Indian village of Kahnawake near Montreal, Canada. The settlement on the St. Lawrence opposite Lachine was established for the Iroquois converts to Christianity who wanted to withdraw from the "moral corruption" of their pagan kinsmen. In 1679, Kateri pronounced a vow to God of perpetual virginity. Known for her gentleness, kindness and good humor, her life of piety ended when she died on April 17th, 1680 at the tender age of 24. Her short life was devoted to penance and a ministry to serve others. After her death, her scarred face reportedly became beautiful. Pope Pius XII recognized her heroic virtues in 1943, and declared Kateri Venerable. In 1980, Pope John Paul

▲ A Blessed Kateri statue at Fonda.

II declared Kateri, born of strife and one who preached love and healing, Blessed. Now there is a growing movement to try get Kateri canonized as a Saint.

> The Auriesville and Fonda shrines commemorate the birthplace and baptism of Kateri Tekakwitha, the most famous of all Native American Jesuit converts. Her two shrines, associated with the establishment of Christianity in New York, attract thousands of pilgrims every year.

Besides becoming the first laywoman in North America to be honored as Blessed, the popularity of Kateri Tekakwitha also lies in the fact that she lived such a troubled life yet maintained her faith through such harsh adversity. Although banished by her people, she came to be known as the "Lily of the Mohawks." Blessed Kateri is also considered the patroness of peace and ecology. In the words of the church, she lived an "exemplary life," engaging in severe penances, and proposed to start a colony of Indian nuns. It is said that at the time of her death her face radiated with bliss and many miracles were reported. Today, pilgrims from all over the world come by the thousands to pray at the site where Blessed Kateri was born and baptized.

Along with the Blessed Kateri shrine in Fonda, the Martyrs' Shine in Auriesville commemorates several Jesuits who were killed during their missionary work. In 1642, 14 years before Kateri was born, two French missionaries were captured and brought to her village. One of the men was killed; the other was allowed to live and finally escaped a year later. He returned to the Mohawks in 1646 and was martyred. The next day his young companion was also killed. Martyrs' Shrine was begun in 1885 as a monument to these first saints of North America to be canonized. The various outdoor shrines and the unique Coliseum Church mark the hallowed ground where the blood of the missionaries was spilled. Pope Pius XII called Auriesville "nature's own reliquary—the verdant hills that slope up from the quiet, easy-flowing river of the Mohawks." In 1930, the Catholic Church canonized the three Auriesville martyrs, along with five other Jesuit missionaries martyred in Canada. In 1969, Pope

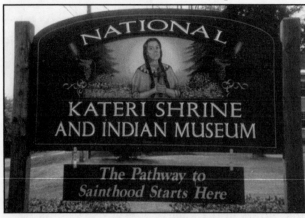

▲ Fonda is the beginning of the Blessed Kateri trail.

Paul VI appointed October 19<sup>th</sup> as the date to observe their feast day throughout the world. Also celebrated every year on July 14<sup>th</sup> (or the closest weekend) is Kateri's feast day, including Mohawk rituals during mass, a blessing of the four directions, and a pipe ceremony.

### Getting to the Auriesville and Fonda shrines

The Shrine of the North American Martyrs is located in the picturesque Mohawk Valley in eastern New York, about 40 miles (64 km) west of the New York state capital Albany. If coming from the east on the Thruway, exit at Amsterdam Interchange 27 and continue westward on Route 5-S. If coming from the west, exit at Fultonville Interchange 28 and continue eastward along Route 5-S. Exit 28 is also the turnoff for the Tekakwitha Shrine located on Route 5, just southwest of the small town of Fonda. Auriesville and Fonda are only 6 miles (9.6 km) apart. The fully excavated village of Caughnawaga is located at the National Tekakwitha Shrine in Fonda. The Kateri gift shop in Fonda is open daily from 10 a.m. until 4 P.M. from May 1<sup>st</sup> to October 31<sup>st</sup>. The Kateri Shrine is open from 9 a.m. to 7 P.M. everyday.

## Chautauqua and Lily Dale

The shores around both Chautauqua Lake and Cassadaga Lake once contained dozens of Native American features, including ritual sites, mounds and prehistoric campsites, all since destroyed by development. Early farmers and settlers held little respect for Native American earthworks and wantonly plowed them over or looted the mounds with no regard for preservation. An excavation on Bemus Point jutting out of Chautauqua Lake has revealed evidence for a prehistoric settlement up to 10,000 years old. Cassadaga Lake is much smaller, but the ruins around it seem more significant. The "Mound City of Cassadaga Lake" has been charted based on remaining archaeological evidence. Two rows of earthwork

▲ Areal view of the Chautauqua Institution.

palisades created a fortified enclosure to protect an ancient city surrounding a large mound, likely a temple mound, on a prominent peninsula where the current Lake's End Marina now resides. The Mound City of Cassadaga Lake also featured an ancient causeway leading to a ritual fire bed compound, along with scattered Native American caches, fire pits and other mounds surrounding the lake.

The word Chautauqua, hard as it is to say or spell, holds several distinct meanings. As a Seneca Indian word it likely translated as "bag tied in the middle" based on the shape of the lake of the same name, but there are other Seneca translations so nobody really knows for certain. As the Methodist summer camp with the original purpose of educating Sunday school teachers, the Chautauqua Institution evolved into a campus for learning, the arts, philosophical discussion, music concerts, and recreation. More than a resort or spa, coming to Chautauqua (pronounced Sha-*talk*-wa) is about lifetime education and personal growth. Sister institutions continue to operate in Ohio and Colorado. Since its founding in the 19th century by Protestant leaders, it has always placed importance on openness by including all Protestant faiths. The Institution fully integrated Catholics and Jews in the 20th century, and the push now is to include Muslims, Orthodox Christians, Buddhist and Hindu leaders. All these people would "take a chautauqua" to come here. Robert Pirsig in *Zen and the Art of Motorcycle Maintenance* instructed his son as they traveled across America on their own chautauqua. A "Traveling Chautauqua" toured across America from 1904 to 1933, setting up a weekly learning and cultural event in large and small towns alike. Even Elvis Presley played the role of a Traveling Chautauqua manager in his 1969 film *Trouble with Girls*.

Native Americans utilized the 18-mile (29-km) glacial-carved Chautauqua Lake for 10,000 years as a strategic portage between Lake Erie and the river systems that feed into the Ohio and Mississippi River valleys. Indian mounds and campsites once scattered around the lake. It didn't take long before the new European settlers discovered the beauty of Chautauqua Lake. Pastor John Vincent and

inventor Lewis Miller started the Chautauqua Institution in 1874 with tents on the lakeshore under a cathedral-like canopy of stately trees. U.S. President Grant arrived the following year and the first Victorian home was constructed for his visit. After the regal Athenaeum Hotel was

▲ The grand Athenaeum Hotel is the Victorian centerpiece of the Chautauqua Institution.

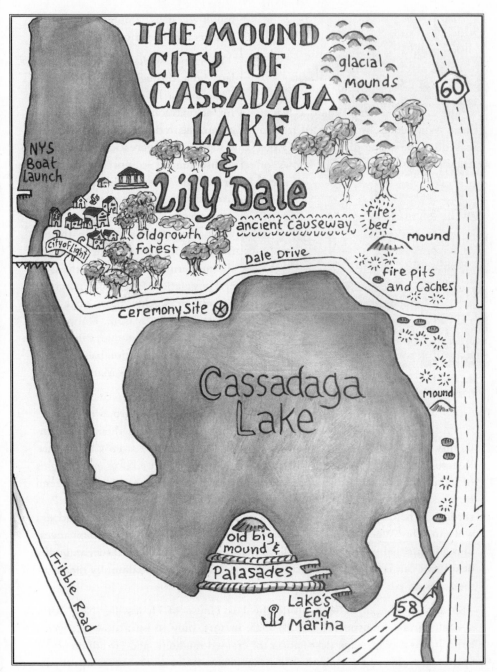

constructed in 1881, the Chautauqua Institution experienced a building boom of Victorian-era structures. Different Christian denominations added their own homes to the village, and private homes continue to dominate the nearly 800 acres (320 ha) of Institution grounds. Within a few decades the village spread across the lakefront and up the hill for several city blocks, sprinkled with civic

▲ The Lily Dale Museum is a treasure-trove of history from the colorful past of summer assemblies.

buildings, halls, amphitheaters, and centers for the various arts.

For nine weeks each year, from late June through late August, the Chautauqua Institution comes alive for an extraordinary blend of programming in the arts, education, philosophy, and recreation. Car travel is discouraged so most visitors walk or bicycle around the pedestrian-friendly village on their way to catch a concert or listen to a lecture. Each week centers on a separate theme, ranging from global warming to how the modern media impacts the general population. Guests can purchase a daily or weekly pass, or a pass for the whole season. During the two months of summer events the Chautauqua Institution has the same population density as Manhattan.

In the Chautauqua spirit of "summer assembly," another group of inspired free thinkers began their own community called Lily Dale in 1879, only 15 miles (24 km) away from Chautauqua. Where Chautauqua attracts U.S. presidents, Supreme Court justices and captains of industry, Lily Dale hosts those who wish to meet with a medium, or attend lectures on the subject of UFOs, chakras, or alternative healing methods. Pass through "The City of Light" front gate on the shore of Cassadaga Lake and you will enter the "World's Largest Center of Spiritualism." Lily Dale Assembly members are Spiritualists, those who believe that spirits of the deceased survive bodily death and can communicate with the living, usually via a medium by means of messages, or paranormal physical effects.

Spiritualism began in 1848 inside the Fox House of Hydesville, New York, a small cottage transported to Lily Dale in 1915, only to burn down 40 years later. It was a pilgrimage destination for trained mediums and lay adherents of Spiritualism alike. And while the old steam engine trains no longer transport passengers to Cassadaga, Lily Dale continues its summer program of special events. Visitors to Lily Dale are attracted primarily for the daily healing and message services, as well as to meet with a medium or attend the various workshops or lectures. A healing service at Lily Dale is basically an opportunity to meet with energy healers in a community setting. Participants sit in pews and await a turn to sit with a trained "healer" who surrounds them with energy using their hands. It should be noted that the healers do not actually touch the "sitter." A message service is very similar to a regular church service with hymns, prayers, and a sermon (or lecture) with the addition of a time for "messages." Prominent guests to Lily Dale included Arthur Conan Doyle, Susan B. Anthony, Harry Houdini, Mae West, Deepak Chopra, and Wayne Dyer.

> The summer assemblies of Chautauqua and Lily Dale were a product of 19th century Industrial Revolution rethinking by those who wished to develop a new meaning to life. Both locations have survived by changing with the times and keeping with the basic concept that learning lasts an entire lifetime.

What is most impressive of the two surviving summer assemblies of Chautauqua County is the sheer amount of events per season they both offer. The Chautauqua Institution offers approximately 2,000 unique events in a mere 65 days. It would be impossible to do even a fraction of all the events that are offered. Both summer assemblies hold the basic premise that their events be open to people of all faiths or belief systems. At Chautauqua the "four pillars" are art, recreation, religion, and education with each featuring a wide array of related activities to choose from during the season. Lily Dale is a smaller community and hosts a smaller summer assembly, but offers a well-balanced schedule of alternative speakers and varied events such as sweat lodges, astrology roundtables, yoga, reiki, astral travel, meditation, and other New Age coursework. For the past few years Buddhist monks of Tibet's Loseling Temple have come to Lily Dale to perform a Mandala Ceremony. The concept of learning in community and reading circles live on at both locations. Although still retaining a strong Christian foundation, the Chautauqua Institution is a community renowned for the performing arts and a resource for the discussion of important issues of our time. One 2007 lecture in the Hall of Philosophy was entitled "Are the Sacred Texts Sacred? The Atheist Challenge"—proving that Chautauqua remains a bastion of tolerance, truth, and the open discourse of challenging ideas.

## Getting to Chautauqua and Lily Dale

The nonprofit Chautauqua Institution and Lily Dale Assembly are both located in the southwestern corner of New York state. Chautauqua is easily located along Highway 394, 15 miles (24 km) north of Jamestown, which features a regional airport. Lily Dale is near the town of Cassadaga, just off Highway 60. Both communities are located about one hour south of Buffalo, NY; three hours north of Pittsburgh, PA; three hours east of Cleveland, OH; four hours south of Toronto, Canada; and eight hours west of New York City. Gate tickets are required at both locations for seasonal activities, but they are both free to enter during the off season. Also worth seeing is the unusual Panama Rocks scenic park, located about 10 miles (16 km) south of Chautauqua on Route 10. Chautauqua winter residents number only 400, as compared to the 150,000 attendees during peak season from late June to late August. Consider staying at the century-old Spencer Hotel any time of the year when planning a visit to the Chautauqua Institution.

# RHODE ISLAND

The smallest of all the United States, Rhode Island was originally settled in 1636, only 16 years after the first colony was established by the English Pilgrims at Plymouth, Massachusetts. The colony grew up as a haven for dissidents, such as the religious maverick Roger Williams who was a refugee from the Massachusetts Bay Colony, where, because he so passionately and publicly opposed the right of a civil government to dictate to the human conscience, the Puritans had him banished. They had tried to deport him to prevent his founding a new colony on such "dangerous" principles, but Williams escaped into the forests and founded Providence "especially for such as are troubled elsewhere about the worship of God." Other liberals followed in 1638, establishing Portsmouth on the island of Aquidneck and Newport the following year. After 1700, the population expanded rapidly along with a lucrative maritime trade that made Newport one of the wealthiest cities in America. Testaments of this great wealth are preserved in the many lavish mansions built in Newport as millionaires' summer homes.

## Newport Tower

Located in a small park above the harbor on Aquidneck Island is a weathered stone tower uniformly regarded as the oldest structure in Newport. The antiquity of the tower is where the unanimous opinions abruptly end. The original sign at the site described the monument as: "Old Stone Mill built probably about 1660 by Benedict Arnold first Governor of Rhode Island (Under the Charter of 1643) referred to in his will as 'My Stone Built Windmill.' Legends ascribe its erection to the Norsemen during their supposed visit about 1000 A.D." This dualistic description is indicative of the heated debate that rages on to this day about the true origin of who built the Newport Tower. Part of the mystery is that there is room for doubt on all claims of when and by whom and for what purpose it was built. Indeed, there are few other historic sites in North America that are the subject of such a fundamental level of disagreement. Isolationist historians, who seem to have a vested interest in keeping any pre-Columbian Europeans out of New England, routinely dismiss some basic evidence about the tower's elusive identity.

The Newport Historical Society does not recognize the structure as anything more than a colonial mill, yet the design would be impractical for a windmill, nor does anything like it exist anywhere else in New England. Windmills have a strong torquing force and a heavy stone mass on top of eight pillars is a poor engineering design, as compared to a round tower built of solid walls. Furthermore, the open area on the ground level would be impractical for working on windy days, which are regular at Newport. While excavations around the tower have not produced any conclusive Norse artifacts, they have not produced a single grain shard or any other organic matter that would have been mass-processed at a mill.

▲ The Newport Tower.
An old stone mill or America's oldest church?

Curious nooks add interest to the tower, including small alcoves built into the wall both above and below the channel which likely held relics and items of religious import. The design and orientation of the largest Newport altar is consistent with the practices of Catholic worship. However, there were no Catholics present among the early colonists of Newport during the 17th century. Directly behind the small window on the second floor is a fireplace, allowing a bright fire to warm the room and cast a light out to the harbor in two directions. A fireplace would be completely unfeasible in a mill because the fine powder produced is prone to explosion if exposed to fire. Besides being a year round observation tower and lighthouse, the structure may have acted as a safe house in times of conflict, or had been used as a religious building just as identical structures were utilized in medieval Scandinavia. The Newport Tower may have been the farthest western outpost of Catholicism in a land called Vinland. Substantiating this claim are inscriptions carved into the tower spelling "HNKRS," meaning stool or seat, as in a Bishop's seat. The runic inscriptions are very faint after centuries of weathering, yet can be located on the outer wall above the southwest pillar. Another runic inscription, 14 feet (4.2 m) above the ground, on the west side of the tower is translated as the date "1010." Further dispelling the Benedict Arnold stone mill theory are several early maps and documents denoting the tower and surrounding area under Norse influence. The Mercator map of 1569 clearly depicts the tower a full 67 years before the British settled in Rhode Island. The map accurately portrays several important rivers and the Appalachians as a continuous mountain range stretching along the Eastern Seaboard. The Mercator map shows Narragansett Bay as a region called "Norombega," which may have been a spelling for Norway in the 14th century. The tower is identifiable on Mercator's map, depicting a conical roof intact along with a now lost adjoining structure. Italian explorer Giovanni de Verrazano's map of 1542 denoted a settlement called "Norman Vilia" on the New England coast—the name "Norman" derives from Norsemen, or Northmen. Seven years before Newport was founded, a New York historical document refers to a "rownd stone towre" on the opposite shore from eastern Long Island.

> Newport Tower is the most hotly disputed
> structure in New England. Some believe it's a
> poorly designed English windmill, others the
> Bishop's seat for an early Catholic settlement.
> The latter theory would make it the oldest
> Christian building in North America.

The circular tower was originally three stories tall, but the top portions are now partially blown off. The solid upper stories are supported by eight stone pillars with neatly executed arches between each pillar. There are four windows and

"THE OLD STONE MILL"
NEWPORT, RHODE ISLAND
POPULARLY SUPPOSED TO BE A VIKING TOWER,
BUT POSSIBLY THE "STONE-BUILT WINDMILL"
OF GOVERNOR BENEDICT ARNOLD, ca1677.

▲ A view of the tower as it would have appeared before development in Newport.

a fireplace on the second level. Above it, log hole depressions indicate a third floor. Unlike other colonial structures that were built exclusively using the English foot, the tower is apparently built using the Rhineland foot (12.35 modern inches), a unit of measurement contemporaneous with 12th century Scandinavian measurements. Another suspected unit of measurement could have been based using an ancient Scottish unit of measurement known as an ell which is equivalent to three Norse feet. Several identical towers remain in Norway, Sweden, the Orkney Islands and the German Low Countries, and if the Newport Tower had been located in northern Europe no one would question its medieval antiquity. Noted similar structures include the Church of the Holy Sepulcher in Cambridge, England and the Church of Saint Olaf in Tunsberg, Norway. The Newport Tower is located on a ridge crest with strategically placed sighting windows facing four different directions. The largest window faces south, looking beyond the headlands to the Atlantic Ocean 11 miles (18 km) away, and another faces the entrance to Newport Harbor. The vantage would allow detection of incoming ships into Narragansett Bay. It is advantageously located on the highest hill in Newport, making the design and placement of this structure ideal for maritime navigational purposes.

There is an ancient document from 1121 that tells of a Bishop from Greenland named Eric Gnupsson arriving in Vinland hoping to Christianize the inhabitants. Some cultural diffusionists attribute the building date of Newport Tower to him, and this is about the time when other round towers in

▲ This internal view of the Newport Tower shows the second level fireplace, several viewing windows, and postholes for the second and third floor.

northern Europe were being constructed. Another popular diffusionist theory is that Henry Sinclair, a wealthy earl of Scotland's Orkney Islands, built the Newport Tower in 1398. Sinclair sailed with a Venetian admiral named Zeno who documented their trip in the *Zeno Narrative*. The manuscript describes the journey to Nova Scotia (New Scotland) and then to Narragansett Bay. The Sinclair family had Norse connections through marriage, and thus knew of previous Viking trips across the Atlantic. Henry Sinclair never claimed to be the discoverer of America because he knew his Viking forebears had been there before him. Far across the ocean in Scotland is the famous Rosslyn Chapel built by the Sinclair family, who were part of the powerful Freemason fraternity. In the chapel are images of native North America maize (corn) and the aloe cacti, which were carved in stone before Christopher Columbus was born. Some have compared the Newport Tower to Scottish or Templar architecture of the 14th century. As noted, one Scottish ell equals three Norse feet, which corresponds precisely to the unit of measurement used. Regardless if the Vikings or the Scottish built it, Aquidneck Island where the tower is perched would have made an excellent location for a sanctuary, allowing the water channel to provide protection from Indian raids. When the Narragansett Indians were asked who built the Newport Tower, they replied: "They were fire-haired men with green eyes who sailed up river in a ship like a gull with a broken wing."

## Getting to Newport Tower

The "Old Stone Mill" is located above Newport Harbor in Touro Park on Bellevue Avenue, between Mill and Pelam Streets. Founded in 1639, Newport was partially destroyed by the British during the Revolutionary War because it was one of the leading colonial cities, yet the tower remained. In 1790, George Washington proclaimed America's commitment to religious freedom at the nearby Touro Synagogue, North America's oldest synagogue, built in 1763. Today Newport is a fashionable summer resort and historic seaport city. Newport is Rhode Island's second largest city and is easily reached by public transportation on Route 138 or Route 114 into the historic city. Touro Park is centrally located in the old section of town, a few blocks above the yacht harbor on Aquidneck Island.

# THE SOUTH

*And in these ancient lands; Enchased and lettered as a tomb*
*And scorned with prints of perished hands; and chronicled with*
*dates of doom ... I trace the lives such scenes enshrine; and*
*their experience count as mine.* **-Thomas Hardy**

THE FIRST DEFINITE PALEO-INDIANS ENTERED THE SOUTHERN region of what is now the United States during the last Ice Age when massive glaciers gripped the upper half of North America. Although Clovis, Preclovis, and Pleistocene era artifacts dating back 50,000 years old have been found at the Topper Site in South Carolina, these findings are not universally agreed upon in archaeological circles. The discovery in 2007 of a Clovis spear point tip at a dig site in Alexandria, Virginia dated to be at least 13,000 years old establishes the first known migration. Clovis points are recognized by their distinctive shape and serve as one of the diagnostic markers for an era known to archaeologists as the Paleo-Indian period that lasted from as early as 18,000 to about 12,000 years ago. The Archaic Period started around 10,000 years ago when environmental change allowed a larger hunting range and social interactions became more complex. Sometime during the transition into the early Woodland period came the appearance of artificial mounds, first as small burials, later as complex geometric earthworks.

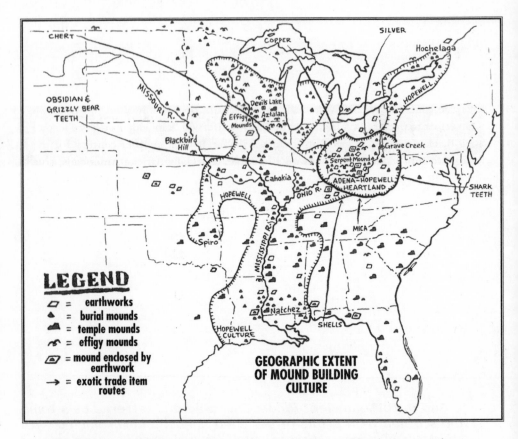

LEGEND

- 🗆 = earthworks
- ▲ = burial mounds
- ⛰ = temple mounds
- 🐚 = effigy mounds
- 🗆 = mound enclosed by earthwork
- → = exotic trade item routes

GEOGRAPHIC EXTENT
OF MOUND BUILDING
CULTURE

The earliest phase of earthen mound construction in North America began around 5,400 years ago at a mound site called Watson Brake in northern Louisiana, almost certainly influenced by the high civilizations of Central America. Not far away the Olmec-influenced Poverty Point was the next phase of mound building, but on a much larger scale. Carbon dating revealed that the people who developed what has become known as the Poverty Point Culture lived there by 2500 BCE. They constructed a massive bird effigy mound, hundreds of circular houses on raised horseshoe-shaped embankments, and used wooden poles to determine astronomical alignments. Several avenues leading into the site were used for observations of the rising and setting sun on the equinoxes. Other alignments to solar, lunar, and stellar alignments are suspected at the site. Similar to the Great Pyramids in Egypt, Poverty Point emerged as a highly sophisticated civilization very early on and likely influenced other mound builder traditions in North America.

Mound complexes continued to be built in the South sporadically for thousands of years, until gold-seeking Spaniards in the 14th century inadvertently unleashed deadly diseases upon a native population with no natural immunities. The mound building tradition was all but lost by 1720 CE when the French began setting up garrisons and trading posts along the Mississippi River. Hostilities with the

French and other colonists were inevitable and the end result was most Native Americans being either killed off, dying of new diseases, or being relocated to reservations. After the French and Spanish ceded their territories to the newly established United States, the South went through a period of rapid economic expansion largely as a result of the millions of African slaves imported to work the fertile land. In the Civil War, the southern states broke away from the Union in an effort to preserve their entrenched way of life, which included slavery. Despite all black slaves being freed after the Civil War, it took another century for the Civil Rights Movement to ensure all people, especially African Americans, true equality in the United States.

## Temple Mounds of the South

Along the many tributaries of the Mississippi River are the remnants of a once grand Indian culture that constructed large platform and conical-shaped mounds. The culture has been termed "Mississippian" because of the many mound cities that were located near the extensive waterway. The original name of what these people might have called themselves has been lost to history. The temple mounds of the Mississippian Culture were directly influenced by the advanced societies of pre-contact Mexico. Artifacts recovered at Poverty Point closely resemble artifacts found at early Olmec sites. The layout of Poverty Point appears to be based upon the Olmec cities of La Venta and Corral in the Tabasco and Vera Cruz regions of southern Mexico, both of which were occupied during the same time-frame. Maize, beans, chili and squash were grown in abundance and elaborate ceremonies, several of which were associated with death and human sacrifice, were held every year. These characteristics clearly suggest a Central American influence, possibly under the stimulus of exotic traders who introduced ideas, customs, religious beliefs, as well as plants and animals from prehistoric Mexico.

Early settlers were surprised to come across the large mounds with flat tops as they began to explore southern Indian lands. Some complexes were used for ceremonial purposes, others as burial grounds, and still others were designed as fortresses. The author of the Constitution and the third president of the United States, Thomas Jefferson, took a keen interest in native sites. Jefferson was among the first to seriously document Indian mound building, and wrote the following passage in 1782 in his book *Notes on the State of Virginia:* "Appearances certainly indicate that (the mound) has derived both origin and growth from the accustomary collection of bones, and the deposition of them together; that the first collection had been deposited on the common surface of the earth, a few stones put over it, and then a covering of earth, that the second had been laid on this, had covered more or less of it in proportion to the number of bones, and then also covered with earth; and so on." Jefferson's documentation of prehistoric mounds earned him the title "Father of American Archaeology."

▲ A conical mound with moat in Greenup County, Kentucky, and several
Mississippi Valley burial mounds.
Lithographs circa 1847.

Temple mounds of the South had sometimes
been used successively by overlapping cultures
at different times. Some sites have a history of
continuous usage for over 2,000 years.

The southeastern United States was, and still is, punctuated with clusters of
mounds, some small, others enormous, but all manmade and once used for burial or
ceremonial purposes. Originally numbering in the thousands, the many mounds of
the South have been reduced to a few hundred largely due to desecration of treasure seekers and urban expansion. While most mounds are protected as national,
state or county parks, some are on private land and may not be accessible to the
general public. Others have been completely obliterated, but early maps and records
allow a glimpse into their design and layout. Most Mississippian earthworks were
orientated to the east. Over half of all temple mounds reveal alignments with the
brightest summer stars, along with lunar alignments. Not only do the Mississippian
mound sites resemble Central American city layouts, but some arrangements are
very similar to Stonehenge and other Neolithic sites in Europe.

### Getting to important Temple Mounds of the South

The following are some of the most notable southern archaeological and ceremonial mound sites listed state by state. In **Alabama,** there are six extant temple
mounds in Baldwin County called the Bottle Creek Indian Mounds. Florence
Indian Mound in the Tennessee Valley is one of the largest mounds in the South.
Near Fort Toulouse are two forts and a single platform mound called Jackson
Park. Mound State Monument near Moundville, about 13 miles (20 km) south
of Tuscaloosa, was a private tourist attraction vulnerable to exploitation until
local conservationists succeeded in restoring it to its natural state. Mound State
Monument contains 20 truncated earthen pyramids roughly arranged in a huge
circle. Complex rituals were held at Mound State Monument and the site was
known as the center of "The Southern Death Cult."

**Arkansas** is home to a 1,000-year continuously used ceremonial village, erroneously called Toltec Mounds, and is located southeast of Little Rock. Stellar, lunar
and solar alignments have been recorded at the 18 mounds that encompass Toltec,
most notably the southern setting point of the moon. Parkin was a mound site
known to have been visited by De Soto in 1541.

In **Florida**, Bickel Ceremonial Mound near Bradenton is one of the oldest sites in the state dating from 500 BCE. Big Mound City in Indiantown was once a vast 23 mound ceremonial complex. Crystal River Indian Mounds in Citrus County was perhaps the most significant site in Florida with 1,600 years of continual usage. Lake Jackson Mounds and Lake Lafayette Mound are both located near Tallahassee. Mound Key in Fort Meyers and Safety Harbor Mound in Old Tampa Bay were both positioned near prehistoric ports. Temple Mound Museum at Fort Walton Beach is a fully restored mound and temple site which spanned a succession of cultures over a period of 1,700 years. The Tequesta tribe thrived for 2,500 years before succumbing in the 1700s to European germs, but not before creating the 38-foot (11.4-m) wide stone Miami Circle in what is now downtown Miami.

**Georgia** was once home to the former political and religious mound builder center called Etowah Mounds in Bartow County, three miles (5 km) from Cartersville. Etowah is a classic example of a stockaded Mississippian town centered around three large, flat-topped mounds. A 24-foot (8-m) wide moat surrounded the tall wooden walls of the Etowah stockade. The Kolomoki Mounds State Park in Early County near Blakely was put to use by both Mississippian and Late Woodland cultures. Nacoochee Mound in White County is uniquely elliptical in shape. Ocmulgee National Monument in Macon County is a reconstructed ceremonial lodge. The massive Rock Eagle Mound in Putnam County is made entirely of milky quartz boulders. Several other eagle effigy mounds made from milky quartz once existed in Georgia.

▲ The Kolomoki Mounds, and the Etowah Mounds. Both groups are in Georgia.
(Photos courtesy Georgia State Parks)

In **Kentucky,** the Ancient Buried City (King Mounds) in Wickliffe was once a huge community of temples and burial mounds. Three rectangular altars were found in chambers inside the mounds. The Portsmouth Earthworks included long, embanked walkways connecting three different ritual complexes in two states. The first complex was a triple ringed compound with a large conical mound in the center, avenues led away from and crossed the Ohio River to several geometric mounds dominated by a pair of U-shaped embankments on the Ohio side, then crossed back to Kentucky to a square enclosure from which two nearly identical elongated rectangular enclosures extended in opposite directions. It is

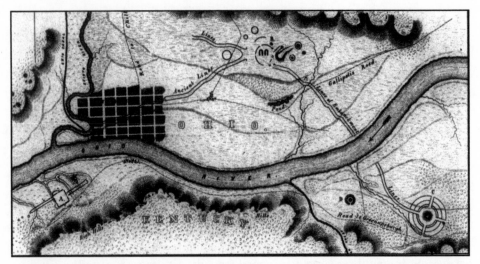

▲ Spanning both sides of the Ohio River, the Portsmouth Earthworks extended for several miles between Ohio and Kentucky. The square and circular earthworks in Kentucky are lost, but a few features remain in Ohio. The purpose of this elaborate complex is described by archaeologists as "ritualistic." From Squier & Davis (1848) "Ancient Monuments of the Mississippi Valley."

likely that Hopewell seasonal processions, similar to Avebury in England, took place at Portsmouth. Unfortunately very little has survived, except for a few components in the Mound Park of Portsmouth, Ohio.

**Louisiana** has several temple and burial mounds in Marksville Prehistoric Indian Park State Monument, which is a southern variant of the Ohio Hopewell. Marksville featured seven conical burial mounds flanked around a central plaza featuring three dominant temple mounds. Watson Brake near Monroe, Louisiana is gigantic, oval embankment containing 11 mounds, but none were used for burials. It has been dated as the first genuine mound builder site. Only 60 miles (100 km) away near Epps, Louisiana is Poverty Point, the only ancient American site recognized by academics to hold the distinction of being directly linked with the Olmec in Mexico. Artifacts found at Poverty Point prove that the people traveled and traded widely. Semi-octagonal earthen embankments focused on a huge bird effigy mound.

The state of **Mississippi** has the largest concentration of mound sites in the South. A series of impressive mound sites that stretch along the Mississippi River include Holly Bluff Site, Pocahontas Mound B, Rolling Fork Mounds, and Winterville Mounds Historic Site. The Emerald Mound, Magnum Mound, Boyd Mounds, Bynum Mounds, Pharr Mounds, and the 8,000 BCE Bear Creek Mound village (at milepost 308.8)—all can be found along the Natchez Trace Parkway. The Choctaw believed that their ancestors emerged from the Nanih Waiya mound in the remote past at a time when the earth was covered with water. The

Choctaw traditional name for ancient mounds is *Nanne-yah*, literally the "hills of God" or "mounts of God" (also see: Natchez, MS).

**North Carolina** has the famous Nikwasi Mounds built by Late Mississippian mound builders, and was used at a later time by the Cherokee who infused the site with many mythological tales. The Town Creek Indian Mounds near Mount Gilead is a State Historic Site. Town Creek has a partly reconstructed stockade and sanctuary to illustrate how the complex was a fortress surrounding a temple mound and plaza.

In **South Carolina**, the overlapping culture on Blair Mound near Winnsboro spanned several centuries. The Fort Watson Mound in Clarendon County was so strategically situated that the British used it as a base during the Revolutionary War. Indian Hill on St. Helena Island is a truncated cone-shaped mound used as a platform for a large temple. Scotts Creek Temple Mound is a traditional platform mound located in the southern Appalachians. The Topper Site in Allendale County has produced the astonishing radiocarbon date of 50,000 years old as the earliest habitation in North America. Still awaiting full confirmation, the Topper Site along the Savannah River has produced artifacts from the Clovis, Preclovis, and the Pleistocene era, which occurs before the last Ice Age.

In **Tennessee** there are four large and several smaller mounds surrounding a large plaza called Duck River Temple Mounds near Hurricane Mills. A central mound flanked by 13 smaller mounds is called Mound Bottom near Kingston Springs. The earliest site in the state is called Obion Mounds near Paris and is also situated around a central plaza. There is a cluster of 30 mounds at the Civil War site Shiloh National Military Park near Pittsburgh Landing. The Chucalissa and the De Soto Mounds in Memphis were most certainly visited by the famous Spaniard during his ill-fated expedition of 1541. The Pinson site, 10 miles (16 km) south of Jackson, is modeled upon the same grid system found at Teotihuacán near Mexico City. Pinson was the largest ceremonial mound site in all of ancient America, containing at least 12 mounds including four truncated platform pyramids, and also features an earthen effigy mound depicting an eagle. Various alignments to solar and stellar events can be determined by the arrangement of mounds at the Pinson site.

**West Virginia** once supported a high a density of mounds and earthworks along a 10-mile (16-km) stretch of the Kanawha Valley from Charleston to Saint Albans. One of these mounds, the Shawnee Reservation Mound in Institute, once contained two skeletons of very tall people found in a sitting position facing each other. Two copper bracelets were on the left wrist of one skeleton, a hematite celt and lancehead with the other. Hyer Mound near the town of Huttonsville contained 20 bodies, some possibly executed in a death rite ritual. Pipes, vessels, copper beads, and a large cache of flint were included as Hyer burial items (also see: Grave Creek, WV).

# ALABAMA

Early settlers dubbed this region of the Deep South (later to become known as Alabama), as the "Black Belt" because of its distinctively dark and nutrient-rich soil. The rapid growth of this new agricultural and commercial center in the 16th and 17th centuries came with a heavy price—slavery. The southern part of the United States grew to become an economic powerhouse, mostly by the labor of millions of black men and women transported from Africa against their will. Even though Abraham Lincoln issued the Emancipation Proclamation freeing the slaves in 1863, the problem of getting true equality for all races, especially African Americans, continued to exist in Alabama and other southern states more than a century later.

## Selma

The small riverside city of Selma played a vital role in creating the history of racial equality in the United States. From the Voting Rights Movement which started here, to a bitter confrontation with law enforcement officers, Selma has come to represent the heart of the African American struggle in the nation. In the 1960s, Selma became the focal point for equal voting rights which was dramatized in the Selma to Montgomery march. Enduring angry demonstrations, mass arrests and even the violence of the Bloody Sunday March, the pacifists held firm in their conviction that nonviolent action was the only moral course.

Selma was a major Civil Rights flashpoint in 1965 when a passive protest for voting rights was brutally repressed by authorities and thus received worldwide media attention.

▲ Edmund Pettus Bridge, Selma. The Bloody Sunday March in 1965 was a turning point for the Civil Rights Movement.

As the Civil Rights Movement gained momentum in the United States, African American leaders requested that Dr. Martin Luther King Jr. lead the campaign for equal voting rights. In early 1965, demonstrators led by Dr. King and others left Brown Chapel and marched to the Dallas County Courthouse in an effort to register to vote. An ongoing confrontation developed between the marchers and sheriff's deputies under the command of Sheriff Jim Clark. This struggle climaxed in a show of force by state troopers, deputies, and Clark's posse at the Edmund Pettus Bridge on Sunday, March 7th, 1965. The marchers were physically assaulted by the officers and driven back into the city. Subsequently, Selma became the focus of national media attention. On March 15th, President Lyndon B. Johnson compared the events to Revolutionary War Lexington and Concord: "At times, history and fate meet at a single time, in a single place to shape a turning point in man's unending search for freedom. So it was last week in Selma, Alabama." A short time after Johnson's speech, hundreds of new marchers came to Selma to join in solidarity. Due to national attention, federalized National Guardsmen kept a watchful eye as Dr. King and others were finally allowed peaceful passage to the capital Montgomery. The successful completion of the voting rights march ended the centuries-old intimidation of African Americans from exercising their rights.

Every spring, hundreds of African Americans and peace activists from around the world converge upon Selma to commemorate the heroics of the 1965 nonviolent demonstrators. Civil Rights leader Jessie Jackson and Democratic Senators and Congressmen often join the mass demonstration across the Edmund Pettus Bridge on the anniversary of the Bloody Sunday March. The city's history tells an important story of our nation: A story of a struggle for what is right and moral. Selma has come far since the early days of slavery, and with each day, moves closer to realizing Dr. King's dream of true racial equality. The year 2000 marked the election of Selma's first black mayor James Perkins Jr., defeating 9-term incumbent Joe Smitherman who was the newly elected mayor in 1964 during the voting rights era demonstrations.

### Getting to Selma

Selma is situated along the banks of the Alabama River in the south-central part of the state. The Edmund Pettus Bridge is located where Highway 80 crosses the river at the intersection of Broad Street and Water Avenue. Selma is also home to the National Voting Rights Museum and Institute; the Martin Luther King Jr. Street Historic Walking Tour; and several prominent churches that played key roles in the Civil Rights Movement. The Bridge Crossing Jubilee Festival is held on the first weekend of March every year. With signposts along the way, the Selma to Montgomery Voting Rights Trail is a 54-mile (87-km) route along Highway 80 that has been designated a National Historic Trail. The Civil Rights Movement was born in Montgomery in 1955, when a woman named Rosa Parks refused to give up her public bus seat for boarding whites, thus spurning the Montgomery Bus Boycott and the start of the struggle for racial equality.

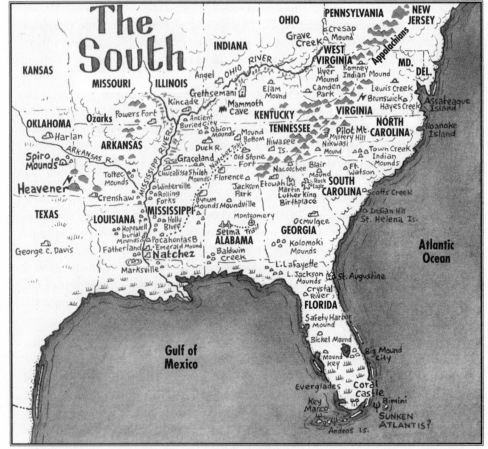

# FLORIDA

According to legend, Florida was discovered by the Spanish explorer Ponce de Léon on his quest to find the mythical fountain of youth. History will never know if Ponce de Léon actually found the fountain, but what is known is that the eminent explorer organized an expedition from Puerto Rico in 1513 CE to a land he named *Pascua Florida*. While the Ponce de Léon expedition was exploring the Florida coast it discovered the Gulf Stream and several islands in the Bahamas, and was the first to chart the Yucatán Peninsula. The northeastern Florida city St. Augustine was one of the landing sites for Ponce de Léon in 1513, and in 1565 it became occupied continuously, making it North America's oldest permanent city.

## Bimini and Atlantis

Whether fact or fiction, southeastern Florida has been the focus of mysterious phenomenon since Ponce de Léon dropped anchor. One southern gentleman with an amazing ability to recall events in the very distant past spoke of a high civilization that was destroyed when earth changes toppled it into the sea. In 1932, the "Sleeping Prophet" Edgar Cayce spoke these words in one of his trances: "The position ... the continent of Atlantis occupied is between the Gulf of Mexico on the one hand and the Mediterranean upon the other. Evidence of this lost civilization can be found in the Pyrenees and Morocco, British Honduras (Belize), Yucatán and America. There are some protruding portions ... that must have at one time or another been a portion of this great continent. The British West Indies, or the Bahamas, are a portion of same that may be seen at present. If the geological survey would be made in some of these especially, or notably in Bimini and in the Gulf Stream through this vicinity, these may be even yet determined" (reference 364-3).

▲ The "Sleeping Prophet" Edgar Cayce.

Narratives of a sunken continent called Atlantis, whispers of a Fountain of Youth and mysterious manifestations have all been attributed to Bimini and the Florida coast since it was first charted by Spanish explorers.

No supporting evidence for Cayce's Atlantis came until 1968, when crude steps were found leading down under the ocean at the island of Bimini in the Bahamas. Other elaborate underwater ruins were soon discovered off the tiny island near the Florida coast. In the same year, a series of closely arranged underwater stone blocks called "Bimini Road" or "Bimini Wall" were located in 30 feet (9 m) of water, along with sections of fluted pillars. The stretches of this collapsed "wall" are composed of square blocks measuring as large as 20 feet (6 m) by 10 feet (3 m) and weighing approximately 25 tons (25,400 kg) each. The "road" stretches around North Bimini in the shape of the letter "J," and the pillars form a circular portico seaward from the site. Some of the 44 marble pillars are still standing in their original positions, while others were found lying in a jumble on the sea floor. Both the wall and pillars reveal a high degree of engineering skill in their manufacture. Other profound underwater discoveries continue to "arise" near Bimini, pointing the way to Atlantis. Off the shore of East Bimini divers have uncovered a half-mile (.8 km) long "dyke," extending a quarter-mile (.4 km) in length. Also found at East Bimini are rectangle shapes carved into the sea floor, straight and

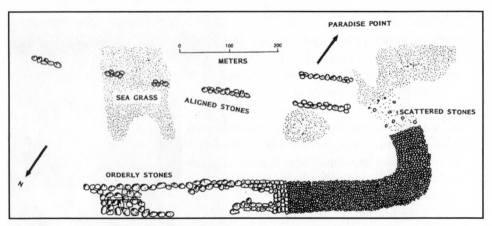

▲ Underwater map of the square blocks that comprise the Bimini Road.

intersecting lines, in addition to a huge circular stone construction that appears (when it existed above sea level) to be a water reservoir. Also uncovered near Bimini were a stylized marble animal head artifact, a dressed stone slab with a "tongue and groove" pattern on the sides, the "keystone" artifact (divisible by 10 cm at every measurement), and a stone clearly protruded with drill holes.

Further evidence for Atlantis predicted by Cayce are recent seismographic surveys carried out across the Atlantic Basin. Several of these independent studies have revealed many "deviations" and unexplained "contours" to be found at the bottom of the Atlantic and Caribbean. The most exciting discovery is the recent "underwater city" found on a large plateau in 2,200 feet (660 m) of water off the southwest coast of Cuba. *Reuters* ran an article in May 2001, reporting on treasure seekers using a side-scan sonar who described "clear manmade architectural designs" that (when seen from above) "resemble pyramids, roads and buildings." About 75 miles (120 km) from Bimini at Cay Sal there is an underwater cave that appears to be an ancient quarry with cut rectangular stones. All these discoveries match no known culture. Yet the finds do correspond with Cayce's prophecies that portions of Atlantis would be discovered in or near the island of Bimini. Cayce related in 1933, "As indicated, the records as to ways of constructing same are in three places in the Earth, as it stands today: in the sunken portion of Atlantis, or Poseidia, where a portion of the temples may yet be discovered under the slime of ages of seawater—near what is known as Bimini, off the coast of Florida" (reference 440-5).

It is very unlikely that any Mesoamerican or North American Indian culture could have constructed the underwater features near Bimini. This region of the world contains no other megalithic ruins, except additional submerged sites such as the triple concentric circle of stones at Andros Island near Pine Key, Florida, and numerous other ruins along the Great Bahama Bank. Still more sunken ruins can be found off the coasts of Anguilla, Hispaniola, Venezuela, Mexico and Belize. One logical conclusion is that a highly advanced culture sank under the ocean during the last polar shift when the continents started to drift. Jacques Coustéau confirms this finding with his research conducted inside submerged Caribbean caves. In certain underwater caves there are found stalactites and other calcium carbonate structures that could only have been formed above water. Furthermore, the Coustéau team noted that the stalactites in the "Blue Hole" off Belize had a tilt incline of 15 degrees, suggesting some type of major geological movement.

Further suggestions of Atlantis can be found within the infamous Bermuda Triangle. The confines of the triangle run from Melbourne, Florida, to the island of Bermuda, to the island of Puerto Rico, while encapsulating most of the Bahamas, including Bimini. Strange manifestations, UFO sightings and time warps are just a few of the unexplained phenomenon said to take place within the Bermuda Triangle. One theory suggests that

▲ It is unlikely that nature created the uniform and right-angled blocks of the Bimini Roads that appear to be fitted together.

damaged 12,000-year-old Atlantean "fire-stone" crystals on the sea floor have been left generating power out of control, thus having an effect on some of the airplanes and ships passing through the region. Whatever phenomenon the Bermuda Triangle may represent, these finds only enhance the legacy of Atlantis and may someday vindicate Edgar Cayce's prophecy about a portion of the fabled sunken continent being located off the shores of Bimini.

### Getting to Bimini

The Bimini group of islands in the Straits of Florida is a mere 50 miles (80 km) off the coast of Florida, yet there is something remotely detached about the islands. The small islands seem completely removed from North America. Perhaps this has something to do with Biminians relatively low population, only 1,600, compared to the over 2 million people living in Miami, whose lights of industry on the nighttime horizon never seem to dim. Chartered boats, ferries and flights leave daily from most south Florida cities. A tour operator on the northern bank of Bimini takes snorkelers and divers out to view the famous "Bimini Road" underwater ruins, and to swim with dolphins often spotted at the site.

## Coral Castle

How the Coral Castle in south Florida was built single-handedly by a tiny Latvian man remains one of North America's biggest mysteries. The builder was Ed Leedskalnin who was only 5-foot-tall (1.5 m), and weighed a mere 100 pounds (45 kg). Ed was born in 1887, and at the age of 26 was engaged to marry a 16-year old Latvian girl named Agnes Scuffs. The day before the wedding young Agnes decided to cancel because she thought Ed was too old, or maybe she was in love with someone else. Heartbroken and alone, Ed left his beloved Latvia for the United States always thinking of Agnes as his "Sweet Sixteen." With only a 4th grade education, he drifted from job to job until he came down with tuberculosis and moved to Florida for its more favorable climate. During his travels he became interested in science, astronomy, and Egyptian history, spending most of his time reading books on magnetic currents and cosmic forces. Ed was a frugal man, collecting old mechanical pieces and saving money any way he could. Eventually he bought a 10-acre (4-ha) plot of land in Homestead, Florida and set about excavating, carving, and moving many tons of coral rock all by himself. His monument would be devoted to his lost love, his Sweet Sixteen.

> Using only simple tools, a slight immigrant from Latvia single-handedly moved over 1,100 tons (997,700 kg) of coral blocks and constructed an engineering marvel called the Coral Castle.

Ed's coral carvings are symbolic of everything that mattered to him: love, astronomy, nationalism, family and magnetism. He created huge block walls surrounding a courtyard of theme tables and other whimsical stone attractions. Many people witnessed Ed hauling his original sculptures from Florida City to Homestead, but no one ever saw how he loaded or unloaded the trailer. He refused to allow visitors while he worked and had a kind of sixth sense which alerted him when someone was coming to spy. Ed was a very private man who did much of his work entirely alone in the dark of night. For 28 years, with only crude winches, block tackles, and iron wedges, Ed labored tirelessly on his monument. He cut coral from a quarry in front of the castle and moved enormous stones by lantern light. The Obelisk stone weighs 28.5 tons (25,850 kg / 57,000 pounds) and is taller than the Great Upright stone at Stonehenge, positioned single-handedly into place by Ed. The Tower consists of 243 tons (220,400 kg) of coral rock with each block weighing four to nine tons (3,630-8,170 kg). The average weight of the individual stones at Coral Castle is greater than those used on the Great Pyramids in Egypt. Perhaps the most astonishing characteristic is the perfectly balanced Nine-Ton Gate that can be turned by the touch of a child. Although the gate is uneven in its dimensions, Ed was able to locate the precise center of balance so the heavy stone could easily swing on top of a recycled automotive gear.

Ed had a keen interest in astronomy and his sculptures were inspired in part by celestial objects and their movements. Always pointing to the North Star in Ursa Minor, the Polaris Telescope stands 25 feet (7.5 m) high and weighs 25 tons (22,675 kg). Polaris is a fixed star that is always visible at night through the opening in the telescope. It helped Ed plot the earth's path around the sun and enabled

362

him to design and construct a sundial that also indicated the solstice and equinox days. The sundial is so accurate that it is possible to determine Standard time within one or two minutes any time of the year. His celestial sculptures range from an 18-ton (16,330-kg) carving of Mars and another of Saturn, to enormous crescent moons, a Sun Couch, a Throne Room, and a Moon Fountain. Since Ed had a personal belief that there was life on Mars, he placed a Palmetto plant in the Mars sculpture as a symbol life.

▲ Ed Leedskalnin poses in front of one of his massive carved stones.

The extraction and lifting of such incredible amounts of coral stone—without the use of electricity or modern cranes and using only handmade tools—seems impossible for a single man who was known to be an eccentric loner. Baffled engineers have compared Ed's secret method of construction to the enigmatic megalithic buildings of prehistory. Many people asked the diminutive Latvian how he was able to excavate and position such heavy objects. He would only say that he understood the secrets of how the Great Pyramids were built. Was it possible that Ed was a reincarnated Egyptian architect who retained past life knowledge of secret levitation techniques? Some would argue there is no other explanation.

### Getting to the Coral Castle

Nestled between the Florida Keys and Miami, the privately owned Coral Castle is open for self-guided tours from 9 a.m. to 9 P.M. every day. Conveniently located at 28655 South Dixie Highway on the main drag in Homestead, the Coral Castle is centrally located only "a stones throw away from Exit 5 South," according to the tourist brochure. Just outside of Homestead are the fantastic natural preserves of Everglades National Park and John Pennekamp Coral Reef State Park.

# GEORGIA

The modern history of Georgia started in 1733 as the brainchild of English general and philanthropist James Oglethorpe as an opportunity for debtors to gain a fresh start. King George II granted the charter for the new colony, mostly so it would serve as a buffer between the British Carolinas and Spanish Florida. The colonial city Savannah reflects most of the state's history from its time as an English colony, to a booming slave plantation town, to Civil War flash point where General Sherman concluded his famous march to the sea. At war's end many of Georgia's proud plantations lay in ashes, and much of its great wealth lost. Besides bearing the shame of the African slave trade, Georgia is also tainted with one of the largest Indian forced relocations in history. Touched off by the Dahlonega gold rush in the 1820s and 1830s, the infamous "Trail of Tears" uprooted all the native Creek and Cherokee people as encroaching settlers usurped their homeland.

## Martin Luther King, Jr. Birthplace

The most influential African American leader of the 20th century, Martin Luther King, Jr. was born on January 15th, 1929, a date now recognized as a national holiday in the United States. The future clergyman and Civil Rights leader was raised in a neighborhood called Sweet Auburn in the heart of Atlanta's former ghetto. Growing up, young Martin was segregated from white children according to the customs of the South in the early and mid-20th century. Born into a family of Baptist ministers who pioneered in resisting racial discrimination, Martin Jr. gained national recognition at age 26 for his leadership of the 382-day Montgomery, Alabama bus boycott. He felt his nonviolent Gandhian tactics of civil disobedience were the only way to bring freedom to his people, despite death threats and segregationists' fire bombing his house. He consoled love and forgiveness: "All humanity is involved in a single process, and all men are brothers. To the degree that I harm my brother, no matter what he is doing to me, to that extent I am harming myself."

▲ Reverend Martin Luther King, Jr. advanced the Civil Rights Movement because of his firm conviction in promoting nonviolence.

In his utopian speech "I Have a Dream!" delivered on the steps of the Lincoln Memorial in August, 1963 King envisioned a racially just society where "little black boys and black girls will be able to join hands with little white boys and white girls and walk together as sisters and brothers." He reminded us that the Founding Fathers intended a land where all people were created equal, thus guaranteeing all Americans life, liberty and the pursuit of happiness. The speech went on to articulate for the country a vision of what America was not, but what it could and should become. "A place where a person would not be judged by the color of their skin, but of the content of their character." Yet King could not neglect citing the deep segregation dividing the nation, and commented that black people were like "a bad check that has come back marked 'insufficient funds.'" At the end of his prepared speech on that sweltering August day in Washington D.C., King began to preach as he had done so well and so often at the Ebenezer Baptist Church, improvising in the moment. He concluded with a message of hope and optimism: "Go back to Mississippi, go back to Alabama, go back to Georgia, go back to Louisiana, go back to the slums and ghettos of our northern cities, knowing that somehow this situation can be changed." The "I Have a Dream!" speech went on to be rated as the greatest political address of the 20th century based on its historical impact and rhetorical artistry.

> The birthplace of slain Civil Rights leader
> Martin Luther King, Jr. features an eternal
> flame of hope burning in front of his tomb.

At the pinnacle of his career, and after having received numerous death threats, King knew he had to persist in his work despite the dangers. On the early morning of April 4th, 1968 Reverend Martin Luther King, Jr. was shot and killed on a motel balcony in Memphis, Tennessee. The American clergyman, civil rights leader and Nobel Peace Prize Laureate (1964) was assassinated by a lone gunman named James Earl Ray who was intent on destroying King's dream of racial equality for all persons. The Irish rock band U2 wrote the song "In the Name of Love" memorializing King: "free at last, they took your life, they could not take your pride." Despite his urgent message of nonviolence and racial unity, riots erupted in cities across the nation in the evening and subsequent days following his assassination.

▲ Civil Rights leader Martin Luther King, Jr. delivers his famous "I Have a Dream" speech in 1963 to a huge crowd gathered around the Reflecting Pool in Washington D.C. The speech helped inspire most Americans to believe in equal rights for all.

The Martin Luther King, Jr. memorial near downtown Atlanta draws huge crowds in mid-January on the national holiday honoring King's birthday. The memorial is popular with international visitors who come from all points on the globe to honor America's most famous peacemaker. The National Historic Site is also a neighborhood gathering place, featuring monthly gospel concerts and lectures in the church where King occupied the pulpit. The National Park Service started restoring the Sweet Auburn neighborhood in the early 1980s, in an effort spearheaded by the King family. It includes his childhood Queen Anne-style wooden home, a memorial garden surrounding his grave, and the 1999 addition of the original Ebenezer Baptist Church—King's most famous speaking location. The Park Service also works with King's alma mater, nearby Morehouse College, to educate students on the Civil Rights Movement and train them in nonviolent conflict resolution.

### Getting to the Martin Luther King, Jr. Birthplace

The Martin Luther King, Jr. National Historic Site is located at 501 Auburn Avenue in the middle of the Sweet Auburn neighborhood. The National Historic Site includes the Queen Anne style house where King was born and raised, his gravesite, and the Ebenezer Baptist Church where King began his career as a preacher. The Sweet Auburn neighborhood is located near downtown Atlanta, in one of the oldest residential neighborhoods in the city. There is a year-round schedule of attractions and activities at the Historic Site. The national holiday commemorating Dr. King's birthday is celebrated in mid-January when crowds gather in large numbers at the various neighborhood locations.

# KENTUCKY

Originally an extension of Virginia known as Kentucky County, the first settlers led by Daniel Boone migrated over the Appalachians along the Wilderness Road. Isolated by the mountains and from the protection of the eastern colonies, the first settlers were vulnerable to Indian attacks until 1778, when George Rogers Clark launched a campaign to force the Indians from their land once and for all. In 1792, Kentucky became the 15th state in the United States. Its farmers thrived on the cultivation of hemp, tobacco, and grains used to manufacture whiskey and feed the soon-to-be-famous thoroughbred horses. Tourism is modern Kentucky's third largest revenue producer and its second largest private employer.

## Gethsemani

The origin of America's oldest Catholic monastery traces back to 1098 CE and the New Monastery of Citeaux, near Dijon in eastern France. A Middle Age reform in the monastic order led several monks to return to the rule of Saint Benedict in its ideal simplicity and silence. From these humble beginnings the Cistercian Order arose. Its expansion was rapid and far-reaching, including hundreds of monasteries being founded across Europe during the Middle Ages. The name "Trappist" comes from the Cistercian Abbey of La Trappe in Normandy, France where a significant reform took place in the 17th century. When the French Revolution suppressed all religious houses in 1790, the monks of La Trappe dispersed across Europe to as far away as Russia, and also to North America. After the revolution the monks returned to France in 1815 to repurchase and repopulate La Trappe. The Abbey of Mount Melleray in southern Ireland was another early foundation, and this community eventually established Gethsemani after overcrowded conditions and unrest in the land forced several of the younger monks to seek a new home. The Abbey of Melleray dispatched the 45 founders of Gethsemani via ship, steamboat and wagon to again establish a new Order of Trappists in the New World.

> Gethsemani Abbey is the oldest monastery in the United States still in continuous use, founded by French Trappist monks on December 21, 1848.

From the earliest days of Christianity, men and women ascetics have been drawn to the devotional and simple ways of monastery life. Saint Benedict of Nursia, father of Western monasticism, established the abbey of Monte Cassino in southern Italy around 530 CE, where he wrote the *Rule of Saint Benedict*. This manual outlines the regulation for community living, but is especially noted for its devotion to discipline, balance, prayer and service. The "Rule" has remained to the present day the living code for most of the monks in the Western Hemisphere. Based on the Benedictine tradition, the New Monastery of Citeaux was founded, and this tradition has passed on to Gethsemani. Saint Benedict's Rule makes clear: "when they live by the labor of their hands, then they are really monks." Gethsemani Abbey's principal source of income is the production of cheese, fudge and fruitcake sold on site and by mail order.

▲ Gethsemani Abbey
in rural Kentucky.
(Photo courtesy Gethsemani)

Just as Citeaux is the origin of the Cistercian Order, the Abbey of our Lady of Gethsemani is considered the "motherhouse" of the 13 monasteries of Trappist monks and five convents of Trappistine nuns in the United States. It is therefore more contemplative, laborious and stricter than all the others. Gethsemani is most famous for being the abbey where Thomas Merton lived and later became a hermit. His writings grace the abbey, including the monastic milieu, which offers a place apart "to entertain silence in the heart and listen for the voice of God—to pray for your own discovery." From Citeaux to Melleray to Gethsemani, the search for God and Christ under the rule of a single abbot continues its French tradition in the school of brotherly love, labor and silence.

### Getting to Gethsemani

The Abbey of our Lady of Gethsemani is located in the community of Trappist, just off Highway 247 in central Kentucky. Take Exit 21 on the Blue Grass Parkway near Bardstown and head south about 10 miles (16 km). All are welcome to visit the chapel, walk the grounds or stay for Mass. There is a guesthouse for men and women, but segregated by the week. Accommodations are by reservation only: (502) 549-3117.

## Mammoth Cave

The Mammoth Cave National Park is the longest known cave system in the world. Deep within the cave's vast subterranean world there are five overlapping and interlinked levels, with four rivers, eight waterfalls, one lake and one "Dead Sea." Mammoth Cave maintains the constant temperature of 54 degrees Fahrenheit (21° C) every day of the year. There are giant vertical shafts, from the towering 192-foot (58-m) high Mammoth Dome to the 105-foot (32-m) deep Bottomless Pit. The Green and Nolin Rivers course though the system creating new caverns, as well as the underground Echo River and the River Styx that flow through Mammoth Cave's deepest chambers. Some passages and rooms are decorated with sparkling white gypsum crystals, while others are filled with the colorful, sculpted shapes of stalactites, stalagmites, and other cave formations. And in the absolute blackness of the cave dwell many rare and unusual animals, including eyeless fish, ghostly white spiders, and blind beetles. The Kentucky Cave Shrimp is an endangered species that is only found in Mammoth Cave National Park.

> Mammoth Cave is the most elaborate and longest recorded cave system in the world with the oldest human artifacts dating back 4,000 years. The cave system has more than 336 miles (541 km) of explored and mapped passages.

Some of the first people to explore Mammoth Cave were the Adena mound builders and migrating Woodland Indians who first wandered into the cave around 4,000 years ago. It is not likely that they lived in the cave but only explored it and extracted various minerals useful for making their medicines or paints. At one location in the cave two Indian mummies were found, along with well-preserved prehistoric artifacts including woven sandals. By locating several other Indian artifacts in different parts of the cave, archaeologists can determine that the early explorers ventured almost a mile into the cave. It is believed that the early explorers were primarily in search of the mineral gypsum to make paint. In 1935, some early guides accidentally discovered a mummified body of an ancient gypsum miner. He was killed when a five-ton (4,535-kg) boulder landed on him as he was

▲ The author as a teenager on the "Wild Cave" tour of Mammoth Cave. (circa 1984)

chipping away minerals from the cave wall. The ancient miner's body, affectionately known as Lost John, was remarkably well-preserved because of the constantly cool temperatures and stable humidity of the cave.

Although explored by Indians as early as 2,000 BCE, the "Historic Entrance" to the cave was not re-discovered until a hunter stumbled upon it in 1790 while tracking down a bear. Rumors and stories proliferated for a decade about the massive cave until verified reports announced it to the rest of the world. During the War of 1812, slaves were put to work mining the cave for saltpeter, a main ingredient in gunpowder. It also served briefly as the site of an experimental tuberculosis hospital during the winter of 1842-43. A local landowner, Frank Gorin, acquired the cave in 1838. One of his black slaves, Stephen Bishop, became one of the first guides and made many important discoveries within Mammoth Cave. Stephen Bishop was one of the first people to draw an accurate map of Mammoth Cave and is credited for discovering the Echo River, Mammoth Dome, the Snowball Room, and the blind fish from Echo River. Mr. Gorin sold the cave to Dr. John Croghan who made further improvements upon Mammoth Cave as a tourist attraction. In 1908, Ed Bishop, a grandnephew of Stephen Bishop, made some more important discoveries within the cave. He discovered the Violet City, Kaemper Hall, Bishop's Pit, and with the help of a German visitor, Ed Bishop made an even more detailed and accurate map of Mammoth Cave. The complete history and most of the famous caverns are covered on the "Historic Cave Tour" given by National Park Service guides. As a testament to its importance, Mammoth Cave was authorized as a natural park in 1926, received National Park status on July 1, 1941, became a World Heritage Site on October 27, 1981, and was designated an International Biosphere Reserve on September 26, 1990.

### Getting to Mammoth Cave

Mammoth Cave National Park is located in the town of Mammoth Cave off Interstate 65 on Highway 259 in central Kentucky. There is an admission fee for the various cave tours and advance reservations, especially for the popular "Wild Cave Tour," are strongly recommended. It is very simple to book tours via the toll free 1-800-967-CAVE (2283) reservation line.

# MISSISSIPPI

Cutting its way clear through the state of Mississippi into Alabama and Tennessee is the prehistoric Natchez Trace, a name given by French traders, meaning "Natchez Indian Trail." The 440-mile (708-km) long pathway was opened by Archaic Indians over 8,000 years ago. The various mound building cultures of the South including the Woodland Indians continuously used the trail for thousands of years. Early Christian missionaries called it the "Devil's Backbone" because of the importance Native Americans put upon its use. European traders and trappers trampled down the rough road to settle the "Old Southwest." The state of Mississippi began to take a modern appearance largely due to the access provided by the Natchez Trace. From 1800-1820, the frontier brimmed with trade and new settlements, and the Natchez Trace became the busiest byway in the South. Today's modern Parkway closely follows the original trail with markers of important sites along the way.

## Natchez

The last documented earthen temple mound builders were the prehistoric Natchez of the lower Mississippi River Valley. The citizens of ancient Natchez, it was observed by the French, were "devout worshipers of the sun." Each of their seven villages had its own mound, but the group as a whole was focused on the larger Emerald Mound. The elaborate Emerald Mound was a truncated mound with terraced altars and temples on several levels below a dominant temple at the highest level. All the flat-topped mounds of Natchez contained individual thatched-roof buildings, upon which effigies of birds or other symbols were placed. Arts and crafts flourished immediately before the abrupt decline of the Mississippians. The Natchez practiced a religion based on the solar disc, similar

▲ Emerald Mound near Natchez was the central location of a large prehistoric city.
(Photo courtesy MS State Parks)

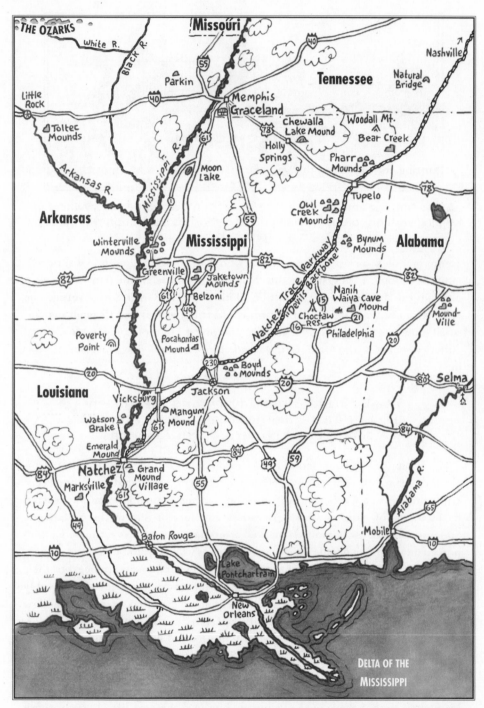

to the Toltec, Aztec, and Inca peoples of Central and South America. Their chief was known as the Great Sun, and his relatives were called Little Suns and stood in the noble rank above the commoners. "Honored men" were those within the

▲ The Natchez king known as the "Great Sun" was carried everywhere in keeping with his role as an omnipotent deity. This illustration was made by DuPratz in 1758.

commoner rank, a class open to anyone who distinguished himself in war or religious devotion. Membership in the "Sun" family was determined by inheritance through the female line, or a matrilineal kinship. The Great Sun governed the tribe with the help of his relatives who held tribal offices and through his personal knowledge of tribal politics. Like the priest-kings of comparable Central America societies, the Great Sun was worshipped as a divine possessor of solar energy.

### The Emerald Mound crowning the ancient city of Natchez is the second largest temple mound of its kind in North America.

Those people who belonged to the Mississippian Culture became expert farmers and organizers. Populations grew tremendously large around ceremonial centers, and between harvesting seasons huge earthen pyramids were constructed by hundreds of workers who moved vast amounts of dirt in thatch baskets. Sometimes 20 or more mounds marked a ceremonial site. It is estimated a phenomenal 57.3 million people lived in the Americas when Columbus arrived in 1492. The Mississippian people were known practitioners of human sacrifice, but their religious ceremonies surrounding it, if any, are unknown. Sacrifices were possibly made to conserve resources for the elite, eliminate captured enemies, or follow the grisly killing practices of their Toltec and Aztec contacts in Central America. Human sacrifice, as practiced by the Natchez mound builders, was quite different than that practiced by the Aztec or any other Mexican group. Upon death of a chief, those people who had served the chief in life were expected to continue to serve him in death. Members of the Great Sun's court were killed during his funeral so that they could accompany him into the next life. As such, those prehistoric Indians known to have performed human sacrifices are called the "Southern Death Cult," or the "Buzzard's Cult."

The first modern European explorer to march through the South was Hernando De Soto in 1539-1542, on his unsuccessful quest to find gold. The De Soto Expedition failed miserably in its efforts to duplicate the success of similar conquests in Mexico and Peru. On the long overland journey from the Florida Gulf Coast

▲ Hernando De Soto and his men meet the Natchez Indians in 1540.

to Georgia, north to what is today Memphis, Tennessee and then west to the Arkansas Ozarks, the De Soto Expedition came across some mound builder sites abandoned only recently. When the Expedition arrived at any inhabited Indian settlement, they demanded enormous quantities of food for hundreds of soldiers and slaves, for 200 horses, and their livestock. Surprisingly, he and his band of Spaniards came across Natchez while occupied and still under construction. They called it Quigualtum, which may include a string of provincial settlements extending north into the Yazoo River Basin. De Soto did view some of the densely populated mound cities lining the lower Mississippi, but since riches were not to be found, the conquistadors continued traveling in their circuitous trail of destruction. The weary party reached Quigualtum near the end of their disastrous three-year campaign. De Soto died in the spring of 1542, either in the vicinity of Natchez or near the mouth of the Arkansas River. Confronted by the sheer numbers of angry Indians determined to fight back, the remnants of De Soto's battered army left everything behind in a hasty retreat to Florida via homemade rafts. One of the last things the De Soto survivors noted of the Natchez Indians was their instant slaughter of the abandoned Spanish horses, butchering the animals for meat rather than keeping them as beasts of burden. It would be a long time before Europeans again reached the Mississippi Valley.

Most of the powerful mound building societies were still largely intact when Columbus reached the New World in 1492, and their hasty demise is directly attributed to the spread of foreign diseases that came with the earliest European explorers. The Mississippian mound cities were abandoned and all but forgotten by the Woodland Indians who moved into the region centuries later. By the time French explorers came down the Mississippi in 1673, almost all of the large Indian cities had vanished, largely due to continued Eurasian microbes spreading across the continent. Natchez, however, was still a functioning society when the French arrived. It is surmised that the majority of the Mississippian culture died off in devastating epidemics of smallpox, measles, tuberculosis, and the common cold. Thus the De Soto Expedition contributed less to the mound building societies' direct downfall than the earlier Spanish conquests of the Aztec and Inca empires, yet Eurasian germs, particularly smallpox, did the real destruction. In some cases, the deadly microbes spread up the southern Mississippi Valley in advance of the Spaniards themselves.

### Getting to Natchez

Modern Natchez is a small city on the Mississippi River, but the Natchez mound builders lived in villages along the Saint Catherine's Creek outside the modern city limits. The place the French called "The Grand Village of the Natchez Indians" is located in the town of Natchez at 400 Jefferson Davis Blvd., just off Highway 61. The Emerald Mound site is located 10 miles (16 km) north of Natchez off Highway 61. There are other Natchez-related sites near Tupelo.

# NORTH CAROLINA

Decades before English pilgrims established the Plymouth, Massachusetts colony in 1620, two unsuccessful British settlements faltered on the North Carolina coast in 1585 and 1587. The tiny outposts on Roanoke Island were short lived, and the second containing 116 men, women and children vanished completely within three years, becoming known as the Lost Colony. The first recorded English baby to be born on American soil, a girl named Virginia Dare, was delivered in North Carolina on August 18th, 1587. The state is also famous for the aviation pioneers, Orville and his brother Wilbur Wright, two bicycle makers who crafted the world's first powered airplane flight at Kitty Hawk in 1903.

## Pilot Mountain

In the eastern foothills of the Appalachian Range is a state park devoted to a rounded-top mountain and its sister pinnacle. The two prominent peaks soar above the surrounding landscape and were used by Native American scouts as a navigational marker. The nomadic Saura tribe passed through the region frequently and used the mountain as a landmark. Sacred to the Cherokee as a gathering place for initiating young tribal members, Pilot Mountain is home to a spirit guide they named Jomeoki who resides within this hallowed mountain. "Jo-me-okee" literally means "Great Guide," or "Pilot." The Cherokee came to Pilot Mountain for many centuries to commune with the spirit of the mountain (Jomeoki), seek a vision quest, and collect the rose quartz found abundantly in the surrounding region. Pilot Mountain is one of two known nesting places for the common raven (*CORVUS corax*) in North Carolina. Some New Age adherents claim that the large ravens frequently seen flying over the peak are very much alive with the spirit of Jomeoki and can communicate the language of the Cherokee.

Once used for Cherokee initiation rites, Pilot Mountain is perhaps best know today for rock climbing and the occasional incidence of UFO sightings above the peak.

When the first Europeans arrived in the New World, there were approximately 950 million acres (380 ha) of woodlands in what would become the lower 48 states. The Chattahoochee Forest, in which Pilot Mountain is included, was part of an immense, unbroken canopy stretching from southern Alabama to the northern reaches of Canada, and from the sandy shores of the Atlantic Ocean to the grasslands of the Missouri River. In 1751, the mountain and surrounding region was mapped by Joshua Frye and Peter Jefferson, the father of President Thomas Jefferson. Early settlers originally called the peak Mount Ararat or Stonehead Mountain, but in 1753, the Moravians translated the word "Pilot" from the spirit guide Jomeoki and the name has stuck ever since.

Pilot Mountain is located along the southeastern reaches of the rounded Appalachian Mountains—one of the oldest mountain ranges on earth. The Appalachians also hold the distinction of supporting one of the world's most extensive hardwood forests—an expansive relic of the richest, most diversified sweep of woodland ever to grace the temperate world—but that forest is in serious danger. The elms and chestnuts have already succumbed to foreign diseases, while the hemlock, dogwoods,

▲ Pilot Mountain soars above all other mountains in the area.
(Photo courtesy NC Tourism)

mountain ashes, red spruces, Fraser firs, and sugar maples have all indicated signs of stress. If global warming continues and global temperatures rise even a few degrees, the whole of the Appalachian wilderness below New England could become savanna.

Pilot Mountain can be seen from several counties on a clear day. The summit is 2,421 feet (726 m) above sea level capped by two pinnacles, one slightly larger than the other. The Big Pinnacle, with walls of bare rock and a rounded top covered by vegetation, rises 1,400 feet (420 m) above the valley floor and the sheer walls of the knob juts skyward some 200 feet (60 m) from its base. It is connected to Little Pinnacle by a narrow saddle. Rock climbing and rappelling are favorite activities at Pilot Mountain State Park. Visitors have easy access to Little Pinnacle via a park road and a series of maintained hiking trails. Pilot Mountain is probably best known as "Mount Pilot" from the *Andy Griffith Show*.

## Climbing Pilot Mountain

Climbing and rappelling are not permitted on Big Pinnacle. Climbers are required to register before starting, and must climb in designated areas only. Contact the park office for more information: (336) 325-2355. The State Park is only a few minutes drive from the town of Mount Airy, NC, and is located about 30 minutes north of Winston-Salem on Highway 52. Another section of the park extends along a scenic section of the Yadkin River and connects to the larger section of the park via a hiking and equestrian trail.

# The Cherokee Indians

The United States government passed the official "Indian Removal Act" in 1830, which called for the forced displacement of all remaining eastern native tribes. The noble Cherokee people were forced to leave their homeland even

though they had accommodated to the presence of white settlers who continued to press for more and more land. This disgraceful chapter of American history is know as the "Trail of Tears" where, under Army supervision, some 18,000 Cherokee were forced to walk to Oklahoma in the frigid winter of 1838-1839. Starving, sick and despondent, almost one in four died before reaching a land completely unfamiliar to the displaced people. In all, an estimated 4,000 died en route, including 300 who perished in a steamboat disaster. Before the march began, a few hundred brave Cherokee eluded their captors by disappearing into the Blue Ridge Mountains. Those who escaped formed the core of the Eastern band of Cherokee, which remains the largest Native American population of any state east of the Mississippi River. Today the Cherokee land is 50 miles (80 km) west of Asheville, has a population of around 9,000 on their 56,000-acre (22,400-ha) reservation. The Cheorkee reservation also hosts museums and casinos. The most famous Cherokee descendent is the singer / actress Cher, who had a hit single in the 1970s called "Half Breed."

# TENNESSEE

Regarded as a backcountry territory during the time of the 13 original British colonies, the region was claimed at different times by France, Spain, and England before being usurped by the British colony of North Carolina. In 1790 it became annexed as United States territory south of the Ohio River, and in 1796 Tennessee became the nation's 16th state. The name Tennessee is derived from the Cherokee name *Tanasi*, for the long dissecting river that runs through the middle of the state. Memphis is the state's largest city, whose growth was fueled by the area's prodigious slave-driven cotton plantations, and the crossroads for riverboats and railroads. The city's wealthy cotton brokers, bankers, and other tycoons built their grand mansions in the Victorian Village Historic District, now one of the largest tourist attractions in Memphis.

## Graceland

From abject poverty to superstardom, Elvis Aaron Presley lived the proverbial American Dream. Growing up in Tupelo, Mississippi the youthful Elvis was exposed to many musical styles that later became the crux of his creative force. His musical aspirations crossed the spectrum from blues, country, gospel, to the emerging sounds of rock and roll. When the teenager Elvis walked into the Memphis Recording Service (part of the now-legendary Sun Studio) in July, 1954 he was employed as a truck driver for an electric company. After his first recording session produced the songs "I Love You Because," "Blue Moon of Kentucky," and "That's All Right," little did he know that he was only days away from becoming famous. His early contributions to rock music earned him the title "The King of Rock and Roll." Within a decade "Elvis the Pelvis" became America's most beloved homegrown musician, and after his death, the nation's greatest tourist celebrity. His fame has only increased since his untimely death at the age of 42 on August 16th, 1977 inside the mansion he named Graceland.

▲ The Jungle Room features a flowing waterfall, various animal figures, tiki statues, and shag carpeting on the ceiling. It was one of Elvis Presley's favorite rooms in Graceland.

From the first day in 1957 when he moved into the residence with his parents, Graceland became Elvis Presley's oasis away from megastardom. Elvis spent much of his adult life in the friendly confines of Graceland—a refuge from the outside world of adoring fans. Although he loved his home, Elvis was not confined to Graceland. He toured in concert, made movies, recorded new material and traveled around Memphis for entertainment quite often. The "prisoner at Graceland" perception is a myth. Some of the rooms at Graceland testify to the brilliance and quirkiness of Elvis Presley, featuring his taste for crystal chandeliers, shag carpets, gilt mirrors and stained-glass windows. The basement TV room is where he often watched three televisions at once, and was within close reach of a wet bar. The Jungle Room was designed by Elvis himself and features lampshades that look like leopard skins, zebra-striped sofas, and green shag carpeting on the ceiling. It was in the Jungle Room where Elvis recorded his final two albums. His living room at Graceland was decorated completely in white. The dining room features his gold-leaf piano. There is a shooting room where Elvis practiced his marksmanship, an auto museum containing 22 cars including his famous 1955 Pink Cadillac. His former racquetball court displays an array of lifetime awards, gold albums, and favorite performance suits. Perhaps the most telling aspect of Elvis' private life is his personal jet collection at Graceland. A recreated 1970s style airport terminal contains two planes—the *Hound Dog II* and the *Lisa Marie* jet, named after his daughter. He referred to the *Lisa Marie* as his "Flying Graceland." After Elvis died the swimming pool area became the Meditation Garden, a solemn location where Elvis is laid to rest alongside his mother, father, and grandmother.

The Life of Elvis Presley is commemorated at his beloved estate called Graceland. Upward near a million visitors arrive annually to pay homage to The King. In 2006, the Graceland Mansion was designated a National Historic Landmark by the U.S. Department of Interior.

▲ Graceland is the final resting place for Elvis Presley and his immediate family.

Elvis Presley was undoubtedly one of the 20th century's most musically influential figures. His recording career became legendary and sparked the admiration of post-World War II America. His spirit is everywhere at Graceland, an estate that has remained frozen in time since his death in 1977, and is now moving beyond his suburban neighborhood into downtown Memphis and even out of state. A certain cult of personality has developed around Elvis since his death. His love for karate earned his pants the centerpiece honor at the Elvis Presley Museum in Kissimmee, Florida. As the sign says, "He achieved 9th degree black belt, making him the highest ranked entertainer." The immediate neighborhood around Graceland has become an institution of its own, fully devoted to all things Elvis. There is the "Heartbreak Hotel" directly across the street, adjacent to the Graceland Plaza memorabilia center. Here the visitor can enjoy Elvis-inspired restaurants, gift shops, additional Graceland museums and a post office where visitors can have their mail stamped with an official Graceland postmark. All this makes Elvis Presley's Graceland Mansion the most visited home in America.

## Getting to Graceland

Graceland is located approximately 10 miles (16 km) due south of downtown Memphis. Driving from I-55 take Exit 5-B on to Elvis Presley Boulevard, then travel south about 1 mile (1.6 km) to Graceland. Parking is located across the street from the mansion, at 3717 Elvis Presley Boulevard. Elvis tribute gift stores, museums and restaurants line the street across from the mansion. In downtown Memphis, be sure to visit the Sun Records Studio at 706 Union Avenue where the careers of Elvis Presley, Jerry Lee Lewis, B. B. King, Johnny Cash, and Roy Orbison were launched. "Elvis Presley's Memphis" is a restaurant and nightclub district on Beale Street, where neon-lit clubs stay hopping until the wee hours.

There are two major annual events in Memphis to honor The King: the Elvis Presley Birthday Celebration in January and Elvis "Tribute" Week in August. Also in downtown Memphis is the National Civil Rights Museum, located at the Lorraine Motel (450 Mulberry Street) where Dr. Martin Luther King Jr. was assassinated in April, 1968.

# VIRGINIA

On April 20th, 1607 a band of British colonists arrived on the Virginia coast to establish a toehold on the continent. The colony was called Jamestown and after a shaky start they went on to become the first English colony to survive, following the mysterious disappearance of the Roanoke, North Carolina colony 20 years earlier. Although the Jamestown colony seemed destined to fail like its predecessors, everything changed when a young man named John Rolfe managed to hybridize a mellow, smokable tobacco. The lucrative European export launched the original tobacco baron plantations in the South along the James River, the first of which, the Shirley Plantation, was established in 1613 and survives to this day. After a rough start, early Virginian colonists struck upon rice, indigo, sugar, and cotton as cash crops that allowed the South to grow in leaps and bounds. In 1619, the first African slaves landed in Virginia, starting a development that would define the region for generations to come.

## Assateague Island

The Virginia shoreline has long been a menace to mariners who named the many sandspit splinters "The Graveyard." The shallow water hazards are compounded by the angry, unpredictable merging of two strong currents in the Atlantic Ocean. Here the Cold Stream pouring south from Labrador and the warm Gulf Stream thrusting north mingle with a fury that has sunk or disabled thousands of ships. Stretching along the Maryland and Virginia coasts, Assateague Island National Seashore is a beautiful low-lying sandspit island fronting the Atlantic Ocean. Best known for its wild horses called the Chincoteague ponies, this picturesque area is also said to be the Eastern Gate spiritual entryway for the Woodland Indians. Similar to Point Conception in California, Assateague Island is an ultra-sacred portal for Native American souls entering and exiting the earth plane.

The name *Assateague* is derived from a Native American term meaning "A Running Stream Between," or "Swiftly Moving Water." Prehistoric tools have been unearthed on the island indicating that the Indians raised vegetables and hunted the abundant wildlife on the island long before the first white settlers arrived in 1688. There is no evidence however, that Native Americans lived permanently on this narrow sacred island. At the time of first contact, British colonists observed very peculiar burial practices among the Native Americans living near Assateague Island. The Assateague, Choptank, and Nanticoke Indians held a deep reverence for the bones of their recently deceased kin. The bones were placed on a specially constructed *Chiacason* House, built of logs and containing shelves as a repository for the remains. The bones were first scraped clean of all flesh before being deposited in the holy temple. All the dead person's material riches, such as beads, pipes, and ornaments, were placed on shelves with the bones. After a lapse of time, the bones were gathered and reburied in a permanent tomb where they were not disturbed again. The items of the deceased were then distributed among the persons' friends and relatives during a solemn ceremony. Early records indicated that when the Indians were being removed from Maryland in the years 1759 and 1760, they made a great effort to take the unburied bones with them much to the consternation of the Puritan colonists.

> Assateague Island is a revered Native American location where recently deceased and newborn souls would depart and enter the cosmos. Farther south at Roanoke Island, along the Outer Banks island chain, the first British colony of settlers mysteriously disappeared and became known as the Lost Colony.

The first effort made by the British to establish a colony in North America began in the late 16th century at Roanoke Island in North Carolina. Sir Walter Raleigh commissioned a colonization party, first of soldiers to build a fort in 1585, then a permanent group composed of 116 men, women and children in 1587. All seemed to proceed favorably for the colony until supplies and protection were delayed for three years because of a war between England and Spain. When relief finally came in 1590, the Roanoke colony was completely abandoned. Clues indicated that the English were starving and the "Lost Colony" had moved inland, perhaps to trade with the natives. It was not until the Jamestown, Virginia settlement 20 years later that an effort was made to locate the Roanoke settlers. Because the investigation came decades

▲ The wild ponies of Assateague Island.
(Photo courtesy National Park Service)

later, no conclusive answer was established with academics and the Lost Colony was relegated to either being massacred entirely or loosely assimilated into various native groupings.

The Lumbee (or Croatan) tribe of North Carolina cannot completely understand why historians persist in calling the Roanoke colony the "Lost Colony," since they left information telling the British where they were going. The colonists had carved the word "Croatoan" onto a wooden post, indicating that they were going inland to live with the friendly Cheraw Indians. When the descendents of the Croatan Cheraw were found some 50 years later speaking English, practicing Christianity, and using about 75% of the last names that the colonists had brought with them, it was accepted that these were the descendents of the Roanoke colony. These descendents—who call themselves the Lumbee after the Lumber River running through their traditional land—were a mixed-race, with so many Caucasian features that they were spared the forced relocation to Oklahoma with the Cherokee and other tribes in the 1820s and 1830s. The Lumbee anthropological model is an excellent example of cultural diffusion in North America, when a numerically dominant tribe adopts a racially distinct group and over the years they merge into a single identifiable culture.

### Getting to Assateague Island

The entire 35-mile (56-km) barrier island spanning two states is part of the Assateague Island National Seashore, and the Virginia side contains the Chincoteague National Wildlife Refuge. Assateague Island is a barrier beach built by sand that persistent waves have raised from the Atlantic Ocean's gently sloping floor. Almost the entire island is undeveloped wilderness, perfect for waterfowl and the two herds of wild "ponies," but difficult for travel. There are two bridges accessing the island—Route 611 on the Maryland side and Route 175 on the Virginia side—but no single road connects the two coastal access areas. Instead, visitors can enjoy over 10 miles (17 km) of uninterrupted shell-strewn public beaches.

# WEST VIRGINIA

At the beginning of the Civil War, in a public referendum, voters overwhelmingly supported the creation of the new state, to be called Kanawha. Never dependent on slave labor, the pro-Union counties in the northern part of western Virginia seceded from eastern Virginia and applied to the federal government to accept them as a new state. President Lincoln signed the West Virginia Statehood Proclamation in June 1863, making it the only state created by carving out territory from another state, without that state's permission. Largely associated by its coal mining industry, West Virginia has the highest average elevation of any state east of the Mississippi River, and the most irregular boundary of any state.

## Grave Creek

One of North America's most curious monuments was once surrounded by a moat within a vast complex of now-lost burial mounds and earthworks. The Grave Creek Mound, also know as Mammoth Mound, is regarded as the largest earthwork created by the Adena people (600 BCE – 100 CE) of the middle Ohio River Valley. Not long after the Grave Creek Mound was constructed the Adena culture began to slowly assimilate into the more sophisticated Hopewell culture. Unlike the irregular shape of Hopewell mounds usually assembled all at once, Adena mounds were symmetrical in shape and built up in stages over time. Adena mounds began as ground level graves covered with a slight dirt hill. Successive burials were made on top of the original mound, again covered with soil, so that over the decades a sizable mound was constructed with several layers of graves.

The two largest burial mounds in North America are Miamisburg Mound in Miamisburg, Ohio and Grave Creek Mound in Moundsville, West Virginia. Both were massive undertakings, requiring the movement of more than 60,000 tons (54,420,000 kg), or some three million basket loads, of earth. Grave Creek Mound is of the late Adena Period and was built in successive stages over a period of 100 years or more from about 250 to 150 BCE. It is not know why the Adena chose to build this particular mound on such a huge scale compared with other burial mounds in the area, all of which generally range in size from 20 to 300 feet (6 to 90 m) in diameter. The Grave Creek Mound was originally 65 feet (19.5 m) tall with an outer circumference of 910 feet (273 m). Adding to the mystery was the discovery of a moat with a south-facing causeway accessing the mound. The moat had been about 40 feet (12 m) wide and five feet deep encircling the Grave Creek Mound, buried over in 1838 when the mound was excavated. Grave Creek

Mound is remarkably similar in design to the prehistoric earthen Silbury Hill, moat and causeway located at Avebury, England. Although little remains of their villages, the Adena left grand monuments to mark their passing, and one of the greatest of these is the Grave Creek Mound.

▲ The Grave Creek Mound has always been a curiosity.
(Squier & Davis, 1847)

Grave Creek Mound was constructed
in successive stages as indicated by the
multiple burials at different levels within
the structure. In one of these tombs the
Grave Creek Tablet was found with an
enigmatic script, deciphered to be Iberian
in the Punic language.

The first recorded excavation of the mound took place in 1838, conducted by local amateurs. To gain entrance into the mound, two long shafts were dug, one vertical and one horizontal. The tunnels led to the discovery of two log burial vaults, one situated directly over the other. Another horizontal shaft dug from the outer base of the mound revealed 10 skeletons in sitting positions, and masses of charcoal including cremated human bones. The first chamber was discovered at a depth of 60 feet (18 m), while the second was found at the 77-foot (23-m) level, that is, 12 feet (3.6 m) below the "bottom" of the mound itself. The subsurface log chamber was found covered by stone slabs. A male and female skeleton were retrieved along with mica sheets, copper ornaments and nearly 700 shell beads. A single male skeleton wearing copper arm rings and various ornaments was found in the upper vault, which also contained a flat sandstone disk inscribed with an ancient Semitic script. The Grave Creek Tablet is a small inscribed stone, about 1 7/8" (4.8 cm) wide, and 1 1/2" (3.6 cm) high. The reverse side was not inscribed. Ever since its discovery the tablet has created quite a stir in historic and archaeological circles, with most academics casually dismissing it as a hoax. In 1976, Harvard professor and epigrapher Barry Fell declared the tablet to be genuine. Fell professed that its symbols derive from an ancient Punic, or Phoenician, alphabet used on the Iberian Peninsula during the first millennium BCE. At the time of the stone's discovery in 1838 the script had not yet been deciphered by any scholar, and thus could not have been a forgery. Despite the heated controversy over a rune-like text associated with Celtic Europeans, the find was well documented and indicates that the Adena were either a literate people, or had strong cultural ties with seafaring Europeans. The Iberian translation of the inscription is as follows: "The mound raised-on-high for Tasach—this tile—(His) queen caused-to-be-made." The inscription is an exchange of greetings from the Queen of a Celtic culture to the east and the king of the local Adena nation. Other similar stones written in ancient Celtic / Punic have been found in the area, but none so conclusively known to come from a dateable burial mound such as Grave Creek. The real historical anomaly is the presence of Semitic inscriptions in ancient American tombs.

The town of Moundsville adopted the name from the multitude of burial mounds in the vicinity when the town was founded in the late 1700s. Grave Creek Mound was the largest of 47 mounds within the city limits of Moundsville, which included other elaborate earthworks, now lost. The only known shaped earthwork was a 5-acre (2-ha) octagon near the bank of the Ohio River, also

ruined by centuries of farming and development. Grave Creek Mound is all that
survives today, the last remnant of a massive Adena necropolis of sorts. Some in
town claim it was the ghosts of the ancient
mounds who were responsible for the
plague of hauntings to beset the town in
the 20th century. Many strange phenomena have been recorded in Moundsville,
including frequent UFO sightings, Men
In Black, phantom cars on the road late at
night and inexplicable interference with
telephones and televisions. A period of

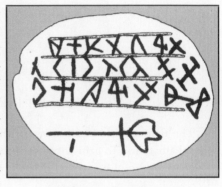

▲ The Grave Creek Stone
inscription.

bizarre events culminated in 1966 when a huge winged man with glowing red
eyes called Mothman haunted Moundsville. The unearthly entity was said to take
off straight up in the air without using its wings, and would chase cars near the
Chief Cornstalk Hunting Grounds, the location of an abandoned World War II
ammunition dump. Mothman would emit a loud squeaking noise like a gigantic
mouse and utterly terrified all who encountered him. Most of the witnesses to
the Mothman sightings were killed in an unsettling accident when a bridge spanning the Ohio River collapsed.

### Getting to Grave Creek

The most important prehistoric monument in West Virginia is located in the
quiet, middle-class town of Moundsville near the Ohio River. Moundsville is
conveniently located 15 minutes south of Wheeling, on the northern arm of
West Virginia between Ohio and Pennsylvania. Grave Creek Mound State Park
and Delf Norona Museum are located just east of Route 2 on Jefferson Avenue.
Artifacts and exhibits interpreting the lifestyle of the Adena people are displayed
in the museum, adjacent to the 2,200-year-old mound. The Iberian translation
of the Grave Creek Tablet is incorporated into an exhibit about the stone in the
Delf Norona Museum. An entrance fee is required for the museum and access to
the trail leading to the top of the mound.

# CONCLUSION

*"The whole of science consists of data that, at one time or another, were inexplicable."*
-Brendan O'Regan

THE modern science of archaeology was developed in the early 19th century by a famous authority on ancient coins named Christian Thomsen. For many decades, out of place artifacts (or "OOPAS" as they are called) were being retrieved in Scandinavia, leading the King of Denmark to appoint a Royal Commission for the Preservation and Collection of National Antiquities. In 1816, Thomsen headed the commission and set forth interpreting the numerous amounts of stone and metal artifacts recovered from Danish soil and ancient burial mounds. He divided the vast collection into three parts: one group comprised of stone artifacts, another of those made in bronze and copper, and a third group consisting of cast iron objects. To each of these groups he added other objects such as textiles or wooden fragments, pottery shards, or leather garments into the appropriate piles when such objects were known to be associated with any of the stone or metal artifacts. Then, by reading the oldest texts he could find, Thomsen noted that the oldest books contained no references to iron, yet many for copper and bronze. He inferred from the ancient Greek texts, mainly Homer's *Iliad* and *Odyssey*, that the art of smelting iron ore must have been a subsequent discovery after the bronze alloys had been developed. We know now that around 800 BCE, the shift from Bronze Age to Iron Age had started in the region of Europe north of Greece. Thomsen then reasoned by common sense that stone tools, quite obviously, would have been utilized by primitive peoples long before the art of working metals arose. In 1819, the collection was opened to the public in Copenhagen, and the explanatory labels offered the revolutionary suggestion that there had at first been a Stone Age, followed by a Bronze Age, which in turn was followed by an Iron Age. The essential basis of modern archaeology is now classified as the original Three-Age System.

At the same time in history, archaeologists from the United States rejected the Three-Age System, for the reason that Native American artifacts presented anomalous cultural features. Indian arrowheads chipped from stone, for example, fit the grouping of "Paleolithic," yet were sometimes mixed with copper bracelets, knives, and polished amulets—a veritable jumble of "ages" on the European dating system. These anomalies, together with a growing cache of misinformation on the supposed uniqueness of Columbus' "first contact" voyages, led to a deep schism of American archaeological thinking away from its European counterparts, and ultimately to the impasse in which North American historians now find themselves. This tight grip of dogma prejudges all newly discovered Old World connections as forgeries, misinterpretations, and covert importations of ancient objects in modern times. Such misguided views have hindered investigators attempting to restore the long-neglected evidence, to add new evidence, or to make inferences accordingly.

An example of misguided American archaeological reasoning is the mystery of Michigan's vast reserves of pure copper. Where did it go in prehistory and who took it? North American archaeologists continue to puzzle over who mined the millions of pounds of pure raw copper from Michigan's Upper Peninsula and Isle Royale in Lake Superior. The time period it was extracted is calculated between 3000 BCE and 1200 BCE. Certainly some copper mining can be attributed to Native Americans, but indigenous use of copper was limited and does not account for the phenomenal quantities extracted. Conversely, in European and Middle Eastern archeological circles one of the greatest enigmas is where did all the copper come from to sustain the Bronze Age cultures? Again, the time periods match between 3000 BCE and 1200 BCE. Local copper mines were not sufficient enough, nor of the necessary quality to supply these emerging cultural demands. Bronze Age people valued copper as much as gold or silver, so the profit motive for copper procurement would have been very strong—a motive strong enough to send willing sailors across vast oceans to far-away lands in search of this prized commodity.

# CONCLUSION

Some of the greatest misconceptions about North American prehistory stem from the overly simplistic history lessons we were taught in school. Contrary to the convenient record of Christopher Columbus being the first European explorer to arrive in the New World, Viking explorers beat him here by at least 500 years, and the Celts / Phoenicians by another 2,500 years or more. Ironically, the misguided "Discoverer of America" erroneously believed he had located islands near India in south-central Asia—hence the term "Indian" for indigenous people and "West Indies" for the Caribbean islands—an incorrect assumption that Columbus held

▲ Christopher Columbus, the disputed "discoverer" of America.

his entire lifetime. While Columbus and the Spaniards preferred to colonize in tropical latitudes, the Vikings were prolific explorers of northern lands—their river and sea expeditions into the far reaches of Eurasia are well documented. It would seem the Vikings and their predecessors had a much greater role in exploring the continent and influencing Native American culture than is currently accepted. New finds are emerging almost every year. For example, scattered around parts of eastern North America are Viking runestones, along with various relics and "mooring holes" found in areas of eastern Canada, New England, and the Great Lakes region, lending evidence to the idea that there were significant Norse incursions into the continent long before Columbus. Assorted Viking relics found in North America include iron-cast halberds, swords, spears, boat hooks, various metal tools and iron smelting furnaces. Archaic Irish and Iberian Phoenician inscriptions in the Ogam script, along with various stone carvings, have also been found and dated. The chiseled mooring holes into large waterside boulders are more prolific, especially along rivers and ocean access waterways. The Vikings used these mooring holes by fitting a peg attached to a line from the ship to securely anchor the vessel front and aft, and allow for a hasty retreat if necessary. There have been more than 200 pairs of such holes found, from South Dakota and Michigan to Massachusetts and the Canadian Atlantic Provinces. The mooring holes alone indicate a significant Viking presence in North America from at least 1000 to 1400 CE. Rising before and contemporary with the Viking incursions into the continent are the mysterious mound builder people, especially the Mississippian Culture, who reached one of the most refined states of civilization in North America, before all but disappearing by the time of the second wave of European explorers. While most academics will

▲ Sailing vessels like this one circled the globe in the 15th century. Were they the first?

regard the Mississippian Culture as an isolated indigenous American culture to emerge, other evidence suggests that they assimilated with outside influences ranging from the Aztec, Toltec, or Maya in present-day Mexico, to the Norsemen of Scandinavia, or Phoenician / Celtic traders who came in the centuries before Christ. Whoever they were they erected fantastic earthen temple mounds, elaborate burial sites, enormous geometric earthworks, and highly organized mound cities throughout most of eastern North America. Some of the most famous earthworks of the Mississippian Culture and others include features such as game yards, public plazas, ceremonial courts, platform pyramids, elaborate burial complexes, earthen defensive walls and effigy animal figures.

Archaeologists and historians have been frustrated by these strange findings for centuries, but were unable to write up their interpretations because of preconceived notions and the popular dogma among their colleagues. As tempting as the all-OOPAS-are-forgeries explanation may be, nothing should be called a fake until it is absolutely proven to be a fake. All the pieces of the puzzle, no matter how obscure, no matter how out of place, absolutely need to be considered in their entirety instead of being wantonly discarded because they might not fit. Without a doubt, the prehistory of North America remains an incomplete puzzle. At best, the fakes won't fit when the puzzle is completed. When the cultural diffusionist picture is given its proper place in history—as it well deserves—a new conception of North American prehistory will emerge much different than the simplistic cookie-cutter history mold we were taught in school. Indeed, sometimes the truth is stranger than fiction.

I designed this book to be used for an objective historical background to the sites, as a navigational and directional guide, and to set the stage for individual self-discovery. Many times the places described in this book will tell their own stories to the people who take the time to experience them. Talk to the historians and curators at the sites and open yourself to what these places might have to offer. In other words, keep an open mind and let the experiential value of visiting these sacred sites influence your own opinion. Discovering the sacred places in this volume should be considered an interpersonal and spiritual quest. Happy trailblazing!

# ABOUT THE AUTHOR:

BRAD OLSEN's *World Stompers: A Global Travel Manifesto*, now in its Fifth Edition, was lauded by film director Oliver Stone as a "subversive masterpiece" and Publisher's Weekly as a "quirky pleaser." He is Contributing Editor for *World Explorer* magazine and writes a bi-monthly travel column called "Sacred Destinations" for *Heartland Healing Magazine*. He is the author/illustrator of *Extreme Adventures Hawaii* and *Extreme Adventures Northern California* (Hunter Publishing). His popular travel website (www.stompers.com) was Microsoft Network's 'Site of the Week' and regularly ranks in the Top 10% Travel Sites on Lycos. Brad is the President of CCC Publishing in San Francisco, which publishes *In Search of Adventure: A Wild Travel Anthology; The Key to Solomon's Key* and the *Sacred Places: 108 Destinations* series. His commentaries have appeared on National Public Radio, CNN and the Travel Channel. Brad enjoys lecturing on the subject of journeys to sacred places and extended global travel.

Brad usually spends his summers in the Midwest and the rest of the year in sunny California. Brad is an avid downhill skier, scuba diver, and ultimate frisbee player. He goes to the Burning Man Festival every year and occasionally builds an art project to burn. As a result of researching this book, Brad has started writing his first historical screenplay about the Viking excursions to North America. In between projects, or when the weather is really nice, he can usually be found playing frisbee or volleyball with his friends down on San Francisco's Baker Beach.

Brad is Executive Director of the World Peace Through Technology Organization, a 501 (c) 3 nonprofit corporation, and the founder of the How Weird Street Faire. Both projects are based out of San Francisco. He is 42 years old.

To learn more about this 21st century world traveler have a look at his various web sites:

www.bradolsen.com

www.stompers.com

www.peacetour.org

www.howwierd.org

www.cccpublishing.com

▲ Brad Olsen examines a heiau on Oahu, Hawaii.

# ACKNOWLEDGMENTS

This work was greatly enhanced by the fine suggestions from the following editors: Ed Taylor, Jennifer Bolm, Kristen Fourier, Mark Maxam, Mara Rogers, Ben Wolff, and family members Chris Olsen (brother), Marsi Olsen (sister) and Elaine Olsen (mother). Hats off to the page design and publishing direction from Mark Maxam and cover assistance by Eric Stampfli—my old San Francisco studio mates. Gratuitous support came from Aunt Bonnie and Uncle Bud Hausman, my father Marshall Olsen and his wife Susan, Joe Firmage and the ISSO, Michael O'Rourke, Peter Bartsch, David Templeman, Justin Smith, Justin Weiner and Randy Barris from the Peace Tour organization, Vera Ginzbourg and Jennifer Fahey. Mike Boyd and Harry O from the World Explorers Club directly aided my research. Regards to Calum Grant, Talia Nero-Turk, Tommy Peloquin, Harry Pariser, Bruce Northam, Ben Adair, and Jerry Nardini. Special thanks to Daniel Polikoff and our wonderful CCC friends and family, Stewart and Roseanne Fallin, Travis "Neo" Winn, Kun & Erika, Antione, Paul and Jovis. Three cheers for the wonderful books, inspiration and advice from maverick archaeologist David Hatcher Childress.

This book would not be possible without the ample information gathered from the National Park Service (NPS) brochures, photographs, and committed Park Rangers at all the National Parks extending across the United States and Canada. The online Wikipedia website was an invaluable resource for second opinions. Special thanks go out to the museum curators, historians, tour guides and archaeologists who took a personal interest in this research project. Those people are Larry Harvey of the Burning Man Organization; Larry Henry of the Highlands Nature Sanctuary which includes Spruce Hill; Richard Gould from the Pawnee Indian Village State Historic Site in Kansas; Natchez historian Jim Barnett; the Shakers at Sabbathday Lake; Leslie Lewis of the Manitou Springs Mineral Springs Foundation; Bobby Davis of Elvis Presley Enterprises; David Wells at Naturally Superior Adventures; Dennis Peterson at Spiro Mounds State Park; Gloria Farley at Heavener Runestone State Park; Stephanie Burdo from Tour Chautauqua; and Basil Northam who fearlessly navigated the far corners of the earth, including the Queen Charlotte Islands.

Special promotional thanks to the Big Sky Chamber of Commerce in Big Sky, Montana; Poco Diablo Resort in Sedona, Arizona; Royal Hawaiian Resort in Waikiki, Hawaii; The Chamber of Commerce at Moab, Utah; Chautauqua Visitor's Bureau, and the Alabama Bureau of Tourism and Travel.

# BIBLIOGRAPHY

## Author's Karma Statement

**Dillard,** Annie, "The Wreck Of Time: Taking Our Century's Measure." *Harper's,* (New York), January 1998.

## Introduction

**Adams,** Russell B., Series Director, *Mystic Places: Mysteries of the Unknown.* Alexandria, VA: Time-Life Books, 1987.

**Childress,** David Hatcher, *Anti-Gravity & The World Grid.* Stelle, IL: Adventures Unlimited Press, 1995.

**Frejer**, Ernest B., Compiler, *The Edgar Cayce Companion.* Virginia Beach, VA, 1995.

**Metzner,** Ralph, *The Unfolding Self.* Navato, CA: Origin Press, 1998.

**Westward,** Jennifer, Editor, *The Atlas of Mysterious Places.* London, UK: Weidenfeld & Nicolson, 1987.

## Alaska and Hawaii

**Herb,** Angela M., *Alaska A to Z.* Bellevue, WA: Vernon Publications, 1993.

**Geis,** Darlene, *Let's Travel in Hawaii.* New York, NY: Columbia Record Club, 1960.

**Noone,** Richard, *5/5/2000 Ice: The Ultimate Disaster.* New York, NY: Three Rivers Press, 1982.

**Otteson,** Paul, *Alaska: Adventures in Nature.* Santa Fe, NM: John Muir Publications, 1998.

**Suggs,** Robert C., *The Island Civilizations of Polynesia.* New York, NY: Mentor Books, 1960.

**Ward,** Greg, *Hawaii.* London, UK: The Rough Guides, 1996.

**Wheeler,** Mortimer, Editor, *Splendors of the East.* New York, NY: G.P. Putnam's Sons, 1965.

## Central Plains

**Childress,** David Hatcher, *Lost Cities of North and Central America.* Stelle, IL: Adventures Unlimited Press, 1992.

**Doubleday,** Nelson, Editor, *Encyclopedia of World Travel Volume 2.* Garden City, NY: Doubleday & Company, 1967.

**Erdoes,** Richard, Alfonso Ortiz, *American Indian Myths and Legends.* New York, NY: Pantheon Books, 1984.

**Farley,** Gloria, *In Plain Sight.* Columbus, GA: ISAC Press, 1994.

**Fell,** Barry, *Saga America.* New York, NY: Times Books, 1980.

**Sullivan,** Walter, et. al, *The World's Last Mysteries.* Pleasantville, NY: The Reader's Digest Association, 1981.

**Walsh,** Tom, *This One Dear Place.* Peosta, IA: New Melleray Abbey, 1999.

**Wedel,** Waldo R., *Central Plains Prehistory.* Lincoln, NB: University of Nebraska Press, 1986.

**Wyckoff,** Don, Dennis Peterson, *Spiro Mounds: Prehistoric Gateway, Present-Day Enigma.* Oklahoma Foundation for the Humanities, 1978.

## Eastern Canada

**Bayly,** C. A., et. al. *Light in the East.* Alexandria, VA: Time-Life Books, 1988.

**Fell,** Barry, *Bronze Age America.* New York, NY: Little Brown, 1982.

**Breining,** Greg, "The Power of Rock." *Sierra,* (San Francisco, CA), Jan. Feb. 2001.

**Gibbs,** Walter, "Did the Vikings Stay? Vatican Files May Offer Clues." *New York Times: SCIENCE,* (New York, NY), December 19, 2000.

**Jewell,** Roger, *Ancient Mines of Kitchi-Gummi.* Jewell Histories: Fairfield, PA, 2000.

**Lefebvre,** Eugene, *Saint Anne's Pilgrim People.* Québec, Canada: Charrier et Dugal, 1981.

**Mallery,** Arlington, Mary Roberts Harrison, *The Rediscovery of Lost America.* New York, NY: E. P. Dutton, 1979.

**Moloney,** Norah, *The Young Oxford Book of Archaeology.* Oxford, England: Oxford University Press, 1995.

## Great Lakes

**Belliveau,** Jeannette, *An Amateur's Guide to the Planet.* Baltimore, MD: Beau Monde Press, 1996.

**Birmingham,** Robert A., Eisenberg, Leslie E., *Indian Mounds of Wisconsin.* University of Wisconsin Press, 2000.

**Hamilton,** Ross, *The Mystery of the Serpent Mound.* Berkeley, CA: Frog, LTD., 2001.

**Hart,** Carl, "New World Vikings." *World Explorer,* (Kempton, IL), Spring, 1993.

**Howell,** Clark, F., *Early Man.* Alexandria, VA: Time-Life Books, 1968.

**Ingpen,** Robert, et. at. *Encyclopedia of Mysterious Places.* New York, NY: Viking Penguin, 1990.

**Knapp,** Joseph, M., "Hopewell Lunar Astronomy: The Octagon Earthworks." www.copperas.com/octagon © 1998.

**Lepper,** Bradley, T., "The Hopewells: Heath's Earliest Residents." www.heathohio.org/hopewell.html © 2001.

**Little,** Gregory L., Van Auken, John, Little, Lora H., *Mound Builders: Edgar Cayce's Forgotten Record of Ancient America.* Memphis, TN: Eagle Wing Books, 2001.

**Mallery,** Arlington, Mary Roberts Harrison, *The Rediscovery of Lost America.* New York, NY: E. P. Dutton, 1979.

**Massey,** Kevin and Keith, "The Kensington Stone is Genuine!" http://home.att.net/~phaisttosdisc/mystery.PDF © 2000.

**Ross,** Hamilton Nelson, *La Pointe Village Outpost.* St. Paul, MN: North Central Publishing Co. 1960.

**Woodward,** Susan L., McDonald, Jerry N., *Indian Mounds of the Middle Ohio Valley.* Blacksburg, VA: The McDonald & Woodward Publishing Company, 2002.

## New England

**Bahn,** Paul G., Editor, *100 Great Archaeological Discoveries.* London, UK: Barnes & Noble Books, 1995.

**Barker,** Sister R. Mildred, *The Sabbathday Lake Shakers*. New Gloucester, ME: The Shaker Press, 1985.

**Cahill,** Robert Ellis, *New England's Ancient Mysteries*. Salem, MA: Old Salt Box, 1993.

**Fell,** Barry, *America B.C.* New York, NY. Pocket Books, 1989.

**Frank,** Irene M., et. al. *To the Ends of the Earth*. New York: Facts On File Publications, 1984.

**Hartt,** Frederick, et. al. *Art: A History of Painting, Sculpture, and Architecture: Second Edition*. Prentice-Hall: Englewood Cliffs, New Jersey, 1985.

**Longman,** Byron, Sullivan, Walter, et. al, *The World's Last Mysteries*. Pleasantville, NY: The Reader's Digest Association, 1981.

**Taylor,** Colin, *North American Indians*. Bristol, UK: Parragon, 1997.

## The Southwest

**Andres,** Dennis, *What is a Vortex: A Practical Guide to Sedona's Vortex Sites*. Sedona, AZ: Meta Adventures, 2000.

**Gray,** Martin, *Sacred Earth: Places of Pace and Power.* New York, NY: Sterling Publishing, 2007.

**Harvey,** Rankin, et al., *Adventure Guide to New Mexico*. Edison, NJ: Hunter Publishing, 2000.

**Noble,** David Grant, *Ancient Ruins of the Southwest (2nd ed.)*. Flagstaff, AZ: Northland, 2000.

**Plog,** Stephen, *Ancient People of the American Southwest."* London, UK: Thames and Hudson, 1997.

**St. Rain,** Tedd, *Mystery of America: A Guidebook to Ancient Mysteries of North America*. Plan't Publishing, 1999.

**Soleri,** Paolo, *Arcology: The City in the Image of Man*. Phoenix, AZ: Bridgewood Press, 1999.

**Stieber,** Tamar, "Driving into Prehistory." *American Archaeology,* Summer, 2001.

**Tehabi** Books, Editors at Time-Life, *The Way of the Spirit*. New York, NY: Time-Life Books, 1997.

**Winnemucca Hopkins**, Sarah, *Life Among the Paiutes*. 1882.

## The Rocky Mountains

**Black Elk,** Nicholas, *Black Elk Speaks*. University of Nebraska: Bison Books, 1932.

**Childress,** David Hatcher, *Lost Cities of North and Central America*. Stelle, IL: Adventures Unlimited Press, 1992.

**Doubleday,** Nelson, Editor, *Encyclopedia of World Travel Volume 1*. Garden City, NY: Doubleday & Company, 1967.

**Eiseley,** Loren, Editor, *The Epic of Man*. New York, NY: Life Books, 1961.

**Janetski,** Joel C., *Indians of Yellowstone Park*. Salt Lake City, UT: University of Utah Press, 1987.

**Noble,** David Grant, *Ancient Ruins of the Southwest: An Archaeological Guide (1st ed.)*. Flagstaff, AZ: Northland, 1981.

**O'Brien,** Christopher, *Secrets of the Mysterious Valley*. Kempton, IL: Adventures Unlimited Press, 2007.

**Root,** Don, *Idaho Handbook*. Chico, CA: Moon Publications, 1997.

**Young,** John V., *Kokopelli: Casanova of the Cliff Dwellers*. Palmer Lake, CO: Filter Press, 1990.

## The South

**Bryson,** Bill, *A Walk in the Woods: Rediscovering America on the Appalachian Trail*. New York, NY:Anchor Books, 1998.

**Casson,** Lionel, et. al. *Mysteries of the Past*. New York, NY: American Heritage Publishing, 1977.

**Diamond,** Jared, *Guns, Germs, and Steel: The Fates of Human Societies*. New York, NY: W. W. Norton, 1999.

**Donato,** William, "Revisiting Edgar Cayce's Caribbean Atlantis." *Atlantis Rising, #30;* Nov. Dec., 2001.

**Fell,** Barry, *America B.C.: Ancient Settlers in the New World*. New York, NY: Wallaby Books, 1976.

**Frank,** Irene M., et al, *To the Ends of the Earth*. New York: Facts On File Publications, 1984.

**Guiley,** Rosemary Ellen, *Atlas of the Mysterious in North America*. New York, NY: Facts On File, 1995.

## West Coast, USA

**Barlow,** Bernyce, *Sacred Sites of the West*. St. Paul, MN: Llewellyn Worldwide Ltd., 1997.

**Clark,** Ella E., *Indian Legends of the Pacific Northwest*. Berkeley, CA: University of California Press, 1953.

**Coronel,** Antonio, *Tales of Mexican California*. Santa Barbara, CA: Bellerophon Books, 1994.

**Dennett,** Preston, "Mountains of Mystery: Are Shasta and Rainier the Preferred Destinations for Other Worldly Visitors?" *Atlantis Rising,* (Livingston, MT), Issue #25, 2001.

**Mann,** Nicholas R., Sutton, Marcia, *Giants of Gaia*. Albuquerque, NM: Brotherhood of Life, 1995.

**Rogers,** Malcolm J., et al, *Ancient Hunters of the Far West*. San Diego, CA: Union-Tribune Publishing CO., 1966.

**Trento,** Salvatore M., *Field Guide to Mysterious Places of the Pacific Coast*. New York, NY: Henry Holt and Company, 1997.

**Watkins,** T. H., *California: An Illustrated History*. New York, NY: Weathervane Books, 1973.

**Wright,** Ralph B., *California's Missions*. Covina, CA: Herbert A. Lowman, 1950.

**Yogananda,** Paramahansa, *Autobiography of a Yogi*. Los Angeles, CA: Self-Realization Fellowship, 1946.

## Western Canada

**Childress**, David Hatcher, "The Mystery of Thunderbirds." *World Explorer*, (Kempton, IL), Summer, 2007.

**Colombo**, John Robert, *Mysterious Canada: Strange Sights, Extraordinary Events, and Peculiar Places*. Toronto, Canada: Doubleday, 1988.

**Folsom**, Franklin and Mary Elting, *America's Ancient Treasures*. University of New Mexico Press, 1983.

**Giese**, Paula, "Stone Wheels as Analog Star Computers." http://www.kstrom.net/isk/stars © 1995, 1996.

**Goddard**, Pliny Earle, *Indians of the Northwest Coast*. Cooper Square Publishers, New York, NY, 1972.

**Joseph**, Frank, *Sacred Sites of the West*. Surrey, BC: Hancock House, 1997.

**Scarre**, Chris, General Editor, *Past Worlds: The Times Atlas of Archaeology*. London, UK: Times Books Limited, 1988.

**Vickers**, J. Rod "Medicine Wheels: A Mystery in Stone," *Archaeological Survey*, (The Provincial Museum of Alberta), Winter 1992-93.

**Whitehouse**, David & Ruth, *Archaeological Atlas of the World*, San Francisco, CA: W.H. Freeman & CO., 1975.

"Were seafarers living in Canada 16,000 years ago?" Source: *Times Colonist* (21 August 2007)  http://tinyurl.com/2zag8x

# APPENDIX

## Tour Outfitters to North American Sacred Places

Many of the selected outfitters below specialize in one or a few sacred site regions of North America. Call for a free brochure and more information.

**Alaska outfitters and climbing guides for Mount McKinley:**
Alaska Mountaineering School: (907) 733-2649
Alpine Ascents International: (206) 378-1927
American Alpine Institute: (360) 671-1505
National Outdoor Leadership School: (907) 745-4047

**Mount McKinley climbing permits and registration forms:**
Talkeetna Ranger Station
Box 588, Talkeetna, Alaska 99676
PHONE: (907) 733-2231
EMAIL: DENA_Talkeetna_Office@nps.gov

**Adventure Center**
1311 63rd Street, Suite # 200
Emeryville, CA 94608
PHONE: (800) 227-8747
*Specializes in affordable group travel to especially adventurous destinations.*

**Deja Vu Tours**
2018 Aulston Way
Berkeley, CA 94704 USA
PHONE: (800) 204-TOUR
WEB: www.berkeleypsychic.com
*Tours to sacred sites led by graduates of the Berkeley Psychic Institute.*

**Global Exchange REALITY TOURS**
2017 Mission Street # 303
San Francisco, CA 94110
PHONE: (800) 497-1994
WEB: www.globalexchange.org
*Educational, interactive and inspiring excursions dealing with provocative themes, such as peace and conflict, human rights, revolution, history, culture, art and the environment.*

**Journeys Unlimited**
500 Eighth Avenue, Suite # 904
New York, NY 10018
PHONE: (800) 486-8359
*Tour outfitter to sacred Christian sites.*

**Power Places Tours & Conferences**
116 King St.
Fredricksted, Virgin Islands 00840
PHONE: (800) 234-8687
FAX: 340-772-1392
WEB: www.powerplaces.com
*Tours led by modern-day luminaries to power places around the world.*

**Circle The Planet**
PHONE: (800) 799-8888
EMAIL trips@circletheplanet.com
WEB: www.circletheplanet.com
*Lowest-cost tickets to most sacred places worldwide.*

**World Explorers Club**
PO Box 99
403 Kemp Street
Kempton, IL 60946
PHONE: (815) 253-9000
WEB: www.wexclub.com
*Tours/Expeditions/Conferences to more remote sacred sites.*

# INDEX

# SACRED PLACES NORTH AMERICA

# INDEX

# INDEX

# WORLD STOMPERS
## A GLOBAL TRAVEL MANIFESTO (FIFTH EDITION)

When you are ready to leave your day job, load up your backpack and head out to distant lands for extended periods of time, Brad Olsen's "Travel Classic" will lend a helping hand. It will save you hundreds of dollars in travel expenses, prepare you for an extended journey, keep you safe & healthy on the road, find you a job overseas, and get you psyched to travel the world! For a good time, read the book Publishers Weekly called a "Quirky Chain Pleaser" and Library Journal recommended as "A great addition to your collection."

"Travel can be a nightmare when you find yourself in the wrong place at the wrong time. This subversive masterpiece of travel writing might just save your sanity the next time you go out there. Get it. It makes life fun!"—film director Oliver Stone

"This brightly colored post-psychedelic cover conceals what may be more than you ever knew existed about (travel)." — Chicago Tribune

ISBN 1-888729-05-8    288 pages    $17.95    Maps and illustrations by Brad Olsen

### ANCIENT SECRETS OF THE KNIGHTS TEMPLAR AND FREEMASONRY AFFECT THE MODERN WORLD

King Solomon is the central figure of both the secret rituals of Freemasonry and the forbidden rites of sorcery. The sacred traditions of Judaism, Christianity and Islam come together in the person of the wise magician-king of ancient Israel, and his presence in Biblical history is a key element in how these three disparate religions view themselves and each other. The story of Solomon and his magnificent Temple in Jerusalem is the keystone of the Bible that supports and connects the Old Testament to the New. But is it true? Or do myth and tradition hold keys that unlock mysteries of human consciousness infinitely more astounding than history?

"Learn the Masonic teaching by which the human spirit may be elevated — without ignoring either historical reality or scientific fact."
— James Wasserman, author of *The Templars and the Assassins: The Militia of Heaven*
1888729-14-7   206 pages  $14.95   Written by Lon Milo DuQuette

All CCC Publishing titles may be ordered from:
Independent Publishers Group (800) 888-4741

## SACRED PLACES SERIES

*Sacred Places Around the World* is your essential guidebook to 108 unique treasures on the planet. Includes detailed directions, travel restrictions, and hundreds of photos, illustrations and maps.

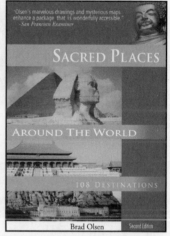

The mystical comes alive in this exciting compilation of 108 spiritual destinations. Whether you are planning a world tour or enjoying a spiritual journey without leaving the comfort of home, "Sacred Places" is your essential guidebook to 108 celebrated holy destinations around the globe.

"(Readers) will thrill to the wonderful history and the vibrations of the world's sacred healing places." — East & West

"108 places that stir the soul." — Chicago Tribune

## SACRED PLACES AROUND THE WORLD: 108 DESTINATIONS
ISBN 1-888729-10-4     288 pages     $17.95     2nd edition includes color photos

## A JOURNEY INTO GODDESS DIVINITY

Discover a book 20,000 years in the making! Travel with author Karen Tate as she examines the varied Divine Feminine traditions as old as the Neolithic temples of Malta or as new as the Goddess Temple of Orange County, in locations as inaccessible as Sedna's Watery Domain near the Arctic Circle or as crowded as Ueno Park in downtown Tokyo.

Meticulously researched, clearly written and comprehensively documented, this book explores the rich tapestry of Goddess worship from prehistoric cultures to modern academic theories. Consider the amazing similarities between age-old pagan rituals and those associated with contemporary religions.

"The book is a user-friendly guide that provides background information on a site's ancient or new importance. Some sections have warnings about deterioration at some sites; these are called "Gaia Alerts," after the Greek goddess personifying Earth."
— *Los Angeles Times*

## SACRED PLACES OF GODDESS:
### 108 DESTINATIONS
ISBN: 1-888729-11-2     $19.95     by: Karen Tate

# SACRED PLACES SERIES

Travel to Europe for 108 uplifting destinations that helped define religion and spirituality in the Western Hemisphere. From Paleolithic and Neolithic sites to underground New Age temples, this is a book many millennium in the making.

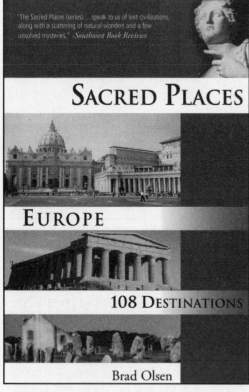

"The Sacred Places (series) ... speak to us of lost civilizations, along with a scattering of natural wonders and a few unsolved mysteries." -*Southwest Book Reviews*

SACRED PLACES

EUROPE

108 DESTINATIONS

Brad Olsen

- Who were the first seafaring Europeans to discover and proselytize in distant continents?

- Why did the Romans copy so much from the ancient Greeks?

- Where are the most-frequently visited Catholic and Protestant locations?

- What celestial orientations did the earliest Europeans incorporate into their megalithic monuments?

- Who were the most popular saints and why were they venerated for centuries?

"Explores the rich cultural, spiritual landscape through all points of the compass." -Nexus

## SACRED PLACES EUROPE: 108 DESTINATIONS
ISBN: 1-888729-12-0     $19.95     Maps and photos by Brad Olsen

### FOR INDIVIDUAL ORDERS INCLUDING FREE SHIPPING:
Indicate quantity ordered and book price only. California residents add 10%. Free shipping! Send a check or money order to: CCC Publishing, 530 8th Avenue #6, San Francisco, CA 94118.
*Signed books available upon request*
or order online at: www.cccpublishing.com

All Consortium of Collective Consciousness Publishing books are distributed by: Independent Publishers Group
(800) 888-4741     www.ipgbook.com